CW98545735

Forging New Partnerships, Breaching New Frontiers

Forging New Partnerships, Breaching New Frontiers

India's Diplomacy during the UPA Rule 2004–14

Edited by

REJAUL KARIM LASKAR

UNIVERSITY PRESS

Great Clarendon Street, Oxford, ox2 6dp,
United Kingdom

Oxford University Press is a department of the University of Oxford.
It furthers the University's objective of excellence in research, scholarship,
and education by publishing worldwide. Oxford is a registered trade mark of
Oxford University Press in the UK and in certain other countries

Published in the United States of America by Oxford University Press
198 Madison Avenue, New York, NY 10016, United States of America

British Library Cataloguing in Publication Data

Data available

Library of Congress Control Number: 2022938084

ISBN 978-0-19-286806-0

DOI: 10.1093/oso/9780192868060.001.0001

Endorsements

'A valuable and timely book. Bringing together reputed international scholars, this comprehensive and readable work on India's significant bilateral, regional, and global initiatives and policies during UPA rule, 2004-14, is a seminal addition to works on Indian diplomacy. The UPA government presided over India's high-growth years, handled significant transitions such as the global financial crisis, expanded India's role abroad, and integrated India into the global polity and economy. If news is only the first rough draft of history, this is a polished final manuscript which will be the basis of serious future academic studies of this pivotal period in India's international relations and transformation.'

—Amb. Shivshankar Menon, Former National Security Advisor of India

'The decade of 2004–14 under UPA rule marked many key transitions for India. It was acknowledged as a major emerging economy with rising military, scientific and technological capabilities and with a vibrant plural democracy. It achieved remarkable diplomatic success with the landmark nuclear deal, a more constructive relationship with China, and a neighbourhood policy which promised both enhanced security and economic benefits. *Forging New Partnerships, Breaching New Frontiers* provides a welcome spotlight on a decisive decade in India's external relations under the leadership of a statesman and visionary, Dr Manmohan Singh. This is a major contribution to contemporary diplomatic history'.

—Amb. Shyam Saran, Former Foreign Secretary of India

'This is a most impressive, thoughtful and insightful volume on the origins and evolution of India's foreign policy during the UPA government. The volume deftly covers relations with key countries and regions as well as addressing a number of critical thematic issues ranging from its nuclear diplomacy to its long-standing quest for a Security Council seat. Those seeking an understanding of the dynamics of foreign policy making during the UPA era will benefit considerably from a careful perusal of this book.'

— *Prof. Sumit Ganguly, Rabindranath Tagore Chair in Indian Cultures and Civilizations, Indiana University, Bloomington*

'*Forging New Partnerships* is a much-needed volume focusing on India's foreign policy under the United Progressive Alliance Government. Covering a sweeping range of issues, the book gathers together diverse perspectives to offer a nuanced picture of a crucial period in diplomatic history'.

—*Prof. Sugata Ray, Director (Interim), Institute for South Asia Studies, University of California, Berkeley*

'The period 2004–14 witnessed a global financial crisis, the beginnings of a backlash against globalization, and the rise of nationalist politics around the world. In the new book *Forging New Partnerships, Breaching New Frontiers: India's Diplomacy during the UPA rule 2004–14*, the editor Rejaul Laskar brings together a diverse set of area specialists from around the world to provide an insightful set of new perspectives on how India's foreign policy contended with this rapidly changing landscape'.

—*Prof. Saumitra Jha, Associate Professor, Stanford University*

'This scholarly, highly readable volume offers a new and detailed assessment of key transformations in India's foreign policy from 2004 to 2014. It should be required reading for policymakers, researchers, and practitioners interested in the emergence of India as a rising power in a volatile region. Its diverse group of contributors also offers valuable insights into the ambivalent relationship between India's domestic politics, regional interests, and global aspirations'.

—*Dr. Vivian S. Walker, Executive Director, United States Advisory Commission on Public Diplomacy*

'The book on India's Foreign Policy during the UPA rule gives a rare holistic insight in an important period of time. A period where geopolitics and geo-economy emerged and impacted the game of diplomacy increasingly—also India. On the one hand, the UPA government had to be loyal to its traditional values and its ideology, and on the other hand, it had to strike a balance with a changing world, especially the rise of China. Eminent scholars and diplomats present to readers a rich and deep dive into Indian diplomacy under PM Manmohan Singh. Perhaps, the most interesting finding is how the calm and soft personality perfectly shaped the most soft diplomacy of any Indian government: a perfect match in the transition from pure non-alignment to a more active caretaking of India's National interests. For an active diplomat, it is a must to know the past while operating in the present and ultimately trying to shape the future. Please read the book if you love diplomacy or you just want to understand India—the emerging global power. It will leave you with a sweet and a spicy taste'.

—*Amb. Freddy Svane, Ambassador of Denmark to India*

'This is an excellent volume on Indian Foreign Policy between 2004 and 2014. An important and informative contribution to the academic and policy literature, the book sheds new light on a range of regional, bilateral, and multilateral engagements made by India in this critical period'.

—*Dr Debak Das, Stanton Nuclear Security Postdoctoral Fellow,*
Stanford University

Preface

This book examines India's diplomacy during the period 2004–14, when the United Progressive Alliance (UPA) Government, led by Prime Minister Manmohan Singh, was in office. Seventeen contributors contribute sixteen chapters which analyse various aspects of India's external relations that evolved during the UPA decade. From important bilateral relations and diplomacy towards important geographical regions to India's diplomacy on key themes of International Relations, the chapters of this book, together, offer a rich and kaleidoscopic view of India's foreign policy under the UPA.

The UPA—a coalition of centrist and centre-left parties—was formed after the general elections of 2004, under the chairpersonship of Smt. Sonia Gandhi, the president of the Indian National Congress—the largest constituent of the alliance. In May 2004, the UPA formed the government with Dr Manmohan Singh, the renowned economist, as the prime minister. After the successful completion of a five-year term, the alliance was successful in getting the mandate of the people for another five years. As a result, the UPA continued to govern India under the leadership of Prime Minister Dr Manmohan Singh until May 2014.

The 10-year-long period of UPA Rule has proved to be a milestone in the evolution of India's diplomacy. The period saw significant activities on the diplomatic front, including establishing strategic partnerships with a number of important powers, strengthening of existing strategic partnerships, and signing of a number of trade, investment, and economic cooperation agreements. The period also saw India playing a prominent part in the global political, trade, and financial decision-making process. It also saw India playing a more proactive role for economic development and socio-political stability in its immediate and extended neighbourhoods.

However, what puzzles an observer of India's foreign policy is the surprising absence of serious scholarly examination of the period. To be sure, there are a plethora of books available on India's foreign policy. However, one may daresay none of these looks exclusively at India's diplomacy during the UPA period, especially through the prism of the objectives that the UPA government sought to achieve through its diplomacy and the extent to which it has been successful in achieving these objectives in its ten-year-long stint.

Seventeen eminent scholars of International Relations belonging to some of the leading universities, think tanks, and scholarly organizations from around the world—including the University of Oxford, New York University, University of Michigan-Ann Arbor, SOAS University of London, University of Paris VIII, Australian National University, Melbourne University, the Fletcher School of Law and Diplomacy, Tufts University, Jawaharlal Nehru University, University of Aberdeen, University of Manchester, French Institute of International Relations, International Institute of Strategic Studies London, and International Political Science Association—came together to bridge this gap in the literature on India's foreign policy. Each of them contributed a chapter that focuses on an area that relates to her or his area of expertise. The result of their painstaking efforts is a book that makes incisive examination and analysis of the important facets of India's diplomacy during the UPA rule, ranging from bilateral relations and policies towards particular geographic regions to India's diplomacy addressing particular issue areas like international trade, energy, UNSC reforms, nuclear cooperation, and maritime security.

This book will be an important and valuable addition to the existing literature on India's foreign policy in the sense that it not only bridges the above-mentioned serious gap in the existing literature but also in the process makes a very thorough and incisive scholarly examination of the developments in India's foreign policy that took place in a decade of remarkable transformations. It will be helpful as a reference resource for academics, scholars, students, analysts, journalists, and researchers working on or studying India's foreign policy. It will also be helpful for diplomats—both Indian and foreign. In particular, it will be a valuable guide to foreign diplomats and policymakers who deal with India or South Asia to develop an insight into the way India's foreign policy has evolved in the recent past and the implications this has for its evolution in the near future. Its simple and accessible language and lucid style will also make it useful for a wider audience.

I would like to take this opportunity to acknowledge my gratitude to all those who have extended kind encouragement and valuable counsel or otherwise helped me in this book project.

First of all, I would like to thank the distinguished contributors for so kindly agreeing to be part of this book project amidst their busy schedule and also for their exceptional patience and forbearance in this long-drawn-out process. Thanks are also due to them for the timely submissions of their chapters under a tight deadline. Their contributions to this book project went far beyond the respective chapters they contributed and often extended to offering valuable ideas and suggestions at various stages and on various aspects of this project. Indeed, more than a mere book, what I have earned from this project is a team of wonderful colleagues with whom it will be a pleasure to work on many such projects in the future.

I would also like to express my gratitude for Mr Salman Khurshid—who was the External Affairs Minister of India for a significant portion of the time period covered by this book—for giving valuable time from his busy schedule for an informal discussion and also for explaining very cogently the ideas that drove the UPA Government's diplomacy.

I would also like to thank the three anonymous external reviewers of the Oxford University Press for their valuable comments and feedback.

Thanks are also due to my relatives and friends for their patience and understanding while I was busy with this project and could not devote sufficient time for them. Special thanks are due to my late father, Asik Ali Laskar—though he left this world before the beginning of this project, the values and spirit instilled by him in me were my constant companions while working on this project. Special thanks are also due to my mother and my two sisters for their constant support and encouragement throughout the process.

Finally, I would like to thank the Oxford University Press for so kindly agreeing to publish this book. Special thanks are due to Ms Moutushi Mukherjee, Commissioning Editor (Sociology and Politics), Oxford University Press, for all her assistance, support, and guidance as our manuscript progressed through the processes in the OUP. I would also like to thank Mr Barun Sarkar, Commissioning Editor, Academic Division, Oxford University Press, India, for his valuable support, assistance, and guidance whenever needed. I would also like to thank Dr Sugata

Ghosh, former Director—Academic Publishing, Oxford University Press, India, Ms Chandrima Chatterjee, former Commissioning Editor (Politics), Academic Division, Oxford University Press, India and Mr Chirag Thakkar, former Assistant Commissioning Editor (Politics), Oxford University Press, India, who have provided valuable support and guidance in this project during their stint in the OUP.

Rejaul Karim Laskar
New Delhi, March 2021

Contents

List of Figures

List of Tables

About the Editor and Contributors

Editor

Rejaul Karim Laskar is former Secretary of the Vichar Vibhag of All India Congress Committee. The 'Vichar Vibhag', which literally translates into English as 'Thought Department', is a Department of the All India Congress Committee. It acts as the think tank of the All India Congress Committee. All India Congress Committee is the highest policy-making body of the Indian National Congress. Indian National Congress was the largest constituent party of the United Progressive Alliance (UPA) Government of India. Over the last one and half decades, Laskar has written extensively on the foreign policy of the two UPA Governments.

Contributors

Mervyn Bain is Professor and Head of the School of Social Sciences, University of Aberdeen, Aberdeen, UK. His notable academic works include *Latin America* (co-authored with Oelsner, A.) in Haerpfer, C.W., Bernhagen, P., Inglehart, R.F., Welzel, C. (eds.) *Democratization* (Oxford University Press, 2009 and 2018).

Thomas P. Cavanna is Assistant Research Professor of Strategic Studies at the Fletcher School of Law and Diplomacy, Tufts University. He holds a French 'Agrégation' in history and an MA and PhD in history from Sciences Po (Paris). He was also Fox Fellow at Yale and Lecturer at the University of Pennsylvania.

John D. Ciorciari is Associate Professor and Director of the Weiser Diplomacy Center and International Policy Center at the Gerald R. Ford School of Public Policy, University of Michigan. He was an Andrew Carnegie Fellow from 2015 to 2018 and previously was Shorenstein Fellow and National Fellow at the Hoover Institution, both at Stanford University. From 2004 to 2007, he served in the United States Treasury Department, including as Deputy Director in the Office of South and Southeast Asia. He has an AB and JD from Harvard University and an MPhil and DPhil in International Relations from the University of Oxford.

Bhavna Dave is Senior Lecturer in Politics of Central Asia at the Department of Politics and International Studies, SOAS University of London. She is the author of *Kazakhstan: Ethnicity, Language and Power* (Routledge, 2007) and editor of *Modern*

Central Asia (Routledge, 2009), a four-volume reference collection which is part of Routledge's series on *Critical Issues in Modern Politics*.

Barnaby Dye is Research Fellow, Global Development Institute, University of Manchester, and Fellow of the Royal Geographical Society, United Kingdom. Barnaby received his BA from the University of Cambridge, MA from King's College London, and DPhil from the University of Oxford. He studies the political economy of development, specializing in the infrastructure, the energy sector, and the role of India and Brazil in Africa.

Carolyn Kissane is Clinical Professor and Academic Director, Center for Global Affairs, School of Professional Studies, New York University. She received her PhD from Columbia University, New York. She is a life-member of the Council on Foreign Relations and Non-Resident Fellow at the Payne Institute, Colorado School of Mines. She is also the Director of the Energy, Climate Justice, and Sustainability (ECJS) Lab of the School of Professional Studies, New York University.

Srikanth Kondapalli is Professor in Chinese Studies at Jawaharlal Nehru University. He has been Chairman of the Centre for East Asian Studies, School of International Studies, Jawaharlal Nehru University four times from 2008 to 2010, 2012 to 2014, 2016 to 2018, and 2018 to 2020. He was a post-Doctoral Visiting Fellow at People's University, Beijing, from 1996 to 1998. He was Visiting Professor at National Chengchi University, Taipei, in 2004 and Visiting Fellow at the China Institute of Contemporary International Relations, Beijing, in May 2007. He received the K. Subramanyam Award in 2010 for Excellence in Research in Strategic and Security Studies.

Timothy J. Lynch is Professor in American Politics at the University of Melbourne. His latest book is *In the Shadow of the Cold War: American Foreign Policy from George Bush Sr. to Donald Trump* (Cambridge, 2020). His other books include *Turf War: The Clinton Administration and Northern Ireland* (Ashgate, 2004) and *US Foreign Policy and Democracy Promotion* (Routledge, 2013). His co-authored book, *After Bush: The Case for Continuity in American Foreign Policy* (Cambridge, 2008), won the Richard Neustadt Book Prize and became a best-selling international security text. He is the editor of the two-volume *Oxford Encyclopedia of American Military and Diplomatic History* (2013).

Babak Moussavi is a researcher at a management consulting firm in London. He has an MSc in Contemporary India from the University of Oxford, as well as a BA in Philosophy and MSc in International Public Policy from University College London. He writes in a private capacity.

Vinícius Rodrigues Vieira is Associate Professor of Economics and International Relations at the Armando Alvares Penteado Foundation (FAAP), São Paulo, Brazil. He also teaches at the School of International Relations of the Getúlio Vargas Foundation (FGV). From 2016 to 2017, he was a Fung Global Fellow at Princeton University,

USA. Currently, he is the Secretary of the International Political Science Association (IPSA) Research Committee on 'International Political Economy'. He earned his DPhil in International Relations from Nuffield College, University of Oxford, and an MA in Latin American Studies from the University of California, Berkeley.

Rahul Roy-Chaudhury is the Head of the South Asia Programme at the International Institute for Strategic Studies (IISS), London. He is also Research Associate at the Oxford School of Global and Area Studies, University of Oxford. Earlier, he served as an official in India's National Security Council, which advises the Prime Minister of India. He has written two books on India and maritime security.

Isabelle Saint-Mézard is Assistant Professor at the French Institute of Geopolitics, the University of Paris VIII. She is also Associate Research Fellow, French Institute of International Relations (IFRI, Paris). Earlier, she was an analyst on South Asia at the Directorate for Strategic Affairs of the French Ministry of Defence (2006–11).

Shutaro Sano is Professor at Nihon University College of International Relations, Japan. Earlier, he was Professor and Deputy Director, Center for International Exchange, National Defense Academy of Japan. His recent academic works include *Japan-India Bilateral Security Cooperation: In Pursuit of a Sound and Pragmatic Partnership* (co-authored) in Rohan Mukherjee and Anthony Yazaki (eds.) *Poised for Partnership: Deepening India-Japan Relations in the Asian Century* (Oxford University Press, 2016). He is the winner of the Inoki Masamichi Honorable Award (Japan Society for Defense Studies) for his publication on private military and security companies in 2015. He did his MPP in Public Policy from the John F Kennedy School of Government, Harvard University, and PhD in International Security from the National Defense Academy of Japan.

Ricardo Soares de Oliveira is Professor of the International Politics of Africa at the Department of Politics and International Relations, University of Oxford, and Khandari Fellow in Politics at St Peter's College, Oxford. He is co-editor of *African Affairs*, the *Journal of the Royal African Society*, and co-director of the Oxford Martin School's Programme on African Governance. He is the author of *Magnificent and Beggar Land: Angola Since the Civil War* (2015) and *Oil and Politics in the Gulf of Guinea* (2007) and the co-editor of *China Returns to Africa* (2008).

Kate Sullivan de Estrada is Director of the Contemporary South Asian Studies Programme at the Oxford School of Global and Area Studies, University of Oxford, and Associate Professor in the International Relations of South Asia at the University of Oxford. Her research focuses on India's rise and role in global governance and on current contestations around maritime security in the Indian Ocean. She has delivered expert testimony on the UK–India relationship to two recent UK parliamentary inquiries and engages regularly with the UK Foreign, Development and Commonwealth Office, including through a period of secondment as a principal research analyst in 2021.

Ramesh Thakur is Emeritus Professor in the Crawford School of Public Policy, Australian National University (ANU), Senior Research Fellow, the Toda Peace Institute, and Fellow of the Australian Institute of International Affairs. His last post was Director of the Centre for Nuclear Non-Proliferation and Disarmament at the ANU. He was formerly Senior Vice-Rector of the United Nations University (and Assistant Secretary-General of the United Nations); Co-Convenor of the Asia-Pacific Leadership Network for Nuclear Non-Proliferation and Disarmament; Editor-in-Chief of Global Governance; and has been a consultant to the Australian, New Zealand, and Norwegian governments on arms control, disarmament, and international security issues.

PART I

INTRODUCTION

This introductory part seeks to put the remaining parts of this book in proper context. It includes a survey of theoretical and empirical literature on foreign policy of coalition governments, an overview of the foreign policy positions and principles of the Congress party, and an overview of the salient features of UPA Government's diplomacy in terms of the broader objectives it sought to achieve and the broader principles it adhered to.

1

Foreign Policy
of Coalition Governments

The Case of Congress party-led United Progressive Alliance, 2004–14

Rejaul Karim Laskar

This chapter seeks to put the remaining chapters of this volume in proper context by giving a brief overview of the overall framework of India's diplomacy during the United Progressive Alliance (UPA) period, especially in terms of the broader objectives that the UPA government pursued in its diplomacy.[1] While the following chapters focus on India's relations with one important country or region, or India's policy and diplomatic initiatives on a particular thematic issue, it goes without saying that diplomacy—while it must be conceptually fragmented for analytical purposes—is an indivisible whole in terms of the broader objectives it serves.

The chapter begins with a survey of theoretical and empirical literature on the role of leadership in foreign policy. It, then, surveys the theoretical and empirical literature on foreign policies of coalition governments. This is followed by an overview of the foreign policy positions and principles of the Indian National Congress (also known as Congress party/Congress)—the leading party of the UPA. The chapter, then, provides a brief overview of the salient features of the UPA government's diplomacy in terms of the broader objectives it sought to achieve and the broader principles it adhered to, thus setting the context for the remaining chapters of this volume. It then goes on to explain the rationale for undertaking this book project. The chapter concludes by providing an overview of the volume.

Rejaul Karim Laskar, *Foreign Policy of Coalition Governments* In: *Forging New Partnerships, Breaching New Frontiers*. Edited by: Rejaul Karim Laskar, Oxford University Press. © Oxford University Press 2022.
DOI: 10.1093/oso/9780192868060.003.0001

Influence of Leadership on Foreign Policy

Agent-Structure debate is as old as the discipline of International Relations itself. While much of the mainstream International Relations theory, to date, has prioritized the influence of international structure on the foreign policy of a nation (Waltz 1959), there also has been a great deal of theoretical literature as well as empirical studies on the influence of individual human agents in shaping the foreign policies of nations. One cannot but agree with the former U.S. Secretary of State, Henry Kissinger, when he says, 'as a professor, I tended to think of history as run by imperial forces. But when you see it in practice, you see the differences personalities make' (quoted in Kaarbo 2018, 37).

Indeed, one has only to glance through the pages of a history book to have an inkling of the important role played by individual human personalities in shaping the course of international relations. Jervis makes this point clear with the rhetorical question, 'Who could doubt that the world would have been very different without Woodrow Wilson, Winston Churchill, Josef Stalin, Franklin Roosevelt, Mao Zedong, Richard Nixon, and George W. Bush?' (Jervis 2013, 154). As Jervis points out, leaders can influence the foreign policy of their respective nations through four 'main channels': (i) foreign policy of a nation will 'reflect the outlook, values, and beliefs' of its leader; (ii) 'distinctive personalities and styles' of a leader can affect the behaviour of the state he leads; (iii) 'political style and skill' of a leader can determine his 'ability to mobilize support' in favour of the foreign policy of the nation he leads; and (iv) different leaders will generate 'different environments' (Jervis 2013, 161). Jervis adds that the end of the Cold War has enhanced the influence of the leaders on the foreign policy of the nations they lead simply because it has provided them with a wider range of choices as compared with the Cold War era (Jervis 2013, 172). Indeed, explaining international relations without reference to important leaders can be compared to explaining art and music without reference to Michelangelo or Mozart (Byman and Pollack 2001, 145).

Since the late seventies of the last century, neorealism has been dominating International Relations theory (Rose 1998, 144). Neorealists argue that it is the international structure that determines the course of international politics and they discount the role of domestic factors such as the personality or psychology of leaders (Horowitz et al. 2005, 662). Although neorealism explains the outcomes of state interactions, it does not explain well the making of the foreign policies of nations (Rose 1998, 145).

The neoclassical realism,[2] on the other hand, acknowledges the role of human agents as 'intervening variables' even though it acknowledges that the foreign policy of a nation is shaped 'first and foremost by its place in the international system and specifically by its relative material power capabilities' (Rose 1998, 146). As Rose puts it, 'there is no immediate or perfect transmission belt linking material capabilities to foreign policy behaviour' (Rose 1998, 146–147). That does not, however, mean that the international structure and material capabilities of a nation do not play any role. Indeed, as Jervis puts it, 'the degree to which there is freedom of choice and room for individual preferences depends in significant measure on how compelling the external environment is' (Jervis 2013, 156). But in the end, foreign policy decisions are made by 'actual political leaders' and therefore their perceptions play a decisive role in the shaping of the foreign policy of a nation (Rose 1998, 146–147). Neoclassical realists acknowledge that over the long term, the relative amount of material power resources of nations will shape their foreign policies. However, they argue that to understand how states respond to their external environment, we must analyse how systemic forces are translated through 'unit level intervening variables' including perceptions of decision-makers (Rose 1998, 152).

Waltz specifies three distinct ways of analysing international politics— that he terms as three images (Waltz 1959). The *first image* looks into international politics through the perspective of the role of human agents that make decisions on behalf of their nations. The *first image* prioritizes the importance of the personality, psychological traits, beliefs, and perception of the statesmen. The *second image* looks into international politics through the perspective of the state. It gives importance to factors like state structure, state ideology, etc., as determinants of the foreign policy of a state. The *third image* looks into international politics through the perspective of the role of international structure. The third image gives importance to systemic factors such as relative material power capabilities of various nations as the principal determinants of international politics (Waltz 1959). Even though Waltz argues that the third image provides the basic framework of international politics, he, nonetheless, acknowledges that without referring to the first and the second images, 'there can be no knowledge of the forces that determine policy…' (Waltz 1959, 238).

One of the notable approaches to international politics which focuses on human agents as the drivers of international politics is the *Decision-Making* approach. The most outstanding work on this approach is that by Snyder, Bruck, and Sapin (1962). This approach looks at international politics from the perspective of decision-making by human agents who act on behalf of their states to steer their respective states through the complex landscape of interactions among nations. This approach to international politics revolves 'around those officials who act for the political society' (Snyder, Bruck, and Sapin 1962, 85).

One of the notable theoretical works that elucidate the crucial role played by leaders in framing the foreign policy of their nations is that of Putnam (1988). By using a metaphor of 'two-level games', Putnam portrays the leader as a negotiator who negotiates in two boards: in one board, he negotiates with his international interlocutors on behalf of his domestic constituency, while on the other board, he negotiates with his domestic constituency on behalf of his foreign interlocutors (Putnam 1988, 434). Putnam points out the divergent interests of the leader and the domestic constituents on behalf of whom he is negotiating with his foreign interlocutors to emphasize the role that the leader can play in determining the outcome of international negotiations (Putnam 1988, 460).

Another notable theoretical work that elucidates the influence of leadership on foreign policies of nations is that of Byman and Pollack (2001). By examining five important cases from world history, Byman and Pollack explain how individual human agents influence the shaping of the contours of international relations.

Empirical Studies

As in any other scientific discipline, in International Relations too, the final arbiter of theoretical contestations over any issue is empirical findings. The Agent-Structure debate is no exception to this general rule. When the leading theorists of International Relations fail to agree on whether, and if yes, then how and to what extent, the leaders influence foreign policies of their nations, we must turn to the empirical findings, if any, which can resolve this contestation.

Fortunately for us, a large number of empirical investigations have been conducted to date to find out whether, how, and to what extent leadership affects foreign policies of nations.

Some of these empirical investigations have looked into the totality of the foreign policy of a country. However, most of them have a narrower focus, looking into a particular domain of foreign policy, such as initiation, continuation, and termination of military disputes; granting of foreign aid; voting behaviour in the United Nations; and signing of treaties and agreements. They also have looked into if and how different aspects of leadership such as the leadership style, psychological traits, prior experience, and age of the leader influence the foreign policy of the nations they lead.

Some of the notable empirical studies on the influence of leadership style on foreign policy are Kaarbo (1997, 2018) and Keller and Yang (2008). In one of the earliest empirical studies in the field, Karbo (1997, 572) finds that leadership style influences the foreign policy decision-making process. In a later study, Karbo (2018) uses *Leadership Trait Analysis* of Turkish and British prime ministers to examine whether their leadership styles affect the extent of parliamentary involvement in security policy. She finds that the leadership styles of prime ministers have a bearing on the extent of parliaments' involvement in the security policies of their respective nations (Karbo 2018).

The most notable empirical studies on the influence of the leaders' psychological traits on foreign policy are Hermann (1980), Crichlow (2001), and Kesgin (2011). Hermann (1980) examines the impact of 6 personal characteristics of 45 heads of government on the foreign policy behaviour of their nations. She finds that 'aggressive' leaders are 'high in need for power, low in conceptual complexity, distrustful of others, nationalistic, and likely to believe that they have some control over the events in which they are involved' (Hermann 1980, 8). Her study also finds that 'conciliatory' leaders are 'high in need for affiliation, high in conceptual complexity, trusting of others, low in nationalism, and likely to exhibit little belief in their own ability to control the events in which they are involved' (Hermann 1980, 8). Crichlow studied how the psychological characteristics of political leaders, their beliefs, and personality traits affect the foreign policy of their nations. He investigated two primary questions: (i) What relationships exist between the psychological characteristics of political leaders and their policy preferences in times of international conflict? and (ii) How are the views of presidents and prime ministers reconciled with those of their key advisors in the creation of a national foreign policy? Crichlow (2001) sought to find answers to these two questions through an examination of sixteen foreign policy decisions that were made by eight governments in three countries—the United States, Israel, and the United Kingdom. He finds that there are a number of linkages between the psychological characteristics of decision-makers and their policy preferences. The study finds that having personality characteristics like 'high levels of distrust and a high need for power' makes it more likely that a decision-maker will support conflictual policy options. The study finds that individuals who see the world as more cooperative have a greater tendency to take risks and to opt for cooperative policy options. It also finds that the linkage between leaders' psychological characteristics and foreign policy is particularly strong in the case of those leaders who have prior expertise in foreign policy (Crichlow 2001). Using 'at-a-distance' measures of personality assessment (specifically, leadership traits analysis and operational code analysis) of Israel's and Turkey's prime ministers from 1991 to 2011, Kesgin (2011) sought to find the effect of leadership styles and belief systems on foreign policy. Interestingly, the study debunks simplistic appraisals of different leaders as 'hawkish' or 'dovish'. The study, however, finds that leaders having the psychological trait of distrusting others tend to show conflictual foreign policy behaviour (Kesgin 2011).

A large number of empirical studies have been conducted on the influence of leaders' beliefs and perceptions about the external world on the foreign policies of their respective nations. Notable among them are Jervis (1970, 1976), Levi and Tetlock (1980), Tetlock (1991, 1992, 1999), Blanton (1996), Post (2003), and Dyson (2009). Dyson (2009) applied 'conceptual complexity content analysis' to British Prime Minister Margaret Thatcher's responses to foreign policy questions in the House of Commons. The study finds that Thatcher's style, which Dyson describes as 'a stark framing of the world based upon essentially dichotomous categorizations', affected her foreign policy decisions (Dyson 2009). Jervis (1976) and Levi and Tetlock (1980) studied the effects of cognitive biases of leaders on the foreign policies of the nations they lead. Levi and Tetlock (1980) find that cognitive bias, once formed, is very difficult to change. Somewhat contrary results are obtained in Blanton's (1996) study of the effect of the 'cognitive images' of U.S. President Ronald Reagan on the U.S. responses to the El Salvador conflict. Using thematic content analysis of the speeches of Ronald Reagan vis-à-vis the El Salvador issue between the years 1980 and 1984, the study finds that 'discordant information' has a cumulative effect upon the tendency of the individual to maintain original images. That is, with the passage of time, the pressure for image change applied by discordant information builds up and may be linked to an increased proclivity on the part of the individual to modify their original images (Blanton 1996, 40).

There has also been a number of empirical studies on the effect of the age and experiences of a leader on the foreign policy of the nation he/she leads. The notables among them are Horowitz et al. (2005), Calin and Prins (2015), Preston (1996), and Bak and Palmer (2010). Horowitz et al. (2005) conducted a study on the relationship between leaders' ages, regime type, and the likelihood of militarized dispute initiation and escalation by the state they lead. By examining more than 100,000 interstate dyads between 1875 and 2002 to systematically test the relationship between leader age and militarized disputes, they find that, in general, as the age of leaders increases, the states they lead become more likely to both initiate and escalate militarized disputes (Horowitz et al. 2005). Interestingly, they find that this relationship between leaders' age and the propensity of conflict initiation and escalation is more pronounced in democratic states than in autocratic ones. In autocratic states, the relationship is actually reversed: as the age of the leader increases, the propensity of conflict initiation and escalation actually declines (Horowitz et al. 2005). Bak and Palmer (2010) conducted an empirical investigation to examine the tenability of the then U.S. Vice President Joe Biden's (currently he is the U.S. President) claim that foreign enemies will test a young and inexperienced leader's resolve and therefore such a leader will lead to greater risk of his nation becoming involved in conflicts. The results of the study challenge Biden's claim. The study finds a correlation between age of the leader and the probability of conflict initiation, but the correlation is in the exact opposite direction of Biden's claim: the more the age of the leader, the greater probability of conflict initiation (Bak and

Palmer 2010). The results of the study bolster the findings of the study by Horowitz et al. (2005) mentioned previously.

Calin and Prins (2015) conducted an empirical study on the relationship between the prior executive experience of a leader and the likelihood of onset, targeting, and initiation of Military International Dispute (MID) involving the state he/she leads. By examining the extent to which previous executive experience of the U.S. presidents affected the use of military force from 1918 to 2001, the study finds that past political executive experience of a leader strongly reduces the probability of MID initiation involving the state he/she leads (Calin and Prins 2015). The study also finds that the higher the level of president's executive experience (no experience, state, federal—in that order), the less likely for the state he/she leads to be targeted, initiate, or to get involved in MIDs (Calin and Prins 2015). Preston (1996) studied the correlation between prior foreign policy experiences/expertise of a leader and his foreign policy behaviour as a president. He finds that leaders with a high degree of prior foreign policy experience/expertise appear to prefer more direct, personal involvement in the policy formulation process, while leaders with less experience have the opposite tendency (Preston 1996). Potter (2007) examined the possible correlation between the time in the office of a U.S. President and the probability of an international crisis involving the United States. His study finds that the probability of an international crisis involving the United States declines as a presidential administration gains time in office (Potter 2007).

The role of prime minister in India's foreign policy has been touched in a few notable works such as Bandyopadhyaya (1979), Tharoor (1982), and Kapur (1994). However, these are more of descriptive analyses rather than systematic and rigorous empirical studies.

The previously mentioned empirical studies make one thing clear: leadership does have an influence on the foreign policy of a nation. To be more specific, the leadership style of a leader; the leader's psychological traits; the leader's belief system, in particular, his/her belief and perception about the external world; the leader's cognitive biases; the age of the leader; the length of time the leader has served in the office; and the leader's prior executive experience, in particular, his/her prior experience of handling foreign policy issues influence, significantly, various aspects of the foreign policy of the nation he/she leads.

Foreign Policies of Coalition Governments

In parliamentary democracies, the government is responsible to the legislature and remains in office till it enjoys the support of majority of the members of the popular house of the legislature. When a single political party has majority, it forms the government. But often arises situations where no single party has majority in the popular house of the legislature. In such circumstances, a coalition of political parties is formed, which constitutes an arithmetic majority in the legislature so that the government is formed by this coalition instead of a single party. Sometimes such coalitions become permanent of sorts so much so that they even contest elections together. Normally, however, the constituent parties of a coalition 'govern jointly' but 'compete for votes separately' (Martin and Vanberg 2011, 11). As the parties compete for votes separately, they have to do a balancing act: on the one hand, to remain in power, they sometimes have to compromise on their principles and ideology in the 'greater interest'; on the other hand, too much of such concessions threatens to undermine their electoral base and endanger their very political survival in future elections. To put it another way, though every party would like the government policies to reflect—as accurately as possible—its own principles and ideology,[3] the very fact that there are more than one party in the coalition makes some sort of compromise inevitable. The question is which party is to make how much concession in terms of principles and policies and thus endanger their future electoral prospect. This dilemma is all the more complex as remaining in power also brings significant benefits to the party concerned.

While this dilemma is present vis-à-vis the spectrum of government policies, one particular case is foreign policy. Traditional realist international relations literature has considered foreign policy to be determined by 'national interest' and therefore beyond partisan politics.[4] Others, however, argue that *national interest* can be defined and interpreted differently by different political parties based on their respective ideological character (Rathbun 2004) and, therefore, foreign policy is very much an arena of domestic political contestation.

Indeed, political parties may differ in their foreign policy positions for three important reasons (Wagnera et al. 2017, 22):

  (i) Foreign policy has an impact on domestic policy as they compete
      for same resources and attention and therefore differences in do-
      mestic policy will, perforce, translate into differences over foreign
      policy.
 (ii) Even in the absence of foreign policy's impact on domestic pol-
      icies, parties may differ on foreign policy due to their different
      worldviews.
(iii) The differences in the core values and principles of parties may
      result in differences over foreign policy.

Findings of empirical investigations seem to largely favour the latter
view. A large number of recent empirical investigations revealed that foreign policy is indeed affected by partisan considerations.[5]

Of course, if foreign policy were determined by a clear and immutable
conception of 'national interest', the foreign policy of a single-party majority government and that of a coalition government would have been
identical, other things remaining same, just as foreign policy of a country
would have remained unchanged with a change in government unless
there is a concurrent significant change in the global milieu. However, as
we will see later in this chapter, a large number of recent empirical studies
find that coalition governments differ from single-party majority governments on the substance of their foreign policies.

In the following sub-section, we will see whether coalition governments are different from single-party majority governments in the substance of their foreign policies. In the next sub-section, we will proceed to
see whether and how the ideological composition of a coalition impacts
its foreign policy.

Difference between Foreign Policies of Coalition and Single-Party Governments

Intuitively, it makes sense that coalition governments should be moderate compared to single-party majority governments in the substance
of their foreign policies as they are subjected to several constraints such
as the pulls and pressures of the different constituent parties of the coalition and the *coalition agenda document*, which constricts the leeway

that such forms of governments have. This is the basic argument of 'Democratic Peace' theory, which predicts that coalition governments will be more peaceful compared to single-party governments (Beasley and Kaarbo 2014, 730). However, the empirical studies conducted in the field give us a different picture. While some of the empirical studies authenticate 'Democratic Peace' theory and show that coalition governments are indeed more peaceful and moderate than their single-party majority counterparts, others, indeed a larger number of them, find that coalition governments actually show extreme behaviour in foreign policy compared to their single-party majority counterparts. Some other studies, interestingly, show no difference between coalition governments and single-party majority governments on the substance of their foreign policies.

Most of the empirical works conducted in the last two decades comparing foreign policies of coalition governments with that of single-party governments have found coalition governments to be more prone to extreme foreign policy—either higher levels of cooperation or higher levels of conflict—than single-party governments (Coticchia and Davidson 2016, 151). Some of these works, such as Kaarbo and Beasley (2008), Clare (2010), and Beasley and Kaarbo (2014), find that coalition governments show both more cooperative and more conflictual behaviour. Some other, such as Palmer et al. (2004) and Prins and Sprecher (1999), find coalition governments to show more conflictual behaviour.

A number of explanations have been offered by scholars to account for these seemingly counterintuitive empirical findings. Three of them are worth noting:

(i) Pressure by extreme right or extreme left parties within the coalition, whose support is indispensable for the survival of the government, compels these governments to take extreme foreign policy measures (Beasley and Kaarbo 2014, 731; Kaarbo and Beasley 2008, 70; Coticchia and Davidson 2016, 150; Clare 2010, 980–981).

(ii) Domestic political weakness of coalition governments tempts them to adopt an extreme foreign policy as a diversionary tactic to bolster legitimacy among domestic audiences in the belief that extreme behaviour towards foreign countries has a 'rally-'round-the-flag-effect' at home (Beasley and Kaarbo 2014, 737; Kaarbo 2008, 62; Hagan 1993, 30–31).

(iii) Diffusion of accountability due to shared authority among multiple parties in a coalition makes risk-taking behaviour in foreign policy less risky for individual parties, thereby tempting parties running a coalition government to take extreme foreign policy (Beasley and Kaarbo 2014, 732; Vertzberger 1997, 282; Prins and Sprecher 1999, 275; Oktay 2014).

However, some of the empirical studies find coalition governments to be more moderate compared to single-party majority governments. These studies indeed confirm the 'Democratic Peace' theory, which contends that institutional constraints prevent coalition governments from pursuing extreme foreign policy (Maoz and Russett 1993; Hagan 1993; Vowles 2010).

Some other, albeit a smaller number of, studies find no substantial difference in foreign policy between coalition governments and single-party majority governments. Notable among them are Reiter and Tillman (2002) and Ireland and Gartner (2001).

Impact of Ideological Composition of Coalition on Foreign Policy

Coalitions are normally forged between a larger centrist leading party and one or more smaller ideologically extreme parties (Kaarbo 2008, 64).

In terms of ideology,[6] the composition of a coalition government can be described by two measures: (i) 'government ideology' and (ii) 'ideological diversity'.

Government Ideology

'Government ideology' can be defined as the mean of the ideologies of all the parties in the government (Calin 2010, 94). Calin (2010, 94) defines 'government ideology' as

$$\text{G.I.} = \Sigma \left\{ \text{Ideology}_i * (\text{Posts}_i / \text{Total Posts}) \right\}$$

where:

Ideology$_i$ = the ideology of party i
Posts$_i$ = the total number of cabinet posts controlled by party i
Total Posts = the total number of posts in the cabinet

While some scholars maintain that the role of ideologies in shaping foreign policy is negligible (Morgenthau 1948), others argue that they act as 'road maps' in foreign policy decision-making (Goldstein and Keohane 1993). Recent empirical studies have shown that there are systematic differences in foreign policies between governments with left-leaning ideology and those with right-leaning ideology (Palmer et al. 2004, 5; Calin 2010, 57). Indeed, the differences between governments with left—and those with right-leaning ideologies begin with a difference in their respective worldviews. The worldview of the governments with right-leaning ideology is based on the belief that conflicts among nations are inevitable and therefore national security is the most important issue for the governments to preoccupy themselves with. The worldview of the governments with left-leaning ideology is based on the belief that equality, redistribution, and justice in the society are the most important issues and international conflicts are a distraction from that pursuit (Calin 2010, 64). Based on this fundamental difference in worldview, the governments with left- and right-leaning ideologies have three significant differences vis-à-vis foreign policy:

(i)   Governments with left-leaning ideology prefer negotiation while governments with right-leaning ideology prefer the use of force to settle differences with other nations.
(ii) Governments with left-leaning ideology prefer multilateralism while governments with right-leaning ideology prefer unilateralism in dealing with international challenges.
(iii) Governments with left-leaning ideology emphasize foreign aid while governments with right-leaning ideology emphasize foreign trade as tools to help poor countries.

Governments composed of left-wing parties normally prefer peaceful methods for the resolution of international disputes, such as diplomacy (Calin 2010, 66). On the other hand, governments composed of right-wing parties rely on punishment or threat of punishments to settle disputes with other nations (Calin 2010, 67). This has been confirmed by a number of recent empirical investigations. The most notable of them are Palmer et al. (2004), Joly and Dandoy (2018, 516), Koch (2009), Klingemann et al. (1994), and Wagnera et al. (2017).

On the question of dealing with international challenges, the governments composed of left-wing parties have been found to be giving more emphasis on multilateralism, that is, coordinating and cooperating with other nations in dealing with international challenges, while the governments composed of right-wing parties have been found to be relying more on unilateral actions in securing their national interests vis a vis such challenges (Calin 2010, 70).

Similarly, on 'aid vs trade' debate, governments composed of left-wing parties have been found to be giving greater emphasis on foreign aid to poor countries compared to governments composed of right-wing parties which apparently believe international trade is a better tool to help poorer nations instead of foreign aid (Joly and Dandoy 2018, 529).

However, as a matter of caution, it must be emphasized that the differences cited above are only general tendencies and not iron laws that know no exception. There are numerous specific instances when a government composed of left-wing party/parties have taken recourse to military means, unilateralism, and emphasis on trade. Similarly, there are numerous specific instances when a government composed of right-wing party/parties have preferred dialogue, multilateralism, and foreign aid to poor nations. Moreover, the left-right dichotomy, as it exists in a western context, might not translate accurately into non-western contexts where ideological differences between parties may not be solely or even mainly based on socio-economic policies but may rather reflect domestic ethnic/religious/cultural cleavages (Oktay 2014, 879). In India, for example, while it is true that the two largest parties—namely the Bharatiya Janata Party (BJP) and the Indian National Congress that lead India's two major coalitions, National Democratic Alliance (NDA) and United Progressive Alliance, respectively—can be considered to be right-leaning and left-leaning, respectively in a western, i.e., socio-economic sense but their emphasis—as expressed through policy documents and public statements—seems to be, to a large measure, on the conception of nationalism—namely 'secular' (multi-religious/multicultural) conception of nationalism and 'Hindu nationalism' (mono-religious/mono-cultural conception of nationalism), respectively—a dichotomy usually not found in western democracies. Therefore, while using the western template to evaluate the foreign policies of NDA and UPA, this difference in the contexts must be kept in mind.

Ideological Diversity

'Ideological diversity' of a coalition may be defined as the ideological difference between the party that is furthest to the right and the party that is furthest to the left in the coalition. The 'ideological diversity', too, has a significant bearing on the foreign policy of a coalition government. To begin with, *ideological diversity* places additional constraints on the government. If the government is ideologically cohesive, i.e., if all the parties in the coalition have the same or nearly same ideology, the government can adopt a foreign policy in accord with that ideology. However, when there are parties with diverse ideologies in the government, it is a hard task to adopt a foreign policy that can satisfy all of these parties and each party tries to put pressure on the government to orient/reorient the foreign policy in a direction that better reflects its own ideology. Moreover, in an ideologically diverse coalition government, often the policy of the government goes against the ideology of one or the other party in the government, putting the party in a dilemma as to whether to compromise on its ideology in order to save the government or to topple the government to show commitment to its ideology which is needed to protect its long-term support base.

A number of empirical studies have been conducted to examine whether *ideological diversity* of government has consequences for foreign policy. A study by Oktay (2014, 871), for example, finds that the foreign policy commitment intensity of ideologically diverse coalition governments is less than that of ideologically cohesive governments. Similar results are found by a number of other empirical studies too. Notable among them is Clare (2010).

The question of the impact of ideological diversity of coalition on foreign policy is, to a large measure, the question of influence of junior parties in the coalition on the foreign policy of the coalition government. As a coalition, a government consists of different political parties, which may differ in their views on foreign policy; they will perforce compete with their coalition partners to ensure that the foreign policy of the government reflects their own ideologies and policies (Joly and Dandoy 2018). While the lesser strength of junior parties may lead one to expect the negligible influence of such parties—surprisingly, a large number of empirical studies show they do have significant influences. However, the findings of these studies are mixed in the sense that they find different conditions for the successful influence of junior parties in foreign policy. Brommesson and Ekengren (2019), for example, find that the influence of junior coalition partners is more on symbolic issues than on substantive issues. Kaarbo (1996, 519), on the other hand, finds that junior party influence is more pronounced in issues where the senior party itself is divided. Kaarbo also finds that junior party influence is more pronounced on issues where the parties sharply differ than on issues on which the difference is moderate (Kaarbo 1996, 519). However, on this issue, a study by Ozkececi-Taner (2005) has exact opposite findings. The study finds that on issues where the coalition partners differ sharply, the junior party's influence is least (Ozkececi-Taner 2005, 264). Apart from this, these two studies have exact opposite findings on another issue. This relates to the so-called 'policy saliency hypothesis', which assumes that a party will have more influence on issues that are more important to it, other things remaining the same. While the study by Ozkececi-Taner confirms this 'saliency hypothesis' (Ozkececi-Taner 2005), the study by Kaarbo (1993) finds no such pattern of influence based on policy saliency. Kaarbo finds an interesting result in her study regarding the successful strategies adopted by the junior party. She finds that junior parties are more successful in influencing foreign policy when they threaten to leave the government (Kaarbo 1993, 323).

Interestingly and somewhat puzzlingly, there is no notable study on the influence of the largest party of the coalition on foreign policy. While there are a number of studies on the influence of the ideology of the party in a single-party majority government and an even larger number of studies on the influence of the junior parties in a coalition, there is no notable study on the influence of the ideology or of party institutions of the largest party of the coalition on government's foreign policy. One possible explanation of this glaring gap in the literature can be the widespread belief that the largest party's influence is too obvious to need any study. However, such beliefs can hardly be justified given the fact that it is not only the political executive which shapes the foreign policy of the country but also many other institutions—most notably among them the permanent bureaucracy, the security and defence establishments, and the strategic experts' community—play important roles in this regard. Once a foreign policy emerges after interactions among these diverse sections, to what extent the influence of the largest political party in the government—as an institution and as an embodiment of an ideology and associated principles and not merely as a support base of the Prime Minister[7]—is visible in the foreign policy is definitely an area that needs systematic empirical investigation.

Congress Party's Foreign Policy Positions and Principles

The Indian National Congress, also known as Congress party, was established in 1885 when India was under British rule (Indian National Congress Undated). During its formative days, the Congress fought for the greater say of the native people of India in the colonial administration. Gradually it became vocal in its demand for India's independence from the British rule. In fact, Indian National Congress was the organization that largely spearheaded the independence movement in India until the latter got independence in 1947.

After independence, for a long time, Congress was the ruling party of India. Indeed, in the first ten general elections held after India's independence, the Congress party got the absolute majority in all but two—1977 and 1989 (Mathur and Kamath 1996, 94). Naturally, under such circumstances, it is difficult to differentiate between the foreign policy of government of India and the foreign policy of the Congress party as most of the time government of India was run by the Congress party (Mathur and Kamath 1996, 94).

In terms of ideology, the Congress party is considered by some scholars as centrist (Hasan 2002, 9). Others consider it as 'left liberal' (Bajpai 2012, 111). The salient principles on which the Congress party is committed are democracy, secularism, and mixed economy (Hasan 2002, 9). The Congress is committed to more equitable distribution of resources and opportunities among different sections of Indian society (Soikham 2019, 36).

In recent times, the Congress has lost its earlier hegemony in the political landscape of India due to, *inter alia*, the rise of Hindu nationalist forces politically represented by the centre-right BJP. However, according to some scholars of Indian politics like Soikham (2019, 35), the Congress still remains the leading force shaping India's 'norm architecture' as three of Congress's major social policies, namely, social inclusivity, social justice, and peaceful and democratic resolution of disputes, still retain their command on India's 'norm architecture'.

Before starting a discussion on the foreign policy positions and principles of the Congress party, it is apt to mention that in India, the ruling party lays down the broad outline of foreign policy, leaving it to the discretion of the permanent government officials to formulate the details of the policy and to interpret and apply such broad policy in different contexts and situations (Bandyopadhyaya 1979, 139). This has been true of all the Congress governments since India's independence, but especially true of those after Nehru. This is so because, in the post-Nehru era, the prime ministers and other party leaders were not as interested in foreign policy as Nehru, which, in effect, left it to the permanent government officials to formulate India's foreign policy within the broad parameters laid down by important party documents and resolutions (Bandyopadhyaya 1979, 139).

It will be apt here to mention the institutions of the Congress party that have a bearing on the foreign policy of the party. The highest policy-making body of the Congress party is the *All India Congress Committee* (AICC) which holds its plenary session once in a few years, normally once in five or six years.[8] The plenary session normally passes several resolutions—including one on foreign policy, which lays down the broad outline of Congress party's position on important foreign policy issues. The *Congress Working Committee* (CWC), which is a much compact body, meets frequently and on short notice but normally takes up only urgent issues that require immediate attention. There is another institution, namely, the *Congress Parliamentary Party* (CPP), which normally meets during or on the eve of parliament sessions to chalk out the party's strategy in the parliament. While the AICC plenary session lays down the broad outline of the Congress party's foreign policy—which is of a permanent or semi-permanent nature—the CWC and the CPP normally take up matters that require immediate attention. To assist the AICC on foreign affairs, there is a department of the AICC named as the *Foreign Affairs Department* headed by a Chairperson and aided by a Secretary and other members appointed by the AICC President. Interestingly, the *Foreign Affairs Department* is one of the oldest existing departments of the AICC. It was established by a resolution of the 40th session of the Indian National Congress held in 1925. Rammanohar Lohia was the first secretary of the department (Bandyopadhyaya 1979, 140).

As the Congress party ruled India for the most part of the history of independent India, there was a semblance of continuity and 'national consensus' on India's foreign policy. However, in recent years, with the rise of the BJP with its own vision of foreign policy distinct from that of the Congress, this consensus seems to be falling apart. In what can be viewed as a manifestation of this development, the 'Foreign Policy Resolution' of the 84th Plenary Session of the Indian National Congress held in 2018, accuses the BJP-led NDA Government of India of disrupting and unravelling this 'national consensus' (Indian National Congress 2018).

The Core Values Underlying Congress Foreign Policy

Foreign policy is dynamic and ever changing in response to changing circumstances. However, some core principles act as sheet anchors to give a permanent character to foreign policy. The foreign policy of Congress is no exception to this general rule. Former Prime Minister Manmohan Singh elucidates this point in the following words, 'While the instruments of our policy and the tactics and strategy we adopt may change with time, the values in which they are embedded are universal and remain true for all time' (Singh 2008). The basic principles that inform the foreign policy of the Congress party were evolved through India's independence movement led by it (Laskar 2004, 8; All India Congress Committee 2019, 27). In fact, soon after independence, the CWC, in 1948, passed a resolution that stipulates, '(t)he foreign policy of India must necessarily be based on the principles that have guided the Congress in past years ...' (quoted in Mathur and Kamath 1996, 95–96). Some of the important foreign policy principles of the Congress, enunciated by the above mentioned CWC session, are promotion of world peace, freedom of all nations, racial equality, and the ending of imperialism and colonialism, to maintaining friendly and cooperative relations with all nations and avoiding entanglement in military or similar alliances, and maintaining India's freedom of action in foreign affairs (Mathur and Kamath 1996, 95–96).

Evolution of Congress Foreign Policy from Pre-independence Days to Manmohan Era

Even before India's independence, the Indian National Congress had laid down the basic outlines of the foreign policy which free India would pursue. In fact, the Indian National Congress showed its interest in international affairs right from its birth in 1885 (Prasad 2013, xxvii). In its very first session held in 1885, the Indian National Congress passed a resolution condemning the British government of India for the annexation of upper Burma to India (Prasad 2013, 18). In 1921, the AICC approved a statement drafted by M. K. Gandhi, which outlines the broad contours of the foreign policy that free India will pursue (Prasad 2013, 43). Some of the notable basic principles of the Congress party's foreign policy that have pre-independence origin are non-alignment, anti-imperialism, closer relations with East and Southeast Asia, and West Asia (Nehru 1972, 361).

The most formative period in the evolution of the Congress party's foreign policy position was the Nehru period. In fact, it will not be an overstatement to say that Jawaharlal Nehru is the architect of the Congress party's foreign policy. Most of the basic tenets of the Congress party's foreign policy have the imprimatur of Nehru. Of course, with time, these tenets have been redefined and re-interpreted but at least semantically, the Congress party still pays obeisance to the principles developed by Nehru. The Nehru period, so far as Congress foreign policy is concerned, began as early as in 1927 when the Congress leadership started to defer to Nehru's expertise on international affairs and thus Nehru became the most influential voice in the Indian National Congress on foreign policy. From then and until his death in 1964, Nehru remained the chief foreign policy-maker of the Congress party. Some of the most distinctive features of Nehru's foreign policy were[9]: commitment to an independent foreign policy, idealistic in tone and tenor, call for 'One World' instead of a world divided between two ideological camps, Panchsheel or the five principles of peaceful coexistence, non-alignment, leadership of the non-aligned movement, India's continued membership of British Commonwealth, leadership of the third world in multilateral institutions, support to the decolonization of European colonies, and closer relations with East and Southeast Asia, Africa, and West Asia. Some of these features have become less relevant with the passage of time, and some remain as relevant as they were during Nehru's time.

The post-Nehru phase in India's foreign policy had actually—and ironically—started during the lifetime of Nehru. During the last two years of his Prime Ministership, i.e., from 1962 Conflict with China and until his demise in 1964, Nehru himself had to significantly revise his foreign policy in light of the bitter experience of that conflict—shedding much of its idealist leanings (Ganguly and Pardesi 2009).

After Nehru's death and a short interlude of Prime Minister Shastri, Nehru's daughter Indira Gandhi held the helm of India, and of course of the Indian National Congress, for a long time. Although Indira Gandhi's foreign policy has been considered more geared towards realism by scholars of India's foreign policy, she did not completely break away from the basic template bequeathed by Nehru. Scholars like Cohen described her foreign policy as 'militant Nehruvianism' (Cohen 2001, 41). 'Militant Nehruvianism', as the term suggests, places greater reliance on military strength even while retaining most of the features of Nehru's foreign policy. Compared to Nehru's emphasis on abstract principles, Indira Gandhi's emphasis was on, to borrow the words of Tharoor, 'hard interests and cost calculations' (Tharoor 1982, 92). Although during the early days of Indira period, India gradually became closer to the

Soviet Union culminating in the Indo-Soviet Treaty of Friendship and Cooperation, in the later stages of her prime ministership, this 'tilt' was shed significantly and India became quite closer to the United States (Tharoor 1982, 96).

When Indira was succeeded by her son Rajiv Gandhi in 1984, while there were noticeable changes in style and he made some notable initiatives such as the 'Action Plan' for global disarmament (Laskar 2014, 47) and the initiative to improve relations with China, in substance, his foreign policy was not much different from his mother and grandfather (Narang and Staniland 2012, 86).

The most substantial change in the foreign policy orientation of the Congress party came with the end of the Cold War, especially during the Congress government headed by P. V. Narasimha Rao. Indeed, scholars prefer to use the term 'transformation' to describe this change in Indian foreign policy during Rao's term (Sridharan 2006, 76). This transformation of foreign policy was, though a response to the drastic changes in the international structure, was further propelled by the economic reforms initiated by the Rao government (Sridharan 2006, 79–80). Some of the notable components of this transformation in foreign policy during Rao's tenure were (Sridharan 2006, 79): establishment of diplomatic relations with Israel; thaw in relations with China leading to the 1993 Agreement 'to maintain peace and tranquillity on the line-of-actual-control'; initiation of a policy of seeking closer relations with the United States; and initiation of a 'Look East' policy to give a major boost to India's relations with the countries of Southeast Asia.

After Rao, following a gap of eight years of the political wilderness, the Congress came back to power again in 2004—for the first time as part of a coalition named as UPA—with Dr Manmohan Singh as the prime minister. Dr Singh, as finance minister in the Rao government, was instrumental in initiating India's economic reforms in the early nineties of the last century. As an economist, the primary foreign policy goal of Prime Minister Manmohan Singh has been giving a boost to economic growth at home (Narang and Staniland 2012, 88). It is not surprising, therefore, that the focus of Manmohan's foreign policy has been on securing for India, foreign investment, overseas markets for India's exports, securing advanced technology from abroad, and seeking a greater role for India in global political and economic institutions.

Five Distinguishing Characteristics of Congress's Foreign Policy

The foreign policy of the Congress party has some distinguishing characteristics. The most notable among them are: a blend of idealism and pragmatism; based on enlightened self-interest; seeks to guard the independence of foreign policy; has an aversion to power politics; and gives highest priority to the economic development of the country.

The Indian National Congress describes its foreign policy as 'a blend of idealism and firm pragmatism' (All India Congress Committee 2010). It rejects the extreme and often self-defeating policy of naked realism/pragmatism. At the same time, it avoids the other extreme—unalloyed idealism of ignoring the hard reality. The Congress party, in its foreign policy approach, rather takes the middle path—the golden mean of idealism tempered by pragmatism.

The idealistic moorings that Congress foreign policy inherited from Nehru, sometimes lead some commentators to think that it is divorced from national interest. But this assessment is patently erroneous. Indeed, Nehru himself clarified this matter in his speech in India's Constituent Assembly in the following words, 'the art of conducting the foreign affairs of a country lies in finding out what is most advantageous to the country' (Nehru 1961, 28). However, the national interest that Congress foreign policy aims to secure is not narrow jingoistic bravado to incite the masses but enlightened national interest based on a wise understanding of the long-term interests of India. In the words of Nehru himself,

> if we have a narrow national policy it may excite the multitude for the moment ... but it is bad for the nation ... because (in this case) we (will) lose sight of the ultimate good and thereby endanger our own good. Therefore, we propose to look after India's interests in the context of world co-operation and world peace. (Nehru 1961, 28)

Nehru understood well that a strong military alone does not guarantee national security. To quote him,

> The normal idea is that security is protected by armies. That is only partly true; it is equally true that security is protected by policies.

A deliberate policy of friendship with other countries goes farther in gaining security than almost anything else. (Nehru 1961, 79)

This commitment to an enlightened self-interest has been upheld by successive Congress governments down to the Manmohan Singh-led UPA government, of course with necessary adjustments in response to changing domestic and international milieu. Indeed, the most misunderstood policy of non-alignment—which the critics of Nehruvian foreign policy cite as a classic example of the latter giving priority to idealism over national interest—has been repeatedly clarified by Congress leaders as actually based on India's *enlightened self-interest* above everything else. In the words of Prime Minister Singh, 'non-alignment was an expression of our enlightened national interest and continues to be so even today' (Singh 2008).

One of the most emphasized features of the Congress party's foreign policy is 'independence of foreign policy'. Nehru, the architect of the Congress party's foreign policy, considered 'independence of foreign policy' as the touchstone of independence of a nation. In his words,

What does independence consist of? … it consists fundamentally and basically of foreign relations. That is the test of independence. All else is local autonomy. Once foreign relations go out of our hand into the charge of somebody else, to that extent and in that measure, you are not independent. Nehru. (Quoted in Laskar 2004)

Subsequent Congress leaders, who succeeded Nehru, continued to emphasize this commitment to 'independence of foreign policy' (Tharoor 1982, 89). This emphasis on independent foreign policy has been conspicuously present during the UPA period too. The Congress, for example, in its manifesto for the 2009 Lok Sabha elections, declares in no uncertain terms that it will continue to pursue an 'independent foreign policy' (Indian National Congress 2009, 19).

Aversion to Power politics is another distinguishing characteristic of Congress's foreign policy. This aversion has been shown by Congress leaders from Nehru onward, down to the current Congress President Sonia Gandhi. Nehru, in his radio broadcast of September 7, 1946, declared that India will 'keep away from the power politics of groups'

(Nehru 1961, 2). His successors largely maintained that aversion. When his daughter Indira Gandhi became prime minister, she, in an interview with Shashi Tharoor, when asked 'Should India ... become a big power?', replied, 'No-why should we? ... All we want is to be strong enough to solve our own problems' (Tharoor 1982, 88). This aversion is not lost even in present times. The current Congress President Sonia Gandhi puts this in a very succinct fashion. Addressing a *leadership summit* held by prominent Indian newspaper *Hindustan Times*, she sums up Congress party's aversion to power politics in the following words,

> Your theme this year is 'India, the Next Global Superpower?' The question mark is certainly appropriate. But while noting the question mark, I am somewhat uneasy with the very word 'Superpower'. For too many of us, it evokes images of hegemony, of aggression, of power politics, of military might, of division and conflict. But that is not what India has been all about through the centuries and it certainly is not what I would like to see India become ... Why should we think of ourselves as a "Global Superpower"? Why not instead work towards becoming a global force for Peace, Progress and Prosperity? (Gandhi 2006, 9)

Right from Nehru, the Congress party's priority has been the economic development of India. All the efforts of Congress governments down the line have been focused on this imperative. It is not surprising, therefore, that the foreign policy of the Congress party, in large measure, is geared to this objective. Nehru himself, in his address to India's Constituent Assembly in December 1947, made this clear in the following words, 'Ultimately, foreign policy is the outcome of economic policy' (Nehru 1961, 24). Later prime ministers such as Indira Gandhi, too, continued to emphasize the 'use of foreign political policy for domestic economic ends' (Tharoor 1982, 89). Later, when Prime Minister Rao initiated the economic reform, economic interest as a driver of foreign policy got an even greater emphasis (Sridharan 2006, 79–80). Manmohan Singh, being an economist and being the architect of India's economic reforms, gave an ever-greater emphasis on foreign policy as a tool to promote domestic economic growth. Unsurprisingly, during his prime ministership, economic growth became even greater an objective of India's foreign policy. Prime Minister Singh gives expression to this *economy-first* focus of

Congress's foreign policy with the following words, 'Our foreign policy must help create an international environment conducive to India's rapid social and economic development' (Singh 2008, 7).

Basic Principles Underlying Congress Foreign Policy

The foreign policy of the Congress party is informed by two basic principles: non-alignment and Panchsheel.

Non-alignment, as a principle, has been the bedrock of the Congress party's foreign policy since its enunciation by Nehru (Laskar 2004, 8). Nehru, in his reply to a debate in the Lok Sabha in 1958, elaborates on the principle of non-alignment thus,

> when we say our policy is one of non-alignment, obviously we mean non-alignment with military blocs. It is not a negative policy. It is a positive one … I hope, a dynamic one … The policy itself can only be a policy of acting according to our best judgement. (Nehru 1961, 79)

In other words, non-alignment, as understood by Nehru, is not a negative and stagnant policy of persistent neutrality, as wrongly understood by some of the watchers of India's foreign policy. Rather, it is a dynamic policy whereby India retains her right to take a stand on any emerging issue based on her own understanding and interests vis-à-vis that particular issue rather than keeping her hands tied to any one military block in advance. Throughout the Cold War period, this policy of non-alignment has been the sheet anchor of Congress party's foreign policy (Encyclopaedia Britannica Undated). So much so that Congress made the alleged departure of the Janata government from the principle of non-alignment an electoral issue in the Lok Sabha elections of 1980 (Patagundi and Rao 1981, 28). Although some commentators of India's foreign policy believe that non-alignment—as a principle of India's foreign policy—has lost its relevance with the end of the Cold War, if we go by the public pronouncements of Congress leaders and public declarations issued by the Congress party, non-alignment continues, to this date, a bedrock of Congress party's vision on foreign policy. Jaipur Declaration, issued in 2013 by the AICC, for example, asserts:

The Indian National Congress ... believe(s) in a policy that is predicated on the enduring principles of non-alignment as enunciated by Pandit Jawaharlal Nehru, yet creatively adapted to meet the needs of relationships between nations in a rapidly changing global scenario. (All India Congress Committee 2013, 18)

Apart from non-alignment, the most important principle on which the foreign policy of the Congress party is based is Panchsheel. The term 'Panchsheel' denotes a combination of five principles of peaceful co-existence that were originally enshrined in an agreement[10] signed by India and China in the early fifties of the last century. The five principles are mutual respect for each other's territorial integrity and sovereignty; mutual non-aggression; mutual non-interference in each other's internal affairs; equality and mutual benefit; and peaceful coexistence (Appadorai 1981, 228). Like non-alignment, Panchsheel has remained a sheet anchor of Congress party's foreign policy to this date. In the words of Pranab Mukherjee, the then Minister of External Affairs in the UPA government, 'Our foreign policy ... (is) based on Panchsheel, propounded by Pandit Jawaharlal Nehru ...' (Mukherjee 2007).

Broad Objectives of Congress's Foreign Policy

Foreign policies are not abstract ideas and principles. They are policies aimed at attaining a set of concrete objectives. The foreign policy that the Congress party espouses is no exception to this general rule. To put it another way, the foreign policy that the Congress party pursues is meant to achieve a set of broad objectives. The most notable among these are securing trade, investment, and energy for India; protecting India's national security; securing global leadership role for India; protecting interests of Indian diaspora; and promoting soft power of India.

Seeking foreign investments to spur India's economic growth and seeking foreign trade to secure export markets for Indian products is one of the most important objectives of Congress's foreign policy (All India Congress Committee 2019, 27). Similarly, securing energy resources to propel India's growing economy is another important objective of Congress's foreign policy (All India Congress Committee 2010, 4). Prime

Minister Manmohan Singh elucidates this major objective of Congress's foreign policy in the following words,

> we seek to sustain annual growth rates of between 8 -10 per cent in the future. These demands have created new challenges for our foreign policy in terms of seeking access to markets, sources of energy and investment and advanced technologies. (Singh 2008)

Protecting national security is a paramount objective of any foreign policy and Congress foreign policy is no exception to this rule. Congress pledges to 'provide maximum possible security to all Indians, against both external and internal threats' (All India Congress Committee 2013).

Congress leadership, right from the days of Nehru, have envisioned and strived for a leadership role of India in the world. This vision has not blurred in recent times. Rather, if anything, with increased economic strength, this vision has become even stronger. This is clear from the emphatic assertions by recent public statements of the Congress party. The 'Foreign Policy Resolution' of the 83rd plenary session of AICC, held in 2010, declares that the Congress party will work 'to ensure that India plays a leadership role in the 21st century world' (All India Congress Committee 2010, 1). Similar sentiments are expressed by the AICC's 2013 Jaipur Declaration too: 'The Indian National Congress believes that India's role as a global power comes with great responsibilities on the global stage' (All India Congress Committee 2013, 18).

Protecting and promoting the interests of Indian Diaspora living in different countries of the world is yet another important objective of the foreign policy of *Indian National Congress*. Indeed, it was the Congress-led UPA government that created the *Ministry of Non-Resident Indians' Affairs*[11] in May 2004. The Congress has, on a number of occasions, publicly asserted that protecting Indian Diaspora 'from exploitation or threats' is 'a paramount concern of the Indian National Congress' (All India Congress Committee 2014, 48).

In recent times, the concept of 'soft power' has been getting increasing attention of scholars and policymakers. The Congress party, too, has been observed recently to give emphasis on projection on India's 'soft power' as a foreign policy objective. The 'Foreign Policy' section of the Congress party's manifesto for the 2019 Lok Sabha elections, for example, pledges to work towards increasing 'the projection of India's soft power globally' (All India Congress Committee 2019, 27).

Major Elements of Congress's Foreign Policy

Among the major elements of the foreign policy of the Congress party, the most notable are reforming the global order; international cooperation to meet global challenges; working for a stable and peaceful South Asia; closer relations with major powers; closer relations with key regions; improving relations with China; maintaining a credible nuclear deterrence; and promoting nuclear disarmament and non-proliferation.

One of the major elements of Congress's foreign policy is to work towards reform of global order through reform of global institutions—both political and economic—to make them 'democratic and representative' so that they 'remain relevant in modern times' (All India Congress Committee 2010, 4). In particular, the congress emphasizes the need to reform the *United Nations Security Council* (All India Congress Committee 2013). Congress has repeatedly committed itself publicly to work towards securing permanent membership of India in the *UN Security Council* (All India Congress Committee 2014, 47; 2019, 27). Similarly, working towards reform of global nuclear order, in particular, securing membership of India in the *Nuclear Suppliers Group* is an important element of Congress's vision for reform of global order (All India Congress Committee 2019, 27).

Congress is in favour of international cooperation to meet global challenges. Congress calls for strengthening of international cooperation in dealing with international challenges such as climate change, nuclear proliferation, and terrorism (All India Congress Committee 2014, 47). In particular, congress calls for 'deep and sustained cooperation' between the members of the international community in fighting terrorism (All India Congress Committee 2013).

Congress realizes that India cannot play a global role as long as relations with its own South Asian neighbours do not improve (Indian National Congress 2018, 3). Therefore, 'a peaceful, stable and economically vibrant South Asia' lies 'at the heart' of Congress foreign policy (All India Congress Committee 2013, 18). Towards this end, Congress calls for 'unilateral economic initiatives (by India) in the region' (All India Congress Committee 2013, 18). However, at the same time, the Congress calls upon India's South Asian neighbours to recognize former's 'legitimate security interests and concerns' (All India Congress Committee 2013, 18). In particular, to normalize relations with Pakistan, Congress calls for dialogue 'on all issues' on the basis of the Shimla Agreement of 1972 (All India Congress Committee 2004). However, Congress is unequivocal in its demand that 'Pakistan's sponsorship of cross-border terrorism must end completely once and for all' (All India Congress Committee 2004).

Closer relations with major powers of the world such as the United States, Russia, and Japan is another major element of Congress's foreign policy (All India Congress Committee 2009, 20). In particular, with the United States, the Congress emphasizes 'scientific, technological, strategic and commercial cooperation' (All India Congress Committee 2004). At the same time, the Congress reaffirms India's 'traditional bonds' with Russia (All India Congress Committee 2004).

Congress is committed to India's closer relations with key regions of importance to India such as East Asia, Southeast Asia, Africa, and West Asia. In particular, the Southeast Asian region has an important place in Congress's foreign policy. Indeed, it was the Congress government in the early nineties that initiated the 'Look East' policy to strengthen India's relations with the region (Laskar 2005, 19). The Congress believes that India has 'a central role to play' in the economic integration process in the region (All India Congress Committee 2013, 18). On Africa, Congress is of the view that 'there is great appreciation' in that region of 'what India has to offer to them' (All India Congress Committee 2009, 20). The congress also calls for the revival of the past 'close ties' with West Asia (All India Congress Committee 2004).

Congress also stands for improving relations with China. India has troubled relations with China since the war of 1962. The process of normalization of relations started with Prime Minister Rajiv Gandhi's China visit in 1988 (Laskar 2014, 47). In present times, while there are some irritants especially with regard to the border demarcation, the two nations are cooperating at the global level to promote common interests on some issues. Congress recognizes these common interests, particularly the common objectives of 'a new global governance architecture' (Indian National Congress 2018, 4).

Commitment to maintain India's nuclear deterrence is another notable element of Congress's foreign policy. Although India declared herself to be a nuclear power during the rule of the NDA government headed by Atal Bihari Vajpayee, the Congress realizes and acknowledges the importance of a credible nuclear deterrence for India's national security. The Congress has publicly committed itself to maintain 'a credible nuclear weapons programme' (All India Congress Committee 2004).

Congress's commitment to maintain India's nuclear deterrence capability does not, however, negate Congress's longstanding commitment to universal nuclear disarmament. Congress has always stood for universal nuclear disarmament. The most notable move by Congress towards universal nuclear disarmament was the 'Action Plan' presented by the then prime minister Rajiv Gandhi in the *United Nations General Assembly* on June 9, 1988 (Laskar 2014, 47). The party is still publicly committed to this 'Action Plan'. Indeed, during the UPA rule, Congress has publicly asserted that the plan 'continues to remain the sheet anchor of India's world view of … nuclear weapon free world' (All India Congress Committee 2010, 1). While remaining committed to this long-term goal of universal nuclear disarmament, the Congress also favours short- and medium-term international measures on non-proliferation of nuclear weapons, until universal disarmament becomes a reality (All India Congress Committee 2014, 47).

UPA Government's Foreign Policy: Objectives and Principles

In the 2004 elections to the Lok Sabha—the lower house of Indian Parliament—the ruling BJP-led NDA of Prime Minister Atal Bihari Vajpayee suffered a surprise defeat and the opposition Congress party emerged as the single largest party (Ramesh 2004). On 22 May 2004, Manmohan Singh—an Oxford-trained economist and former finance minister of India who oversaw the economic liberalization of the country in the early nineties of the last century—took oath as Prime Minister heading UPA—a coalition of centre-left parties led by the Congress party (CNN 2004).

Shortly afterwards, the UPA issued a 'Common Minimum Programme' (CMP) outlining the principles and priorities that will guide the government (*The Hindu* 2004). In the section titled 'Foreign Policy, International Organisations', the CMP declares 'The UPA government will pursue an independent foreign policy keeping in mind its past traditions. This policy will seek to promote multi-polarity in world relations and oppose all attempts at unilateralism' (UPA 2004, 22).

The CMP further asserts:

> The UPA government will give the highest priority to building closer political, economic and other ties with its neighbours in South Asia and to strengthening SAARC...Trade and investment with China will be expanded further and talks on the border issue pursued seriously. Relationships with East Asian countries will be intensified. Traditional ties with West Asia will be given a fresh thrust ... Even as it pursues closer engagement and relations with the USA, the UPA government will maintain the independence of India's foreign policy position on all regional and global issues. The UPA is committed to deepening ties with Russia and Europe as well ... the UPA government will fully protect the national interest, particularly of farmers, in all WTO negotiations ... The UPA government will use the flexibility afforded in existing WTO agreements to fully protect Indian agriculture and industry. The UPA government will play a proactive role in strengthening the emerging solidarity of developing countries in the shape of G-20 in the WTO. (UPA 2004, 23)

From the CMP, it was clear that the major objectives of the UPA government's foreign policy would be: *first*, to improve relations with South Asian neighbours; *second*, strengthen economic relations with China; *third*, forge closer relations with East Asian, West Asian, and European nations; *fourth*, enhancing relations with the United States as well as Russia; *fifth*, in the context of WTO negotiations, protect the interests of Indian farmers; *sixth*, seeking a multipolar world; and *finally*, while pursuing the above objectives, maintaining the independence of foreign policy.

Later, in 2013, towards the end of the two UPA administrations, Prime Minister Manmohan Singh, in his address to a conclave of Indian diplomats, outlined the basic principles and objectives that have underpinned the foreign policy of UPA-I and UPA-II governments since 2004.

Asserting that the two UPA administrations have brought about a 'fundamental reset' in India's foreign policy, Singh identified five principles that have guided and still guiding the foreign policy of his two governments: *first*, India's developmental priorities have been the key to its foreign policy; *second*, greater integration with the world economy; *third*, enhancing relations with major powers; *fourth*, enhancing regional cooperation and connectivity among South Asian countries; and *fifth*, foreign policy of India will not be guided solely by India's interest but also by the values cherished by the Indian people (Singh 2013).

Scholars are divided over the extent to which the UPA government has been successful or otherwise in securing the previously mentioned principles and objectives. Scholars like Ian Hall observe that the foreign policy of the UPA government helped 'maintain and accelerate India's economic development, manage key security challenges, especially those posed by China, provide India with access to regional and global forums at which its voice would be heard, and allow it to promote its own values without committing to a Western normative agenda' (Hall 2016, 279). A similar assessment has been made by Malone et al. (2015, 16), who list the positive outcomes of UPA's foreign policy including India's enhanced 'international profile' and greater role in global economic governance through institutions like the G20 and BRICS. Others like Jacob and Layton listed the 'failings' of UPA's foreign policy, including in its Pakistan policy, neighbourhood policy, China policy, the U.S. policy, and on anti-terror policy (Jacob and Layton 2009, 13–15). Ankit Panda (2013) and C Raja Mohan (2013) have a more balanced assessment. Raja Mohan gives a thumbs up to UPA-I and a thumbs down to UPA-II as far as foreign policy is concerned. While in its first term, feels Raja Mohan (2013), the UPA government 'created unprecedented diplomatic opportunities', in its second term it squandered them. To buttress his argument, Raja Mohan lists three major 'debacles' of UPA-II: the 'mishandling' of the nuclear liability legislation in 2010; failure to improve relations with neighbours; and bringing back 'discredited' non-alignment (Raja Mohan 2013). Panda (2014), too thinks that the record of UPA-I has been better than that of UPA-II in the realm of foreign policy.

Regarding the changes and continuity in India's foreign policy, too, the assessments of scholars are mixed. Ian Hall (2016, 275), for example, observes that the UPA government brought about significant changes in 'driving principles' and practices of India's foreign policy Others like Shivshankar Menon (2016, 4), Harsh pant (2012, 12), and Raviprasad Narayanan (2008, 25) find elements of continuity with the foreign policy of the previous NDA government more marked.

Rationale of the Volume

At this stage, the pertinent question is why a volume on India's diplomacy during the UPA rule? The answer lies in the existence of a glaring gap in the existing literature.

A cursory look at the existing literature on India's foreign policy makes one notice two trends.

First, there are those writings on India's foreign policy—incidentally, they dominate the field—which follows the neorealist tradition and tends to ignore the political complexion of the government and the personality of the prime minister with the assumption that foreign policy is largely determined by systemic factors and the role of the political dispensation or for that matter leadership is marginal. Such writings normally do not periodize their analysis. Notable examples of such literature on India's foreign policy are Cohen (2001), Ganguli (2003), Nayar and Paul (2003), Raja Mohan (2003), Kapur (2006), Sinha and Mohta (2007), Sikri (2009), Pant (2008), Malone (2011), Scott (2011), Bajpai and Pant (2013), and Malone et al. (2015).

Second, there are those that treat foreign policy as solely or at least mainly the product of the ideas, imaginations, and attitudes of a 'great leader'. Such literature were extant during the time of Nehru and to a lesser extent that of Indira Gandhi and Atal Bihari Vajpayee. Examples of such literature are Murti (1953), Thapar and Rajan (1951), Mansingh (1984), and Sondhi and Nanda (1999). What is interesting is that such *first image*-based accounts of the foreign policy of India (for a theoretical overview of three images of foreign policy analysis, see Waltz 1959), after their conspicuous absence in the ten years of two UPA governments, have made a big comeback after the NDA came to power in 2014 with a number of notable volumes including Tremblay and Kapur (2017), Raja Mohan (2015), Chaulia (2016), and Ganguli et al. (2016). I would hesitate to add Sinderpal Singh (2017) to this list as the latter, contrary to what its title suggests, is a much more balanced account than the previously mentioned volumes.

This brings us to the puzzle, why the ten-year-long period of two UPA governments received so little attention of the foreign policy epistemic community? Does the UPA decade lack of sufficient interesting developments in foreign policy so as to deserve a bit more detailed scholarly scrutiny than a few opinion pieces in magazines and newspapers such as Jacob and Layton (2009), Panda (2013), Panda (2014), and Raja Mohan (2013)? The only notable scholarly work on the UPA government's foreign policy is a chapter by Kanti Bajpai (2012). Does the foreign policy of the UPA government show too much of a continuity with the previous NDA Government to merit a bit more detailed scholarly treatment?

This is all the more baffling because during the period, some very interesting developments took place in how India engages the world, including India's entry into the international nuclear cooperation regime and into global economic governance structure in the form of G20.

Therefore, it seems that there is a gap in the literature on India's foreign policy waiting to be filled. This volume is an attempt to bridge this gap.

Apart from the previously mentioned gap, the volume's relevance in the literature on Indian foreign policy stems from one more factor. For the last two decades, India is being ruled alternately by the NDA and the UPA and if the present political scenario in India is any indication, this trend will continue for some time in the near future, at least for the next one or two decades. This makes it critically important for any keen observer of India's foreign policy to understand the commonalities and differences in the foreign policy orientations of the UPA as well as that of the NDA so as to predict accurately the continuities and changes that might be seen over the medium term in India's foreign policy. The current gap in the literature makes it difficult for the scholars and policy-makers to make such a comparison. With the publication of this volume on UPA's foreign policy, the observers of India's foreign policy will have an opportunity to study this volume together with the existing literature on NDA's foreign policy to make a comparison between the foreign policies of the two leading political coalitions in India.

One might ask a question: why to bring out a volume seven years after the end of the period? The answer is—a seven-year period is long enough a distance to develop the hindsight needed for a dispassionate, objective, and scholarly reflection on the ten-year period under study. An immediate exercise would have engendered bias towards the immediate past, that is, the later part of the UPA period, as many of the writings published one or two years after the UPA rule can be seen to give too much weightage to the last one/two years of activity/inactivity of the UPA government and tended to underemphasize the foreign policy activities of initial UPA years, especially its first five-year term. A seven-year gap is a good temporal distance to develop a bird's eye view of the ten-year-long period of UPA rule, giving equal importance to both UPA-I and UPA-II. Also, the seven-year distance is not too long as to decrease the contemporary relevance of the period we are studying. Also, the ten-year period is a long enough timespan for developing a historical analysis of the period with a view to find out the medium-/long-term trends as well as to detect the elements of continuities and changes in foreign policy orientation.

Volume Overview

This volume does not start with *a priory* assumption that the ten years of the UPA government led to a radical shift in India's foreign policy. It rather seeks to examine the shift, if any, along with continuities to develop a more nuanced understanding of the evolution of India's foreign policy. The volume brings together some of the best International Relations scholars of the world. A few of them are at the beginning of their academic careers. The rest are already recognized as eminent IR scholars, having published some of the finest works in the field and holding or have held in the recent past responsible posts in leading universities and think tanks around the world, key government bodies, or at the United Nations Organization. The institutional affiliations of the authors of this volume include some of the leading institutions of higher learning and research around the world, including the University of Oxford, New York University, University of Michigan—Ann Arbor, Fletcher School of Law and Diplomacy—Tufts University, School of Oriental and African Studies—University of London, University of Paris—VIII, Australian National University, University of Melbourne, University of Manchester, University of Aberdeen, Jawaharlal Nehru University, French Institute of International Relations, and International Institute of Strategic Studies

London. The rationale for including authors from this diverse range of institutions is that this will provide a broader perspective of India's foreign policy during the period under study.

The first and introductory part of this volume consists of the present chapter. The remaining fifteen chapters of this volume are organized into four parts. Each of the next three parts examines an important aspect of India's diplomacy during the period under study. The second part of this book examines India's important bilateral relations. The third part examines diplomatic outreach towards key geographic regions of interest to India. The fourth part examines key thematic issues in India's foreign policy. The fifth part concludes this volume by summarizing its findings.

The second part of this volume examines India's key bilateral relations, namely, that with the United States, China, Russia, Japan, and Pakistan.

In Chapter 2, which begins the second part of this volume, Timothy J. Lynch examines India-U.S. relations during the UPA period. Using four levels of analysis—personality, ideology, geopolitics, and economics—Lynch tries to determine what factors drove and hindered the relationship between the world's oldest and the largest democracy during the period. Lynch's conclusion is that while there has been notable progress in the relationship during the period, the progress in implementation of the agreements reached has been less than satisfactory. Lynch explains this anomaly by arguing that while the agreements were the results of the strong political will at the leadership level, the implementation of these agreements became mired in the complexities of the domestic setting.

In Chapter 3, Srikanth Kondapalli assesses the relations between India and China during the UPA period. He finds several similarities in the priorities of the leadership of the two Asian giants during the period, including focus on economic reforms and emphasis on economic growth but also several differences including China's irredentist claim over Arunachal Pradesh. Examining the relations in bilateral as well as multilateral context, Kondapalli finds that the relations were better in the multilateral context than bilateral. He concludes that the relationship was relatively smooth during the period despite some differences. One of the reasons for this, Kondapalli finds, is increased economic interdependence between them. He also finds that 'institutionalization of process of communication at almost all levels' has been the main feature of India's diplomacy towards China during this period.

In Chapter 4, Mervin Bain examines India-Russia relations during the UPA period. Examining the impact of the interplay between 'Putin Doctrine' and 'Manmohan Doctrine', Bain finds out that, despite the seeming contradiction between these two doctrines, they actually helped rather than hindered the progress in relations.

In Chapter 5, Shutaro Sano seeks to assess the relations between Japan and India during the UPA decade by focusing on security issues. Sano makes a detailed examination of the key drivers of the security relations between the two nations as well as the major factors that helped or hindered the security relations during the period. He finds that drastic changes in international and regional security environments were the two main drivers of the enhanced security cooperation between the two nations during the period. In addition to these two drivers, Sano finds three factors that have helped enhance the security relations between the two nations, namely increased closeness between Japan and the United States, Japan's value-oriented diplomacy, and the deepening of India-U.S. relations. However, he also finds three factors that hindered the growth of their security relations, namely wariness on the part of the two nations to antagonize China, different foreign policy orientations of the two nations with Japan's emphasis on its alliance with the United States and India's emphasis on its strategic autonomy, and domestic political instability of Japan.

In Chapter 6, which concludes the second part of this volume, Isabelle Saint-Mézard examines India's relations with its somewhat difficult neighbour—Pakistan. Sketching the trajectory of conflict between the two countries, Saint-Mézard highlights the attempts made by the first UPA government to push multiple formats of negotiations with Pakistan. She underlines the reluctance of the two UPA governments to resort to the use of force in response to Pakistan-based terrorist attacks, and their preference for a diplomatic approach to deal with the issue. The chapter finally identifies the main factors hindering the improvement in the bilateral relationship.

The third part of this volume examines India's diplomatic outreach towards four key geographic regions of interest to India, namely, South Asia, East and Southeast Asia, Africa, and Central Asia.

In Chapter 7, which begins the third part of this volume, Thomas P. Cavanna studies India's policy towards its South Asian neighbourhood during the period. Cavanna finds four factors that frustrated India's

South Asia policy during the UPA period: Pakistan's provocative policies, legacy of mistrust towards India among its South Asian neighbours, India's financial limitations, India's political and bureaucratic constraints, and China's increasing influence in the region.

In Chapter 8, John D. Ciorciari examines the development of India's 'Look East' policy during the UPA period. Ciorciari argues that the policy played a crucial role in reshaping Asia's political geography, helping India move from being a peripheral actor in the Asia-Pacific region to a major node in the ascendant 'Indo-Pacific' area. He finds that the UPA leadership prioritized engagement with Southeast and East Asian partners to promote regional integration—both for its lagging north-eastern states and its economy as a whole—and to address mounting strategic concerns about China. Ciorciari also finds that the UPA's proactive Look East policy, coupled with regional receptiveness to a larger Indian role in the evolving power equilibrium, contributed considerably to the emergence of a more robust Indo-Pacific order.

In Chapter 9, Barnaby Dye and Ricardo Soares de Oliveira trace the evolution of India's relations with Africa during the UPA period. While acknowledging the importance of a number of flagship initiatives that the UPA government launched to give a spur to the relations with the continent accompanied with 'much fanfare, using the grand rhetoric of South-South Cooperation', they ask: 'Has this rhetoric matched actions? And how responsible was the UPA government for the booming India-Africa relationship? ...' The chapter makes three arguments about India-Africa relations during the UPA period. *First*, the chapter emphasizes the role of the Indian private sector, rather than the government, as the central actor driving India-Africa ties. *Second*, the chapter argues that there was a contrast between government rhetoric and reality on the ground vis-à-vis the growth of India's relations with the continent during this period. *Third*, the chapter argues that the drivers for India's interest in the continent lay more in fear of other Asian states, especially China, gaining ground and in a desire to secure natural resources. Finally, Dye and Soares de Oliveira maintain that though India-Africa relations under the UPA administration reached new heights, they essentially followed the established trajectory.

In Chapter 10, Bhavna Dave examines relations between India and Central Asian countries during the ten-year period of the UPA rule.

The chapter identifies the processes shaping India's diplomacy towards Central Asia during the period, leading to the adoption of 'Connect Central Asia' policy in 2012, which Dave argues, was India's first comprehensive attempt to develop a strategy for the region. The chapter analyses the policies and measures adopted by the UPA in four key areas: (i) connectivity, (ii) energy partnerships, (iii) strategic engagement, and (iv) multilateral cooperation. Dave finds that India's Central Asia policy has evolved through adjustments to a number of important geopolitical shifts in the region. She finds that India, during the UPA period, carved out its options in the region through an enhanced multilateral cooperation with a range of actors and institutions and building on the niches where it possessed a distinct edge.

Chapters in the fourth part examine five key thematic issues in India's foreign policy during the period. They are nuclear diplomacy, diplomacy to secure permanent membership of the UN Security Council, maritime diplomacy, energy diplomacy, and India at the WTO negotiations.

In Chapter 11, which begins the fourth part of this volume, Ramesh Thakur examines India's nuclear diplomacy during the UPA rule. Thakur contends that the 'signature nuclear legacy' of the UPA government is the nuclear deal with the United States, which has 'unlocked the global strategic frame' for India. After a thorough examination of the negotiation process that went behind the deal, he concludes that the deal would not have been possible without 'the personal commitment and directives' of President Bush and Prime Minister Singh. Apart from this deal, other salient features of India's nuclear diplomacy during the period, observes Thakur, were its pursuit of membership of four 'key export control regimes', namely the Nuclear Suppliers Group (NSG), Missile Technology Control Regime (MTCR), Australia Group, and Wassenaar Arrangement.

In Chapter 12, Kate Sullivan de Estrada and Babak Moussavi trace the diplomatic efforts that India made during the UPA years to secure permanent membership of the *United Nations Security Council.* Sullivan de Estrada and Moussavi found significant activism by India towards this end—both in terms of forging coalitions in the form of G4 and L69 and in terms of securing Individual country pledges from as many as 82 member states of the UN in support of India's candidature as a permanent member. They also examined India's performance as an elected member of the UNSC for the period 2011–12, which were '(v)iewed by many as

India's dry run for permanent membership,' and found that India adopted a 'proactive stance' in the UNSC as an elected member on some important issues of international concern during the period, including the issues of UN Peacekeeping, Counter-terrorism, and anti-piracy. However, on the issues of Libya and Syria, India adopted a more cautious stand, thus sending 'conflicting signals' to the international community. They also found that the reform process was hindered due to counter moves by opposing coalitions like the 'Uniting for Consensus' as well as due to opposition of some permanent members like China.

In Chapter 13, Rahul Roy-Chaudhury traces India's maritime diplomacy during the UPA period. Roy-Chaudhury finds that the UPA government gave 'greater focus' to maritime affairs compared to its predecessors. He proffers three reasons for this increased focus: growing importance of energy imports through the sea, concern over increasing Chinese presence in the Indian Ocean, and the Mumbai terror attack the perpetrators of which came through the sea. Roy-Chaudhury observes that while the previous NDA government considered India's area of maritime interest to range from the Persian Gulf to the Malacca straits, the UPA government expanded the area of interest to include South China Sea and 'other areas of west pacific'. He finds that India's maritime diplomacy during the period is marked with: accepting greater roles and responsibilities in the maritime domain, announcement of itself as a 'net security provider' in the Indian Ocean, anti-piracy patrols, continuous updation of official maritime doctrine and strategy, deepening of naval cooperation with friendly navies, and naval expansion and modernization.

In Chapter 14, Carolyn Kissane explores India's energy diplomacy during the UPA decade, specifically focusing on how India used various diplomatic initiatives to secure energy resources—fossil fuels and non-conventional sources of energy—and technologies for becoming energy efficient. Examining India's burgeoning energy needs amidst rising global prices during the period, Kissane points out the energy security challenges faced by the UPA in its efforts to fuel a rapidly growing economy. As a result of this, she argues, energy diplomacy became an important, even critical, part of India's diplomacy. The chapter provides an in-depth look at the diplomatic strategies for securing energy resources and technologies employed by India during the period. Kissane finds that the UPA government's energy diplomacy sought to ensure India's energy security through a number of strategies, notably: strengthening relations with oil and gas resource-rich countries through exchange of bilateral visits; hosting of energy conferences and summits; acquiring overseas oil and gas assets through India's state-owned company ONGC Videsh Limited; signing of agreements for the supply of natural gas; investing in power generation projects in coal resource-rich countries through India's state-owned company National Thermal Power Corporation Limited (NTPC); and concluding agreements with nations having advanced nuclear technology as well as those having large deposits of nuclear fuels for securing advanced technology and nuclear fuel for India's nuclear power program.

In Chapter 15, which concludes the fourth part of this volume, Vinícius Rodrigues Vieira studies India's approach towards the WTO negotiations during the UPA period. Rodrigues Vieira finds that the UPA government's approach towards WTO negotiations was based on balancing between defensive interests of Indian agriculture and small-scale industries and the offensive interests of its service sector. Examining how the domestic pressure and international factors interacted to shape India's policy in this context, Rodrigues Vieira concludes that India's position in WTO negotiations during the UPA period should be understood 'less in terms of partisan preferences rather than because of transformation in both international and domestic environments during the period'.

The fifth part concludes this volume. .

In Chapter 16, the only chapter in the fifth part of the volume, the editor Rejaul Karim Laskar sums up the findings of the volume to reach a number of important conclusions about the foreign policy of India during the UPA period. Laskar argues that a number of short- and medium-term foreign policy objectives of the UPA government are clearly discernible from the findings of the previous chapters of this volume. He lists these objectives and also lists the major instruments that the UPA government used to secure these objectives, in light of the findings of the previous chapters of this volume. Laskar argues that the findings of the chapters of this volume clearly indicate that the ten-year period of the UPA government led to a transformation in a number of aspects of India's foreign relations. He sums up the most notable among these transformations. However, Laskar acknowledges that there were significant continuities in some other aspects. Finally, he concludes the chapter with some suggestions for future research.

The objectives of this volume are two-fold: (i) to give the readers a sense of the direction of India's foreign policy during the period of two UPA administrations, including the objectives sought to be achieved, the instruments used to achieve these objectives and the principles adhered to while trying to secure these objectives and (ii) to make an objective assessment of the foreign policy of the two UPA administrations.

India's foreign policy is a vast field and any book—whether monograph or edited volume—cannot be fairly expected to cover it in its entirety. This present volume is no exception. The list of the topics covered in this volume is not exhaustive. Some important bilateral relations of India, including that with the UK, France, Australia, South Africa, Israel, Iran, and South Korea, have not been covered. Similarly, India's policy towards three important regions, namely Europe, West Asia, and Latin America, has been left out. Among the important thematic areas, environmental diplomacy has not been covered. It is hoped that these areas will be covered in a subsequent edition.

The volume will be an essential reading for policymakers, scholars, students, and observers of India's foreign policy. At the same time, the language and style of the volume are simple enough to be accessible to general readers who do not have any special knowledge or training in foreign policy but are interested to have an understanding of India's foreign policy.

Notes

1. The author would like to thank Mr. Salman Khurshid—who was the *External Affairs Minister* of India for a significant portion of the time period covered by this book—for giving valuable time form his busy schedule for an informal discussion and also for explaining very cogently the ideas that drove the UPA government's diplomacy.

2. Notable neoclassical literature include: Thomas J. Christensen. 1996. *Useful Adversaries: Grand Strategy, Domestic Mobilization, and Sino-American Conflict, 1947–1958*. Princeton: Princeton University Press; Michael E. Brown et al. (eds.). 1995. *The Perils of Anarchy: Contemporary Realism and International Security*. Cambridge: MIT Press; Fareed Zakaria. 1998. *From Wealth to Power: The Unusual Origins of Americas World Role*. Princeton: Princeton University Press; William Curti Wohlforth. 1993. *The Elusive Balance: Power and Perceptions during the Cold War*. Ithaca, NY: Cornell University Press; and Randall L. Schweller.

1998. *Deadly Imbalances: Tripolarity and Hitlers Strategy of World Conquest.*
New York: Columbia University Press.

3. Political parties are not mere vote maximizers the way economic firms are profit
maximizers. In fact, they are rooted in certain ideology and policies rooted in that
ideology. They will not adopt a policy even if it is popular to the general voters
and its adoption increases their chance at the upcoming elections if that under-
cuts their ideology. This is so because this will damage their long-term credibility (Hanna Bäck, Marc Debus, and Patrick Dumont. 2011. 'Who Gets What
in Coalition Governments? Predictors of Portfolio Allocation in Parliamentary
Democracies'. *European Journal of Political Research*. Vol. 50: 441–478). In other
words, a party's primary loyalty is to its ideology and resultant policies and it is
these ideology and policies that is the *raison-de-etre* of the party. This is true for
all public policies, including foreign policy.

4. A popular phrase capturing this realist assumption is 'politics stop at the water's
edge' (Jeroen Joly and Regis Dandoy. 2018. 'Beyond the Water's Edge: How
Political Parties Influence Foreign Policy Formulation in Belgium'. *Foreign Policy
Analysis*. Vol. 14: 512–535) which implies that foreign policy is beyond the reach
of domestic politics.

5. Some of the notable empirical studies that find foreign policy to be affected by
partisan domestic politics have been referred to in the previous section while discussing the role of leadership on foreign policy, some more will be referred to in
the present section.

6. Hinich and Munger define ideology as 'complex, dogmatic belief systems by
which individuals interpret, rationalize, and justify behavior and institutions'
(quoted in Costel Calin. 2010. *Hawks Versus Doves: The Influence of Political
Ideology on the Foreign Policy Behavior of Democratic States*. PhD Dissertation.
Knoxville: The University of Tennessee. p. 44).

7. Indeed, to what extent a prime minister acts on the advice of party institutions
and to what extent he acts on the advice of the members of the permanent bureaucracy is another important area that needs empirical study.

8. The last two *plenary sessions* of the AICC were held in 2010 and 2018, respectively.

9. For detailed accounts on Nehru's thinking on foreign policy, the reader may con-
sult the following primary and secondary literature: Jawaharlal Nehru. 1972.
Selected Works of Jawaharlal Nehru. Volume Two. New Delhi: Orient Longman;
Jawaharlal Nehru. 1961. *India's Foreign Policy: Selected Speeches, September 1946–
April 1961.* The Publications Division, Ministry of Information and Broadcasting,
Government of India; Paul F. Power. 1964. 'Indian Foreign Policy: The Age of
Nehru'. *The Review of Politics*. Vol. 26, No. 2: 257–286; Vipin Narang and Paul
Staniland. 2012. 'Institutions and Worldviews in Indian Foreign Security
Policy'. *India Review*. Vol. 11, No. 2: 76–94; Nalini Kant Jha. 2003. 'Nehru and
modern india: impact of his personality on foreign policy', in T. A. Nizami (ed.).
Jawaharlal Nehru and Modern India. Aligarh: Three Way Printers; Sumit Ganguly
and Manjeet S. Pardesi. 2009. 'Explaining Sixty Years of India's Foreign Policy'.

India Review. Vol. 8, No. 1: 4–19; and A. Appadorai. 1981. *The Domestic Roots of India's Foreign Policy: 1947–1972*. New Delhi: Oxford University Press.
10. 'India-China Agreement on Trade and Intercourse between Tibet Region of China and India' signed by Nehru and Chou-en-Lai in 1954.
11. The ministry was renamed as Ministry of Overseas Indian Affairs in September 2004 and played a significant role in protecting and promoting the interests of Indian Diaspora for over a decade before ultimately being abolished by the Narendra Modi-led NDA government in 2016.

References

All India Congress Committee. 2004. *Manifesto of the Indian National Congress for 2004 Lok Sabha Elections*. New Delhi: All India Congress Committee.
All India Congress Committee. 2009. *Lok Sabha Elections 2009: Manifesto of the Indian National Congress*. New Delhi: All India Congress Committee.
All India Congress Committee. 2010. *Foreign Policy Resolution, 83rd Plenary Session of All India Congress Committee*. New Delhi: All India Congress Committee.
All India Congress Committee. 2013. 'The Jaipur Declaration, All India Congress Committee'. *Congress Sandesh*. Vol. XV, No. 5: 14–19.
All India Congress Committee. 2014. *Lok Sabha Elections 2014: Manifesto of the Indian National Congress*. New Delhi: All India Congress Committee.
All India Congress Committee. 2019. Manifesto: *Lok Sabha Elections 2019*. New Delhi: All India Congress Committee.
Appadorai, A. 1981. *The Domestic Roots of India's Foreign Policy: 1947–1972*. New Delhi: Oxford University Press.
Bajpai, Kanti. 2012. 'The UPA's foreign policy, 2004–9' in Lawrence Sáez and Gurharpal Singh (eds). *New Dimensions of Politics in India: The United Progressive Alliance in Power*. 99–112. New York: Routledge.
Bajpai, K.P. and H.V. Pant (eds). 2013. *India's Foreign Policy: A Reader*. New Delhi: Oxford University Press.
Bak, Daehee and Glenn Palmer. 2010. 'Testing the Biden Hypotheses: Leader Tenure, Age, and International Conflict'. *Foreign Policy Analysis*. Vol. 6, No. 3: 257–273.
Bandyopadhyaya, Jayantanuja. 1979. *The Making of India's Foreign Policy: Determinants, Processes and Personalities*. Mumbai: Allied Publishers.
Beasley, Ryan K. and Juliet Kaarbo. 2014. 'Explaining Extremity in the Foreign Policies of Parliamentary Democracies'. *International Studies Quarterly*. No. 58: 729–740.
Blanton, Shannon Lindsey. 1996. 'Images in Conflict: The Case of Ronald Reagan and El Salvador', *International Studies Quarterly*. Vol. 40, No. 1: 23–44.
Brommesson, Douglas and Ann-Marie Ekengren. 2019. 'When, How and Why Are Junior Coalition Parties Able to Affect a Government's Foreign Policy? A Study of Swedish Coalition Governments 2006–2014'. *Scandinavian Political Studies*. Vol. 42, No. 3–4: 203–219.
Byman, Daniel L. and Kenneth M. Pollack. 2001. 'Let Us Now Praise Great Men: Bringing the Statesman Back In'. *International Security*. Vol. 25, No. 4: 107–146.

Calin, Costel. 2010. *Hawks Versus Doves: The Influence of Political Ideology on the Foreign Policy Behavior of Democratic States*. PhD Dissertation. Knoxville: The University of Tennessee.

Calin, Costel and Brandon Prins. 2015. 'The Sources of Presidential Foreign Policy Decision Making: Executive Experience and Militarized Interstate Conflicts'. *International Journal of Peace Studies*. Vol. 20, No. 1: 17–34.

Chaulia, Sreeram. 2016. *Modi Doctrine: The Foreign Policy of India's Prime Minister*. New Delhi: Bloomsbury.

Clare, Joe. 2010. 'Ideological Fractionalization and the International Conflict Behavior of Parliamentary Democracies'. *International Studies Quarterly*. Vol. 54: 965–987.

CNN. 2004. Singh sworn in as India PM. CNN, 22 May 2004. http://edition.cnn.com/2004/WORLD/asiapcf/05/21/india.prime.minister/ (accessed 17 March 2019).

Cohen, Stephen P. 2001. *India: Emerging Power*. Washington, DC: Brookings Institution Press.

Coticchia, Fabrizio and Jason W. Davidson. 2016. 'The Limits of Radical Parties in Coalition Foreign Policy: Italy, Hijacking, and the Extremity Hypothesis'. *Foreign Policy Analysis*. Vol. 14: 149–168.

Crichlow, Robert Scott. 2001. *The Impact of Individuals on Foreign Policy Decision Making*. PhD Dissertation. Baton Rouge: Louisiana State University.

Dyson, Stephen Benedict. 2009. 'Cognitive Style and Foreign Policy: Margaret Thatcher's Black-and-White Thinking'. *International Political Science Review*. Vol. 30, No. 1: 33–48.

Encyclopaedia Britannica. Undated. 'Indian National Congress: Policy and Structure', *Encyclopaedia Britannica*, https://www.britannica.com/topic/Indian-National-Congress/Policy-and-structure (accessed 15 January 2020).

Gandhi, Sonia. 2006. 'A Global Force for Peace, Progress & Prosperity: Address by Smt. Sonia Gandhi in The Hindustan Times Leadership Summit on 17th November, 2006 Held in New Delhi'. *Congress Sandesh*. Vol. 9, No. 4: 9–11.

Ganguly, Anirban, Vijay Chauthaiwale, and Uttam Kumar Sinha (eds). 2016. *The Modi Doctrine: New Paradigms in India's Foreign Policy*. New Delhi: Wisdom Tree.

Ganguli, S. (ed). 2003. *Indian as an Emerging Power*. London: Frank Cass.

Ganguly, Sumit and Manjeet S. Pardesi. 2009. 'Explaining Sixty Years of India's Foreign Policy'. *India Review*. Vol. 8, No. 1: 4–19.

Goldstein, J. and Keohane R. (eds). 1993. *Ideas and Foreign policy*. Ithaca, NY: Cornell University Press.

Hagan, Joe D. 1993. *Political Opposition and Foreign Policy in Comparative Perspective*. Boulder, CO: Lynne Rienner.

Hall, Ian. 2016. 'Multialignment and Indian Foreign Policy under Narendra Modi'. *The Round Table*. Vol. 105, No. 3: 271–286. DOI: 10.1080/00358533.2016.1180760.

Hasan, Zoya. 2002. *Parties and Party Politics in India*. New Delhi: Oxford University Press.

Hermann, Margaret G. 1980. 'Explaining Foreign Policy Behavior Using the Personal Characteristics of Political Leaders'. *International Studies Quarterly*. Vol. 24, No. 1: 7–46.

FOREIGN POLICY OF CONGRESS PARTY-LED UPA 49

Horowitz, Michael, Rose McDermott, and Allan C. Stam. 2005. 'Leader Age, Regime Type, and Violent International Relations'. *The Journal of Conflict Resolution*. Vol. 49, No. 5: 661–685.

Indian National Congress. 2018. *Resolution on Foreign Policy, 84th Plenary Session of Indian National Congress*, New Delhi, 17–19 March 2018. p. 3. https://www.inc.in/en/media/press-releases/foreign-policy-resolution-at-84th-plenary-session-of-indian-national-congress-at-igi-stadium-new-delhi (accessed 12 February 2020).

Indian National Congress. Undated. *First Session of the Congress: The Journey Begins*. https://www.inc.in/en/inc-timeline/1885-1895 (accessed 7 February 2020).

Ireland, Michael J. and Scott Sigmund Gartner. 2001. 'Time to Fight: Government Type and Conflict Initiation in Parliamentary Systems'. *The Journal of Conflict Resolution*. Vol. 45, No. 5: 547–68.

Jacob, Happymon and Kimberley Layton. 2009. 'UPA's Foreign Policy: A Critique'. *Economic & Political Weekly*. Vol. XLIV, No. 25: 13–15.

Jervis, R. 1970. *The Logic of Images in International Relations*. Princeton, NJ: Princeton University Press.

Jervis, R. 1976. *Perception and Misperception in International Politics*. Princeton, NJ: Princeton University Press.

Jervis, Robert. 2013. 'Do Leaders Matter and How Would We Know?'. *Security Studies*. Vol. 22, No. 2: 153–179. DOI: 10.1080/09636412.2013.786909.

Joly, Jeroen and Regis Dandoy. 2018. 'Beyond the Water's Edge: How Political Parties Influence Foreign Policy Formulation in Belgium'. *Foreign Policy Analysis*. Vol. 14: 512–535.

Kaarbo, Juliet. 1993. *Power and Influence in Foreign Policy Decisionmaking: The Role of Junior Parties in Coalition Cabinets*. PhD Dissertation. Columbus, OH: The Ohio State University.

Kaarbo, Juliet. 1996. 'Power and Influence in Foreign Policy Decision Making: The Role of Junior Coalition Partners in German and Israeli Foreign Policy'. *International Studies Quarterly*. Vol. 40: 501–530.

Kaarbo, Juliet. 1997. 'Prime Minister Leadership Styles in Foreign Policy Decision-Making: A Framework for Research'. *Political Psychology*. Vol. 18, No. 3: 553–581.

Kaarbo, Juliet. 2008. 'Coalition Cabinet Decision Making: Institutional and Psychological Factors'. *International Studies Review*. Vol. 10: 57–86.

Kaarbo, Juliet. 2018. 'Prime Minister Leadership Style and the Role of Parliament in Security Policy'. *The British Journal of Politics and International Relations*. Vol. 20, No. 1: 35–51.

Kaarbo, Juliet and Ryan Beasley. 2008. 'Taking It to the Extreme: The Effect of Coalition Cabinets on Foreign Policy'. *Foreign Policy Analysis*. Vol. 4, No. 1: 67–81.

Kapur, A. 2006. *India: From Regional to World Power*. New York: Routledge.

Kapur, H. 1994. *India's Foreign Policy: 1947–1992 Shadows and Substance*. New Delhi: Sage.

Keller, Jonathan and Yi Yang. 2008. 'Leadership Style, Decision Context, and the Poliheuristic Theory of Decision Making: An Experimental Analysis'. *Journal of Conflict Resolution*. Vol. 52, No. 5: 687–712.

Kesgin, Baris. 2011. *Political Leadership and Foreign Policy in Post-Cold War Israel and Turkey*. PhD Dissertation. Lawrence, KS: University of Kansas.

Klingemann, Hans-Dieter, Richard I. Hofferbert, and Ian Budge. 1994. *Parties, Policies, and Democracy*. Boulder, CO: Westview.

Koch, Michael T. 2009. 'Governments, Partisanship, and Foreign Policy: The Case of Dispute Duration'. *Journal of Peace Research*. Vol. 46: 799–817.

Laskar, Rejaul. 2014. 'Rajiv Gandhi's Diplomacy: Historic Significance and Contemporary Relevance'. *Extraordinary and Plenipotentiary Diplomatist*. Vol. 2, No. 9: 46–47.

Laskar, Rejaul Karim. 2004. 'Respite from Disgraceful NDA Foreign Policy'. *Congress Sandesh*. Vol. 6, No. 10. June 2004: 8.

Laskar, Rejaul Karim. 2005. 'Strides in Look East Policy'. *Congress Sandesh*. Vol. 7, No. 11. July 2005: 19.

Levi, Ariel and Philip E. Tetlock. 1980. 'A Cognitive Analysis of Japan's 1941 Decision for War'. *Journal of Conflict Resolution*. Vol. 24, No. 2: 195–211.

Malone, D. 2011. *Does the Elephant Dance? Contemporary Indian Foreign Policy*. Oxford: Oxford University Press.

Malone, David M., C. Raja Mohan, and Srinath Raghavan. 2015. 'India and the world' in David M. Malone, C. Raja Mohan, and Srinath Raghavan (eds). *The Oxford Handbook of Indian Foreign Policy*. 3–20. New York: Oxford University Press.

Mansingh, Surjit. 1984. *India's Search for Power: Indira Gandhi's Foreign Policy: 1966–1982*. New Delhi: Sage.

Maoz, Z. and Russett, B. 1993. 'Normative and Structural Causes of Democratic Peace 1946–1986'. *American Journal of Political Science*. Vol. 87, No. 3: 624–638.

Martin, L. W. and G. Vanberg. 2011. *Parliaments and Coalitions: The Role of Legislative Institutions in Multiparty Governance*. Oxford: Oxford University Press.

Mathur, Krishan D. and P. M. Kamath.1996. *Conduct of India's Foreign Policy*. New Delhi: South Asian Publishers.

Menon, Shivshankar. 2016. *Choices: Inside the Making of India's Foreign Policy*. Washington, DC: Brookings Institution Press.

Morgenthau, Hans J. 1948. *Politics among Nations*. New York: Alfred A. Knopf.

Mukherjee, Pranab. 2007. 'India's Foreign Policy: Peace and Nonviolence (Speech by Shri Pranab Mukherjee, Hon'ble Minister of External Affairs, Government of India, at the International Satyagraha Conference, New Delhi January 29, 2007)'. *Congress Sandesh*. Vol. 9, No. 6: 22–23.

Murti, Bhaskarla Surya Narayana. 1953. *Nehru's Foreign Policy*. New Delhi: Beacon Information & Publications.

Narang, Vipin and Paul Staniland. 2012. 'Institutions and Worldviews in Indian Foreign Security Policy'. *India Review*. Vol. 11, No. 2: 76–94.

Narayanan, Raviprasad. 2008. 'India-China Relations: The United Progressive Alliance (UPA) Phase'. *Harvard Asia Quarterly*. Vol. 11, No. 4 (Fall): 24–31.

Nayar, B.R. and T.V. Paul. 2003. *India in the World Order: Searching for Major Power Status*. Cambridge: Cambridge University Press.

Nehru, Jawaharlal. 1961. *India's Foreign Policy: Selected Speeches, September 1946–April 1961*. The Publications Division, Ministry of Information and Broadcasting, Government of India.

Nehru, Jawaharlal. 1972. *Selected Works of Jawaharlal Nehru. Volume Two*. New Delhi: Orient Longman.

Oktay, Sibel. 2014. 'Constraining or Enabling? The Effects of Government Composition on International Commitments'. *Journal of European Public Policy*. Vol. 21, No. 6: 860–884.

Ozkececi-Taner, Binnur. 2005. 'The Impact of Institutionalized Ideas in Coalition Foreign Policy Making: Turkey as an Example, 1991–2002'. *Foreign Policy Analysis*. Vol. 1: 249–278.

Palmer, Glenn, Tamar R. London, and Patrick M. Regan. 2004. 'What's Stopping You?: The Sources of Political Constraints on International Conflict Behavior in Parliamentary Democracies'. *International Interactions*. Vol. 30: 1–24.

Panda, Ankit. 2013. 'Did India's 'Manmohan Doctrine' Succeed?'. *The Diplomat* (6 November 2013). https://thediplomat.com/2013/11/did-indias-manmohan-doctr ine-succeed/ (accessed 19 March 2019).

Panda, Ankit. 2014. 'India's UPA Government and Foreign Policy'. *The Diplomat* (18 January 2014). https://thediplomat.com/2014/01/indias-upa-government-and- foreign-policy/ (accessed 20 March 2019).

Pant, H. V. 2008. *Contemporary Debates in Indian Foreign and Security Policy: India Negotiates Its Rise in the International System*. New York: Palgrave Macmillan.

Pant, Harsh V. 2012. *Contemporary Debates in Indian Foreign and Security Policy*. Revised and Updated edition. Basingstoke: Palgrave Macmillan.

Patagundi, S.S. and Raghavendra Rao. 1981. 'The Indian Political Parties, Their, Foreign Policy and Strategic Concerns: An Investigation into the Content of the Election Manifestos'. *The Indian Journal of Political Science*. Vol. 42, No. 2: 28–40.

Post, Jerrold M. (ed). 2003. *The Psychological Assessment of Individual Leaders: With Profiles of Saddam Hussein and Bill Clinton*. Ann Arbor, MI: University of Michigan Press.

Potter, Philip B. K. 2007. 'Does Experience Matter? American Presidential Experience, Age, and International Conflict'. *Journal of Conflict Resolution*. Vol. 51 No. 3: 351–378.

Prasad, Bimal. 2013. *The Making of India's Foreign Policy: The Indian National Congress and World Affairs*. New Delhi: Vitasta.

Preston, John Thomas.1996. *The President and His Inner Circle: Leadership Style and the Advisory Process in Foreign Policy Making*. PhD Dissertation. Columbus, OH: Ohio State University.

Prins, Brandon C. and Christopher Sprecher. 1999. 'Institutional Constraints, Political Opposition, and Interstate Dispute Escalation: Evidence from Parliamentary Systems, 1946–89'. *Journal of Peace Research*. No. 36: 271–287.

Putnam, Robert D. 1988. 'Diplomacy and Domestic Politics: The Logic of Two-Level Games'. *International Organization*. Vol. 42, No. 3: 427–460.

Raja Mohan, C. 2003. *Crossing the Rubicon: The Shaping of India's New Foreign Policy*. New Delhi: Viking.

Raja Mohan, C. 2013. 'Won by UPA 1, lost by UPA 2'. *Indian Express* (5 Nov 2013). http://archive.indianexpress.com/news/won-by-upa-1-lost-by-upa-2/1190958 (accessed 16 March 2019).

Raja Mohan, C. 2015. *Modi's World: Expanding India's Sphere of Influence*. New Delhi: Harper Collins.

Ramesh, Randeep. 2004. 'Shock Defeat for India's Hindu Nationalists'. *The Guardian* (14 May 2004). https://www.theguardian.com/world/2004/may/14/india.randee pramesh (accessed 12 March 2019).

Rathbun, Brian C. 2004. *Partisan Interventions: European Party Politics and Peace Enforcement in the Balkans*. Ithaca, NY: Cornell University Press.

Reiter, Dan and Erik R. Tillman. 2002. 'Public, Legislative, and Executive Constraints on the Democratic Initiation of Conflict'. *Journal of Politics*. Vol. 64: 810–826.

Rose, Gideon. 1998. 'Neoclassical Realism and Theories of Foreign Policy'. *World Politics*. Vol. 51, No. 1: 144–172.

Scott, D. (ed). 2011. *Handbook of India's International Relations*. London: Routledge.

Sikri, R. 2009. *Challenge and Strategy: Rethinking India's Foreign Policy*. New Delhi: Sage.

Singh, Manmohan. 2008. 'Jawahar Lal Nehru—The founder of Modern India (Speech by Prime Minister Dr. Manmohan Singh at the Foundation Stone laying ceremony of Jawaharlal Nehru Bhavan, New Delhi)'. *Congress Sandesh*. Vol. 10, No. 5: 7–8.

Singh, Manmohan. 2013. 'Highlights of Prime Minister's Address at the Annual Conclave of Indian Ambassadors/High Commissioners Abroad, New Delhi, November 4, 2013'. https://www.mea.gov.in/Speeches-Statements.htm?dtl/22428/Highlights+of+Prime+Ministers+address+at+the+Annual+Conclave+of+Indian+AmbassadorsHigh+Commissioners+abroad+in+New+Delhi (accessed 22 March 2019).

Singh, Sinderpal. 2017. *Modi and the World: (Re)Constructing Indian Foreign Policy*. Singapore: World Scientific.

Sinha, Atish and Madhup Mohta. eds. 2007. *Indian Foreign Policy: Challenges and Opportunities*. New Delhi: Academic Foundation.

Snyder, R. C., H. W. Bruck, and B. Sapin (eds.) 1962. *Foreign Policy Decision-Making: An Approach to the Study of International Politics*. New York: Free Press.

Soikham, Piyanat. 2019. 'Revisiting a Dominant Party: Normative Dynamics of the Indian National Congress'. *Asian Journal of Comparative Politics*. Vol. 4, No. 1: 23–41.

Sondhi, M. L. and Prakash Nanda. 1999. *Vajpayee's Foreign Policy, Daring the Irreversible*. New Delhi: Har-Anand Publications.

Sridharan, Kripa. 2006. 'Explaining the Phenomenon of Change in Indian Foreign Policy under the National Democratic Alliance Government'. *Contemporary South Asia*. Vol. 15, No. 1: 75–91.

Tetlock, Philip E. 1991. 'Learning in U.S. and Soviet foreign policy: In search of an elusive concept' in G. Breslauer and P. E. Tetlock (eds). *Learning in U.S. and Soviet Foreign Policy*. 20–61. Boulder, CO: Westview.

Tetlock, Philip E. 1992. 'Good Judgment in World Politics: Three Psychological Perspectives'. *Political Psychology*. Vol. 13: 517–40.

Tetlock, Philip E. 1999. 'Theory-driven Reasoning about Plausible Pasts and Probable Futures in World Politics: Prisoners of Our Preconceptions?'. *American Journal of Political Science*. Vol. 43, No. 2: 335–366.

Thapar, Romesh and M. K. Rajan. 1951. *Nehru's Foreign Policy*. New Delhi: Crossroads Publication.

Tharoor, Shashi. 1982. *Reasons of State: Political Development and India's Foreign Policy under Indira Gandhi 1966–1977*. New Delhi: Vikas Publishing House.

The Hindu. 2004. 'UPA Government to Adhere to Six Basic Principles of Governance'. 28 May 2004. https://www.thehindu.com/2004/05/28/stories/2004052807371200. htm (accessed 13 March 2019).

Tremblay, Reeta Chowdhari and Ashok Kapur. 2017. *Modi's Foreign Policy*. New Delhi: Sage.

UPA (United Progressive Alliance). 2004. *National Common Minimum Programme of The Government of India*, May 2004. New Delhi: United Progressive Alliance.

Vertzberger, Yaacov. 1997. 'Collective risk taking: The decision-making group' in Paul T. Hart, Eric K. Stern, and Bengt Sundelius (eds). *Beyond Groupthink*. 275–307. Ann Arbor, MI: University of Michigan Press.

Vowles, J. 2010. 'Making a Difference? Public Perceptions of Coalition, Single-Party, and Minority Governments'. *Electoral Studies*. Vol. 29, No. 3: 370–380.

Wagnera, Wolfgang, Anna Herranz-Surrallésb, Juliet Kaarboc, and Falk Ostermannd. 2017. 'The Party Politics of Legislative-Executive Relations in Security and Defence Policy'. *West European Politics*. Vol. 40, No. 1: 20–41.

Waltz, Kenneth N. 1959. *Man, the State, and War: A Theoretical Analysis*. New York: Columbia University Press.

PART II
IMPORTANT BILATERAL RELATIONS

This part examines India's key bilateral relations, namely, that with the U.S., China, Russia, Japan, and Pakistan.

2

India-United States Relations during the United Progressive Alliance 2004–14

Timothy J. Lynch

Introduction

The relationship between India and the United States from 2004 to 2014 was to be played out against the backdrop of some of the most momentous events of the post-Cold War years. These included the bitter and bloody occupation of Iraq, the intractable Afghanistan war, a global war against terrorism, a great recession, the coming to office of America's first mixed-race president, Chinese expansionism and Russian revanchism. Given these issues, prioritizing a relationship that often did not directly bear on them was difficult for George W. Bush (2001–09) and Barack Obama (2009–17). But this did not preclude some remarkable developments in bilateral relations during the two terms of the United Progressive Alliance (UPA). While India was a priority for neither Bush nor Obama, each man attempted to recast the relationship, and both enjoyed success and failure in so doing.

This chapter audits those efforts at four levels of analysis (see Singer 1961; Yetiv 2004). Each constitutes a set of tools both sides used to advance their interests (see Rose 1998, 157). The first considers the role that leader images of each other and their respective interests played in the relationship. How far did the personal approaches of key leaders matter? The second analyses how far ideology and/or strategic cultural factors should have helped but often hindered progress. How were such issues used to advance relations? Why didn't the fact that both nations are large democracies guarantee cooperation? The third uses geopolitics as a guide to understanding change and continuity in the relationship.

Timothy J. Lynch, *India-United States Relations during the United Progressive Alliance 2004–14* In: *Forging New Partnerships, Breaching New Frontiers*. Edited by: Rejaul Karim Laskar, Oxford University Press. © Oxford University Press 2022. DOI: 10.1093/oso/9780192868060.003.0002

Did a common fear of Islamic extremism and competition with China bring the UPA and Bush and Obama administrations closer together and if so, how? The fourth level suggests that economics and trade provided a platform for a stronger relationship rather than the purpose of better relations itself. The levels are not separate and distinct categories. They blend and blur. One can affect several, and several, one. Each can sustain much longer studies than sketched here.

The years of UPA rule are neatly divided across two U.S. administrations, 2009 being the middle point when Barack Obama replaced George W. Bush and Manmohan Singh's UPA was re-elected (in January and May, respectively). The chapter compares the Indian policy of both American administrations—and its Indian reception—at each level of analysis. The chapter thus proceeds thematically rather than chronologically. Its emphasis is on the interrogation of arguments about what drove the relationship during the UPA years and how far this was a period of success or failure in U.S.-India relations—perhaps better understood in terms of hopes and expectations realized versus not and why. My conclusion is an upbeat one: despite ongoing American frustration at the speed and depth of implementation of some of the agreements, the symbolic achievement of the agreements themselves—from nuclear energy and defence to trade and cultural exchange—is what is remarkable about the 2004–14 period.

The two governments did not suddenly become friendlier. Rather, they reasoned that their respective national interests would be better met by substantive collaboration. Neither side obliged the other to reformulate its interests. Instead, each, to varying degrees, accepted that the symbolic advances would be necessarily subject to internal processes. In so doing, Indian and American decision-makers were conforming to what political scientists have called neoclassical realism (see Ripsman et al. 2009 and 2016). The pursuit of national interest, of power and of security, remained the fundamental objective of both Washington and New Delhi. How they pursued these objectives was conditioned by the character, history, and institutions of the states themselves. Intervening unit-level variables—which include leader perceptions, ideological divisions, bureaucratic traditions, and historical experiences—impacted on how the UPA and Bush and Obama administrations engaged with each other but less why they engaged: to increase the power and security of both. Thus, sentimentality does not explain the 2004–14 transformation. In those ten years, both sides worked out how to advance their respective national interests. Symbolic victories were a crucial part of this effort more than they were evidence of some new-found affection.

Leader Images

The pace of events, from the terrorist attacks of 11 September 2001, to the surge of the U.S. troops into Iraq in 2007, explains why the Middle East was the central focus of the George W. Bush administration. Bush himself gives India only two mentions in his 497-page memoir (Bush 2010, 213–14). These expressed frustration with Pakistan's obsession with India. Dick Cheney's (2011) memoir and Robert Draper's (2007) biography of Bush never mention India. In other texts covering the Bush years, references to India are sparse (see, for example, Baker 2013; Woodward 2008). The historic shift that took place in India's electoral politics in 2004 goes almost entirely unrecorded in the accounts of senior Bush officials (Gates 2014; Rice 2017; Rumsfeld 2011). The Mumbai terrorist attacks of November 2008, despite the potential to fit with Bush's global war on terror narrative, did not resonate much with him. Bush was not legacy hunting with his diplomacy towards New Delhi. In contrast, his initiatives in Africa to counter AIDS receive considerable attention in his memoirs and at his presidential library. He travelled only once to India (in March 2006) to sign the U.S.-India Civil Nuclear Agreement with Prime Minister Singh. Obama was slightly less economical with his Indian outreach, visiting twice. In November 2010, he met with President Pratibha Patil and Singh and, post-UPA, in January 2015 with Narendra Modi. Obama gives India eight (sometimes fulsome) mentions in his 751-page memoir (Obama 2020).Some experts asked whether Bush and Obama had a more ambivalent, even neglectful, rather than an engaged approach to India (Kearn 2014; Burns 2014). Others observed that the United States continued to play a role in Indian politics far greater than India played in America's (Gandhi 2014).

For his part, Manmohan Singh displayed an openness to work with the United States that stood in contrast to some of his predecessors. There seemed a genuine affection towards Bush in the Indian PM's rhetoric. 'The people of India deeply love you', Singh reassured Bush on his final visit to Washington (Giridharadas 2009). The warmth of the Bush-Singh relationship was striking, that with Obama less so. He was Obama's first official state visitor in November 2009, but, some observers claim, the 44th president's interest waned thereafter. Bush set great store in his empathy and feel for his foreign peers, famously declaring that he got a glimpse of Vladimir Putin's soul. Bush and Singh seemed temperamentally different characters–Singh was famed for his taciturn style, whereas Bush was loquacious—but shared enough of a world view to make their diplomacy work. Singh had been struck by Bush's insistence that India, with U.S. help, should join the ranks of the great powers.

The personal connection was, of course, catalysed by both history and events. In Singh, Bush had a counterpart who had direct experience of confronting Islamic extremism—America's renewed task after the 9/11 attacks—and of doing so within the constraints imposed by democratic institutions. 'We can look to the future with confidence', declared Bush, 'because our relationship has never been better. We are global leaders' (Bush 2006). Singh concurred, sharing in the broad parameters of Bush's ideological and universal vision. In 2002, Bush had affirmed that:

> the United States must defend liberty and justice because these principles are right and true for all people everywhere. No nation owns these aspirations, and no nation is exempt from them. Fathers and mothers in all societies want their children to be educated and to live free from poverty and violence. No people on earth yearn to be oppressed, aspire to servitude, or eagerly await the midnight knock of the secret police. America must stand firmly for the nonnegotiable demands of human dignity: the rule of law; limits on the absolute power of the state; free speech; freedom of worship; equal justice; respect for women; religious and ethnic tolerance; and respect for private property. (Bush 2002, 3)

In 2005, Singh echoed this central tenet of the Bush Doctrine for Indian consumption:

> If there is an 'idea of India' by which India should be defined, it is the idea of an inclusive, open, multi-cultural, multi-ethnic, multi-lingual society. I believe that this is the dominant trend of political evolution of all societies in the 21st century. Therefore, we have an obligation to

history and mankind to show that pluralism works. India must show that democracy can deliver development and empower the marginalized. Liberal democracy is the natural order of political organization in today's world. All alternate systems, authoritarian and majoritarian in varying degrees, are an aberration. (Singh 2005a)

It was no surprise, given this ideological kinship, that by the end of Bush's administration in 2009, 'relations between India and the United States were arguably the best they had ever been' (Kearn 2014, 29).

In contrast, according to several sources, Barack Obama neglected the relationship, certainly early on: 'India's strategic elites recognize that no other U.S. president is likely to match Bush's personal commitment to strengthening Indo-U.S. ties, but they worry that Barack Obama's apparent lack of interest could do real harm to the relationship and squander recent hard-won gains' (Ganguly and Kapur 2009; see also Kronstadt et al. 2011, 2). This argument is belied by Obama's evident fondness for Manmohan Singh (he called the Indian prime minister his 'guru') and his goal to build India into his 'rise of the rest' approach. The new Democratic president had been seemingly persuaded by Fareed Zakaria's (2008) book arguing that the United States needed to recognize, facilitate, and adapt to the rise of the BRICS: Brazil, Russia, India, China, and South Africa (Obama 2020, 336-339). There was a certain voguish acceptance in U.S. foreign policy circles during the first Obama administration that the BRICS would inherit the earth. This was not an analysis universally shared or even welcomed by Indian foreign policymakers. According to a senior official in the Indian prime minister's office, Obama's designation of India as a rising power was 'a rope to hang ourselves' (Miller 2013). But the Democratic president was, by disposition, taken with this prediction of where the global balance of power was moving. He had, after all, inherited the most severe economic depression since the 1930s and was pledged to wind-down U.S. military power in the Middle East. It seemed appropriate, even inevitable, to him that other rising (or re-rising) states, especially India and China, should assume a greater load of global social responsibilities. That this burden-sharing was not ultimately embraced, that the BRICS never cohered into anything approaching a new global axis (see Sharma 2012 and Pant 2016, 75–77), and that Obama's hope that India could secure a U.N. Security Council seat was 'far-fetched' (Indyk et al. 2012, 12), does not mean Obama did not intend such 'gains' and viewed his outreach to India through their lens.

Rather than lacking a personal interest and connection to India, Obama saw in the Singh ministry an opportunity to embed his worldview. 'The country,' he said, 'had always held a special place in my imagination' (Obama 2020, 598). Obama saw in Indian political development 'the power of nonviolent resistance' (Obama 2020, 598). Mahatma Ghandi fascinated him (see Obama 2020, 599). More specifically, Obama's assessment of Bush's failure in the Middle East tallied with the UPA's. The wars in Afghanistan and Iraq had been erroneously premised on the notion of a limitless American legitimacy and the latter as a democratic domino. Obama derided Iraq as a 'dumb war' (2020, 47). There was arguably more synergy between Obama and Singh—both of whom wanted a return to traditional stability in the Middle East—than between Bush and Singh—who disagreed on the prospects for democratization there. As India's then Foreign Minister Salman Khurshid noted at the Manama Dialogue (a Middle East security summit) in 2013, the Persian Gulf is India's largest trading partner and home to 7 million Indians. Sixty-five per cent of its oil comes from the region. New Delhi has a vested interest in its stability, not in its revolution (see Joshi 2015).

For Bush, then, India was an opportunity to advance his personally felt 'Freedom Agenda' (see Bush 2010, 395–498). He sought to build India into 'a balance of power that favoured freedom' (Bush 2002), and thus favoured the world's democracies who were its key ballast. For Obama, India was an important agent of a new world order in which the United States would step back as rising others stepped forward. The doctrines of both U.S. presidents found in UPA India an ally that could, respectively, if somewhat paradoxically, further U.S. pre-eminence and manage its decline.

Ideology and Strategic Culture

How far were India-U.S. relations during the UPA years conditioned by ideological and cultural differences and similarities? Singh was keen to play up the similarities. In July 2005, he reminded the U.S. Congress that:

India and the United States have much in common that is very important to both countries. You are the world's oldest democracy, we are its largest. Our shared commitment to democratic values and processes has been a bond that has helped us transcend differences ... As democracies, we must work together to create a world in which democracies can flourish. (Singh 2005b)

Such rhetoric has been boilerplate in the public diplomacy of both nations since independence—to the point of cliché. Jawaharlal Nehru had relayed much the same message in the same forum in 1949 (Nehru 1949). Was Singh's backed by a fuller substance? In part, it did not have to be. The international setting of Bush-Singh relations was especially conditioned by being post-Cold War and post-9/11. The demise of the U.S.S.R. in 1991 weakened American suspicions of India as a Soviet collaborator. Now into the second post-Cold War decade, Singh more fully claimed to have escaped this retarding legacy. However, suspicions of American motives within sections of the Indian polity persisted. Despite the dynamic of Bush's 9/11 response, which privileged democratic ends by means of military power, making India a logical ideological ally in the war on terror, cooperation was hampered by a refusal to accept Bush's world view and to see in it a straitjacketing of India's 'strategic autonomy'—the more modern-sounding version of non-alignment. We might describe this as an ideological resistance to U.S. power that even the war on terror could not dilute and that the UPA had to work within.

Cold War Hangover?

In the Cold War, Washington viewed India as a combination of economic backwardness and Soviet flirtation. India and the United States were 'estranged democracies' (Kux 1992). India's enduring attempt to remain 'unaligned' continued to hamper fuller relations after the collapse of the U.S.S.R. (see Pant and Super 2015). The bounties India had secured by this attempted middle way have never been fully apparent. It did not protect the nation from Mao's China when it attacked India in 1962—forcing Nehru to seek U.S. arms and ammunition. India's remaining above the Cold War fray allowed Pakistan to cultivate Washington and Beijing as sponsors. Nixon backed Islamabad over New Delhi when the two neigh-bours came to blows over East Pakistan (Bangladesh) secession in 1971. Pakistan has subsequently played a much savvier game in maintaining American sponsorship as well as allying with China as a counterweight to India—an act of diplomatic gymnastics that has consistently eluded Indian governments. Only comparatively recently has India realized the necessity of building strategic partnerships (if not yet formal alliances) instead of remaining apart from them. Every post-Cold War Indian gov-ernment has had to deal with the negative consequences rather than the positive benefits of non-alignment. All have found themselves making treaties to advance Indian interests.

The UPA was no exception. With the end of bi-polarity in 1991 came the strategic redundancy of non-alignment but not of its cultural reson-ance. By 2005, the UPA was busily engaged in forging treaties (not alli-ances) across a range of issues, not least defence, with partners (not allies) such as the U.S., U.K., South Africa, and Italy. However, the demands of non-alignment as a cultural value persisted. These, as Kadira Pethiyagoda (2020, 301) has argued, 'have significant explanatory' in Indian foreign policy. The values are often attributed to Indian officials more than they are claimed by them. According to Jeff Smith (2018), at Washington's Heritage Foundation, 'The ghosts of nonalignment still stalk the halls of South Block, erecting bureaucratic roadblocks and conjuring contentious debate over every self-interested shift in America's direction'.

The UPA deserves recognition for working within these nostalgic constraints. Indeed, there is a strong case to be made that the transform-ation of Indo-U.S. relations after 2004 was owed much more to Indian, Singh-inspired, resolve than to anything matching it on the U.S. side. In Washington, there persists a belief that New Delhi will eventually em-brace fuller and formal ties with it—and thus the disappointment when these do not materialize quickly. The UPA faced a much more difficult challenge: to increase its cooperation with the United States without abandoning India's strategic autonomy. The young Indian diplomats that had applauded Fidel Castro's bear hug of Indira Gandhi in 1983 were, by 2004, the senior bureaucrats with whom the UPA had to forge a different direction with Castro's nemesis: the United States. 'Non-alignment 2.0' was proffered as a way to 'maximize our choices' (Khilnani et al. 2012). National Security Advisor, Shivshankar Menon, and the Deputy National

Security Advisors, Alok Prasad and Latha Reddy, were part of these animated debates between 2010 and 2012. It is a measure of the Singh government's success that so much happened within the Indo-U.S. relationship despite strong pockets of internal opposition. Singh had to reshape India's strategic culture and do so within the constraints of internal bureaucratic process.

Bureaucracy and Policymaking Process

The difficulty of engaging with India has a marked bureaucratic dimension. China, despite profound ideological differences with Washington, has a rigid bureaucratic hierarchy enabling discourse. India, paradoxically, because of its democratic character, is harder to engage. 'Indian ministries', observed Robert Kaplan during the UPA era, 'are overbearing and weak reeds compared to China's (2012, 252). In 2012, the Indian Ministry of External Affairs had just 790 diplomats, while China had 6,200 (Medcalf 2013). We will return to this issue while discussing the 2008 Civil Nuclear Agreement later in the chapter. At this juncture, it should be observed how the lofty aspirations that made it possible—from the slowing of climate change to nuclear non-proliferation—were undercut by bureaucratic and legal obstacles imposed on its operation. According to Nicholas Burns, Under-secretary of State for Political Affairs under Bush, this was not the fault of the U.S. officials, or of Barack Obama who inherited the deal in 2009, but of the Indian government:

In 2010, the Indian Parliament passed an ill-advised nuclear liability law that placed excessive responsibility on suppliers for accidents at nuclear power plants. The legislation, which gained support after the 25th anniversary of a horrific chemical spill at an American-owned plant in Bhopal, shattered investor confidence. By deterring the United States and other firms from entering the Indian market, the law made implementation of the Civil Nuclear Agreement (CNA) impossible, undermining what should have been the centrepiece of the two countries' relationship. Washington and New Delhi haven't managed to resolve the impasse (Burns 2014).

Such bureaucratic obfuscation has its origin in the domestic setting of India's policy towards the United States. Indian foreign policymaking is more dependent on executive skill than its American equivalent. In Washington, the foreign policy bureaucracy is entrenched and incentivizes expertise. The nexus between the civil and military—via the Joint Chiefs, for example—is a powerful one. The president appoints men and women to his National Security staff on the basis of their political loyalty and issue expertise. The State Department rewards regional knowledge. Foreign policy can run without the White House having to micro-manage it. In New Delhi, conversely, according to Pant (2016, 18), 'When the Prime Minister has intermittent or little interest in foreign policy, inertia and even uncoordinated improvisation can result within the Ministry of External Affairs, due to the remaining necessity of staking a coherent stance on an issue'. U.S. policymakers have recurrently exaggerated the capacity of Indian prime ministers to drive policy and underappreciated how far bureaucratic inertia can stymy it. The American system, while hardly perfect, has clearly enumerated fast-track career paths for issues experts. There is no equivalent in India. As Pant observes, 'There is no specialized career track into the Ministry for experts; citizens can only join the general civil service through its application process, and are then assigned to the Ministry. This inhibits the recruitment of talented specialists that the Ministry needs' (Pant 2016, 18). The upshot of all this for Indo-U.S. relations, under the UPA but not unique to it, is a set of initiatives that could advance or retard on the basis of prime ministerial championing. When this waned, as it inevitably would, given the scale of issues facing that office, the structures of Indian foreign policy could not compensate, despite a widespread American misapprehension that they could.

Domestic Settings

There are other important distinctions between the respective domestic settings of Indo-U.S. diplomacy. India has low ideological salience in Washington, but Washington has high political salience in India. American policies towards India do not threaten the survival of U.S. administrations. The reciprocal Indian policies towards America can have that power. This is not to argue that the American political class is stoic and wise, and its Indian equivalent the reverse. The U.S. Congress is capable of partisan dysphoria matching anything observable in the Rajya Sabha and Lok Sabha. It is to observe, however, the more fraught passage of diplomatic initiatives involving the United States in India compared to those involving India in the United States. There is no anti-India lobby in Washington. Indeed, frustration with New Delhi, as several congressional hearings during the UPA years attest (see U.S. Congress, House 2009; U.S. Congress, Senate 2006 and 2014), comes from its recurrent refusal to countenance a formal alliance with Washington. American consternation comes from India's not delivering on aspirational bi-lateral agreements.

Contrast this to the reception of Chinese power in the United States. Both major U.S. parties have wings sceptical of the People's Republic of China. Democrats cite Amnesty International reports of human rights abuses. Republicans worry about the enduring strength of communism. India enjoys a deep well of bi-partisan support. Additionally, 'The success of Indian immigrants in the United States over the past generation has made Americans more familiar with Indian culture and generally appreciative of Indian accomplishments' (Rotter 2013, 432). 'The influence of a geographically dispersed and relatively wealthy Indian-American community of some 2.7 million is reflected in Congress's largest country-specific caucus' (Kronstadt et al. 2011). As we will see, this Indian American lobby was important to getting the 2008 Civil Nuclear Agreement passed in Congress (see Kirk 2008). In 2011, more than 100,000 Indian students were enrolled at American universities (a 50 per cent rise since 2000).

The reverse is less true. There was and remains a significant 'nonalignment crowd' (Smith 2018) within Indian politics that reacts adversely against the deepening of Indo-U.S. ties. This was as apparent under the UPA despite—indeed, because of—its outreach to Bush and Obama, as in previous eras. These reactions could have large and small causes. Large causes included making the operation of signature trade agreements subject to zealous policing by Indian authorities. But the relationship could also be unbalanced by Indian reactions to seemingly small slights, to which the U.S. authorities were insufficiently sensitive. In December 2013, for example, India's deputy consul general in New York, Devyani Khobragade, was arrested by U.S. federal agents for concealing the visa status of her housekeeper. The furious reaction in the Indian media to this diplomatic insult served to confirm caricatures of American-bad faith which have animated non-alignment advocates in India for several decades. We should be careful, however, not to exaggerate the effect of these mini eruptions when assessing the foreign policy legacy of the Singh government. At several measurable levels, Indians' attitudes towards the United States improved during the UPA years. In 2013, according to a Lowy poll, 83 per cent of Indians considered their relations with America 'to be strong' (Medcalf 2013). No other country was more liked, according to a warmth index (scored out of 100):

United States 62
Singapore 58
Japan 57
Australia 56

The BRICS scored significantly lower:

Brazil 44
Russia 53
China 44
South Africa 47

In 2007, Americans overtook Britons as the largest source of tourists to India (Madan 2014). In 1993, only 102,339 Indians visited America. Twenty years later, 859,000 did so (Madan 2014). Seventy-eight per cent of Indians thought 'it would be better if India worked more like the United States' (Medcalf 2013). As Jeff Smith (2018) noted, 'the Indian public views the United States more positively than almost any other country, including old friends like Russia and new ones like Japan'. A small, though still sizable, 31 per cent saw the United States as 'a threat'. Nevertheless, an Indian warming towards the United States and vice versa remains an enduring legacy of the UPA years.

Civil Nuclear Agreement

A test case of the new diplomacy, and its respective domestic setting, was the negotiation (in 2005) and passage (in 2008) of the CNA. The deal stands as the fullest expression of attempts made by the United States to forge a new strategic relationship with India—and of the Indian response to those attempts. The Clinton administration had reacted with dismay at the testing of nuclear bombs by India and Pakistan in 1998. Rather than insisting on some sort of pariah status to check India's nuclear ambitions, the Bush administration opted to negotiate. A deal to separate nuclear energy from nuclear weapons technology was negotiated by Bush and Singh teams in July 2005. This opened the door to what Bush called 'full civilian nuclear energy cooperation and trade with India'. Both sides expected a swift ratification. However, it took three years for the agreement to come into effect (in October 2008). As Dinshaw Mistry (2014, 2) has documented, 'In the end, U.S.-India negotiations only advanced when the conditions for nuclear cooperation satisfied key domestic constituents in both countries'.

Though growing the U.S.-India partnership was uncontroversial in Washington, the CNA encountered significant U.S. opposition, not least of which came from the U.S. agencies concerned about the deal's violation of the Nuclear Non-Proliferation Treaty (NPT). In order to enable the nuclear energy trade, India had to be exempted from the NPT—which it had never signed. The temptation for other states to follow, it was argued, would be unstoppable. The American-led nuclear non-proliferation regime would be under threat, potentially compromising decades of U.S. nuclear policy. The key to unlocking the U.S.-India civil nuclear trade, without unravelling the wider non-proliferation framework, was to get a waiver for India's civil nuclear program. Because it had not signed up to the NPT, it was barred by the international Nuclear Suppliers Group from trading in civil nuclear technology. The Bush administration had to bend this rule—entailing a waiver from the NSG—to get the agreement up. 'In essence, Washington conceded ground on one vital national interest—that of upholding a fundamental rule in the nuclear non-proliferation regime—to further another foreign policy objective: that of developing strategic relations with India' (Mistry 2014, 3).

After a three-year waiver struggle, the agreement passed both houses of Congress by large majorities (298-117 and 86-13). In India, opposition to the nuclear deal almost brought down the UPA. In protest at it, the Left Front parties withdrew their support from the alliance. The UPA survived a subsequent confidence vote by a narrow 275-256. The stakes were much higher for the Indian government than they ever were for George W. Bush—the deal raised the concerns of proliferation experts but had little public resonance.

Disgruntlement in Washington over the NSG waiver gave way to annoyance among members of the U.S. nuclear industry with the imperfect progress of such agreements once signed. In 2014, Senator James Risch complained that 'It has been 6 years since the United States-India nuclear deal was completed and we have yet to see United States nuclear companies have the ability to participate in India' (Risch, U.S. Congress, Senate 2014, 3). This echoed a 2013 U.S. Congressional Research Service report: 'there is widespread concurrence among many [U.S.] officials and analysts that the security relationship would benefit from undergirding ambitious rhetoric with more concrete action in areas of mutual agreement' (Kronstadt and Pinto 2013). In India, the opposition had been ideological; in the United States, dissatisfaction was procedural.

However, the subsequent U.S. grumbling should not obscure the ambition of the nuclear deal. That it was realized at all—given the profound ideological, legal, and technical issues standing in its way—represents a case study of the possibilities of Indo-U.S. cooperation. The U.S. congressional griping with its uneven implementation has something of missing the wood for the trees about it. The UPA faced down ideological resistance, putting its own continuance in office on the line. The Bush administration took risks with international law to affirm its strategic friendship with India and to recognize and affirm New Delhi's great power aspirations—an argument powerfully articulated by Ashley J. Tellis (2005), a key U.S. negotiator of the deal. Evaluating the CNA on the basis of its uneven commercial benefits ignores the diplomatic revolution that it constitutes. The CNA symbolized the large possibilities of U.S.-India cooperation, even as it revealed some of the lasting impediments to that cooperation. Crucially, the deal's successful passage suggests that the strategic cultures of both systems are not impervious to adaptation.

Geopolitics

The India-U.S. warming was most obviously manifested in increased geostrategic mutual empathy and material cooperation. India's strategic recalibration after 2004 advanced its relationship with Washington profoundly, even if it did not always meet the expectations of some U.S. officials. It is hard to exaggerate the intensity of foreign policy debates in the United States during the UPA's ascension to office. Between September 2001 and May 2004, President Bush had been transformed from a leader seeking greater humility in his nation's global posture into the key agent of the demise of two autocratic regimes and advocate of a global democratic revolution. What was India's role in Bush's war on terror and freedom agenda? As previously observed, Bush did not retrospectively afford India a significant role in the opening phase of his counterterrorism campaign. Several assumptions were held by the Bush team about India. They were not inaccurate but did assume that the process of Indian foreign policy was more similar than different to America's. If Bush had his own doctrine, enumerated in his National Security Strategy of 2002, there would be Vajpayee and Singh Doctrines that would adapt themselves around his. That we do not speak of such doctrines in an Indian setting, despite Singh's sometimes similar approach to Bush's, whereas in U.S. political history they are ubiquitous, suggests a misunderstanding in successive White Houses over how India makes its foreign policy.

This disjunction explains, in part, the frustration Bush and Obama had with India's foreign policy under the UPA. Despite a highly competitive political system, the U.S. president, as commander-in-chief and as the centre of a large national security state, enjoys wide latitude in foreign policy. His vision establishes a framework for how America engages with the world. Indian foreign policy is much less centrally coordinated. Top-down planning, where visions and grand strategies get articulated, is rarer because institutionally it is much harder (see O'Donnell and Pant 2015). Civil servants, as opposed to political appointees on the U.S. National Security Council Staff, enjoy significant discretionary powers and, as Miller (2013) has documented, are less subject to prime ministerial control. The process is a variation of Robert Putnam's two-level games (1988). Agreements made between Bush and Singh would be subject to implementation by Indian civil servants who did not owe their careers to their prime minister. This phenomenon can, of course, be overstated. The Ministry of External Affairs under UPA was not a hotbed of anti-Singh radicalism. But the independence of many of its officials does highlight why Singh could not initiate bold new initiatives without having to do a job of persuasion that Bush, especially during his war on terror (and armed with a large grant of congressional authority to wage it as he saw fit), could more conformably avoid.

Common strategic objectives could lessen the impact of these structural dissimilarities without eradicating them. The basis for Indo-U.S. co-operation in the war on terror after 2004 was, after all, a strong one. Bush's freedom agenda seemed to fit India's interest (though rarely activism) in promoting the spread of democracy (see Mohan 2007). Nuclear proliferation and the spread of WMD more generally had become a central preoccupation of the Bush White House. The Iraq war had been largely grounded in severing the link between a regime that might have such weapons and the terrorists prepared to use them. In India, Bush surveyed a nuclear weapons state with a vested interest in non-proliferation. India had the experience of confronting nuclear Pakistan and was to endure yet more Islamist terrorism emanating from that rivalrous neighbour. The 2005 'New Framework for the U.S.-India Defense Relationship' made 'defeating terrorism and violent religious extremism' one of its key security interests (see Kronstadt et al. 2011, 83). The other, almost clichéd, commonalities also applied: a British colonial legacy, a shared language, the rule of law, democratic institutions, and increasing bilateral trade. A key reason why a certain Indian circumspection endured, despite these shared values and concerns, was a wariness about how Bush and Obama would alter their approach to China and Pakistan, India's two great rivals, and states with potentially pivotal roles to play in U.S. foreign policy.

China

The geopolitics of the war on terror increased Bush's willingness to warm towards China, India's strategic rival. Beijing was keen to advertise the internal Islamist challenge it claimed to face. Russia did likewise after 11 September 2001. For a time, this commonality altered the tone of the relations with both. However, it was not long before a pre-9/11 continuity reasserted itself. The U.S. grand strategy the UPA observed in 2004 was not a transformation from the 1990s or even the 1970s. However, Bush now afforded India a role more consistent with its rising power. The ends of U.S. power in the Indo-Pacific were not much different from those obtained before 9/11: work to build trade (especially in defence) across both nations. But the means would entail significant revisions to U.S.-India bilateralism. The enhanced military-to-military ties, from joint exercise to arms sales, burgeoned during the UPA years because they were built on a common, though not identical, desire to contain Chinese power.

The cohesion of the India-U.S. response was grounded in a concern that China be contained regionally. Bush and Obama differed with Singh, as Obama did with Modi, however, on how and where. The geography of the 2,100-mile land border between India and China favours the military adventurism of Beijing (as India's predicament in the 1962 war there demonstrates). Prime Minister Singh saw little advantage in joining the U.S. sabre-rattling towards the People's Republic of China; India would have to pay the price on its border, whereas Americans would not have to on theirs. Moreover, its western border with Pakistan would be destabilized by increased Chinese support for Islamabad to counter increased American support for New Delhi. This simple geography of power explains why Singh did not propagandize against Beijing to affirm his friendship with Washington. This 'geographical dilemma', with which India has lived for thousands of years, is often misunderstood by the American political class (see Kaplan 2012, 228).

Obama continued far more than he revised the Bush approach to China and India. His early 'pivot to Asia', and thus implicitly away from the Middle East, masked the essential continuity of approach with his predecessor. The Obama administration increased its arms sales to New Delhi (giving priority to missiles, the utility of which was specific to its Himalayan border with China [see Dasgupta and Cohen 2011]). Beijing, almost as an opposite and equal reaction, reasserted territorial claims in the East China Sea and increased its bilateralism with Pakistan (see Pant 2012). Such manoeuvring was the repetition of Cold War patterns. Similarly, Obama's prioritization of climate change—despite air pollution in Beijing and New Delhi reaching dangerous levels in the 2010s—did not alter the underlying dynamics of the U.S.-India-China relationship.

When India held a non-permanent seat on the United Nations Security Council, from 2011 to 2013—which Obama used as an argument for giving New Delhi a permanent seat—it repaid him by voting with China, Russia, and Brazil, to deny the extension of the 'responsibility to protect' to Syria (Indyk et al. 2012, 249). Such episodes belie claims and lazy American assumptions that India will consistently support its fellow democracy when the United States opposes China simply because it is a democracy. America and India did not lack connections and enthusiasm during 2004–14. But they did lack 'purpose and focus' (Kronstadt and Pinto 2013), which a common fear of China did not provide because it did not really exist—or it existed in a more nuanced form than many U.S. diplomats were willing to concede (see Sen 2014). According to the 2013 Lowy poll, as many Indians believed the United States should give China a larger say in Asia as believed it should not. A majority (64 per cent) of Indians also agreed 'that India should cooperate with China to play a leading role in the world together' (Medcalf 2013).

Contrast this with the Australian-U.S. relationship over the same period. Despite nominal similarities with Indo-U.S. friendship— heritage, language, democracy, and concerns about China—Bush and Obama were able to forge a much closer relationship with Canberra than they were with New Delhi. Australian troops were a small but committed part of Bush's wars. Obama was able to establish a revolving deployment of U.S. Marines through Darwin. Equivalent, formal, burden-sharing between the United States and India was, even during the warm relations of the UPA years, hard to imagine. India and the United States are now partners on some military exercises (more than India does with any other country [Kronstadt et al. 2011, 84]) because of the 2005 defence framework agreement. But American bases on Indian soil seem some way off. Canberra and Washington have both ideology and values and, crucially, a common concern about the character and ambitions of Chinese power, to make their bilateralism almost familial (though this was tested in the Trump era; see Fullilove 2017 and White 2017). They also have the luxury of geography—where India does not.

Pakistan

Pakistan made U.S.-India relations more difficult during the UPA years (see Fair and Ganguly 2015 and Pant 2012). Manmohan Singh (born in Pakistan) grasped that the higher price lay in resisting the U.S. ambitions in the years of military activism after 9/11. This recalculation led to Indian concessions over Pakistan. George W. Bush needed its president, Pervez Musharraf (born in India), to focus on the Taliban rather than on the deeper enmity with India. In 2005, Singh enabled this refocusing by deciding to downgrade Indian assessments of Pakistan 'terrorism' in Kashmir. One immediate effect was the freedom Musharraf then had to move his forces away from his eastern border with India to his western border with Afghanistan. While this tacit cooperation between the UPA and Pakistan did not flower—undone by the implosion of the Musharraf government and subsequent Mumbai attacks in 2008— they did cause a warming in the strategic relationship between New Delhi and Washington. Singh seemed to get what Bush needed in India's backyard and was prepared to wear the domestic political price of providing it to him.

Singh's deftness, however, was part of a very slow gestation by his predecessors. The UPA deserves credit for breaking with a pattern of suspicion that had long stymied US-India strategic cooperation. Pakistan, on the other hand, has displayed a much greater willingness to adapt to Washington's designs. As Fair and Ganguly (2015) observe:

> Ever since its emergence from the end of the British colonial empire in South Asia, [Pakistan] has adroitly exploited its geostrategic location to extract concessions from the United States, successfully harried its arch-rival India, and developed and sustained a long-term strategic relationship with the People's Republic of China.

The sincerity of Pakistan's efforts is open to debate. What is harder to deny is their apparent success. Successive Pakistani regimes have earned the support—moral and financial—of the world's two largest economic and military powers: China and the United States. India, conversely, became mired in an ideological scepticism of American power in the Cold War—pockets of which have endured into the post-1991 decades—and found itself in recurrent hot and cold wars with China. The Singh government decided to play a much cannier diplomatic game. The rewards, as we will examine shortly, were a significant uptick in defence cooperation with the Bush and Obama administrations.

Russia

The reassertion of a more strident Russian nationalism under Vladimir Putin is another case study of the limits of Indo-U.S. friendship under the UPA. Russia invaded Georgia in 2008 and Ukraine in 2014. Rather than an opportunity for the Singh ministry to signal, for American consumption, its disapproval, an awkward neutrality was attempted. As the U.S. scholar Alyssa Ayres observed of the February 2014 annexation of Crimea:

Indian officials walked a tightrope, saying little publicly about it beyond an anodyne tweet from a Ministry of External Affairs spokesperson ('We are closely watching fast evolving situation and hope for a peaceful resolution') rather than clearly condemning Russia's violation of Ukrainian sovereignty (Ayres 2017, 89).

However, while this diplomatic even-handedness strained the credulity of Obama officials—who themselves could do little beyond verbal condemnation of Putin's land grab—it was balanced by a reinvigorated Indian participation in United Nations Peacekeeping Operations (UNPKO). The UPA did not begin this commitment but it did renew it, especially in Africa. By 2014, India was the largest contributor to UNPKO on the continent. It is also worth considering that the UPA's ambivalence towards Russian revanchism was less rooted in a nostalgia for the Indo-Soviet partnership of the Cold War or a reflexive anti-Americanism. Rather, it reflected a desire to retain Moscow (alongside the United States and Israel) as a key supplier of Indian arms. Israel has been able to maintain this diversified source base for its military *and* the friendship of the United States. Manmohan Singh sought to do likewise. As his Cold War predecessors also attempted, Singh wanted to build relationships but not by destroying others. Indian leaders had, largely successfully, cultivated both the United States and the U.S.S.R. without becoming beholden to either. In 1962, Nehru secured U.S. help in resisting a Chinese invasion; in 1971, Indira Gandhi signed a mutual defence treaty with Moscow to hedge against the nascent Sino-American opening. Singh similarly reasoned that deals with the Bush and Obama administrations should not be purchased at the price of Russian disaffection.

Defence Ties

A historic concern with the placation of Russia and China did not, however, stop India from developing closer defence ties with the United States. The UPA inherited and increased the pace of defence partnerships. Between 2000 and 2008, 19 defence agreements were negotiated, 'a staggering change from the seven total agreements secured in the first 53 years of independence' (Pant and Super 2015). Strategic dialogues became basic to how both sides interacted. In 2005, the United States and India signed a ten-year defence framework agreement to expand bilateral security cooperation. Arms sales became a key vehicle for this deepening of U.S.-India bonds. In 2011, $100 billion was committed by New Delhi to American arms manufacturers over the ensuing ten years. 'Arms sales may be the best way for the United States to revive stagnating U.S.-Indian relations' (Dasgupta and Cohen 2011). The deal would make the United States, after Russia and Israel, the third-largest provider of arms to New Delhi. This bilateral military trade also served to bolster Obama's support for a permanent Indian seat on the UN Security Council, which he made central to his November 2010 visit to the country. That was not a good month domestically for the president—his Democratic party suffered a significant defeat in the midterm elections, losing control of the House of Representatives, on 2 November—and the India trip, four days later, was an opportunity to forge an international legacy. Obama and Singh both had to deal with fraught domestic political situations.

In 2012, Leon Panetta, the U.S. defence secretary led the Defense Technology and Trade Initiative (DTTI). In 2014, Obama and Singh endorsed the India-U.S. Declaration on Defense Cooperation. From 2008 to 2014, noted Senator Tim Kaine, 'The United States and India participate[d] in more than three dozen dialogues covering a wide array of cooperative activities: clean energy, peacekeeping, counterterrorism, health' (Kaine, U.S. Congress, Senate 2014, 2). While the defence ties could stumble on issues of implementation (an enduring though hardly unique source of U.S. frustration), their number and scope were impressive. Between 1999 and 2003, the United States supplied only 0.2 per cent of India's imported arms; by 2013, it was supplying 7.4 per cent, second only to Russia. Bilateral military cooperation was transformed during the UPA years. According to Madan (2014), 'India participates in more military exercises with the U.S. than with any other nation'. Those initiated between 2004 and 2014 include Yudh Abhyas, Cope India, and Vajra Prahar.

These military ties were catalysed by the greatest natural disaster of the UPA years: the 26 December 2004 Indian Ocean earthquake and tsunami. Over 200,000 people along the coasts of the Indian Ocean were killed. International humanitarian and recovery efforts brought together the militaries of Australia, India, Japan, and the United States. 'The Quad', as it was colloquially known, helped facilitate defence cooperation among the four regional powers after the emergency had passed.

Domestic Indian resistance to such cooperation was weakened by its connection to tsunami relief. Likewise, the other three participants could posture on its humanitarian genesis: this was a loose strategic partnership built on values; it was not a formal alliance; it was not an attempt to balance Chinese power in the Indo-Pacific. The Malabar naval exercise, involving India, the United States, and Japan, operative since 1992, was given a boost by the Quad's renewed purpose after 2004. The defence cooperation between Washington and New Delhi seemed a natural extension of this values-driven partnership. To indict the UPA for failing to turn it into a fully-fledged 'NATO of the Indo-Pacific' is to ignore geopolitical realities. Not least among these was the Chinese suspicion at any league of democracies claiming the mantle of humanitarian navalism. Singh understood well that too great a partnership with these fellow democracies would be exacted in Chinese economic and military gamesmanship. It was the same geopolitical calculation that the Australian government made, withdrawing from the Malabar joint exercises in 2007 (see Wyeth 2017).

Economics and Trade

The remarkable growth of the Indian economy and its trade relationship with the United States established the basis for cooperation across a range of other issues during the UPA years. Trade between both nations increased five-fold between 2004 and 2014 (see Figure 2.1).

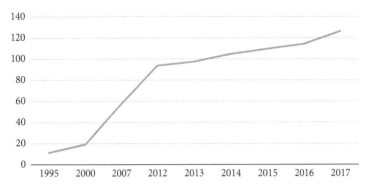

Figure 2.1 US Goods and Services Trade with India (figures in billion US dollars)

Source: United States Trade Representative 2018; https://ustr.gov/countries-regions/south-central-asia/india

A surge in defence contracts was replicated in trade and services. The U.S. imports from India rose from $15.5 billion in 2004 to $45.4 in 2014. Indians spent $6.1 billion on U.S. imports in 2004 and $21.5 by 2014 (U.S. Census Bureau 2021). The Indian IT sector was widely touted as the natural partner to California's Silicon Valley. In 1999, the United States had trade sanctions on India. Fifteen years later, Obama was calling the partnership the most important of the 21st century.

However, what the figures mask is an enduring frustration on both sides, particularly the Americans, expressed about restrictive practices that hampered trade. Despite 'A real sea change [that] has occurred in the last 15 to 20 years, in the way we have dealt with each other', noted Frank G. Wisner, U.S. ambassador to India (1994–97), 'the relationship has … atrophied and requires attention'. The high hopes of bi-lateral initiatives were too often negated, claimed Wisner, by an Indian failure to follow through at a procedural level: 'The criminalization of commercial disputes', said Wisner, 'that has today an American CEO in prison in a Southern Indian state [Andhra Pradesh], the Amway president', was particularly regrettable and indicative of issues that bedevilled economic relations (Wisner, U.S. Congress, Senate 2014, 23–24). The increase in bilateral trade, paradoxically, compounded rather than solved some of these issues. Moves towards a U.S.-India free trade agreement did not proceed during the UPA years.

Economic policy, which delivered strong growth after 2000, stalled after 2012 (see Mehta 2012). India became less attractive to U.S. investors, and thus to their political cheerleaders in the White House and Congress. The United States, of course, suffered a great recession in and after 2008. However, its political response was coordinated in the face of it, despite significant partisan rancour. In India, sometimes haphazard political intervention in the economy served to alienate foreign investors. A 2011 Congressional Research Service report noted the U.S. government complaint that 'India is using sanitary and phytosanitary (SPS) regulations to restrict the import of certain U.S. agricultural goods' (Kronstadt et al. 2011, 77)—a charge India denied. The 2012 decision to retroactively tax the British Vodafone takeover of an Indian phone company, according to a New Delhi think tank, caused many to 'fear that such arbitrary interventions will scare away foreign investment' (Mehta 2012). This discordant economic mood music coloured American perceptions of the U.S.-India relationship during the last years of the UPA.

However, as with nuclear cooperation, the fact that there were so many points of relatively minor economic conflict are testimony to the speed at and the depth to which the trade relationship developed. American critics of Indian intransigence sometimes forget the remarkable challenges facing Indian economic policymakers. Internally, New Delhi faces the consequences of enormous wealth disparities and of the movement of the rural poor into its already congested and polluted cities. Externally, it has poor and/or failing neighbours: Afghanistan, Pakistan, Nepal, Burma, Bangladesh, and Sri Lanka. To treat India as if it is Canada, to expect the smooth execution of all trade deals, and the impartial policing of international trade is to forget that India remains a developing state.

Conclusion

The successes of the UPA's America policy are important to record. Towards the end of the Manmohan Singh ministry, the two countries were 'engaging in unprecedented levels of military-to-military ties, defence trade, and counterterrorism and intelligence cooperation' (Kronstadt and Pinto 2013). The insistence, in sections of both polities, that the historical legacy of Soviet preference and non-alignment persisted is undermined by the strength of the relationship in these areas. By 2014, assertions that neither side could off-load the historical baggage of the Cold War sounded clichéd and shop-worn. Indo-U.S. relations were stronger at every level of analysis in 2014 than they were in 2004.

What proved less successful was the ability and willingness to operationalize, to render routine, the bilateralism that made these developments possible in the first place. This is a complaint heard recurrently from the U.S. officials with experience of the relationship—and domestic Indian opponents of the UPA. To paraphrase their frustration, the UPA was able to talk in lofty terms but often lacked the ability to walk the procedural path that would have solidified them. The Civil Nuclear Agreement is often cited as the central case study of this disconnection between promise and delivery. The agreement was remarkable, reversing three decades of the U.S. non-proliferation policy. It enabled India to pursue a nuclear power future, and thus slow its carbon emissions, in partnership with U.S. experts and investment. It fell victim to a procedural obtuseness within Indian political and legal circles that negated the cooperation it was designed to affect.

But such failures were not exclusively Indian, let alone UPA, in genesis. The Bush and Obama administrations made assumptions about India's capacity to build ever-stronger ties that ignored internal political, bureaucratic, and cultural constraints. Obama was more prone to this than his predecessor but both presidents indulged in it. Bush did not reckon with the differences in democratic character between his nation and Singh's. Positing a 'freedom agenda' in a part of the world, the Middle East, important to India's interests, did not make India an automatic partner in it. Singh's agenda differed there, and Bush made more progress with him when this fact was acknowledged. Obama touted Asia as the next global frontier of human progress and internationalism. He was leading a united, progressive alliance and assumed an India led by a similarly titled government would join it—to the point, claim some, that he became almost disinterested to see if it was actually the case. Obama failed to take into account the longstanding concerns Indians had with being led by any power, let alone the United States, and the disquiet Obama's affection for the 'rising rest' thesis caused in sections of the Indian polity. What Obama thought was empowering to Indians specifically and Asians generally were viewed by many of them as an invitation to failure.

This chapter has argued that the Indo-U.S. relationship evolved across the UPA years into a very strong and positive one. It did not do so by accident but because both sides took seriously how and where to cooperate. They did not simply rely on assertions of goodwill born of their shared democratic character. While this renewed era of good feelings at what political scientists sometimes refer to as Level One—between leaders—was often compromised by internal Indian negation of initiatives and agreements at Level Two—the domestic setting in which implementation had to take place (see Putnam 1988), the fact that there existed agreements to be frustrated at the implementation of is the real story. While the warm relations between Washington and New Delhi could be cooled by national and local pressures within Indian politics and bureaucracy—some of long gestation and deeply rooted—they could not be cooled to an earlier state.

References

Ayres, A. (2017) 'Will India Start Acting Like a Global Power?', *Foreign Affairs* 96(6), 83–92.

Baker P. (2013) *Days of Fire: Bush and Cheney in the White House.* (New York: Doubleday).

Burns, N. (2014) 'Passage to India', *Foreign Affairs* 93, (5) (September/October), 132–141.

Bush, G. W. (2002) 'The National Security Strategy of the United States of America', *White House.* (September 20). https://georgewbush-whitehouse.archives.gov/nsc/nss/2002/ (Online).

Bush, G. W. (2006) *Speech in Purana Qila, New Delhi, India,* March 3.; at https://georgewbush-whitehouse.archives.gov/news/releases/2006/03/20060303-5.html (Online).

Bush, G. W. (2010) *Decision Points.* (New York: Crown Publishing).

Cheney, D. (2011) *In My Time: A Personal and Political Memoir.* (New York: Threshold Editions).

Dasgupta, S. and S. P. Cohen (2011) 'Arms Sales for India: How Military Trade Could Energize U.S.U.S.-Indian Relations', *Foreign Affairs* 90(2) (March/April), 22–26.

Draper, R. (2007) *Dead Certain: The Presidency of George W. Bush* (New York: Free Press).

Fair, C. C., and S. Ganguly (2015) 'Five Dangerous Myths about Pakistan', *Washington Quarterly* 38 (4), 73–97.

Fullilove, M. (2017) 'Down and Out Down Under: Australia's Uneasy American Alliance', *Foreign Affairs* 96(28) (September–October), 28–34. https://www.foreignaffairs.com/articles/2017-08-15/down-and-out-down-under

Gandhi, R. (2014) 'Impacting Each Other: Reflections on the USU.S.-India Relationship', *Comparative American Studies*, 12(1/2), 1–5.

Ganguly, S. and S. P. Kapur (2009) 'The End of the Affair? Washington's Cooling Passion for New Delhi', *Foreign Affairs*. (June 15). https://www.foreignaffairs.com/articles/india/2009-06-15/end-affair.

Gates, R. M. (2014) *Duty: Memoirs of a Secretary at War*. (New York: Alfred A. Knopf).

Giridharadas, A. (2009) 'India Has a Soft Spot for Bush', *New York Times*, (January 10).); at https://www.nytimes.com/2009/01/11/weekinreview/11giridharadas.html

Indyk, M. S., K. G. Lieberthal, and M. E. O'Hanlon (2012) *Bending History: Barack Obama's Foreign Policy* (Washington, DC: Brookings).

Joshi, S. (2015) 'India and the Middle East', *Asian Affairs*, 46(2), 251–269.

Kaplan, R. D. (2012) *The Revenge of Geography* (New York: Random House).

Kearn, D. W. (2014). 'Toward Alliance or Ambivalence: A Theoretical Assessment of U.S.U.S.-India Relations', *India Review* 13(2), 129–148.

Khilnani, S., R. Kumar, P. B. Mehta, P. Menon, N. Nilekani, S. Raghavan, S. Saran, and S. Varadarajan (2012) Nonalignment 2.0: aA Foreign and Strategic Policy for India in the Twenty First Century; https://www.kcl.ac.uk/sspp/departments/kii/documents/nonalignment20.pdf

Kirk, J. (2008) 'Indian Americans and the U.S.U.S.–India Nuclear Agreement: Consolidation of an Ethnic Lobby?' *Foreign Policy Analysis* 4 (May): 275–330.

Kronstadt, K. A., and S. Pinto (2013) *U.S.-India Security Relations: Strategic Issues* (Washington, DC: Congressional Research Service).

Kronstadt, K. A. et al. (2011) *India: Domestic Issues, Strategic Dynamics, and U.S.U.S. Relations* (Washington, DC: Congressional Research Service).

Kronstadt, K. A., Kerr, P. K., M. F. Martin, and B. Vaughn (2011) *India: Domestic Issues, Strategic Dynamics, and U.S.U.S. Relations* (Washington, DC: Congressional Research Service).

Kux, D. (1992) *India and the United States: Estranged Democracies*. (Washington DC: NDU Press).

Madan, T. (2014) India-U.S. Relations in 14 Charts and Graphics, Brookings Institution, Washington DC; https://www.brookings.edu/blog/up-front/2014/09/26/india-u-s-relations-in-14-charts-and-graphics/

Medcalf, R. (2013) '*Lowy Institute India Poll 2013*' (Sydney, NSW: Lowy Institute). https://www.lowyinstitute.org/publications/india-poll-2013

Medcalf, R. (2014) 'Asia's "'Cold Peace'": China and India's Delicate Diplomatic Dance, *National Interest* (24 September 24). https://nationalinterest.org/feature/asias-cold-peace-china-indias-delicate-diplomatic-dance-11338. (Online).

Mehta, P. B. (2012) 'How India Stumbled', *Foreign Affairs*, 91(4), 64–75.

Miller, M. C. (2013) 'India's Feeble Foreign Policy: A Would-Be Great Power Resists Its Own Rise', *Foreign Affairs* 92(, 3) (May/June), 14–19.

Mistry, D. (2014) *The U.S.-India Nuclear Agreement: Diplomacy and Domestic Politics*. (New Delhi: Cambridge University Press).

Mohan, C. R. (2007) 'Balancing Interests and Values: India's Struggle with Democracy Promotion', *Washington Quarterly* 30(3) (Summer), 99–115.

Nehru, J. (1949) Address to Joint Session of U.S. Congress, Washington DC, October 13.

O'Donnell, F. and H. V. Pant (2015) 'Managing Indian Defense Policy: The Missing Grand Strategy Connection,' *Orbis* 59(2), 199-–214.

Obama, B. (2020) *A Promised Land* (New York: Viking).

Pant, H. (2012) 'The Pakistan Thorn in China-India-U.S. Relations', *Washington Quarterly* 35(1) (Winter), 83–95.

Pant, H. V. (2016). *Indian fForeign pPolicy: An oOverview*. (Manchester: Manchester University Press).

Pant, H. V., & and J. M. Super, J. M. (2015) 'India's "Non-Alignment" Conundrum: A Twentieth-Century Policy in a Changing World,' *International Affairs* 91(4), 747–764.

Pethiyagoda, K. (202013) '*Indian Foreign Policy and Cultural Values* (London: Palgrave Macmillan).The Influence of Dominant Cultural Values on India's Foreign Policy,', PhD diss., University of Melbourne.

Putnam, R. (1988) 'Diplomacy and Domestic Politics: The Logic of Two Level Games', *International Organization* 42 (3) (Summer, 1988), 427–460.

Rice, C. (2017) *Democracy: Stories from the Long Road to Freedom.* (New York: Twelvebooks).

Ripsman, N. M., J. W. Taliaferro, J. W., &and S. E. Lobell, S. E. (2016) *Neoclassical Realist Theory of International Politics* (New York, NY:: Oxford University Press).

Ripsman, N. M., J. W. Taliaferro, J. W., & and S. E. Lobell,, S. E., eds. (2009) *Neoclassical Realism, the State, and Foreign Policy* (New York, NY: Oxford University Press).

Rose, G. (1998) 'Neoclassical Realism and Theories of Foreign Policy', *World Politics* 51(1) (October), 144–172.

Rotter, A. J. (2013) 'United States Foreign Relations: India,' in Timothy J. Lynch, ed., *The Oxford Encyclopedia of American Military and Diplomatic History.* 428–433 (New York: Oxford University Press).

Rumsfeld, D. (2011) *Known and Unknown: A Memoir* (New York: Penguin).

Sen, T. (2014) 'The Bhai-Bhai Lie: The False Narrative of Chinese-Indian Friendship', *Foreign Affairs* (July. 11). https://www.foreignaffairs.com/reviews/review-essay/2014-07-11/bhai-bhai-lie (Online).

Sharma, R. (2012) 'Broken BRICs: Why the Rest Stopped Rising', *Foreign Affairs* 91(6) (November/December), 2–7.

Singer, J. D. (1961) 'The Level-of-Analysis Problem in International Relations', *World Politics* 14(1) (October), 77–92.

Singh, M. (2005a) Speech at India Today Conclave, New Delhi, February 25; at https://www.mea.gov.in/speeches-statements.htm?dtl/2464/

Singh, M. (2005b) Address to Joint Session of U.S. Congress, Washington DC, July 19: at https://archivepmo.nic.in/drmanmohansingh/speech-details.php?nodeid=145.

Smith, J. M. (2018) 'Seven Myths are Keeping India and the United States from Pursuing Closer Ties', *National Interest*, (October 29). https://nationalinterest.org/feature/seven-myths-are-keeping-india-and-united-states-pursuing-closer-ties-34627 (Online).

Tellis, A. (2005) 'The U.S.U.S.-India "Global Partnership": How Significant for American Interests?' Testimony before the House International Relations Committee, (November 16); at https://carnegieendowment.org/publications/index.cfm?fa=view&id=17693&prog=zgp&proj=znpp,zsa,zusr

U.S. Census Bureau. (2021) '2004: U.S. trade in goods with India'. https://www.census.gov/foreign-trade/balance/c5330.html#2005

U.S. Congress, House (2009) 'Building a Strategic Partnership: U.S.-India Relations in the Wake of Mumbai', Hearing before the Subcommittee on the Middle East and South Asia of the Committee on Foreign Affairs, House of Representatives, 111th Congress, First Session, February 26 (Washington: GPO).

U.S. Congress. Senate (2006) United States-India Peaceful Atomic Energy Cooperation and Additional Protocol Implementation Act: Report of the Committee on Foreign Relations, 109th Congress, 2d Session (Washington DC: GPO).

U.S. Congress. Senate (2014) 'Indispensable Partners—Reenergizing U.S.–India Ties', Hearing before the Subcommittee on Near Eastern and South and Central Asian Affairs, Committee on Foreign Relations, 113th Congress, July 16 (Washington DC: GPO).

White, H. (2017) 'Without America: Australia in the New Asia', Quarterly Essay 68 (November), 1–81.

Woodward, B. (2008) The War Within: A Secret White House History 2006-2008 (New York: Simon and Schuster).

Wyeth, G. (2017) 'Why Has Australia Shifted Back to the Quad?', The Diplomat, (November 16). https://thediplomat.com/2017/11/why-has-australia-shifted-back-to-the-quad/ (Online).

Yetiv, S. (2004) Explaining Foreign Policy: USU.S. dDecision-making and the Persian Gulf War (Baltimore, MD: Johns Hopkins University Press).

Zakaria, F. (2008) The Post-American World. (New York: W. W. Norton).

3

India-China Relations

2004–14

Srikanth Kondapalli

Introduction

A decade in the relations of two large countries with over 2 billion people
together may not be a decisive period. However, 2004–14 could also be
considered to be a building block in the bilateral relations between India
and China given the number of issues thrown out for their consideration,
the number of agreements arrived at, and also the number of problems
that tested the relations between two largest emerging countries in Asia.
There are also the larger issues at the regional and global level that needed
responses yet at the same time balancing the bilateral relations, if not syn-
chronizing them. All of these were reflected in the relations between India
and China. At a minimum they both were straddled with the unresolved
territorial dispute—a legacy of decades of discussions and conflict as in
1962—and both trying to protect their perceived sovereignty and territorial integrity with China focused on Tibet in the run-up to and during
the Beijing Olympics in 2008 and India on Kashmir and its Northeast
from insurgency and terror incidents. Both were also in the throes of globalization, reflected in China joining World Trade Organization and not
only enhancing its exports and imports but becoming the second-largest
economy in the world in this decade. A string of economic agreements
followed, for instance, with the Southeast Asian grouping, the ASEAN,
and with Japan and South Korea. This aspect of economic integration of
India and China also was to make a significant mark on their bilateral
relations, including mounting trade deficits in favour of China. At the regional and global level, as the Indian growth story rekindled, it had also

Srikanth Kondapalli, *India-China Relations* In: *Forging New Partnerships, Breaching New Frontiers*.
Edited by: Rejaul Karim Laskar, Oxford University Press. © Oxford University Press 2022.
DOI: 10.1093/oso/9780192868060.003.0003

brought in additional responsibilities in the neighbourhood and beyond. As China began expanding its footprint in the Indian Ocean through the Gulf of Aden counter-piracy operations since 2008, India also unveiled its 'primary operational area' from the Persian Gulf to the Straits of Malacca's while the 'secondary area of operation' extending into the South China Sea. Another competitive element that soon became prominent was—as India's relations with the United States improved in 2005–06 on 123 agreement—there was also the pushback from China on the nuclear 'clean waiver' at the International Atomic Energy Agency and Nuclear Suppliers Group in 2008. Nevertheless, the hallmark of multilateral cooperation since the 1950s is also reflected in this decade when both began extensive consultations, coordination, and cooperation in G-20 on countering trade protectionism and investment flows, multipolarity, BRICS, climate change, and the like. Thus broadly 'cooperation and competition' characterized the bilateral relations in this decade.[1] Below is an assessment of the many facets of the bilateral relations in the context of numerous regional and global interventions in the India-China equations. All the above have created a 'cooperative and competitive' cycle in the bilateral relations between India and China which is elaborated below.

The period 2004–14 had a new political dispensation in India under Dr Manmohan Singh led United Progressive Alliance (UPA) and a change of guard in China from Hu Jintao (2002–12) and Xi Jinping (2012–). There are several similarities in these political dispensations, viz., sharp focus on economic reforms and structural adjustments, emphasis on enhancing economic growth rates, and overall comprehensive national power. Dr Manmohan Singh had earlier been the finance minister in P.V. Narasimha Rao government and had begun the liberalization programme and was also instrumental in the launching of the 'Look East' Policy in the early 1990s. Under Hu Jintao, as well, China began the 'go out' policy based on years of reform and opening up policies since 1978. The entry into the World Trade Organization had catapulted the country into the largest trading nation, displacing Germany and the second-largest economy displacing Japan in this decade. Both leaderships were also ambitious, trying to regain the lost glory of the yore. However, at a fundamental level they both were focused on the domestic economic revival.[2] There are also several differences between the two, including an irredentist agenda in China that revived 'historical claims' to over 80% of 3 million square km in the South China Sea and incorporated Arunachal Pradesh into a 'Southern Tibet' construct by 2005. Also, unlike the Chinese Communist Party, which has been ruling China since 1949 single-handedly, Dr Manmohan Singh's government was a coalition, suggesting the decision-making and implementation of policies may not be swifter.

When Dr Manmohan Singh took over as the Prime Minister in 2004, he was guided by his party, the Congress Party's election eve manifesto, as well as the Constitution of India. The former suggested that the foreign policies will take South Asian neighbourhood as the basis and 'Trade and investment with China will be expanded further and talks on the border issue pursued seriously'.[3] The 2009 elections saw a manifesto that has the following provisions: 'India's relationships with countries like the USA, Russia, China and Japan and with countries of Europe have been transformed by sustained diplomatic efforts since 2004. These relationships will be further deepened...'[4] Taking over as the Prime Minister a second time in June 2009, Dr Manmohan Singh, while thanking the Indian President's speech to the Parliament on 9 June 2009, stated:

> ... China is our strategic partner. We have a multi-faceted relationship with China. There is enough space—I have said so often—for both China and India to develop and contribute to global peace, stability and prosperity. We do not see our relations with China in antagonistic terms. We have a large trading relationship, we consult each other on global issues, whether in the G-20 process on climate change or terrorism, and we share a common commitment to maintain peace and tranquillity on our border.... There are, of course, issues which are complex such as the boundary question. But we have agreed upon a mechanism to address this matter. We wish to build a strong and stable relationship with China.... But whether it is China or any country, we will ensure the territorial integrity and unity of our country and protect the security in every manner necessary. The House should have no misgiving on that score.[5]

Likewise, in China, when Hu Jintao took over from Jiang Zemin in 2002, the foreign policy section of the 16th Communist Party Congress emphasized relations with major powers, neighbours, and developing countries.[6] Subsequently, the 17th (2007), 18th (2012), and the recent 19th

(2017) party congresses had the above three priorities, in addition to expanding multilateralism and soft power.[7] None of these party work reports spoke about policy options explicitly for India, though. Of course, India was configured as a neighbour, developing country and in the format of multilateral interactions. By this time, China has become the sixth-largest economy and the fourth largest trader of the world. Its trade volume touched about a trillion dollars, with ASEAN alone accounting for nearly a hundred billion. China continued to be the manufacturing powerhouse of the global economy and became the largest importer from Asian countries, including India, specifically raw materials. As President Hu Jintao mentioned in his address to the Boao Forum in April 2004, the Chinese government intends to 'quadruple the 2000 GDP to 4 trillion US dollars with a per capita GDP of 3,000 US dollars'. It has undertaken several ambitious infrastructure projects including the Three Gorges project, railway project from Golmud to Lhasa (completed in 2006), and East-West gas pipeline project. These infrastructure projects were reaching the border of India in the Himalayas—becoming a new factor in the India-China context.

Bilateral Relations

The first formal meeting between the two premiers of India and China, after the UPA government was installed in 2004, took place in Vientiane on 30 November 2004, on the side lines of the third India-ASEAN summit meeting.[8] The foreign ministers of the two countries—Natwar Singh and Li Zhaoxing—met four times in the same year to enhance understanding on various issues, including preparations for Premier Wen Jiabao's visit to India. As stated by Wen at a press conference in Beijing on 14 March 2005, three issues were to be deliberated during his visit to New Delhi, viz., to view relations from 'strategic and comprehensive perspective', setting principles to solve the border dispute, and 'tap[ping] into the tremendous potential, expand cooperation and strive for common development'.

The reasons for elevating India in the Chinese calculus are many to include burgeoning trade contacts, identical views related to protecting the sovereignty of the countries under the United Nations Charter, close collaboration in the Group 20 developing countries in the discussion on trade barriers and other related economic issues, etc. Also, China's commentators have noticed the continuous stream of visitors to New Delhi with high-level delegations from the United States, Russia, Japan, European Union countries, and South Korea. After Wen's visit, New Delhi received the Japanese Prime Minister Koizumi and the United States President Bush. Landmark agreements were signed with the United States on the nuclear issue that had liberated the bilateral relations from several difficulties since the Cold War period. China's policy analysts also noted U.S. Secretary of State Condoleezza Rice's statement at Sophia University in Tokyo in early 2005 that the United States wants to 'help India to become a major power in 21st century'.

Chinese military writers have noted increasing challenges posed by the U.S. military deployments at its peripheries in not only the traditional areas like Japan, South Korea, Australia, and New Zealand but also the Philippines, Singapore, Pakistan, and Central Asian Republics. They point to an 'Asian NATO' in the making with its operational focus on not only counter-terrorism campaign but dread the prospect of China becoming the target during the second administration of President Bush. The events of the April 2001 EP-3 surveillance plane incident at Hainan Island appear to be still fresh. Hence, it was advocated, China needs to wean away countries planning to join this club. It is not out of context that China has revived the 1954 'good neighbourliness' policy in the last few years and working to enlarge its own club of countries that oppose unilateralism.

Beijing was then aware of the shifting balance of power equations in the region and it had to readjust itself from confining diplomatically India in the South Asian box, as it did during the Cold War and after the 1962 border clashes. To what extent this shift was real rather than only responding to the circumstances was not clear at that moment, but increasingly, in the Chinese lexicon, a new strategy has been added, viz., 'strategic and cooperative partnership' with India.[9]

The January 2005 'strategic dialogue' in a way covered preliminary ground in discussing economic globalization and multipolarity, reforming the United Nations, and non-traditional security issues.[10] During Wen's visit, China also expressed its willingness to cooperate effectively with India in the World Trade Organization and in other areas.

Table 3.1 provides details about the high-level visits between India and China in this decade.

Eventually, during Premier Wen's visit a 'Strategic and Cooperative Partnership' was signed in 2005. A number of agreements were signed touching upon the territorial dispute, 'managing' borders through confidence-building measures, macro-economic issues, people-to-people and cultural relations. The 50th anniversary of the adoption of Panchsheel principles was celebrated as with the 55th anniversary of the establishment of diplomatic relations. Three talks were held on the border dispute by the Special Representatives in this year (more below on this issue). Differences exist between the two sides on the exact location of the Line of Actual Control on the borders though peace and tranquility prevailed over a period of time in these areas. Also, through talks, the perceived disputed area reduced to only a few areas. On the positive side, confidence-building measures have increased over a period of time and the military personnel of the two sides exchanged greetings at Bumla Pass. In April defence minister Gen. Cao Gangchuan visited New Delhi and other places in India. It was followed in October by Tang Jiaxuan, the foreign minister. U.S. Secretary of State Colin Powell acknowledged in

Table 3.1 India-China High Level Visits 2004–14

Year	Visits	Remarks
2005	Premier Wen Jiabao visited on 9–12 April	Strategic and Cooperative Partnership for peace and prosperity signed
2006	20–23 November, State visit by President Hu Jintao	10-point strategy to upgrade relations
2008	13–15 January, PM Manmohan Singh's visit	A Shared Vision for the 21st Century of the Republic of India and the People's Republic of China was issued
2010	16 December, Premier Wen Jiabao's visit	
2013	20 May, Premier Li Keqiang's visit 22–24 October 2013, PM Manmohan Singh's visit	Border Defence Cooperation Agreement; power equipment services centre; agreement on Nalanda University

Source: MEA website.

November that China played a 'very helpful role' in diffusing Indo-Pak tensions. More progress is visible in the trade field (more of this aspect below). Chinese State Councillor Chen Zhili visited India in November to sign a deal on IT. Earlier, in August, a Yunnanese trade delegation came to India to sign a joint declaration with the Confederation of Indian Industry. Henan Province delegation headed by the Governor also visited India in the same month.

The April 2005 joint statement between PM Manmohan Singh and Premier Wen Jiabao outlined cooperation between the two countries at bilateral, regional, and, more significantly, for the first time, at global levels. The latter is a departure from the earlier Chinese stance that aimed to confine the Indian role to the South Asian region in almost three decades after the 'united front' of supporting Afro-Asian unity of the 1950s ended in the 1962 war. The 2005 'Strategic and Co-operative Partnership for Peace and Prosperity' went beyond the 'Cooperative and Constructive Security' strategy crafted by the path-breaking visit of Rajiv Gandhi in late 1988.

From the hype created in both countries, it appeared that the visit would revive the 1950s bonhomie. However, the contexts have changed. Despite several agreements, proposals for confidence-building measures and a joint statement on building 'long term constructive and cooperative partnership' in several spheres, nevertheless, hard ground realities are staring at both India and China. The joint statement between the two countries stated as much when it noted 'incremental progress in addressing outstanding issues'. One major aspect is the inability to resolve the border dispute, as has been suggested before the visit. Instead, 'political parameters and guiding principles' were enunciated. The fact that it took more than 24 years, eight rounds of talks, 15 Joint Working Group meetings, and several Special Representative meetings to arrive at these principles only suggest not only the complicated nature of this issue but also the disinterest of either of the two parties. Clearly, China has been stalling a solution to the border dispute. Nevertheless, the joint statement called for a 'proactive manner' of settling such disputes and that it should be 'pursued as a strategic objective'.

Another major concern in India-China relations is the role played by China in Pakistan, especially in the proliferation of weapons of mass destruction. The joint statement issued by India and China obliquely refers to this when it states that relations between the two should be based on 'sensitivity for each other's concerns ....'

On the 'strategic' aspects of India-China relations, progress achieved during this visit appears to be minimal, though both tried to chart out future possibilities. On the crucial issue of the reform of the United Nations, Beijing's position appeared to be ambiguous. While China stated that it 'supports' enlarged Indian role in the international arena, it did not categorically support Indian claim to the United Nations Security Council permanent membership with veto. Instead, much like its 'all-weather' friend Pakistan's position, Beijing is for 'gradual' and 'consensual' approach and indefinite postponement of the UN reform. In addition, both India and China had different views about each other's entry into Shanghai Cooperation Organization and South Asian Association for Regional Cooperation, respectively. There had also been no visible and concrete progress in arriving at a 'de-targeting' agreement between the two in terms of strategic weapons.

The next major event was the visit in November 2006 of President Hu Jintao, which was significant for its stress on exploring joint cooperation at the Asian levels. Civilian nuclear cooperation between the two has also been highlighted in the 2006 joint statement. Reportedly, President Hu had elevated India in all the three categories of Chinese foreign policy guidelines set by the 16th Party Congress, viz., emphasis on major powers, neighbouring and developing countries. However, the visit was marred by a controversy generated by China's Ambassador to Delhi. In November 2006, on the eve of the Chinese President Hu Jintao's visit to India, Ambassador Sun Yuxi made a statement stating Beijing's claim to a major portion of Arunachal Pradesh. Nevertheless, the takeaway of the 2006 visit remains its strategic content. Previously, the strategic partnership and cooperation formulation in April 2005 alluded to cooperation at the Asian levels (such as in para 43 of the November 2006 joint declaration between the two leaderships).[11] Later, during the visit of Premier Wen Jiabao in December 2010, both have agreed to work together for Afghanistan reconstruction and countering piracy in the Gulf of Aden, although no concrete programme to carry forward effectively these proposals was made.[12] Also, during Hu's visit, China successfully elicited concessions from India (as in November 2006 joint statement) in opposing its version of 'three evils', viz., opposing separatism, extremism, and splittism. This is a Chinese formulation to counter the movements of Taiwan, Uighurs, and Tibetans.[13] It is not clear what diplomatic reciprocal concession was made by China towards India, specifically on cross-border terror incidents from Pakistan. This issue was to haunt subsequent governments later.

Prime Minister Singh visited China twice for improving bilateral relations in 2008 and 2013. During the 2008 visit, on the minimalist foreign policy objectives, the joint declaration (which is incidentally one of the shortest between the two countries) is relatively conducive for China. For instance, on the border dispute, while the aim is said to build a 'boundary of peace and friendship' and that an agreed framework is to be completed at an 'early date', no fixed deadlines were mentioned. Again, while India agreed to abide by the 'one China principle', the joint declaration goes beyond the 'India model' of 1950. The 2008 declaration binds India to 'oppose any activity that is against one China principle'. This appears to be a major Indian concession to China in this round, although short of declaring allegiance to the Chinese anti-secession law of March 2005.

The Congress Party President and ruling UPA Chairperson Sonia Gandhi visited China from 25 to 29 October 2007 to Beijing, Xian, and Shanghai for improving the atmospherics between the two countries. She had earlier visited China in 1996 and a 2003 proposal visit could not take place. Gandhi referred to her trip as a 'milestone' in bilateral relations, while Chinese Premier Wen Jiabao termed her work in improving bilateral relations as 'of great importance'.

Strategic Dialogue

One of the results of Premier Wen's visit to India in 2005 was the institutionalization process at a number of levels: the Prime Minister's Office continues to hold the Special Representative talks, foreign ministry began strategic dialogues, defence ministries the annual defence dialogue, and the like. Foreign Secretary Shyam Saran's first strategic dialogue with Chinese Vice Foreign Minister Wu Dawei took place in January 2005 in New Delhi[14] and the second from 10 to 11 January 2006, in Beijing. These dialogues stressed India and China 'working together in terms of the evolving regional situation in Asia as well as the global situation'.

While multipolarity, multilateralism, World Trade Organization, and countering trans-national phenomena like terrorism, drug trafficking, and environmental degradation were mentioned as possible areas of co-operation in the enlarged envelope of bilateral concerns, it appeared that India's stature had been elevated in Asia.

A hotline between the two foreign ministers was instituted in February 2007. 2006 was observed as a Year of India-China Friendship. The next year saw India-China Friendship through Tourism year 2007. Border trade through Nathu La began in 2006 and Kolkata-Guangzhou consulate offices were opened in the same year. Similarly, later the year 2012 had been designated as the 'Year of India-China Friendship and Cooperation'. This proposal of President Hu Jintao, during his visit to Delhi to attend the 4th BRICS meeting in March 2012, was accepted by India after Indian foreign minister Krishna discussed the issue during his visit to Beijing in February. In these, both organized a series of cultural exchanges of troupes, media, and business interactions, an Indian expedition to Mount Everest from the China side, and middle-level interactions.

Later, Premier Li Keqiang visited India in May 2013. Indian Prime Minister had stated that he had 'wide-ranging and candid' discussions with his counterpart Li Keqiang.[15] In his speech, he had specifically mentioned the Depsang Plains transgression, sharing of river waters, and bridging trade imbalance. Dr Manmohan Singh frankly told Li that 'The basis for continued growth and expansion of our ties is peace and tranquility on our borders'.

Water-related issues emerged as a bone of contention recently. Water sharing or flows from China to the lower riparian states such as India, Bangladesh and Pakistan have become a contentious issue. The Prime Minister had stated in the Lok Sabha that we should 'trust the Chinese, but verify' on this issue. Later, however, he raised Indian concerns at the BRICS meeting in March 2013 to President Xi Jinping. After the Pareechu lake incident—when the artificial lake in Tibet burst, washing off the apple cultivation in Himachal Pradesh—an MoU on hydrological data exchange on River Sutlej was signed. An MoU on Brahmaputra hydrological data exchange was signed in June 2008. On this matter, five meetings between China and India were held by 2011 at the expert levels. Nevertheless, it was reported that several dams were commissioned on the Yarlung Zangbo by China in Tibet. Indian officials termed these as 'run-of-the-river projects' in the light of their talks with their Chinese counterparts.

On another issue, so far, China had been reluctant to acknowledge Indian nuclear weapon status after the 1998 tests. Para 21 of the joint statement between Singh and Li welcomed universal disarmament, while para 20 welcomed the expansion of the civil nuclear energy programmes. After the November 2006 joint statement between the then President Hu Jintao and Singh, the civilian nuclear cooperation issue was reiterated again in 2013. The dialogue process with China on Afghanistan and Central and West Asia was mentioned with counter-terrorism issues. While the Indian government had been reluctant to upgrade the Bangladesh-China-India-Myanmar sub-regional cooperation to the track 1 level, now the joint statement suggested the establishment of a joint study group to go into the connectivity issues in this grouping. While India was also reluctant to expand border trade through Nathu La except in the 2006 formulation of about 28 items, the joint statement agreed to consider the strengthening of trade through this post.

Territorial Dispute

The sovereignty and territorial issues were to bog down many governments in India. The UPA government as well faced this dilemma with China. After the UPA government was installed, it held the fifteenth Joint Working Group meeting on 30–31 March 2005, after the last one in November 2002. Indian Foreign Secretary Shyam Saran and Chinese official Wu Dawei represented the two sides in the meeting. The Chinese foreign ministry restated that 'mutual understanding and mutual accommodation' principles have to be upheld in solving this dispute. At this meeting, the JWG finalized a 'Protocol on Modalities for the Implementation of CBMs in the Military Field Along the Line of Actual Control in the India-China Border Areas'. However, the most important mechanism to resolve this issue is the Special Representative mechanism. Table 3.2 shows the meetings of the Special Representatives during the UPA rule.

The Agreement on Political Parameters and Guiding Principles on the boundary question includes three phases—the first phase of knowing

Table 3.2 India-China Special Representatives' Meetings 2004–14

Period	Place	Remarks
3rd round (26–27 July 2004)	New Delhi	JN Dixit and Dai Bingguo met in talks that were held 'in a friendly, constructive and cooperative atmosphere'.
4th round	Beijing	JN Dixit met Dai Bingguo.
5th round (2005)	New Delhi	MK Narayanan met Dai Bingguo. After these talks, both sides signed in April 2005 'political parameters and guiding principles' for resolving border dispute.
6th round (25–28 September 2005)	Beijing	MK Narayanan met Dai Bingguo. This marked the 'beginning of the second phase of negotiations'.
7th round (11–13 March 2006)	New Delhi and Kumarakom	MK Narayanan met Dai Bingguo in talks that were termed as 'constructive and [conducted in] friendly atmosphere'. Chinese Foreign Ministry spokesman Kong said the two sides 'will proceed from the overall situation of developing friendly relations'.
8th round (25–26 June 2006)	Beijing and Xian	Talks were held in 'friendly, cooperative and constructive atmosphere' between Narayanan and Dai Bingguo.
9th round (25–27 June 2006)	New Delhi	MK Narayanan met Dai Bingguo in talks that were held in 'open, friendly, cooperative and constructive atmosphere'. China argued for preferential border trade, while India reportedly insisted on step-by-step approach.
10th round (17–18 January 2006)	Beijing	MK Narayanan met Dai Bingguo. The 'talks were held in an open, friendly, cooperative and constructive atmosphere'. Narayanan stated that the talks were 'good', while Dai Bingguo stated that these were part of 'achieving the goal of common development for the benefit of people of both the countries'. Chinese Foreign Ministry spokesman, Liu Jianchao, stated, 'They had in-depth exchange of views and the two sides are committed to make joint efforts to promote the process'.
11th round (26–27 September 2007)	New Delhi	MK Narayanan met Dai Bingguo and 'held useful and positive discussions on the framework for the settlement of the India-China boundary question'.
12th round (September 2008)	Beijing	MK Narayanan met Dai Bingguo and decided to pursue their goal for a 'fair and reasonable' solution.

Continued

Table 3.2 *Continued*

Period	Place	Remarks
13th round (7–8 August 2009)	New Delhi	MK Narayanan met Dai Bingguo. Talks were held in 'a cordial and friendly atmosphere'. Both discussed the 'entire gamut of bilateral relations and regional and international issues of mutual interest'. Both sides said they would 'press ahead with the framework negotiations' in accordance with the political parameters and guiding principles.
14th round (29–30 November 2010)	Beijing	Shivshankar Menon and Dai Bingguo's joint call to 'seek a fair and reasonable solution acceptable to both sides'. 'Dai and Menon had an in-depth exchange of views on how to properly solve the China-India boundary issue to safeguard peace and tranquility along the border'.
15th round (15–17 January 2012)	New Delhi	Shivshankar Menon and Dai Bingguo met. Discussions were held on a 'wide ranging, productive, forward-looking and marked by a commonality of views on many issues'. 'Working Mechanism for Consultation and Coordination on India-China Border Affairs' established.
16th round (28 June 2013)	Beijing	Shivshankar Menon and Yang Jiechi talked 'in a practical and in-depth way'.
17th round (10–11 February 2014)	New Delhi	Shivshankar Menon and Yang Jiechi 'made in-depth exchanges of views'. Both 'maintained a good momentum in border talks and effectively controlled and managed their differences concerning the boundary question'.

Sources: Press reports and MEA.

each other's positions on the border dispute and exploring the framework of the boundary through the five SR talks from 2003 ended and the second phase began in September 2005 'to engage in exploring the political framework and the specifics of adjustments to be made by both sides for the boundary settlement'.[16] After five meetings between the SRs of both countries, in a Joint Statement in April 2005 between the Chinese Premier and Indian Prime Minister, the two countries decided to solve the border dispute based on agreed 'political parameters and guiding principles'. The second phase explored possibilities for initiating an 'agreed framework' on the boundary dispute settlement. This was to form the basis for delineation and demarcation of the boundary in future. The third phase of the SR talks is to make actual delineation and demarcation of the boundary on the map and on the ground by the concerned officials. However, differences existed between the two sides. For instance, in late May 2007, the new Chinese Foreign Minister Yang Jiechi reportedly conveyed to Indian counterpart Pranab Mukherjee in Hamburg, at the sidelines of the Asia-Europe Meeting, that 'mere presence' of populated areas would not affect Chinese claims on the boundary. But Article 7 in the bilateral agreement on 'political parameters' between India and China in April 2005 stated: 'In reaching a boundary settlement, the two sides shall safeguard due interests of their settled populations in the border areas'. This was included following the Indian Prime Minister's statement that populated areas would not be disturbed in arriving at a solution to the border dispute.

The above suggest scarce information on the actual progress of the Special Representative mechanism. The issue of the increasing number of border transgressions by both sides in venturing into the grey Line of Actual Control areas of the borders had affected not only the border areas but also the bilateral relations. The April–May 2013 transgression in the Depsang Plains when China mobilized 200 troops accommodated in five tents—in what Indian Defence Secretary testified to a Parliamentary Committee as intrusion of 19 kilometres inside the Indian territory—had rattled the bilateral relations. The then foreign minister Salman Khurshid insisted that these tents be vacated before Premier Li Keqiang could visit New Delhi in May 2013.

Related to the unresolved territorial dispute is the gradual increase in the infrastructure projects across China's peripheral regions, including in Tibet bordering India and Bhutan. While China continued to make border domination efforts through dual-use facilities, including in Aksai Chin—an area of over 38,000 sq. km (and 5,200 sq. km of Shaksgam it secured from Pakistan in 1963) it occupied—Beijing also began exerting pressure on India's Arunachal Pradesh. It had incorporated Arunachal Pradesh into a new construct of 'southern Tibet' and began demanding a share of the territory in the border discussions. It began a two-pronged approach—diplomatic escalation on Indian leaders' visits to these areas and denial of visas to official visitors from the region, issuing 'stapled visas' for ordinary passport holders from the region. This measure was to test the bilateral relations. The issuing of 'stapled visas' to Kashmir residents, however, became more controversial with the UPA government taking retaliatory measures.

The then foreign minister Pranab Mukherjee visited Tawang in Arunachal Pradesh in November 2008 and stated that two elected representatives from the state are represented in the Indian Parliament with a vibrant democratic system in the state. He stated, 'The question of parting company of Arunachal or any of its part does not arise'. China regretted the visit. Prime Minister Dr Manmohan Singh visited Arunachal Pradesh on 3 October 2009. China's foreign ministry spokesman stated: 'We demand the Indian side address China's serious concerns and not trigger a disturbance in the disputed region so as to facilitate the healthy development of China-India relations'.[17] Similar were the Chinese responses to the Indian defence minister's visit in 2012 and then President Pranab Mukherjee's visit in 2013.[18]

For officials from the state—howsoever higher they are—China began denying visas. A former Chief Minister of the state could not visit China, as with several administrative officers from the state. For ordinary people of Arunachal Pradesh, however, China began issuing stapled visas. India quickly issued a travel advisory in November 2009 cautioning Indian citizens that Chinese visas stapled to passports were not valid for travel outside the country. Nevertheless, China's stapled visas to Arunachal Pradesh residents have created much inconvenience and disappointment. In 2011, a Karate team was stopped at the Delhi airport for planning to travel to China with stapled visas. Likewise, in 2012, a weightlifter team was denied permission to travel with stapled visas. In October 2013, an archer's team has to skip a visit to Wuxi for lack of proper visas.

On Kashmir, China adopted a twin-pronged strategy as well. On the one hand, it revised its Kashmir policy of equidistance from Islamabad and New Delhi in its 'sanctity of the Line of Control' policies since Deng Xiaoping time to that of the recent active intervention in not only infrastructure (specifically hydro-electric projects) in Pakistan Occupied Kashmir, Gilgit, and Baltistan. These projects were to become more pronounced since 2014 China-Pakistan Economic Corridor construction in the region. On the other hand, it either denied visas to high-level officials—like in Arunachal Pradesh—or issued 'stapled visas' to Kashmir residents. Thus, China denied a visa to Gen Jaswal, who hailed from

Jammu but an Army Commander as a part of the military-to-military visits to China.

Dr Manmohan Singh's responses on the visa issue were swift. He raised this issue with his counterpart at various fora, began insisting on diplomatic reciprocity from China for recognizing 'one China' policy to that of compliance on Kashmir by Beijing, dispatched his defence minister AK Anthony to Seoul in September 2009 to discuss defence cooperation agreement and the like. Since 2010, it was clear that India had not reiterated the 'one China' policy in its joint statements, although the 2008 joint statement during the visit by Dr Singh to Beijing had assurances from the Indian side on Taiwan. Nevertheless, Dr Singh raised concerns about China's rise in the neighbourhood of India. In his speech at the Council on Foreign Relations in New York, as well as in his interactions with the editorial members of the Indian press, he had suggested to the 'low level equilibrium' that China is striving for in South Asia to the detriment of Indian interests.

Bilateral Trade

One of the issues that exhibited cooperation between India and China is related to growing economic relations. Prime Minister Rajiv Gandhi's visit to Beijing in 1988 opened bilateral economic relations as both sides decided to keep aside the territorial dispute. During Prime Minister Vajpayee's visit to Beijing in June 2003, the fiscal and financial dialogue process was initiated. A border trade agreement through Nathu La was signed at this time (and inaugurated in July 2006 after 44 years).[19] Also a joint study group of officials and experts on expanding trade was conceived.[20] A year earlier, in 2002, direct flights began between the two capitals.[21] In 2003–04, India became the largest trading partner of China in South Asia, with bilateral trade worth $7.5 billion in 2003 and over $13 billion in 2004. Table 3.3 provides figures related to bilateral trade during the decade under study.

From this period, both sides began the process of shifting from commodity trade to also include project contracts, investments, and technology trade. Both sides set up a Joint Study Group that drew up 'five-year' plan targets to expand trade. China began also exploring project contracts in India from this period.[22] Subsequently, in April 2005, during Premier Wen Jiabao's visit to India, both sides released a report on expanding trade and economic cooperation.[23] This year also witnessed China becoming the top import supplier and the third largest export market for India.[24] During President Hu Jintao's visit to New Delhi in November 2006, several agreements were signed related to the economy, one among which was the investment promotion and protection agreement.[25] Early that year, the first Financial Dialogue was held in New Delhi in April 2006. The Dialogue was mooted during Premier Wen Jiabao's visit in 2005 to learn from each other on sustainable development processes. In July 2006, both opened up the Nathu La for border trade.[26] To broad base the business links, the first CEO Forum meeting was held in Mumbai in November 2006.

Later, in April 2007, Indian Commerce and Industry Minister Kamal Nath visited his counterpart Bo Xilai in Beijing and both signed a joint statement on expanding trade. Subsequently, Deputy Chairman of the Planning Commission M. S. Ahluwalia visited China. In October 2007, both countries completed the joint study on exploring regional trade

Table 3.3 India-China Trade 2004–14 (in U.S.$ billion)

Year	India's Exports	India's Imports	Total Trade
2004	7.67	5.92	13.60
2005	9.78	8.93	18.71
2006	10.27	14.58	24.86
2007	14.63	24.01	38.64
2008	20.25	31.48	51.73
2009	13.71	29.65	43.37
2010	20.85	40.91	61.73
2011	23.37	50.54	73.91
2012	18.79	47.61	66.46
2013	17.02	48.44	65.47
2014	16.37	54.22	70.59

Source: China's Foreign Affairs (relevant Yearbooks).

agreement. In December of the same year, the 2nd Financial Dialogue between the two was held in Beijing.[27]

Subsequently, in October 2008, Vice Commerce Minister Gao Hucheng visited India to sign the MoU on Establishment of Technical Level Expert Group of India-China on Trade remedy to Promote Mutual Cooperation.[28] In 2009, Vice Commerce Minister Zhong Shan visited India for trade promotion and Commerce Minister Chen Deming led a delegation to the WTO Ministerial meeting held in New Delhi in September.[29] Indian Commerce and Industry Minister Anand Sharma visited Beijing in January 2010 to attend the 8th meeting of the India-China Joint Group on Trade, Science and Technology. MoUs on trade were signed in this context.[30] However, as the Table 3.3 indicates, trade imbalance, which was in favour of India during the first two years of the UPA government, began adversely affecting India henceforth. During the period 2006–14, the trade imbalance drastically shifted in favour of China. Moreover, this trade deficit began to affect the Indian economy. To address this, India began conveying to China that in order to address trade deficits, China needs to invest in the manufacturing sector, purchase more value-added goods from India, remove non-tariff barriers and observe market economy status as enshrined in the WTO. President Pratibha Patil, during her visit to Beijing in 2010 raised this issue with the Chinese leadership but in vain. Commerce Secretary Khullar prepared a report for the government in August 2011 to overcome the trade deficit and protect Indian companies such as BHEL and Larson & Toubro. While direct bilateral investments were negligible during this decade (with India investing over $400 million in China and China $300 million in India), the value of the contracted projects is substantial at more than $50 billion by China in India. As Dr Manmohan Singh announced $1 trillion in investments in the infrastructure projects across the country, China, with its large-scale projects in this sphere, is a major beneficiary of such investments. Secondly, India also announced increasing its manufacturing sector's role in the GDP from the current 14% to about 29%. This move is also an opportunity for China, given its strength in this field. Yet, no concrete progress was achieved in this regard. Bilateral trade issues also witnessed their lows with the Yiwu incident in December 2011 when Indian businessmen and a Consulate official were manhandled by the locals.

Nevertheless, two sectors have come under increasing Chinese domination. In the power sector, it was reported that out of a demand of nearly 320,000 MW of electricity requirements in India, China was able to sell equipment worth about 80,000 MW, including by Pan Song of Shanghai Electric. The Reliance Group had secured nearly $10 billion in loans from China Development Bank and others. Another sector that saw an upward momentum was the telecommunications sector, with Huawei and ZTE playing an increasing role. This is in the background of the number of mobile phone users in India increasing by leaps and bounds. By 2012, India had 900 million mobile phone users—indicating the growing demand in this sector.

The next phase of high-level discussions on macro-economic issues started with the first Strategic Economic Dialogue (SED) at Beijing between the Indian Planning Commission and China's National Development Reform Commission (NDRC) on 26 September 2011—a decision taken during Premier Wen's visit to India in December 2010.[31] During this meeting both agreed 'to strengthen communication on macro-economic policies, share development experiences and enhance coordination in addressing economic challenges'.[32] Five working groups on economic policy coordination, infrastructure, energy, environment protection, and high-technology were formed after this meeting. They agreed to initiate projects in the infrastructure, specifically in the railways sector.[33] The second meeting in this format was held on 26 November 2012, in New Delhi.[34] The following were the points of the agreement arrived at this meeting and indicate the widespread nature of the discussion:

reform of international monetary and financial systems, stabilizing the volatility in global commodity markets, working towards sustainable development and climate change goals, and ensuring food and energy security ... improve trade and investment environments, work towards removing market barriers, enhance cooperation in project contracting, deepen business to business exchanges ... improve transportation links, encourage greater bilateral investment in high-speed rail development programme, heavy haul and station development ... the possibility of Chinese power equipment manufacturers setting up service centres in India ...[35]

The third SED meeting was held on March 18, 2014, in Beijing.[36]

Another aspect—though marginalized—is related to border trade. Three border posts were opened in the last few decades in Shipki La, Lipulekh, and Nathu La. The latter was to be opened up for trade on 2 October 2005, but postponed on Chinese request. On 18 June 2006, at Lhasa, a six-member Indian delegation agreed with the chairman of the Tibetan Autonomous Region government that Nathu La should be opened for trading from 8 July. It appeared that the Chinese side wanted to complete the Golmud to Lhasa railway line and other over and under-ground defence networks works before Nathu La can be used for trading. China has constructed a 6,400 square metre market at Dongqinggang, about 16 km from the Nathu La. On the Indian side, a trade mart at Sherathang (nearly 7 km from Nathula) was constructed for business. Prior to this, India estimated that it needs to spend Rs 2,122 crores for infrastructure building at Nathu La. A mock trading was carried out by India at Nathu La in April this year to test various parameters of border trade including infrastructure facilities, customs, banking, accommodation, and security. Overall, the border trade is estimated to be in a few hundred million dollars, with maritime trade dominating the overall trade figures.

Broadly, another dimension that has been added during this period was the January 2006 agreement on energy cooperation that the then minister Manishankar Aiyar promoted between India and China as both became the largest consumers of hydrocarbon resources.[37]

Terrorism

Another issue that is close to the national security of India and China is the issue of terrorism. Both India and China were bogged down in Kashmir and Xinjiang on this issue. While all their joint statements during this decade referred to counter-terror efforts, Pakistan's position in the 'all weather' relations with China had complicated the matter. Nevertheless, India's Home Minister Shivraj Patil visited China on 7–11 September 2005, and an MoU was signed for counter-terrorism cooperation.[38] Later, during Hu's visit, India had accepted efforts to counter 'three evils'. Later, the third meeting of the Joint Working Group on counter-terrorism was held at New Delhi in July 2008.[39] As explained below, two defence ministries began counter-terror joint army operations.

South China Sea Issue

The decade under the UPA also saw the emergence of maritime issues for cooperation with China as reflected in the maritime dialogue process, but increasingly of competition both in the Indian Ocean as well as in the South China Sea.[40] China had stepped up its pressure on New Delhi to vacate commercial operations in the South China Sea region. According to the official website of the Oil and Natural Gas Commission (ONGC), it has energy cooperation with Vietnam dating back to 1988—a year when China grabbed the Filipino-held Mischief reef in the South China Sea. The ONGC Videsh Ltd (OVL) acquired the license of exploration in Vietnam for Block 06.1 (located 370 km southeast of Vietnam and with an area of 955 sq. km) in 1988 and production started in 2003. Another Block 127 is located in the deep-sea waters (at a water depth of 400 meters and an area of 9246 sq. km) and was acquired in 2006. Drilling started in 2009 and the block was abandoned due to the non-availability of hydro-carbon resources. The eye of the storm between India and China—Block 128—is at a water depth of 400 meters and has an area of 7,000 sq. km, under the Vietnamese jurisdiction. Vietnam had cited the 1982 UN laws in this regard which India had considered while acquiring the block in 2006 and deployed drilling rigs in 2009. Due to the hard sea bed, the actual operations of the rig were affected. However, China had not objected earlier to the OVL on these operations. Nevertheless, a series of events had resulted in twists and turns and in upsetting the bilateral equations between New Delhi and Beijing.

India have declared that the South China Sea should be part of the high-seas free navigation zone without any interruption to trade and commerce by any disputant to the islands dispute. As nearly half of Indian trade transits through the region, this is crucial sea lane of communication for India. India, in its interactions with China, had also suggested that the Indian role should be seen as commercial in nature and for energy exploration. This was conveyed by Indian Prime Minister Manmohan Singh to his Chinese counterpart Wen Jiabao at the Bali meeting in November 2011. This was preceded by the reported chasing away of INS Airavat in July 2011 by China's naval vessels.

In this background, foreign minister SM Krishna declared that 'The South China Sea is not China's Sea' and in April 2012, his colleague

Minister Ashwani Kumar stated 'South China Sea is the property of the world. Nobody has a unilateral control over it and India is capable enough of safeguarding its interests'. Nevertheless, on April 13, 2012, the issue was discussed between the two foreign ministers in Moscow in the backdrop of the Russia-India-China trilateral meeting. During the early June visit of U.S. Defence Secretary Panetta to New Delhi and his meeting with his Indian counterpart AK Anthony, the latter suggested that disputes in Asia-Pacific should be resolved bilaterally—implying a negative view of the U.S. 'rebalancing' role in the region but more significantly, in the backdrop of the South China Sea islands dispute, suggesting that the dispute be resolved without the U.S. intervention. This position may have been prompted by the India-China discussions on the territorial dispute as well as Kashmir developments. It was also reported that the Chinese leaders had promised the Indian side of investment opportunities in the Chinese-controlled areas in the future, in lieu of India vacating such blocks from Vietnam. This appears to have been the discussion at the G20 meeting in Mexico on 18–19 June 2012. On 18 June 2012, the OVL and China National Petroleum Corp. (CNPC) also had signed an agreement for joint bidding overseas. Both co-operated in the energy extraction in Sudan. However, not much progress was achieved on the cooperation front and the competitive angle increased since the Hanoi meeting of the ASEAN in 2010.

Defence Relations

The unresolved territorial dispute and China's major dual-use infrastructure development in border areas, in addition to China's forays in the Indian Ocean, necessitated active defence postures from India. India followed a dual-track policy—that of engaging China in CBMs approach in maintaining peace and tranquility in the border areas on the one hand, and strengthening conventional and strategic capabilities, on the other. Defence Minister Pranab Mukherjee visited China on 28 May–1 June 2006, and signed an MoU for an Annual Defence Dialogue with China.[41] This called for expanding military contacts between China and India. As a result of the protocol on CBMs of April 2005, Kibithu-Damai Border Personnel Meetings began in the Eastern Sector in November 2006 (the other three are at Nathu La, Spangur, and Bumla) with one more at Lipulekh also came up later.

Nevertheless, the MoU implementation was not without its share of problems as the Chinese side reportedly downgraded the level of military exchanges from Lieutenant General to Major General. Both sides also dragged their feet on the geographical location (given the fact that the border problem was not resolved), level of training and integration of command, etc. This impacted on the repeated postponement of Indian army-Chinese army joint operations, as with the joint air and naval forces operations, although finally both countries decided to conduct 'hand-in-hand' operations with the participation of 206-strong ground forces equally at Kunming in 2007 and Belgaum in 2008. On 28 August 2004, a joint mountaineering activity was conducted between the two armies. Indian army officers were also invited to witness Chinese ground forces exercises in Henan province. In November 2003, both navies conducted a search and rescue operation in Shanghai for the first time; in December 2005, both the navies conducted once again a search and rescue operation at Cochin, while in April 2006, Indian naval ships visited Qingdao. The December 2010 joint declaration between the two premiers commits their respective navies to conduct joint naval operations against piracy incidents in the Indian Ocean.

On the other hand, given the proactive thrust of China in Tibet and Pakistan Occupied Kashmir region, the Indian armed force identified China as the long-term challenge that needs to be addressed first rather than Pakistan. In this background, Army Chief Gen. Deepak Kapoor observed in October 2009 (reiterated by his successors) that India is preparing for a two-front (Pakistan and China) war under nuclear conditions. This was followed by the Indian defence minister AK Anthony's observations to the standing committee of defence of the parliament that the strategic assets (possibly nuclear or ballistic missiles) of the country would be shifted to northeast India. On 16 February 2010, the Indian Defence Minister remarked that the Army will deploy two additional mountain divisions to the China-India border. Thus the Indian government had lifted a 37-year-old freeze on making fresh recruitment for the China-centric mountain division. The Indian Air Force also deployed one Su30MKI squadron each at Tezpur and Chabua, in addition to refurbishing Nyoma, Fukche advanced landing grounds in Ladakh opposite to

China. Indian Air Force orders for the purchase of heavy-lift transports from the United States further augmented Indian military capabilities against China.

Further, to address security issues of widening asymmetries in power, and given the extensive work by China in Tibet military logistics build-up and outreach, India planned to counter these with conventional and strategic deterrence. A new Strike Corps to address the China challenge in the border areas was in principle accepted by the Cabinet Committee but later asked the three armed services to send proposals in this regard for better coordination among them. This proposed Strike Corps began with a provisional headquarter at Panagarh in West Bengal with about 89,000 troops, with an estimated expenditure for raising it at Rs 65,000 crores. India also tested the over 5,000-km radius Agni V ballistic missile in April 2012 and planned to operationalize these by 2014. In addition, the UPA government also commissioned the INS Arihant project once such deployments by the Chinese came to light at the Yulin base in Hainan province.

Multilateral Relations

One area where cooperation is reflected on a larger scale is in the multilateralism—a trend visible during the 1950s as well. With both upholding the UN Charter and non-interference policies, this aspect is obvious. Both have coordinated their positions in the UN, G20, WTO, Russia-India-China trilateral meetings, Shanghai Cooperation Organization, and others. The first test came during the formation of the East Asian Summit in 2005. In the event, the reported Chinese opposition to the expansion of Association of Southeast Asian Nations plus three (to include the 10 Southeast Asian countries, China, Japan, and South Korea) gave way to ASEAN plus six (to include not only ASEAN, China, Japan, South Korea but also India, Australia, and New Zealand) at Kuala Lumpur. India's Look East policy and continuous engagement with the region had positioned India as a 'balancer' in the region that is attractive to the ASEAN to counter the growing assertiveness of China. China, on the other hand, joined as an observer at the 14th South Asian Association for Regional Cooperation summit meeting at New Delhi in

April 2007. Another institution that came under increasing attention was the Shanghai Cooperation Organisation (SCO). During the UPA period, India joined this institution as an observer given the grouping's focus on counter-terror, energy, economic cooperative efforts. It was clear that China had viewed the Indian role in the SCO as competitive in nature. Hence it brought in Pakistan as well to counter India, despite Russian support to India. A significant statement was that of Dr Manmohan Singh that a representative of over a billion people will not be standing outside when the SCO deliberates. In arms control and disarmament institutions as well, China's opposition to India continued including in the Nuclear Suppliers Group and International Atomic Agency meetings.

Nevertheless, India-China cooperation in the BRICS has been significant. Since the Yekaterinburg meeting, India and China have coordinated in the BRICS extensively on a number of issues—including the setting up of New Development Bank for infrastructure projects and climate change as a part of the BASIC (Brazil, South Africa, India, and China) format since the Copenhagen meeting in 2009 and on regional security issues such as on Afghanistan, Iraq, North Korea, Syria, and others.

Conclusions

The UPA decade in the bilateral relations between India and China has been relatively smooth despite core interests becoming a bone of contention at the latter period. Institutionalization of the process of communication at almost all levels has been the main feature during this period, despite at times the other side refusing to budge as in the 2008 IAEA and NSG deliberations on the nuclear issue or on terrorism. Strategic dialogues, Special Representative meetings, financial dialogues, Strategic and Economic Dialogues, MoUs on water, annual defence dialogues, maritime dialogue, and others have enhanced communication and knowledge of each other's positions. Institutionalization of interactions, on the other hand, could also resolve some conflict situations, such as the Depsang Plains incident in 2013. Also, economic interdependence increased, reducing possibilities for conflict. Bilateral trade witnessed major growth during this period, although here again, mounting trade deficits stared in India's eyes. Significantly, India appeared to be catering to its larger northern neighbour without seeking reciprocity on many issues such as Kashmir, water, terrorism, to name a few. Predominantly, then this decade had exhibited cooperation and competition, without graduating into a conflict situation.

Notes

1. See Jairam Ramesh, *Making Sense of Chindia: Reflections on China and India* (New Delhi: India Research Press, 2006); Vincent Wei-cheng Wang, "'Chindia" or Rivalry? Rising China, Rising India, and Contending Perspectives on India-China Relations'. *Asian Perspective* vol 35 (2011) pp. 437–69; Waheguru Pal Singh Sidhu, and Jing-dong Yuan, *China and India: Cooperation or Conflict?* (Boulder, CO: Lynne Rienner, 2003); and Jonathan Holstag, *China + India: Prospect for Peace* (New York: Columbia University Press, 2010).

2. For in-depth comparisons between the two countries, see David Smith, *The Dragon and the Elephant: China, India and the New World Order* (London: Profile Books, 2007) (Indian edition); Prem Shankar Jha, *India and China: The Battle between Soft and Hard Power* (New Delhi: Penguin Viking, 2010); Prem Shankar Jha, *Managed Chaos: The Fragility of the Chinese Miracle* (New Delhi: Sage Publications, 2009); Shalendra D. Sharma, *China and India in the Age of Globalization* (Cambridge: Cambridge University Press, 2009); Ashok Kundra, *India-China: A Comparative Analysis of FDI Policy and Performance* (New Delhi: Academic Foundation, 2009) and Mohan Guruswamy, Zorawar Daulet Singh, *Chasing the Dragon: Will India Catch Up with China?* (Delhi: Longman. 2010); Arvind Panagariya, *India: The Emerging Giant* (New York: Oxford University Press, 2008) and Tarun Khanna, *Billions of Entrepreneurs: How China and India Are Reshaping Their Future and Yours* (Boston: Harvard Business School Press, 2007).

3. 'Text of Draft of Common Minimum Programme', Rediff.com, 22 May 2004, accessed at <https://www.rediff.com/election/2004/may/21cmptext.htm>

4. 'Congress Manifesto for General Elections 2009', 24 March 2009, accessed at <https://www.news18.com/news/politics/in-full-congress-manifesto-for-gene ral-elections-2009-311973.html>. Later during the 2014 elections, which it lost, the Congress Party stated: 'India has emerged as a critical bridge between the developed world and the developing world, along with Brazil, China and South Africa …. We expect to proceed with our mutual efforts with China to work through established instruments towards a resolution of differences of perception about the border and the Line of Actual Control (LAC), even as our economic cooperation and multi-lateral cooperation continue to grow'. See Indian National

Congress, 'Your Voice, Our Pledge', accessed at < https://cdn.inc.in/manifestos/pdf_documents/000/000/001/original/Manifesto-2014.pdf?1506426027 >

5. See 'PM's Reply to the Debate in the Lok Sabha on the President's Address', 9 June 2009, accessed at <http://pmindia.nic.in/speech/content.asp?id = 787>. A few decades ago, in the late 1960s, similar views were expressed by Dinesh Singh, the then Indian External Affairs Minister, in a statement in Lok Sabha on 8 April 1969. He said: '[W]e have no enmity with the people of China; we wish them well. We also do not wish to interfere in China's internal affairs, but where China violates the norms of international behaviour and threatens our security or when China attempts subversion in our country we must be ready to meet them'. See MEA, *Annual Report 1969–70* (New Delhi: Government of India, 1969) p. 9. See also for the 'enough space in Asia' theme, the then Indian defence minister George Fernandez's speech in K. Santhanam and Srikanth Kondapalli (eds), *Asian Security and China 2000–2010* (New Delhi: Shipra Publications, 2003).

6. Jiang Zemin, 'Build a Well-off Society in an All-Round Way and Create a New Situation in Building Socialism with Chinese Characteristics', 18 November 2002, accessed at <https://www.fmprc.gov.cn/mfa_eng/topics_665678/3698_665962/t18872.shtml>

7. See Hu Jintao, 'Hold High the Great Banner of Socialism with Chinese Characteristics and Strive for New Victories in Building a Moderately Prosperous Society in all', 15 October 2007, accessed at <http://www.china.org.cn/english/congress/229611.htm>; Hu Jintao, 'Firmly March on the Path of Socialism With Chinese Characteristics and Strive to Complete the Building of a Moderately Prosperous Society in all respects', 8 November 2012, accessed at <http://www.china.org.cn/china/18th_cpc_congress/2012-11/16/content_27137540_11.htm>; and Xi Jinping, 'Secure a Decisive Victory in Building a Moderately Prosperous Society in All Respects and Strive for the Great Success of Socialism with Chinese Characteristics for a New Era', 18 October 2017, accessed at <http://www.xinhuanet.com/english/download/Xi_Jinping's_report_at_19th_CPC_National_Congress.pdf>

8. Ministry of External Affairs (MEA), *Government of India, Annual Report, 2004–2005* (New Delhi, 2005) pp. iii and 6.

9. For the view that there is no real strategic partnership between the two, despite the rhetoric, see Jean-François Huchet, 'Emergence of a Pragmatic India-China Relationship'. *China Perspectives* no. 3 (2008) pp. 50–67 and for the overall context, John W. Garver, *Protracted Contest: Sino-Indian Rivalry in the Twentieth Century* (Seattle: University of Washington Press, 2002).

10. Jagannath P. Panda, *India-China Relations: Politics of Resources, Identity and Authority in a Multipolar World Order* (Abingdon, Oxon: Routledge, 2017).

11. See 'Joint Declaration by the Republic of India and the People's Republic of China', 21 November 2006, accessed at < https://www.mea.gov.in/bilateral-documents.htm?dtl/6363/Joint+Declaration+by+the+Republic+of+India+an>

12. See 'Joint Communiqué of the Republic of India and the People's Republic of China', 16 December 2010, accessed at < https://mea.gov.in/bilateral-documents. htm?dtl/5158/Joint+Communiqu+of+the+Republic+of+India+and+the+ Peoples+Republic+of+China>

13. There are over 160,000 Tibetans living in India since the Dalai Lama's flight to India in 1959. India had agreed that Tibet was a part of China in 1954. It had also put restrictions on Tibetans in any 'anti-China' activities from the Indian soil. However, given the popularity of the Dalai Lama and his non-violent philosophy, Tibetans have a huge following in Indian society. The Government of India recognizes the 'spiritual' leadership of the Dalai Lama. As China began speculating about his successor in the years following the Beijing Olympics, this issue has become controversial. See Adrien Frossard, 'Reincarnation Under Stress: The Dalai Lama's Succession and India–China Relations'. *Strategic Analysis* vol. 34, no. 4 (2013) pp. 463–73.

14. 'India, China Hold First-Ever Strategic Dialogue', Rediff.com, 24 January 2005, accessed at <https://www.rediff.com/news/2005/jan/24talks.htm>

15. For the joint statement between the two, see 'Joint Statement on the State Visit of Chinese Premier Li Keqiang to India', 20 May 2013, accessed at <https://mea. gov.in/bilateral-documents.htm?dtl/21723/Joint + Statement+on + the+State + Visit+of + Chinese++Li + Keqiang+to + India>

16. MEA, *Annual Report 2005–2006*, p. 6.

17. 'China "Deeply Upset" over Arunachal Pradesh Visit', *The Hindu*, 13 October 2009, accessed at <https://www.thehindu.com/news/international/China-ldquodeeply-upsetrdquo-over-Arunachal-Pradesh-visit/article16886519.ece>

18. See DS Rajan, 'Why China's Objections to Modi's Arunachal Visit Were Muted', Rediff.com, 24 February 2015, accessed at <https://www.rediff.com/news/ column/why-chinas-objections-to-modis-arunachal-visit-were-muted/ 20150224.htm>

19. See 'Declaration on Principles for Relations and Comprehensive Cooperation between the People's Republic of China and the Republic of India', 23 June 2003, accessed at < https://www.mea.gov.in/in-focus-article.htm?7679/Declaration+ on+Principles+for+Relations+and+Comprehensive+Cooperation+Between+ the+Republic+of+India+and+the+Peoples+Republic+of+China>.   However, since the Chinese side violated the 2006 understanding on trading 'local' products and attempted to export electronic and other goods produced elsewhere in mainland China, these were swiftly sent back. Soon China accused India of limiting the items of trade through this border point. See '' 'India accused of erecting barriers at Nathu La', 11 August 2006, accessed at < https://www. hindustantimes.com/india/india-accused-of-erecting-barriers-at-nathu-la/ story-0H860eknnFKowOnWAispPL.html>

20. 'India, China moot economic group to boost trade', accessed at < https:// timesofindia.indiatimes.com/india-china-moot-economic-group-to-boost-trade/articleshow/40396.cms>

21. *China's Foreign Affairs 2004* (Beijing: World Affairs Press, 2004) p. 171.
22. *China's Foreign Affairs 2005* (Beijing: World Affairs Press, 2005) pp. 173–74.
23. 'Joint Statement of the Republic of India and the People's Republic of China', 11 April 2005, accessed at <http://pib.nic.in/newsite/AdvSearch.aspx>
24. *China's Foreign Affairs 2006* (Beijing: World Affairs Press, 2006) p. 184.
25. 'Joint Declaration by the Republic of India and the People's Republic of China', 21 November 2006, accessed at <http://pib.nic.in/newsite/erelease. aspx?relid = 22168>
26. *China's Foreign Affairs 2007* (Beijing: World Affairs Press, 2007) p. 209.
27. The five financial dialogues were in April 2006, December 2007, January 2009, September 2010, and November 2011. See *China's Foreign Affairs 2008* (Beijing: World Affairs Press, 2008) p. 159.
28. *China's Foreign Affairs 2009* (Beijing: World Affairs Press, 2009) p. 186.
29. *China's Foreign Affairs 2010* (Beijing: World Affairs Press, 2010) p. 180.
30. *China's Foreign Affairs 2011* (Beijing: World Affairs Press, 2011) p. 197.
31. 'Joint Communiqué of the Republic of India and the People's Republic of China', December 16 2010, accessed at <http://mea.gov.in/bilateral-documents.htm?dtl/ 5158/Joint + Communiqu+of + the+Republic + of+India + and+the + Peoples+ Republic + of+China>
32. Specifically, the development of railways was noted at this meeting. See 'Agreed Minutes of the 1st India-China Strategic Economic Dialogue', 26 September 2011, accessed at <http://mea.gov.in/bilateral-documents.htm?dtl/5100/Agreed + Minutes+of + the+1st + IndiaChina+Strategic + Economic+Dialogue>
33. 'Agreed Minutes of the 1st India-China Strategic Economic Dialogue', 26 September 2011, accessed at <https://www.mea.gov.in/bilateral-documents. htm?dtl/5100/agreed + minutes+of + the+1st + indiachina+strategic + eco-nomic+dialogue>
34. The 2nd meeting resulted in setting up working groups on policy coordination, infrastructure, energy, environmental protection, and hi-tech sectors. See 'Agreed Minutes of the 2nd India-China Strategic Economic Dialogue', 26 November 2012, accessed at <https://www.mea.gov.in/bilateral-documents.htm?dtl/20848/ agreed + minutes+of + the+2nd + indiachina+strategic + economic+dialogue>
35. 'Agreed Minutes of the 2nd India-China Strategic Economic Dialogue', 26 November 2012, accessed at <http://www.mea.gov.in/bilateral-documents. htm?dtl/20848/Agreed + Minutes+of + the+2nd + IndiaChina+Strategic + Economic+Dialogue>
36. The 3rd dialogue had set up a task force to encourage Chinese investment in India to study sustainable urbanization process; explore projects in heavy-haul, increasing engine speed, redevelopment of stations, etc.; and contract energy management, sewage treatment, water-efficient irrigation, ICT, and others. See 'Minutes of the third India-China Strategic Economic Dialogue', 18 March 2014, accessed at <https://www.mea.gov.in/bilateral-documents.htm?dtl/23125/minu tes + of+the + third+indiachina + strategic+economic + dialogue>

37. MEA, *Annual Report 2005–2006*, p. 8.
38. MEA, *Annual Report 2005–2006*, p. 7.
39. MEA, *Annual Report 2008–2009*, p. 6.
40. Lou Chunhao, 'US–India–China Relations in the Indian Ocean: A Chinese Perspective'. *Strategic Analysis* vol. 36, no. 4 (2012) pp. 624–39.
41. MEA, *Annual Report 2006–2007*, p. 9.

4

India-Russia Relations during the United Progressive Alliance Governments, 2004–14

Mervyn Bain

Introduction

During the period in which Manmohan Singh was Prime Minister of India (2004–14), New Delhi's relationship with Moscow appeared to be somewhat different from the bilateral relationship which had developed between India and the Soviet Union/Russia over the previous 60 years. This chapter will analyse the pressures and issues at play within Indo-Russian relations in the years of Singh's Prime Ministership that explain this apparent altered relationship with the Kremlin.

Notwithstanding this seeming changed relationship, this chapter will posit that despite the perceptible disparities between what were termed the 'Manmohan Doctrine' and 'Putin Doctrine' that emerged in Indian and Russian foreign policies, respectively, the bilateral relationship developed in the years from 2004 to 2014 in which the United Progressive Alliance (UPA) government was in power in accordance with both these doctrines despite, as stated, their seeming contradictions. Consequently, economics, geopolitical considerations (particularly the role of the United States in the international system and Washington's respective relationships with both New Delhi and Moscow), and the realist paradigm of international relations were highly important for bilateral Indo-Russian relations in the years from 2004 to 2014. The significance of the appearance of the BRICS nations, the acronym for the alliance of five

Mervyn Bain, *India-Russia Relations during the United Progressive Alliance Governments, 2004–14* In: *Forging New Partnerships, Breaching New Frontiers*. Edited by: Rejaul Karim Laskar, Oxford University Press.
© Oxford University Press 2022. DOI: 10.1093/oso/9780192868060.003.0004

emerging national economies (Brazil, Russia, India, China, and South Africa), will also be given appropriate consideration.

To illustrate these arguments, this chapter's first section 'Russian Strategic Thought' will examine both Russian Strategic Thought and also the analytical framework that will be used throughout the chapter (the analytical framework will be defensive realism despite the apparent significance of offensive realism in the 'Putin doctrine' with the differences between offensive and defensive realism also being detailed); section 'Indo-Soviet Relations' will chart the character of the traditional bilateral relationship between New Delhi and Moscow from the time of Indian independence in August 1947 until the disintegration of the Soviet Union in December 1991; 'Indo-Russian Relations in the Early Post-Soviet Era' will examine the bilateral relationship in the early post-Soviet period and the effect of Moscow's pivot to the West; the sections the 'Manmohan Doctrine' and the 'Putin Doctrine' focus on the foundations of the both 'Manmohan Doctrine' and 'Putin Doctrine', respectively; while 'Indo-Russian Relations and Manmohan Singh' examines Indo-Russian relations during the 10-year period in which Manmohan Singh was Prime Minister of India and the chapter concludes that despite both their apparent differences which at first made it appear that bilateral relations were of less importance to both New Delhi and Moscow, the relationship actually strengthened during the period under study.

Russian Strategic Thought

Throughout its history, a number of factors have impacted Russian foreign policy, including a wish for warm-water harbours and Russia's place in the international system (White 1991, 179–180; Caldwell 2007, 280–283). Subsequently, Tsygankov has iterated that three 'schools of thought' have historically competed for supremacy within Russian foreign policy; the ideas of westernists (the desire for membership of the 'family of European monarchies'), statists (due to an inferiority complex, statists are willing to sacrifice themselves for independence and sovereignty) and civilizationists (the belief that Russian values are superior to Western values and should be expanded) (Tsygankov 2006, 6).

These 'schools of thought' have resonance for contemporary Russian foreign policy and will be returned to, but at the time of Indian independence Marxist-Leninism also underpinned Moscow's foreign policy. Additionally, realism, or defensive realism, was significant within Soviet foreign policy. Realism postulates that the state's primary aim is their own survival, and consequently, they are power maximizers. Various forms of realism exist with Waltz detailing defensive realism when he wrote, '... the ultimate concern of states is not power, rather security' (Waltz 1979, 4). Contrariwise, offensive realism postulates that states maximize their relative power at the expense of other states (Mearsheimer 2001). Due to its expansive nature, offensive realism would appear key to Moscow's foreign policy. However, defensive realism dominated Moscow's Cold War thinking because Moscow continuously strove to counter the West's anti-Soviet policies. Furthermore, defensive realism is also central to the 'Putin Doctrine', which emerged in the twenty-first century and is detailed later.

Indo-Soviet Relations

Indo-Soviet relations evolved after India's independence in August 1947. The Soviet Union's lack of a colonial past and earlier rapid industrialization were important for the burgeoning relationship (this was repeated with other newly independent countries). Indo-Soviet relations were further aided by Moscow's increased interest in the Developing World after Joseph Stalin's death in March 1953. This increased interest, in part, took the form of financial aid. Indo-Soviet relations were no different.

As noted previously, Marxist-Leninism was important for the Kremlin's foreign policy at this time, with geopolitics also impacting Indo-Soviet relations. In the bipolarity of the Cold War, India aligned itself with Moscow, with India also being geostrategically significant for Moscow as Indo-Soviet relations countervailed the U.S. power in Asia, highlighting the importance in Soviet foreign policy of realism, or defensive realism, as noted previously.

In 1955, Jawaharlal Nehru visited Moscow and Nikita Khrushchev travelled to New Delhi (Khrushchev 1970, 507). Moreover, the relationship became increasingly geopolitically significant for both countries as the U.S.-Pakistan relations developed and the Sino-Soviet split deepened. Additionally, an economic aspect materialized (India predominantly exported raw materials to the Soviet Union while importing machinery), with Soviet aid also being important. By the late 1970s, Moscow was India's sixth-largest aid provider (Mehrotra & Clawson 1979, 1373–1376). The Soviet invasion of Afghanistan in December 1979 further increased India's geostrategic importance for Moscow.

Indo-Russian Relations in the Early Post-Soviet Era

Boris Yeltsin's desire for improved relations with Washington (in the hope of financial aid in Russia's economic transition) in the early to mid-1990s fundamentally altered New Delhi-Moscow relations. Westernists were dominating Russian foreign policy (White 2004, 222–229). The poor economic performances of India, but particularly of Russia, also adversely affected Indo-Russian relations (Khripunov & Srivastava 1999, 154). Significantly, Manmohan Singh, the then Indian Finance Minister, liberalized the Indian economy in an attempt to resolve its balance of payment crunch (Panda 2014). This liberalization would be important for Indo-Russian relations once Singh became the Indian Prime Minister in May 2004.

However, from the mid-1990s, Indo-Russian relations improved. Key was a further alteration in Moscow's foreign policy with statists coming to the fore due to Russian unhappiness at its treatment by the West. This included a lack of financial aid during Russia's traumatic economic transition, North Atlantic Treaty Organisation (NATO) expansion to the East, and the West's conduct towards their fellow Serbs in the former Yugoslavia that culminated in the NATO bombing of Belgrade in March 1999. Russian nationalism had been offended and Moscow wished to reassert itself in global politics.

Moreover, after December 1995 and Yevgeny Primakov's appointment as Russian Foreign Minister, 'spheres of influence' were of increasing significance in Russian foreign policy (White 2004, 230; Lynch 1990, 9–12). Concerning Indo-Russian relations, this manifested itself in Moscow's endeavours to create a 'security axis' with India and China to countervail

Washington in Asia (Tsygankov 2006, 98). Additionally, bilateral trade also increased. Energy and military hardware were at the forefront of increased trade with a $3 billion arms agreement being signed in 1997 (Tsygankov 2006, 109; Khripunov & Srivastava 1999). Furthermore, in the year 2000, Vladimir Putin travelled to India and signed the 'Deceleration on the India-Russia Strategic Partnership' (India-Russia Relations 2016).

The 'Manmohan Doctrine'

As detailed previously, Singh's tenure as Indian Finance Minister had provided some indicators of what would become underlying principles of the foreign policy that his government would pursue from 2004 to 2014. This was only accentuated by his academic background with Panda noting that the notion of a 'Manmohan Doctrine' was apparent in Indian foreign policy. Concerning this apparent doctrine, Panda has written, ' … the notion of a "Manmohan Doctrine" is helpful in understanding what India's technocratic professor-prime minister had in mind when he rose to the helm in 2004' (Panda 2014). More specifically, Panda observes, 'Singh was no realist; as an economist, his "doctrine" was that Indian foreign policy should privilege economic goals as the driver of India's national interest' (Panda 2014). At the start of the twenty-first century, a 'Putin Doctrine' would also emerge in Russian foreign policy, detailed later, with both doctrines impacting Indo-Russian relations. Additionally, Chaudhury has stated that Singh continued the process of increased international engagement initiated by his predecessor Atal Bihari Vajpayee (Chaudhury 2014).

This increased engagement and the 'Manmohan Doctrine', saw India conclude a number of free trade agreements. It also saw more emphasis being placed on Indo-U.S. relations despite minor irritants like the tension that arose between New Delhi and Washington over the U.S. State Department's handling of the Devyani Khobragade issue in 2013 (Chaudhury 2014). The culmination of improved Indo-U.S. relations was both the civil nuclear cooperation deal concluded in 2006, approved by the U.S. House of Representatives in 2008, and also President Barack Obama's visit to India in November 2010 (Panda 2014). However, it was not just with the United States that Indian engagement improved but also with both China and Japan. Chaudhury has described this as part of a 'look east policy' pursued by New Delhi, with improved relations between New Delhi and Washington, further augmented by India's backing of the U.S. action in Afghanistan (Chaudhury 2014). This scenario led Panda to write,

> Other positive indicators that India and the United States converged under the UPA's watch include the increased frequency of bilateral security consultations, and military exercises (see the Malabar series of maritime interdiction exercises). A burgeoning trilateral security process between the U.S., Japan, and India—the first of which took place at the end of 2011—suggests that India is beginning to link its cooperation with the United States to its cooperation with Japan, a major partner. (Panda 2014)

However, it would impinge on New Delhi's relationship with Moscow. Simply, for the reasons detailed previously, under Singh's Prime Ministership, it would appear that more emphasis was placed on relations with Washington than Moscow, unlike the traditional New Delhi-Moscow relationship outlined previously.

Notwithstanding this, New Delhi-Washington relations did not continuously trend in an upward trajectory at this time. Writing in 2009, Muni states,

> The launching and consolidation of India's strategic partnership with the United States during the Bush administration and the first Manmohan government certainly added weight to India in its relations with China as it alerted China towards new power equations in Asia. Under the Obama administration, there are creeping questions on the evolving nature of India-United States strategic partnership. A feeling has slowly started gaining ground in India that in the Obama administration's priorities, China and Pakistan are gaining ascendance and India's concerns, if not completely overlooked, were not being adequately factored and appreciated. India's absence from the itinerary of the United States' Secretary of State, Hillary Clinton's first visit to Asia in February 2009, when allies and non-allies such as China, Japan,

South Korea and Indonesia were covered, left New Delhi uncomfortable. (Muni 2009, 6)

This element of uncertainty within Indo-U.S. relations would be significant for New Delhi's relationship with Washington under Singh's Prime Ministership.

The 'Putin Doctrine'

As noted, in the twenty-first century, a 'Putin Doctrine' in Russian foreign policy also began to materialize, which appeared to be underscored by very different principles to the 'Manmohan Doctrine'. As detailed, while the 'Manmohan Doctrine' was driven by economic reasons whereas the 'Putin Doctrine' strove to return Russia to great power status, desired a multipolar world, is expansionist in nature but is ultimately underpinned by defensive realism (Aron 2013; Grachev 2005, 262–264). Essential to the 'Putin Doctrine' was the emergence in Russia of what has been termed as the 'Weimar syndrome' or 'besieged fortress' mentality, which has at its centre the idea that Russia is surrounded by steadily encroaching enemies (Shevtsova 2015, 2; Aron 2013, 2–3). This returns to the 1990s and the expansion of NATO to the East and the West's treatment of Serbia, detailed previously. However, both Shevtsova and Aron believe that the Russian government has attempted to garner support for itself by trying to counter these humiliations, which had resulted in the appearance of the 'Weimar syndrome' and the 'besieged fortress' mentality (Shevtsova 2015, 3; Aron 2013, 2). Moreover, statists (who, due to the historical Russian psychological inferiority complex, are prepared to fight for their independence and sovereignty) also became more prominent within Russian foreign policy circles. Furthermore, Zevlev also believes that since the year 2000, the ideas of realist–statists and the nationalist school of Russian foreign policy have merged. The nationalist school of Russian foreign policy, which Zevlev has separated into neo-imperialists and ethnic nationalists, desires the creation of a 'buffer zone of post-Soviet protectorates along Russia's borders', while realist–statists strive for increased Russian influence in the post-Soviet space, reduction in the U.S. global power and creation of a multipolar world (Zevlev 2014).

Although this is the case, the 'Putin Doctrine' was ultimately under-pinned by defensive realism as its ultimate goal was to acquire increased support for the Russian government.

Importantly the 'Putin Doctrine' can both be perceived as a con-tinuation of the policies synonymous with Primakov's appointment as Russian Foreign Minister in December 1995, outlined previously, and it also persisted while Dmitry Medvedev was President of Russia between 2008 and 2012. In summation, the 'Manmohan Doctrine' attempted to increase links between India and the United States, whereas the 'Putin Doctrine' was a further rejection of Moscow's turn to the West of the early 1990s. The outcome of these two doctrines would negatively impinge Indo-Russian relations, which as previously detailed, appeared to be of less significance during the Prime Ministership of Manmohan Singh than had traditionally been the case.

Indo-Russian Relations and Manmohan Singh

However, the juxtaposition between these two doctrines did not mean that India and Russia 'turned their backs' on each other. Trade was key for the relationship, with, as noted, economics underpinning the 'Manmohan Doctrine', but Moscow also attempted to increase its global influence, a key component of the 'Putin Doctrine', by utilizing trade links with strategically important partners, especially in energy and military hardware. Writing in 2009, significantly, Muni observes, 'Russia also con-tinues to be India's major defense partner' (Muni 2009, 7). In this manner, during Singh's trip to Moscow in October 2013, detailed later, both the Indian Prime Minister and Russian President spoke of the refurbishment of the aircraft carrier Admiral Gorshkov, renamed Vikramaditya, which was delivered to India in mid-November 2013 (One India October 22, 2013). Moreover, the appearance of the BRICS benefitted Indo-Russian relations (Muni 2009, 7). Not only did this association of countries have a common position on a number of international issues but it also meant that their respective leaders were, from 2009 onwards, meeting on an an-nual basis. The outcome of this was that Singh travelled to Yekaterinburg in June 2009 and Medvedev visited New Delhi in March 2012. Moreover, Putin had also visited New Delhi in the first months of Singh's Prime

Ministership when he travelled to India in December 2004 and the Russian President returned to the Indian capital in January 2007 (India-Russia Relations 2016; President of Russia January 25, 2007). At the conclusion of the January 2007 talks, the Russian government press release stated,

> Following the talks the Russian President and Indian Prime Minister adopted a joint declaration in which they define Russian-Indian relations as a strategic partnership that is not only in both countries' long-term interests but also supports strengthening stability and security in Asia and the world. Both parties confirmed their intention to make active efforts to develop and diversify trade and economic cooperation, and emphasised the need to pay special attention to developing bilateral trade and investments, including in energy and high-tech sectors. The document confirms the parties' agreement to develop a direct dialogue between the two countries' oil and gas companies. (President of Russia January 25, 2007)

In addition to this, Singh visited Russia again in October 2013 when he met Putin for over four hours in the Kremlin. Trade was again at the forefront of bilateral talks with it being agreed that the possibility of an Economic Cooperation Agreement (CECA) between India, Belarus, Kazakhstan, and Russia should be explored. In a similar manner, the opportunity of trade in hydrocarbons was also discussed with a desire to increase cooperation in science, technology, space cooperation, pharmaceuticals, education, and culture. Additionally, Russia remained a strategic partner for India with regards to nuclear energy with discussions over the construction of 12 Russian nuclear plants in India having taken place (Sarkar 2013, 515). The significance of bilateral trade was demonstrated in 2014 when Indo-Russian trade amounted to $9.51 billion, which comprised $3.17 billion of Indian exports and $6.34 billion of Russian imports (*The Economic Times* October 21, 2015).

The importance, and history, of the bilateral relationship for both countries, also became apparent by comments made by both leaders during Singh's October 2013 visit. At the start of the visit, the Indian Prime Minister is credited with having said,

We cherish our true and time-tested friendship with Russia, which has remained strong and relevant despite changes in the world at large, … The level of trust and confidence that we have in our relations with Russia is unmatched by any of our other relationship. I would like to reaffirm that our relations with Russia remain a strategic priority for us and will continue to grow, not only bilaterally but also on the global and regional issues … Ours is truly a special and privileged strategic partnership to which Mr President you have contributed a lot during past years. (*The Economic Times* October 21, 2013)

Quite simply, Singh was highlighting not just the magnitude and strategic importance of the relationship for India but also its multifaceted nature (Sputnik News August 26, 2017). Moreover, Putin commented, 'India is our strategic partner. Most of our mutual achievements have been achieved under your leadership and I am grateful to you' (*The Economic Times* October 21, 2013). Additionally, the Russian President appeared to go beyond normal diplomatic protocol when he both presented Singh with a lithograph painting of Russian tsar Nicholas II who had travelled to India in the nineteenth century, a map of nineteenth-century India, a Mughal coin, and he also spoke of Russia trying to open a Russian consulate in India in the early twentieth century (One India October 22, 2013). These Russian attempts may have been thwarted by the United Kingdom, but these gestures from Putin highlighted not only the importance of the bilateral relationship with Moscow but also its considerable heritage. Furthermore, while in Moscow, Singh was awarded an Honorary Doctorate by the prestigious Moscow State Institute of International Relations, on which he commented was a 'great honour' (One India October 22, 2013).

Additionally, during their meeting in the Kremlin, Singh and Putin also discussed the global geopolitical situation with particular focus being given to the situation in Afghanistan, how to 'prevent the effects of terrorism from spilling over' but also the situations in Iran, Pakistan, and Syria (One India October 22, 2013). It became apparent that both governments had a number of common positions concerning international and regional issues, while they also desired a strengthening of cooperation amongst the BRICS countries (Sarkar 2013, 515). Moreover, the bilateral relationship between New Delhi and Moscow also benefitted from the fact that, unlike Washington, the Kremlin has (1) never felt the need to maintain good relations with India's neighbour and rival, Pakistan, or (2) attempted to gain concessions on Kashmir, the Muslim majority province which is the centre of a longstanding dispute between New Delhi and Islamabad. For its part, India never publically criticized Russia over the Chechen situation (Sengupta 2007). Furthermore, in the immediate aftermath of Russian action in Crimea in March 2014, Putin telephoned Singh to explain the situation, further evidencing the significance of the bilateral relationship as this telephone conversation would have been designed to try and bolster international support for Moscow due to the global reaction to these events in the Crimea (India Today March 19, 2014).

Not only would this level of engagement, official visits by both government's leaders and cooperation seem contrary to the idea of a downturn in relations between New Delhi and Moscow, but they would also appear to be in accordance with both the ideas of the 'Manmohan Doctrine' and the 'Putin Doctrine', despite their apparent contradictions detailed previously. For India, this is in line with the principles of increased international engagement underpinned by economics, evidenced during top-level governmental discussions by the prominence of bilateral trade opportunities in many different sectors. For Russia, a relationship with New Delhi demonstrated its growing international influence, with this apparent assertiveness suggesting the primacy of offensive realism within the Kremlin's thinking. However, the desire for an improved relationship with New Delhi was ultimately underpinned by defensive realism as it was designed to buttress support for the Russian government by countering the 'Weimar syndrome' and 'besieged fortress' mentality that had become prominent in 1990s Russia. Furthermore, it evidenced the increasing role of statists (due to a Russian inferiority complex, statists were prepared to fight in an attempt to preserve Russian sovereignty and independence) in Russian foreign policy. Furthermore, as global politics changed, the bilateral relationship had geostrategic significance for both New Delhi and Moscow, with both governments also highlighting the longevity and history of the relationship. In short, Indo-Russian relations remained mutually beneficial for both countries.

Conclusions

In the period in which Manmohan Singh was Prime Minister of India, i.e., from 2004 to 2014, on the surface, New Delhi's relationship with Moscow appeared to be different from the relationship that had evolved between the two countries over the previous 60 years. The main reason for this was the emergence of a 'Manmohan Doctrine', which seemed to be both at odds with the prominence of the 'Putin Doctrine' in Russian foreign policy at this time, and also attached more importance to India-U.S. relations. Although apparently, this was the case, in reality, the bilateral relationship was not overly different from that which had existed prior to 2004. It remained mutually beneficial for both countries and, despite their apparent differences, developed in this 10-year period in accordance with both the 'Manmohan Doctrine' (a wish for increased international engagement underpinned by economics) and the 'Putin Doctrine' (driven by a desire to have increased international influence calculated to garner support for the Russian government and therefore underscored by defensive realism with this countering the emergence of 'Weimar syndrome' and 'besieged fortress' mentality in 1990s Russia while also highlighting the increasing prominence of statists within Russian foreign policy). Moreover, the emergence of the BRICS only further aided Indo-Russian relations. The outcome is that although the bilateral relationship did appear altered from its previous incarnation during Singh's Prime Ministership, resulting from emphasis being focused elsewhere and subsequently it being 'overshadowed' by these other relationships, in reality, it remained significant for both New Delhi and Moscow. This significance was both economic and political, despite these apparent differences.

References

Aron, Leon, 2013, 'The Putin Doctrine. Russia's Quest to Rebuild the Soviet State', *Foreign Affairs*, 8 March, http://www.foreignaffairs.com/print/136255 (accessed 12 February 2015).

Caldwell Laurence, 2007, 'Russian Concepts of National Security'. In *Russian Foreign Policy in the Twenty-first Century and the Shadow of the Past*, ed. Robert Legvold, 279–342, New York: Colombia University Press.

Chaudhury, Dipanjan Roy, 2014, 'India's Foreign Policy: With Landmark Deals, Manmohan Singh Government Promised Much, Delivered Little', *The Economic*

Times, 23 February, http://economictimes.indiatimes.com/news/politics-and-nation/indias-fireign-policy-with-landmark-deals-manmohan-singh-governm ent-promised-much-delivered-little/articleshow/30864051.cms (accessed 29 October 2018).

Grachev, Andrei, 2005, 'Putin's Foreign Policy Choices'. In: *Leading Russia. Putin in Perspective. Essays in Honour of Archie Brown*, ed. Alex Pravda, 255–273, Oxford: Oxford University Press.

Khrushchev, Nikita, 1970, *Khrushchev Remembers*. Boston: Little, Brown & Company.

'India, Russia Decide to Boost Trade Ties', 2015, *The Economic Times*, 21 October, https://economictimes.indiatimes.com/news/economy/foreign-trade/india-russia-decide-to-boost-trade-ties/articleshow/49473228.cms (accessed 30 October 2018).

'India-Russia Relations', 2016, India Ministry of Foreign Affairs, December, 1–6, http://www.mea.gov.in/Portal/ForeignRelations/India_Russia_Relations_DEC2 016.pdf (accessed 29 October 2018).

Khripunov, Igor, & Srivastava, Anupam, 1999, 'Russian-Indian Relations: Alliance, Partnership, or?', *Comparative Strategy*, 18, 153–171.

Lynch, A., 1990, 'Does Gorbachev Matter Anymore?', *Foreign Affairs*, 69 (Summer), 19–32.

'Manmohan Singh, Indian PM Who Reasserted Indo-Russian Legacy, Turns 85', 2017, Sputnik News, 26 August, https://sputniknews.com/asia/201709261057726 053-manmohan-singh-prime-minister-birthday/ (accessed 19 November 2018).

Mearsheimer, John, 2001, *The Tragedy of Great Power Politics*. New York: W.W. Norton.

Mehrotra, Santosh, K., & Clawson, Patrick, 1979, 'Soviet Economic Relations with India and Other Third World Countries', *Economic and Political Weekly*, 14, No. 30/ 32, August, 1367–1392.

Muni, S.D., 2009, 'Manmohan Singh-II: The Foreign Policy Challenges', *ISAS Insights*, No. 69, 1–7, 26 May, https://www.files.ethz.ch/isn/101116/70.pdf (accessed 2 November 2018),.

Panda, Ankit, 2014, 'How Did India's UPA Government Perform in Terms of Foreign Policy during Its 10 Years in Power?', *The Diplomat*, 18 January, http://thediplo mat.com/2014/01/indias-upa-government-and-foreign-policy/ (accessed 2 November 2018).

'PM Manmohan Singh, Vladimir Putin Praise Each Other for Bolstering Bilateral Ties', 2013, *The Economic Times*, 21 October, https://economictimes.indiatimes. com/news/politics-and-nation/pm-manmohan-singh-vladimir-putin-praise-each-other-for-bolstering-bilateral-ties/articleshow/24493810.cms (accessed 19 November 2018).

'Putin Goes Beyond Protocol: Gives 'Special Gift' to PM Manmohan Singh', 2013, One India, 22 October, https://www.oneindia.com/international/putin-goes-bey ond-protocol-gives-special-gift-to-manmohan-singh-1328237.html (accessed 20 November 2018).

Sarkar, Badal, 2013, 'India's Foreign Policy Under the Prime Minister of Dr. Manmohan Singh', *International Journal of Scientific Research*, 2, No. 12, December, 514–515.

Sengupta, Somini, 2007, 'Putin Visit to India Highlights Enduring Alliance', *The New York Times*, 24 January, https://www.nytimes.com/2007/01/24/world/asia/24cnd-india.html (accessed 20 November 2018).

Shevtsova, Lilia, 2015, *The Kremlin Is Winning*, 12 February, Brookings Institution, http://www.brookings.edu/research/articles/2015/02/12-kremlin-is-winning-shevtsova (accessed 23 February 2015).

Tsygankov, Andrei, P., 2006, *Russia's Foreign Policy. Change and Continuity in National Identity*. Lanham: Rowan and Littlefield Publishers.

Waltz, Kenneth, 1979, *Theory of International Politics*. New York: Random House.

White, Stephen, 1991, *Gorbachev and After*. Cambridge: Cambridge University Press.

White, Stephen, 2004, *Russia's New Politics. The Management of a Postcommunist Society*. Cambridge: Cambridge University Press.

'Vladimir Putin Calls PM Manmohan Singh, Discusses Situation in Ukraine', 2014, India Today, 19 March, https://www.indiatoday.in/world/story/putin-calls-pm-manmohan-discusses-situation-in-ukraine-185357-2014-03-19#close-overlay (accessed 19 November 2018).

'Vladimir Putin Held Talks with Indian Prime Minister Manmohan Singh', 2007, Russian President, 25 January, http://en.kremlin.ru/events/president/news/37070 (accessed 20 November 2018).

Zevlev, Igor, 2014, 'The Russian World Boundaries. Russia's National Transformation and New Foreign Policy Doctrine', *Global Affairs*, 7 June, http://eng.globalaffairs.ru/print/number/The-Russian-World-Boundaries-1607 (accessed 14 September 2014).

5

Quest for Security and Stability in the Asia-Pacific

Japan-India Security Cooperation under the UPA Rule

Shutaro Sano

Introduction

Today, the Japan-India partnership has become one of the key drivers for maintaining the stability and prosperity in the Asia-Pacific region as well as the international environment as a whole. Presently both countries are seeking deeper synergy between Japan's 'Free and Open Indo-Pacific Strategy' and India's 'Act East' policy and have upgraded their relationship to a 'Special Strategic and Global Partnership'. The foundation for this strong partnership was laid during the ten years of the United Progressive Alliance (UPA) administration led by Prime Minister Manmohan Singh in India. In fact, it was during this time that Japan and India were able to overcome the legacy of the Cold War and shed the bitterness that crept into the relations in the aftermath of India's nuclear tests in 1998. Notably in the security realm, India became geopolitically important for Japan during Singh's tenure in response to the growing need to cope with the various regional and international security challenges as well as issues related to national defence. This chapter aims to clarify the ways in which Japan and India endeavoured to stimulate their relationship during the period 2004–14 by primarily focusing on security issues. First, it examines how Japan's position towards India evolved, especially after the Cold War. Second, it considers the main drivers and the underlying factors that propelled and the obstacles that may have hindered the

Shutaro Sano, *Quest for Security and Stability in the Asia-Pacific* In: *Forging New Partnerships, Breaching New Frontiers*. Edited by: Rejaul Karim Laskar, Oxford University Press. © Oxford University Press 2022.
DOI: 10.1093/oso/9780192868060.003.0005

Japan-India partnership under the UPA rule. Finally, the chapter clarifies the unsolved and underdeveloped issues during the UPA term, which have been inherited by the Abe and Modi administrations.

In Pursuit of a Firm Foundation for the Japan-India Security Cooperation

The 21st century has thus far witnessed a promising development in Japan-India relations. Yet, the momentum to form a strategic partnership emerged only after the turn of the 21st century.[1] Indeed, both Tokyo and New Delhi have sought to establish strong diplomatic ties since the end of the Second World War. Notably, India encouraged Japan's prompt return to the international community. Not only did New Delhi refuse to demand war reparations from Japan, but it was also one of the first countries to establish a diplomatic relationship with Tokyo and promote the latter's participation in the 1951 Asian Games and the 1955 Bandung Conference. Subsequently, Tokyo and New Delhi strengthened their relations when Japan's first official development assistance (ODA) was provided to India in 1958. Despite these interactions, the Japan-India relationship did not develop into a strategic partnership during the Cold War and was restricted to the economic domain. In the midst of the East-West confrontation, political relations were not a top priority for both countries as Japan deepened its relationship with the United States while India followed the path of non-alignment and moved closer to the Soviet Union. Japan's neutral positions during the Sino-Indian and Indo-Pakistani wars in the 1960s, as well as its antipathy against India's nuclear test in 1974, also prevented both countries from seeking stronger cooperation in the security realm.

The end of the Cold War provided opportunities for Tokyo and New Delhi to pursue a deeper relationship, but a strategic partnership did not materialize in the 1990s. Initially, the bilateral relationship developed in the economic realm when Japan became the first and only country to provide emergency foreign exchange loans to India after the latter's foreign exchange reserves plummeted to U.S.\$1.1 billion during the financial crisis in 1991. Prime Minister Narasimha Rao's visit to Japan on the 40th anniversary of Japan-India diplomatic relations in 1992 was another valuable opportunity for the two countries to deepen their relationship. Tokyo and New Delhi, however, were unable to establish a firm strategic partnership due to their differences in policy priorities at the time. Notably, New Delhi had high hopes for Tokyo's continued direct investment in India, which was expected to facilitate India's economic liberalization agenda launched in 1991. In 1992, then-Finance Minister Manmohan Singh initiated India's 'Look East' policy to develop economic ties with the ASEAN and major East Asian economies including Japan. There were also expectations within New Delhi that Japan would serve as a bridge between India and the Asia-Pacific (Horimoto 2015, 7). In contrast, Japan primarily aimed to encourage India's participation in the Nuclear Non-Proliferation Treaty (NPT) regime with the desire to boost the momentum of its nuclear-free initiative. Subsequently, Tokyo's expectations towards New Delhi plunged when the latter decided to abstain from signing the Comprehensive Nuclear-Test-Ban Treaty (CTBT) in 1996 and proceeded instead to conduct a series of nuclear tests in 1998.

In addition to the differences noted above, the stagnation of the Japan-India relationship in the 1990s was also a result of Tokyo's lack of attention towards India at the time. Toshiki Kaifu was the only Japanese prime minister to visit India in the 1990s. Likewise, Yukihiko Ikeda was the only foreign minister who visited India during the same period of time. Furthermore, Prime Minister Ryutaro Hashimoto failed to refer to India when he introduced his new foreign policy, Eurasian diplomacy, during his speech to the National Diet in September 1997 (PM&C 1997). Indeed, the top policy priority for Tokyo during the 1990s was the urgent need to redefine the roles and functions of the Japan-U.S. alliance, which came into question with the collapse of the Soviet Union. After the Gulf War, Japan was no longer able to enjoy its traditional low-cost security policy, which heavily rested on an unequal balance in its relationship with the United States. The U.S. expectation for Japan's increased international contribution was clearly reflected, for example, in the bipartisan document which argued that 'we see the special relationship between the United States and Great Britain as a model for the [Japan-U.S.] alliance ... it is time for burdensharing [sic] to evolve into power-sharing' (INSS 2000). In light of these expectations and its determination to fulfil the responsibilities in the international community, Tokyo gradually expanded its defence posture to focus not only on national defence but also on contributing to a stable Asia-Pacific region as well as securing a peaceful international environment as a whole.

The push for a Japan-India rapprochement emerged when Prime Minister Yoshiro Mori visited India in August 2000 to alleviate the tensions between Tokyo and New Delhi following India's nuclear tests in 1998. Mori's visit marked a significant event as it was the first time for a Japanese prime minister to visit India in a decade. During the visit, Prime Ministers Mori and Atal Bihari Vajpayee agreed to strengthen the relationship in the fields of economics and information technology and establish a bilateral Global Partnership that would enable Japan and India to cooperate deeper in global issues, which included mutual support for their permanent membership in the United Nations (UN) Security Council. The subsequent Prime Minister Vajpayee's visit to Japan in December 2001 was also an important occasion that laid the groundwork for the two countries to pursue their Global Partnership that would 'contribute towards the stability and prosperity of Asia and the world in the 21st century' (MOFA of Japan 2001).

Yet, it was during the UPA rule led by Prime Minister Manmohan Singh that Japan and India were able to gain momentum to develop the foundation for their multidimensional strategic partnership. Notably, the two countries signed the 'Eight-fold Initiative for Strengthening Japan-India Global Partnership' when Prime Minister Junichiro Koizumi visited India in April 2005. These included the importance to enhance security dialogue and cooperation and to respond to international challenges such as counter-terrorism, non-proliferation, energy, and environment. Since this visit, summit meetings have been held annually in the capitals of the two respective countries. The relationship strengthened further during Prime Minister Shinzo Abe's first administration when the two countries elevated the relationship to the 'Global and Strategic Partnership' in December 2006. His 'Confluence of the Two Seas' speech to the Indian Parliament in August 2007 was also a milestone event during which Abe emphasized the importance of 'broader Asia' with Japan and India playing pivotal roles. The first Japan-India Foreign Minsters' Strategic Dialogue was held when Minister of External Affairs Pranab Mukherjee visited Japan and met his counterpart Taro Aso in March 2007. During the UPA era, seven rounds of meetings of this kind took place. The relationship attained bipartisan support in Japan when the Democratic Party of Japan (DPJ) came to power under the leadership of Prime Minister Yukio Hatoyama and signed the Action Plan in December 2009 to advance the Japan-India security relations based on the Joint Declaration on Security Cooperation which was signed by the previous Liberal Democratic Party (LDP) government led by Prime Minister Taro Aso in October 2008. Prime Minister Yoshihiko Noda's visit to New Delhi in December 2011 was also a significant event for the two countries with the signing of a Joint Statement entitled, 'Vision for the Enhancement of Japan-India Strategic and Global Partnership upon entering the year of the 60th Anniversary of the Establishment of Diplomatic Relations'. When Prime Minister Abe returned to power in December 2012, he reaffirmed India as an important security partner for Tokyo as well as for the stability in the Asia-Pacific and the international community as a whole as reflected in his idea of establishing a 'Democratic Security Diamond', and in Japan's first-ever National Security Strategy (NSS) issued in December 2013 (GOJ 2013a). The developments during the UPA era established the basis for stronger security ties and deepened Japan-India relations, which later became known as the 'Special Strategic and Global Partnership' during the Modi administration.

Key Drivers for the Deepening of Japan-India Security Cooperation

There are several important drivers which led to the deepening of the Japan-India security cooperation during the UPA government in India. These drivers can be categorized into three dimensions: contribution to securing a peaceful international environment as a whole; contribution to a stable Asia-Pacific region; and cooperation in the national defence of Japan and India (narrowly defined). While the drivers are interconnected and have an overlapping influence upon the level of Japan-India security relationship, the main influential drivers seemed to have gradually shifted over time: i.e., at the beginning of the UPA administration in 2004, the main drivers were related more to the international security environment with the spread of international terrorism and piracy; by the latter period of the first UPA term, the main drivers were related more to regional peace and stability with the increasing assertiveness of China's maritime activities. There was also a push for stronger mutual engagement in the national defence of the two countries during the latter period of the second UPA administration by the challenges imposed by Pyongyang and Beijing.

Securing a Peaceful International Environment

Economic factors have been key components in the deepening of bilateral relations between Japan and India. This trend continued during the UPA administration, as highlighted by the Manmohan Singh doctrine (MEA of India 2013a). Yet the two countries began to engage themselves with one another in response to the drastic changes in the international security environment since the turn of the 21st century. From a security perspective, the importance of India stemmed from the urgent need for the international community to cope with the various global 'non-traditional' security challenges such as the rise of international terrorism and piracy. While New Delhi, unlike Tokyo, refused to join in the U.S.-led campaign in Iraq, Japan and India shared interests in securing a peaceful international environment and remained engaged in international efforts in countering terrorism and piracy since September 2001. Notably, the Indian Ocean region became a greater concern for both countries as well as the international community as it constituted the ground zero for the war on terror and formed 'the intersection of two main reservoirs of Islamic extremism, the Middle East and Southeast Asia' (Ladwig et al. 2014, 135). The region is also closely geographically connected with Central Asia, which continues to face both internal and external challenges from the Three Evil Forces (terrorism, ethnic separatism, and religious extremism). In line with international efforts to eradicate what some call 'a lake of Jihadi terrorism' (Khurana 2004, 414), the Japan Maritime Self Defense Force (MSDF) engaged in refuelling operations and assisted the United States and others in the Indian Ocean during Operation Enduring Freedom (MOFA of Japan 2005).[2] Later in 2009, Japan dispatched two destroyers along with P-3C patrol aircraft to counter piracy and protected Japanese vessels in the waters off the coast of Somalia and in the Gulf of Aden. Since 2013, the MSDF has taken part in Combined Task Force 151 (CTF 151), and in 2015 a Japanese officer took command of the operation, which was the first time ever for Japan to command a multinational force. India, on the other hand, has deployed its naval ship to the Gulf of Aden since 2008. India remained independent of multinational organizations such as CTF 151, but its navy continued to interact with the MSDF through, for example, professional exchanges on counter-piracy operations. The Singh and the successive Japanese administrations, both the LDP and the DPJ, developed their relationship extensively in counter-terrorism/piracy. This was specifically reflected in the 2008 Joint Declaration on Security Cooperation which stated that Tokyo and New Delhi affirmed their commitment to fighting against terrorism and acknowledged that 'counter-terrorism efforts by Japan and India, including the Japan Maritime Self Defense Force's replenishment activities in the Indian Ocean, constitute an important part in the international community's efforts to eradicate terrorism' (MOFA of Japan 2008a). Furthermore, Tokyo and New Delhi began to utilize the Japan-India Joint Working Group on Counter-Terrorism and enhanced greater cooperation in combating terrorism through information sharing.

Closely related to the issue of international terrorism, ensuring peace and stability in Afghanistan also became one of the major issues for the international community including Tokyo and New Delhi during the UPA administration. There has been a growing need to enhance the rule of law, promote regional development, strengthen the crackdown on narcotics trafficking, and prevent corruption (MOD of Japan 2016a, 123). From the very beginning, Japan and India have engaged themselves extensively in the reconstruction efforts in Afghanistan to facilitate the development of the country. Tokyo organized landmark meetings including the first major international conference in 2002 and has taken a comprehensive approach in its effort (MOFA of Japan 2015a, 2).[3] Tokyo also played significant roles in security-sector reform programs, notably the Disarmament, Demobilization, and Reintegration (DDR) initiative and the Disbandment of Illegal Armed Groups (DIAG), both of which aimed to support Afghanistan's self-reliance and prevent the country from becoming a hotbed of terrorism. For India, the political and security situations in Afghanistan have been a vital and sensitive issue due to proximity and history. Afghanistan not only rests at the core of New Delhi's Central Asia strategy, which seeks to secure important trade, transport, and energy access routes but also has become a potentially vital economic hub connecting Central and South Asia after gaining membership in the South Asian Association for Regional Cooperation (SAARC) in 2007. Furthermore, Afghanistan is geostrategically important for countries including New Delhi's archrival Pakistan and regional powers—China, Russia, and Iran—as well as Europe and the United States. Consequently, India has been one of the largest contributors, offering over $2 billion in aid. The Singh government was also one of the lead organizers for the Delhi Investment Summit in Afghanistan in June 2012.

Under the UPA rule, India's assistance in Afghanistan was initially reconstruction-oriented. But with the withdrawal of the International Security Assistance Force (ISAF), New Delhi became more involved in security-related matters. In October 2011, for example, the Singh administration signed a security and trade pact with Afghanistan, agreeing to boost cooperation in counter-terrorism, training of security forces, trade, and other political and cultural engagements (Lakshmi 2011). Although Japan and India have not been involved heavily in bilateral activities in Afghanistan, the two countries have shared their views on the significance of ensuring peace and stability of the region and its effects on the international environment, driving Tokyo and New Delhi to commit themselves deeply to the development of Afghanistan as responsible Asian actors. This is evident from the Joint Statement between Prime Ministers Abe and Singh in December 2006, which noted, 'deep respect for each other's contributions in promoting peace, stability and development in Asia and beyond, unencumbered by any historical differences' (MOFA of Japan 2006a).

In addition to the issue on the UN reform, notably the reform of the Security Council, international peace activities, including UN-mandated peacekeeping operations (PKO) and humanitarian assistance and disaster relief (HADR) missions, also became areas for greater cooperation between Japan and India during the UPA rule. The steady but continuous efforts by both Tokyo and New Delhi throughout the UPA term have contributed to not only securing the peace and stability in the international security environment but also establishing a firm foundation for deeper Japan-India cooperation in the security domain as well as increasing the level of support from the international and regional community for developing the Japan-India partnership.

Regarding PKO, the UN has been expanding its missions to include multiple duties such as the Protection of Civilians (POC), the promotion of political processes, and assistance in DDR in addition to traditional ceasefire monitoring. With the growing opportunities for cooperation in PKO missions, both Japan and India have made steady efforts and continued, although to a different degree, their contributions to these activities. In the case of Japan, its contribution to UN peacekeeping began in Cambodia in 1992, and since then, Tokyo has engaged in multiple missions along with New Delhi.[4] During the UPA administration in India, Japan also dispatched Self Defense Forces (SDF) personnel to leadership positions at mission headquarters as well as the Department of Peacekeeping Operations at the UN Headquarters. In addition, SDF officers were dispatched to seven PKO Centers in Africa as instructors.[5] These past records established a strong foothold for the future deployment of SDF personnel to countries including India and Indonesia.[6] India, on the other hand, came to view itself as a 'leading power' in the non-traditional security sector rather than just manoeuvring as a balancing power (MEA of India 2015). India continued to play a leading role in UN PKO during the UPA term. The successive Indian governments have dispatched nearly 195,000 troops—the largest number from any country—to more than 49 missions, making major sacrifices including losing 168 of its peacekeepers (Permanent Mission of India to the United Nations 2019). As of January 2018, India is the third largest contributor, with approximately 6,700 deployed personnel in nine out of 15 active UN PKO missions (United Nations 2018). Furthermore, India has thus far provided 15 force commanders to various UN missions. In addition to their increased cooperation in PKO, it is important to highlight that Japan and India, along with Brazil and Germany, have cooperated continuously on the issue of UN reform, most notably the reform of the Security Council.

HADR is another field that provided a good platform for Japan-India cooperation during the UPA term. Today, roughly 70% of all natural disasters occur in the Asia-Pacific, costing the region U.S.$68 billion annually over the past ten years (U.S. DOS 2015). In light of this natural disaster-prone environment, Japan and India have played significant roles in HADR both within and beyond the region. Japan continued to engage heavily in HADR activities since the introduction of the 'Law Concerning the Dispatch of Japan Disaster Relief Team[s]' in 1987, with the Japan International Cooperation Agency (JICA) playing a primary role in Japan's HADR efforts.[7] These include activities during the spread of Ebola in 2014 (JICA 2015). Meanwhile, Japan's SDF have also engaged actively in HADR missions since 1998 including the activities in the wake of the Indian Ocean earthquake and tsunami in 2004 and the Typhoon Haiyan in the Philippines in 2013.[8] The SDF have also earnestly participated in multiple exercises such as the Pacific Reach and the Western Pacific Mine Countermeasure Exercise and Diving Exercise (MCMEX/DIVEX) led by the U.S. Pacific Command (Izuyama 2013, 186–7). Likewise, India has also been increasingly involved in HADR missions. New Delhi views itself as a 'net security provider' in the maritime neighbourhood including HADA operations (MOD of India 2015, 8). During the UPA administration, New Delhi provided aid to post-conflict situations in Sri Lanka and Afghanistan and also engaged in disaster relief operations after the 2004 and 2013 natural disasters noted above.[9] In the wake of the 2004 earthquake and tsunami, the creation of the Tsunami Core Group—consisting of Australia, India, Japan, and the United States—proved critical, as one analysis notes, 'in providing the overarching political support for effective disaster relief' (Samaranayake et al. 2014, 4). The Indian forces have also engaged deeply in multilateral and bilateral HADR exercises, which include the Pacific Reach and Western Pacific MCMEX/DIVEX. These efforts provided sufficient grounds for India to engage further with other militaries in future HADR exercises such as the India-Thailand Siam Bharat HADR Table Top Exercise, which was later held for the first time in May 2017. Furthermore, India strengthened its HADR capabilities with the United States during the Singh government (Samaranayake et al. 2014). In July 2005, New Delhi and Washington signed the U.S.-India Disaster Relief Initiative and pledged to 'strengthen their military capabilities to respond effectively to future disasters by joint and combined military exercise' (U.S. DOS 2005). In 2007, India acquired a Landing Platform Dock from the United States (Parmer 2012, 91–101).[10] Meanwhile, regional organizations such as the ASEAN Regional Forum (ARF), in which Japan and India are ASEAN Dialogue Partners, have served as venues for Tokyo and New Delhi to cooperate in HADR activities as well as other key issues such as counter-terrorism and transnational crime (CTTC), maritime security, and non-proliferation and disarmament. The ARF has made considerable progress in disaster re-lief, especially in strengthening the capabilities of ASEAN's Coordination Centre for Humanitarian Assistance on Disaster Management (AHA Centre) (U.S. DOS 2015).

The Arctic also became a promising factor for a deeper Japan-India co-operation, notably during the latter period of the second UPA term. The increasing strategic importance of the Arctic has driven both Arctic and non-Arctic states to cooperate more closely in their approaches to the region. Specifically, the rapid melting of the Arctic ice provided greater opportunities for natural resource development and new commercial sea routes. At the same time, it has damaged the Arctic ecosystem and became the cause for a global rise in sea levels and an increase in extreme wea-ther events. There are also security-related issues with the unsolved issues over the demarcation of maritime boundaries and the extension of states' continental shelves, which have resulted in new territorial claims by some Arctic Ocean states such as Russia (Kramer 2015).[11] Moscow has also in-tensified its military capabilities for securing Russia's national interests in the region (MOD of Japan 2017, 120–1).[12] Meanwhile, non-Arctic Ocean states have signalled their own interests in the development of the region. China, for example, has developed the specific routes in the Arctic (MOD of Japan 2016a, 143).[13] Beijing has also formally added the Arctic route to its $1 trillion cross-border infrastructure development project, Belt and Road Initiative (BRI), by June 2017 (State Council of China 2017). In light of this situation, effective governance has become key to sustain-able development in the Arctic. Opportunities for cooperation opened up during the Abe and Singh administrations in 2013 when Japan and India were among those accepted to serve as permanent observers to the Arctic Council (Headquarters for Ocean Policy 2015; NDTV 2015).[14] Proactive contribution to the international community by Japan and India would support and preserve the international legal principles of freedom of navi-gation and over-flight as well as other uses of the sea and airspace.

Contributing to a Stable Asia-Pacific Region

Maritime security has always been a major issue for countries in the Asia-Pacific including not only Japan and India but also China. Notably, the protection of sea lanes of communication (SLOCs)—including against piracy—has been a critical issue to these countries as they depend heavily on maritime routes to import various natural resources, including oil from the Middle East. In addition, the protection of SLOCs has become even more critical for the region with the growing importance in strengthening regional connectivity, which would provide vital networks to stimulate economic cooperation and integration for the Asia-Pacific as a whole.

For Beijing, active engagement in maritime security is closely linked with its energy strategy, which aims in part to alleviate its heavy dependence on SLOCs through the South China Sea and the Strait of Malacca (U.S. DOD 2016, 47).[15] China has gradually increased its overland oil supply from Russia and Central Asia including Kazakhstan, but its annual volume of imported oil and liquefied natural gas from the Middle East and Africa has been on the rise due to its rapid economic growth, increasing the strategic significance of these SLOCs. Yet, Japan and India, along with other Asia-Pacific countries, have become increasingly concerned over China's actions from the mid-2000s. The modernization of the People's Liberation Army (PLA), the lack of transparency over China's military budget, the growing aggressiveness of its military and paramilitary forces in the South China Sea and the Indian Ocean, and more recently, the geostrategic implications of China's BRI have all become the cause for their concerns. China's assertiveness gradually intensified from the latter period of the first UPA term and continued throughout the second UPA administration.

Specifically in the South China Sea, China escalated its activities in waters around the disputed Spratly Islands, Paracel Islands, and Scarborough Shoal. Satellite imagery has revealed that Beijing has built and strengthened its artificial islands by constructing runways and deploying anti-aircraft missile systems on all seven of China's outposts in the Spratlys (Asia Maritime Transparency Initiative 2016). There have also been direct confrontations between China and other claimant countries as well as the United States (BBC 2015).[16] Likewise, China has steadily increased its naval operations in more distant waters such as the Indian Ocean. Not only have Chinese navy vessels sailed to the Gulf of Aden to engage in international anti-piracy efforts, but its submarines have also been spotted operating in the region, making port calls in Sri

Lanka and Pakistan (MOD of Japan 2016a, 59).[17] Deepwater port at Gwadar in Pakistan, along with the military base in Djibouti, has become the cornerstones of China's regional posture (Gertz 2018).[18] Situations in Sri Lanka, Myanmar, the Maldives, and Seychelles have also generated anxieties in India. Against this backdrop, Indian Navy chief Admiral R.K. Dhowan expressed concerns in December 2014 towards Chinese deployments (NDTV 2014). The anxiety is shared by the United States military today (*Economic Times* 2017).[19]

China's increasing assertiveness has ultimately pushed Tokyo and New Delhi to cooperate more closely in maritime security. This is evident from the Japanese official documents and the various events that took place during the UPA administration. The 2010 National Defense Program Guidelines (NDPG) of Japan, for example, emphasized the global shift in the balance of power with the rise of powers such as China, India, and Russia, along with the relative change of influence of the United States, and reaffirmed the importance of India and the safety of the Indian Ocean by stating that Japan would 'enhance cooperation with India and other countries that share common interests in ensuring the security of maritime navigation from Africa and the Middle East to East Asia' (GOJ 2010, 9). Furthermore, their heads of state and defence ministers have held regular high-level talks (MOFA of Japan 2019a).

Progress on cooperation between their navies and coast guards has also been considerable. Information sharing between the two navies was strengthened by, for example, initiating a mutual exchange of schedules of escort operations in the Gulf of Aden. Moreover, Tokyo and New Delhi agreed on launching bilateral maritime exercise during Defence Minister AK Antony's visit to Japan in November 2011. Subsequently, the first Japan-India Maritime Exercise (JIMEX) took place in Japan in January 2012. In December 2013, the exercise was held for the first time in the Indian Ocean. This later developed Japan's status in Exercise Malabar—initially a bilateral India-U.S. exercise held since 1992—which was upgraded to that of a permanent participant by 2015, making it a trilateral exercise. In regards to coast guards, the two sides have held combined exercises since 2000 with a view to promoting mutual capabilities through joint working procedures for search and rescue operations and combating piracy at sea. During the UPA administration, exchanges in coast guards were strengthened with the signing of a Memorandum on Cooperation in 2006, which solidified the foundation for the Sahayog-Kaijin bilateral exercises, which have been held every two years. It is also important to note that senior-level visits took place eight times between the two coast guards during the ten years of UPA rule. Equally important was the launch of the Japan-India Shipping Policy Forum in 2010, which deepened cooperation in the maritime sector such as the development of ship recycling facilities, ports and inland water transport, ship building, and repair.

Additionally, Japan expanded the number of its defence attachés posted in India, from one Ground Self Defense Force (GSDF) officer to one from each service (three total) by 2015.[20] These developments have solidified the foundation for further military exchanges. As one Indian commodore noted, Japan and India are seeking to engage each other as mutual 'offshore balancers' against common strategic challenges (Sano 2017a).

Capacity building assistance is also an area in which Japan and India engaged actively for a stable Asia-Pacific region during the UPA rule. Capacity-building requirements have increased in areas such as maritime security as well as UN PKO and HADR missions. Japan's Ministry of Defense strengthened its capacity-building assistance capabilities with the establishment of the Capacity-Building Assistance Office (CBAO) in 2011. It stepped up its capacity-building efforts towards the ASEAN countries in particular and in 2016 released the 'Vientiane Vision', which highlights capacity-building cooperation as one of the three main pillars for future Japan-ASEAN defence cooperation (MOD of Japan 2016b). At the same time, the SDF have continuously held human resource development programs, training, and seminars with other Asia-Pacific countries as well (MOD of Japan 2016c).[21] Meanwhile, India has also been active in capacity-building assistance. The Indian Navy has, for example, engaged in training, technical support and maintenance, provision of platforms and equipment, and hydrographic surveys. In particular, cooperation on hydrographic surveys has been a key feature of the Indian Navy's regional engagement initiatives (MOD of India 2015, 91-4). These continuous efforts by both Tokyo and New Delhi have set the ground for deeper cooperation also in the area of capacity-building assistance.

Cooperating in National Defence of Japan and India

Compared to the level of their cooperation in the international and regional security domains, cooperation in national defence remained rather marginal, especially during the first UPA government. However,
challenges related specifically to North Korea and China have driven
Tokyo and New Delhi to seek deeper cooperation also in national defence. This move became more apparent during the latter period of the
second UPA term. Indeed, North Korea's continuous nuclear and missile
development has been a grave threat to both Tokyo and New Delhi as
well as to international peace and security. Since Kim Jong-un assumed
leadership of the country in 2012, Pyongyang has strengthened its nuclear and missile development programs. In 2013, it also threatened the
U.S. forces stationed in Japan by listing specific Japanese cities such as
Yokosuka, Misawa, and Okinawa as potential targets. Furthermore, the
abduction issue remains as an urgent issue for Tokyo. Meanwhile, North
Korea's nuclear and missile development has been a serious concern also
for successive Indian governments including the UPA administration
due to Pyongyang's close collaboration with Pakistan and China. Despite
the differences in the threat perception towards North Korea, Tokyo, and
New Delhi have continuously expressed their concerns over Pyongyang.
In their Joint Statement in January 2014, Prime Ministers Abe and Singh
denounced North Korea's uranium enrichment activities and strongly
urged Pyongyang to take concrete actions towards denuclearization as
well as to fully comply with its international obligations under all relevant
UN Security Council Resolutions and its commitments under the 2005
Six-Party Talks Joint Statement. The two leaders also addressed their concerns over the abduction issue (PM&C 2014).

China's assertiveness along the maritime boundary with Japan in the
East China Sea and along the land border with India in the Himalayas
also drove Tokyo and New Delhi to seek deeper security cooperation
through diplomatic efforts. A concern for Tokyo has been the intrusion of Chinese government vessels into the territorial waters of the
Senkaku Islands since December 2008 (MOFA of Japan 2019b). Tokyo
sees Beijing's announcement of an Air Defense Identification Zone over
the East China Sea in 2013 as a violation of Japan's sovereignty over these
Islands. India, on the other hand, continues to face tensions with China

over their shared border in Arunachal Pradesh and the Aksai Chin region. While the Singh administration succeeded in signing a Border Defense Cooperation Agreement with Beijing in October 2013, New Delhi and Beijing have criticized each other continuously for frequent border incursions and military buildups near the disputed territories. During the summit meeting in January 2014, Prime Ministers Abe and Singh did not touch upon China specifically but reaffirmed their resolve to contribute jointly to the peace, stability, and prosperity of the region and the world, remain committed to the freedom of navigation, and respect the importance of freedom of over-flight and civil aviation safety (PM&C 2014).

Finally, efforts to pursue the transfer of defence technologies also contributed to the deepening of cooperation between Japan and India during the UPA era. Indian defence equipment is old and India remains heavily dependent on Russian technology, which accounts for 70% of Indian defence imports. Consequently, the Abe and Singh administrations held their first meeting of the Joint Working Group (JWG) in December 2013 on the US-2 amphibious aircraft, which would enable India to conduct effective surveillance patrols and search and rescue operations due to its short takeoff capability and long flight range.[22] Tokyo's 2014 decision to relax its arms export controls would also enable Japan to develop arms with allies and partners, including India.

It is also important to note that, unlike China, the rise of India has not been a worrisome issue for most of the countries in the world (Mathur 2012, 36). Consequently, India's rise during the UPA rule has greatly contributed to the deepening of the Japan-India security cooperation. Today, India has become a geopolitically influential partner for Japan and the two countries have now elevated the relations to a 'Special Strategic and Global Partnership'. While its alliance with the United States remains the central pillar of Japan's security strategy, India is now the fifth most important country for Japan, only behind the United States, the Republic of Korea, Australia, and the ASEAN members (GOJ 2013a, 23–4).

In sum, the urgent need for both the Singh government and the successive Japanese administrations to respond to the imminent challenges that emerged from the drastic changes in the international and regional security environment has driven the two countries to develop their relations in the security domain. The major areas of cooperation included counter-terrorism/piracy and maritime security, of which the latter became more prominent with the increasing assertiveness of China's maritime activities from the latter period of the first UPA term. The steady but continuous engagements in international peace activities such as PKO and HADR have also helped the two countries to work more closely together.

Underlying Factors behind the Japan-India Cooperation

While the drivers described above have certainly played a critical role in the development of the Japan-India security partnership, these alone are insufficient to explain the momentum for this development during the UPA administration. Equally important were the underlying factors such as the strong incentives to establish a new rationale for the Japan-U.S. alliance immediately after the Cold War, the introduction of Tokyo's value-oriented diplomacy in the mid-2000s, the deepening of the India-U.S. relations since the turn of the 21st century, and India's complex strategic thinking on the emerging security architecture in the Asia-Pacific region.

First, the deepening of the Japan-India relationship was, in part, a result of the improvement in the India-U.S. relations (Horimoto 2015, 8–9). Initially, it was Prime Minister Rao who sought to improve India's relations with the United States, which were hindered as a result of mutual suspicion and mistrust during the Cold War. The efforts were in line with his economic liberalization agenda, which aimed to gain access to the U.S. markets, technologies, and capital. Subsequently, the India-U.S. relations improved further when President Bill Clinton became the first U.S. president to visit India in 22 years in March 2000. More importantly, the 9/11 attacks on the United States in 2001 became key drivers for the two countries to seek a deeper relationship as reflected in the 2002 U.S. National Security Strategy, which noted that 'U.S. interests require a strong relationship with India' (U.S. White House 2002, 27). In January 2004, Prime Minister Vajpayee and President Bush elevated the relationship to a 'Next Steps in Strategic Partnership' (NSSP), which aimed to strengthen cooperation in areas such as easing restrictions on dual-use technology export to India, increasing cooperation in civil nuclear and space cooperation, and expanding dialogue on missile defence. The efforts in deepening the India-U.S. relations were succeeded by Prime Minister Manmohan Singh when he came to power in May 2004. Notably, the India-U.S. joint statements issued during Prime Minister Singh's visit to the United States in July 2005 and during President Bush's visit to India in March 2006 further set the scene for a stronger strategic partnership. The India-U.S. relations reached a major milestone when the historic civil nuclear cooperation agreement was signed in October 2008. Efforts to deepen the India-U.S. relationship were also carried out by the Obama administration when Secretary of State Hillary Clinton visited India in July 2009 and called for an upgrade of the India-U.S. relationship, which she had earlier referred to as 'U.S.-India 3.0' version. During her visit, the two countries decided to begin the first round of annual strategic dialogue in Washington in the following year, which continued subsequently in alternate capitals. In defence, the India-U.S. relations were also strengthened during the UPA rule. In June 2005, India's Defence Minister Pranab Mukherjee and the United States Secretary of Defense Donald Rumsfeld signed a ten-year defence agreement, the 'New Framework for the U.S.-India Defense Relationship', which called for an expansion in cooperation in defence technology transfer, joint research, development, and production programs. Moreover, India has engaged in joint military exercises, including the Malabar, with the United States more than with any other country in the world.

Development in the India-U.S. relations during the UPA administration helped Tokyo to seek stronger cooperation with New Delhi. Admittedly, opportunities for India's engagement with Japan and the United States emerged when both President Clinton and Prime Minister Mori visited India in 2000, respectively. Yet it was the deepening of the India-U.S. relationship in coping with the various international and regional challenges that drove the three countries to work more closely together. The conclusion of the India-U.S. civil nuclear cooperation in 2008, for example, helped to improve the Japan-India relations over the nuclear issue. The deal opened the door for India's waiver at the Nuclear Suppliers Group (NSG), which in part encouraged the Hatoyama cabinet in Japan to pursue negotiations with the Singh government over the Japan-India civil nuclear cooperation.

Moreover, the developments in the Japan-India and India-U.S. relations, as well as the deepening of the Japan-U.S. alliance, have led to stronger cooperation among the three countries. Initially, Tokyo, New Delhi, and Washington all took an incremental approach on formalizing the trilateral or a quadrilateral relationship with Canberra due to sensitivities about other important relationships they had in the Asia-Pacific region (CSIS 2007). However, the three countries began to acknowledge the advantages of enhanced trilateral cooperation through their common experience, for example, in leading the 2004 tsunami relief with the creation of the Tsunami Core Group. Notably, in maritime security, the close India-U.S. military ties contributed to the strengthening of Tokyo's relations with New Delhi. The bilateral Malabar Exercise between India and the United States since 1992 and the JIMEX initiated in January 2012 led to Japan's permanent membership in the Malabar exercise by 2015. As one Indian commodore noted, cooperation between the Japanese and Indian navies has progressed primarily due to India's own closer strategic engagement with the United States, although sufficient strategic rationale exists for the Japan-India relationship to develop on its own (Sano 2017a). Furthermore, the Joint Statement of the Japan-U.S. Security Consultative Committee meeting in June 2011 referred to the common strategic objectives for Tokyo and Washington and noted that the two countries 'welcome India as a strong and enduring Asia-Pacific partner and encourage India's growing engagement with the region and participation in regional architecture ... promote trilateral dialogue among the United States, Japan, and India' (MOD of Japan 2011). The first trilateral foreign ministerial-level talk between Tokyo, New Delhi, and Washington took place later in September 2015 during which the ministers collectively expressed the importance of close cooperation in maritime security in the Indo-Pacific region (MOFA of Japan 2015b).

The second underlying factor was Tokyo's value-oriented diplomacy which developed in the mid-2000s. From the very beginning of the UPA term in 2004, there was a growing need for both Japan and India to engage themselves more deeply in the international security issues through their diplomatic efforts. In the early 2000s, Tokyo had already begun to acknowledge India's potential and great possibility, and in 2002 Prime Minister Koizumi proposed the creation of a 'community that acts together and advances together' that would include cooperation with Southwest Asia including India. By 2004, Tokyo recognized the importance of elevating the two countries into 'true global partners'

(Gentleman 2005). Koizumi's proposal later developed into Japan's new foreign policy initiative, the 'Arc of Freedom and Prosperity', which was first addressed by then-Foreign Minister Taro Aso in November 2006 (MOFA of Japan 2006b) and reiterated in March 2007 (MOFA of Japan 2007a). The foundation of this new initiative rested on value-oriented diplomacy, which placed high importance on universal values such as democracy, freedom, human rights, the rule of law, and market economy, all of which Japan and India shared together. Furthermore, these values were designed to form an arc by connecting the values with the outer rim of the Eurasian continent. The 'Arc of Freedom and Prosperity' policy presented a fresh approach that focused more on value-oriented cooperation rather than on interest-oriented ties (Hosoya 2013, 149–50). Yet, as the special advisor to the second Abe cabinet Shōtarō Yachi later noted, the policy was not an encirclement strategy that targeted a specific country (Nippon.com 2013). Furthermore, it is worth noting that the spirit of this value-oriented diplomacy was also imbedded in Japan's relationship with Central Asia, a key region also for India, when the previous Koizumi administration launched the Central Asia plus Japan Dialogue in August 2004 (MOFA of Japan 2004). Tokyo's growing acknowledgement of Central Asia was highlighted a decade later, in October 2015, when Prime Minister Abe became the first Japanese leader to visit all five Central Asian countries.

Meanwhile, realpolitik in East and Southeast Asia also contributed to the deepening in the Japan-India relationship at this time. Specifically, bilateral cooperation developed over the composition of the East Asia Summit, which was first held in December 2005. Japan supported the participation of six countries including India in the summit to join the ASEAN ten countries in the midst of the bitter Japan-China struggle and the long-standing rivalry between India and China. This was staged in conjunction with the earlier event when India supported Japan and also China to participate in the SAARC as observers.

The third underlying factor was the strong incentives for Japan and the United States to establish a new rationale in order to continue their alliance after the Cold War. Since the mid-1990s, Tokyo gradually expanded its defence posture to focus not only on national defence but also on contributing to a stable Asia-Pacific region as well as securing a peaceful international environment as a whole in response to the growing expectations from the United States and, more importantly, due to its own determination to carry out more proactively the responsibilities in the international community. This inevitably enabled Tokyo to broaden the roles and functions of the SDF.

With the expansion of Japan's defence posture as well as the emergence of imminent security challenges noted above, the roles and functions of the SDF expanded dramatically during the UPA administration. In 2004, Tokyo clarified its plan to establish the SDF that would function as a 'multifunctional, flexible, effective defense force'. This enabled the SDF to respond more effectively to new threats and diverse situations while maintaining those elements of the Basic Defense Force Concept that emphasized deterrence by the existence of a defence force (GOJ 2004, 5). Furthermore, in 2010, Tokyo authorized the SDF to become a 'Dynamic Defense Force' with capabilities that would enable the force to carry out the various activities proactively rather than to focus on the Basic Defense Force Concept (MOD of Japan 2013, 109). This meant that the SDF were now willing to engage in a variety of military operations both domestically and internationally during peacetime as well as in contingency situations. These new roles and functions of the SDF were also emphasized in the 2013 NDPG (GOJ 2013b), which draws on fundamental concepts reflected in the first NSS issued in December 2013 (GOJ 2013a).

Furthermore, during this period, drastic changes took place in the defence organization in Japan. Along with the changes in the roles and functions of the SDF, the Defense Agency was upgraded to the Ministry of Defense in 2007. In the same year, the Joint Staff Office was established to strengthen the joint operations of the SDF. The Central Readiness Force, which has now become the Ground Component Command, was also established in 2007 to expedite the readiness of the GSDF in both international and domestic missions. International peace cooperation and other activities were upgraded to primary missions of the SDF. Furthermore, the National Security Council was established in 2013 to provide a forum that would undertake strategic discussions on various national security issues on a regular basis and, as necessary, under the strong political leadership of the prime minister (MOFA of Japan 2016). The changes in the defence posture, the expansion of roles and functions of the SDF, and the organizational changes in the Ministry of Defense and the SDF opened the window of opportunity for Tokyo to seek deeper cooperation with other counties including India in the security domain.

The fourth underlying factor was India's complex strategic thinking on the emerging security architecture in the Asia-Pacific region. Similar to Japan, the issue of the establishment of a regional order also became one of the major foreign policy issues for the Singh administration by the mid-2000s, but with different policy priorities. In the case of Japan, as noted above, the primary reason for Tokyo to establish a strong relationship with New Delhi was its strong determination to construct a peaceful and stable Asia-Pacific region as well as the international community as a whole together with other democracies including India. Meanwhile, the importance of Japan-India relations to India remained to rest primarily on the need to enhance cooperation in economic development. A related issue was the importance for New Delhi to maintain closer economic relations with Beijing. The significance of economic development for the UPA government is reflected in the so-called Manmohan Doctrine of 2013 when Prime Minister Singh stated, ' [T]he single most important objective of Indian foreign policy has to be to create a global environment conducive to the well-being of our great country ... greater integration with the world economy will benefit India and enable our people to realize their creative potential' (MOE of India 2013a).

Furthermore, as elaborated by one scholar, there has been a divergence of opinions in India's strategic thinking at the time regarding the regional security architecture or the regional rules-based order (Khan 2015). Arguably, the ten years under the UPA rule have been a period of drastic geopolitical change in the Asia-Pacific region. In the midst of the various security challenges surrounding India, some saw the regional security mechanism purely from a realist perspective and viewed the Japan-India relationship as a byproduct of an assertive China, asserting the need to hedge China. In supporting the relevance of a deeper Japan-India partnership through the balance of power calculations, K. Shankar Bajpai, a former ambassador, states that 'Japan has emerged as one country that looks actively to its realization ... We [Japan and India] can both honestly say that we are not building relations in hostility against China, but it is right and proper for us to examine what to do if China acts in hostility against us' (Bajpai 2014).

Others believed in the value of establishing an inclusive regional security architecture in the Asia-Pacific region and prioritized both Japan
and China equally for India. In this context, there were those who
stressed the importance of including Washington in the paradigm, such
as Rajesh Rajagopalan, who warned the danger of overemphasizing the
benefits of the economic side of diplomacy with China (Rajagopalan
2014). On the other hand, there were those who viewed the United States
as an outsider in the emerging security architecture in the Asia-Pacific.
Siddharth Varadarajan, for example, states that 'Without these four countries [India, Japan, South Korea, and China]—and Russia—establishing
a relationship of comfort among and between themselves, it will not be
possible to develop the security architecture Asia needs to deal with future challenges' (Varadarajan 2006).

Still others have suggested the importance of maintaining New Delhi's
strategic autonomy through its traditional non-alignment. The policy
paper 'Non-Alignment 2.0' stresses the significance of maintaining a balanced approach and emphasizes the need to 'give India maximum options in its relations with the outside world—that is, to enhance India's
strategic space and capacity for the independent agency—which in turn
will give it maximum options for its own internal development' (Khilnani
et al. 2012, 8).

While the centre of attention for Prime Minister Singh soon shifted to
the need of deepening Japan-India cooperation not only in the economic
development realm but also in the 'quest for stability and peace in the vast
region in Asia ...' (MEA of India 2013b), the complexity of the views, as
well as Singh's heavy emphasis on economic development in Indian foreign policy, may have affected, in part, the pace and scope of pursuing a
closer Japan-India relationship during the UPA rule.

Lingering Obstacles

Despite the development of the Japan-India security partnership mentioned above, some obstacles have lingered, which may have slowed
the pace of cooperation between Japan and India. The first issue was
the sensitivities required for both Tokyo and New Delhi to cope with
Beijing. While concerns have increased over China's assertiveness in

the Asia-Pacific region, Beijing remains a vital partner for the two countries. For Tokyo, its relationship with Beijing deteriorated primarily due to Prime Minister Koizumi's visit to the Yasukuni shrine, resulting in large-scale anti-Japanese demonstrations in China. There was also a dramatic shift in Japan's economic engagement with China when Tokyo announced in 2005 that Beijing would not receive yen loans from 2008.[23] However, successive Japanese administrations have endeavoured to improve their relations with Beijing. When Prime Minister Abe met President Hu Jintao and Premier of State Council Wen Jiabao in Beijing in October 2006, for example, Tokyo and Beijing pledged that the two sides would strive to build a 'mutually beneficial relationship based on common strategic interests' (MOFA of Japan 2006c). This was reaffirmed in April 2007 (MOFA of Japan 2007b) and also by the subsequent Fukuda cabinet in May 2008 (MOFA of Japan 2008b). Yet, both sides face difficulties, notably over the Senkaku Islands today. Meanwhile India acknowledges that its economic development depends on its cooperation not only with the United States and Japan but also China. In April 2005, the Singh administration established the 'India-China Strategic and Cooperative Partnership for Peace and Prosperity' with Beijing based on their 2003 'Declaration on Principles for Relations and Comprehensive Cooperation'. India-China bilateral trade reached an all-time high of U.S.$73.9 billion in 2011, an impressive increase from just U.S.$3 billion in 2000. Since 2008, China has become India's largest trading partner in goods, replacing the United States (Embassy of India in Beijing 2018). Furthermore, the two countries have cooperated on global issues such as climate change, sustainable development, and trade liberalization despite major border disputes over Arunachal Pradesh and Aksai Chin.

In light of the growing challenges posed by China, the most important issue for both India and Japan has been the need to hedge China while at the same time maintaining their economic engagement with Beijing. However, the sensitivities towards China have prevented Japan and India from establishing, for example, a strong multilateral partnership, as it became evident when India refused to join in the Tokyo-initiated Quad in 2007. Furthermore, there seem to be differences in the level of the so-called 'threat' perceptions of Japan and India towards China. It remains doubtful whether Tokyo and New Delhi truly share any specific threat perceptions against Beijing due to their different geographic and policy priorities (Ito 2013, 122–5). Both Japan and India have had to confront the assertiveness of China along their respective borders. For Tokyo, the situations in the East China Sea—notably over the Senkaku Islands—and the China-North Korea relations remain as vital national interests, but these issues are of secondary importance to New Delhi, although the latter has expressed serious concerns over ongoing North Korea's nuclear and missile development. Likewise, situations in the Indian Ocean and the China-Pakistan relations are of vital national interest to New Delhi but remain secondary to Tokyo, although the successive Japanese administrations have increasingly voiced concerns over these issues.

Regarding the South China Sea, Japan has taken a deeper interest than India (MOD of India 2015).[24] Notably, this became apparent in the Hague's Permanent Court of Arbitration ruling on the South China Sea in July 2016. Tokyo supports Washington's efforts to protect rules and norms including freedom of navigation and over-flight and has called on China to respect the July 12 ruling by the arbitral tribunal. On the other hand, New Delhi has taken a more careful stance over issues related to the South China Sea. Indeed India's navy, air force, and army have engaged in military exercises and training with both coastal and non-coastal nations, demonstrating its increased power projection capabilities beyond the Indian Ocean region including the South China Sea. Yet New Delhi did not directly join Tokyo and Washington in calling on Beijing to respect the tribunal's judgment. In regards to the Indian Ocean, the Singh administration was concerned over China's String of Pearls strategy from the mid-2000s, with a strong belief that the strategy would endanger the national security of India by containing the subcontinent through constructions of huge ports in places such as Gwadar in Pakistan, Hambantota in Sri Lanka, Chittagong in Bangladesh as well as Kyaukpyu in Myanmar (Thorne and Spevack, 2017). Moreover, India has become increasingly concerned over China's mega infrastructure development project, the BRI, but it initially had a positive view towards the initiative when it was first announced in 2013. Japan, on the other hand, initially shared its scepticism with the United States towards the initiative, but has reversed its original position in June 2017 and announced that it would now provide cooperation and financial backing for the project under certain conditions with the expectation that the move would 'improve connectivity between Asia and Africa … and promote stability and prosperity of the region as a whole' in line with its 'Free and Open Indo-Pacific Strategy' (MOFA of Japan 2017).

Furthermore, it must also be kept in mind that the depths of Japan-China and Japan-India relations have not been viewed by the Japanese government at the same level in terms of people-to-people exchange: the former being viewed much deeper than the latter. In his 2006 speech, then-Foreign Minister Taro Aso pointed out these differences with the expectation to improve the Japan-India relationship in this area (MOFA of Japan 2006a).[25]

The second issue is the different political foundations of the two countries. Japan's reliance on the Japan-U.S. alliance and India's emphasis on its strategic autonomy may have affected the level and pace of cooperation between Tokyo and New Delhi. In India, there has been a strong support base for non-alignment. As noted in the influential document, *Nonalignment 2.0*, strategic autonomy has been 'the defining value and continuous goal of India's international policy … that value we believe continues to remain at the core of India's global engagements' (Khilnani et. al. 2012). The document further notes that the 'historical record of the United States bears out that powers that form formal alliances with it have tended to see an erosion of their strategic autonomy'. While there has been development in both Japan-India and India-U.S. relationships during the UPA term, New Delhi has been cautious in developing a strategic relationship in particular with the United States.

Finally, the Japanese domestic politics had, to some extent, affected Japan's foreign relations including India. The Japanese administrations changed nine times, of which seven lasted for approximately one year only during the ten years of the UPA administration in India. Above all, the biggest issue emerged when the DPJ, under the leadership of Prime Minister Hatoyama, came to power in September 2009. The Hatoyama administration prioritized an East Asian Community based on the Japan-China relationship, failing to acknowledge the importance of cooperation with like-minded countries as envisioned in the 'Arc of Freedom and Prosperity' scheme (Hosoya 2013, 151–2). It also gave the impression that it wanted to shift the axis of Japan's foreign policy from the Japan-U.S. alliance to its partnership with Asia, notably China. Subsequently, with Prime Minister Abe's return to power in December 2012, Tokyo made it clear, as special advisor Yachi noted, that its Asian diplomatic initiative is premised on the centrality on the Japan-U.S. alliance (Nippon.com 2013).

Unsolved/Underdeveloped Issues during the UPA Government

It is no exaggeration to state that the foundation for a deeper Japan-India security relationship was laid during the ten years of UPA administration in India. But the following issues remained either unsolved or underdeveloped in their relations. The first issue is, from a Japanese perspective, related to nuclear. Indeed, Japan and India have been able to shed the bitterness in their relationship, which lingered in their relations after India's nuclear tests in 1998. As noted earlier, the conclusion of the India-U.S. civil nuclear cooperation agreement in 2008 has indirectly helped to improve the Japan-India relations over the nuclear issue. Eventually, the subsequent Abe and Modi administrations were able to strike a deal in July 2017 with the underlying conditions set during the UPA term. Yet, Japan has always felt uncomfortable with India's status as a non-signatory to the NPT, the CTBT, and the Fissile Material Cutoff Treaty (FMCT). In the early 2000s, prior to the official declaration of the 'Strategic and Global Partnership' in 2006, Japanese diplomats formally requested that India participate in negotiations for these treaties (Panda 2013). Furthermore, Japan has encouraged India to become full member of the Proliferation Security Initiative (PSI), which aims to stop the trafficking of weapons of mass destruction. These have not been accomplished. Tokyo believes that New Delhi's admission would enable India to commit itself further to the international non-proliferation framework.

The second issue is related to economic development. There has been a growing need from the UPA term to link security issues more closely with economic development issues which increasingly gained greater strategic significance with the various cross-border infrastructure developments in the Asia-Pacific region. Notably, the development of India's Andaman and Nicobar Islands (ANI) has become a vital area of cooperation for Tokyo and New Delhi in light of China's increasing engagements in the Indian Ocean through its BRI. New Delhi had acknowledged the strategic importance of ANI since the turn of the 21st century when it established the Andaman and Nicobar Command (ANC), the first joint theatre command with headquarters at Port Blair. There have been increasing concerns within the Indian military over the islands as noted by Navy chief Admiral Dhowan in December 2015 when he acknowledged that ANI have become a 'very, very important aspect' of India's security (*Economic Times* 2015). Yet the Singh government seemed to have paid little attention to the development of the islands. It was not until February 2016 that Tokyo and New Delhi started to discuss about a plan to upgrade India's civilian infrastructure on the island chain (Barry 2016). The grant aid is modest in size,[26] but the development of the islands has strategic significance given their location in the Bay of Bengal, located northwest of the maritime chokepoint at the Strait of Malacca. Meanwhile, the Indian military has become increasingly engaged in ANI after the UPA administration. In January 2016, two Indian P-8I aircraft were deployed to the archipelago to engage in their first-ever two-week anti-submarine operations. Searcher-II UAVs have also been temporarily deployed to the islands (Pandit 2016). In November 2017, the Indian military conducted a major exercise in the islands. In March 2018, the multilateral naval exercise, MILAN 2018, was conducted in the Andaman Sea. With Japanese economic assistance as well as the conclusion of the US-2 deal, the archipelago could become a significant platform for aerial maritime surveillance.[27] For Tokyo, on the other hand, there has been a growing need to converge more extensively the MSDF's peacetime commitment strategy with Japan's economic development assistance such as the Asia Africa Growth Corridor, which also involves the Bay states including India (Chotani and Sano 2018).

The third issue regards the need to maximize the effectiveness and efficiency of the Japan-India partnership (Sano 2017b, 20–1). Tokyo and New Delhi have engaged deeply in areas such as capacity-building assistance in maritime security and HADR. Yet, the two countries need to exert more effort in clarifying the division of roles in these areas. Japan can, for example, focus on consolidating information-sharing mechanisms in the Asia-Pacific region as well as offering defence equipment to the regional navies and coast guards. Japan has a proven record in this regard. Specifically, Tokyo agreed in May 2016 to lease the Philippines up to five MSDF's TC-90 aircraft (*Japan Times* 2016) and, in a related move, started to offer training to six Philippine naval pilots to fly the TC-90 aircraft in November 2016 before the leasing deal took effect.[28] One such aircraft has already been deployed to Scarborough Shoal in the South China Sea (*Naval Today* 2018). Meanwhile, India can focus on providing skills related to hydrographic surveys, in which India excels. PKO is another area where clarification of roles has become imminent for both Tokyo and New Delhi, especially with President Trump's determination to cut U.S. contribution to the United Nations activities.

Moreover, the strengthening of military interoperability between the SDF and the Indian forces is also an area in which the two countries could develop more. During the UPA administration, cooperation progressed primarily between the Japanese and Indian navies and coast guards. However, with the growing opportunities for bilateral and multilateral military engagements, cooperation between the ground forces and between the air forces has become a critical issue for both countries as it would enhance the capabilities of Japanese and Indian forces to engage in tri-service joint operations more effectively. Deeper cooperation is also needed regarding the transfer of defence equipment, notably US-2 amphibious aircraft. Both the Singh and Modi administrations seemed to have difficulties negotiating with their Japanese counterparts on this issue (Gady 2016). In April 2018, it was reported that India's Mahindra Group signed a memorandum of understanding with Japan's Shin Maywa Industries to manufacture and assemble US-2s in India (Ayyappan 2018). Cooperation in this area would stimulate the defence industry in both countries, provide better balance in India's arms imports, improve interoperability between Japanese and Indian forces, and could serve as a precedent for transfers of other defence equipment such as submarines and minesweepers (Parameswaran 2015). Japan is well-known for its advanced technologies and extensive know-how in these areas. It is still, however, unclear how the US-2 issue would develop, but both Tokyo and New Delhi would need to find a way to expedite the procedure if they want to deepen the level of their cooperation in this area. Furthermore, the two countries were unable to conclude an agreement on the Acquisition and Cross-Serving Agreement (ACSA) during the UPA rule. The agreement was signed later in September 2020, enabling the SDF and Indian forces to significantly increase not only their interoperability but also enhance operational readiness as well as reduce logistical burdens in mutual support for food, fuel, and transportation..

Fourth, Japan and India need to widen support for bilateral cooperation across the policy spectrum. There are various security and defence frameworks in place between the two countries. These include regular summit meetings, Defense Policy Dialogues, Military-to-Military Talks, and Coast Guard-to-Coast Guard cooperation, as well as vice-minister/secretary-level '2 plus 2' Dialogues. However, Tokyo and New Delhi were unable to hold the '2 plus 2' dialogue at the minister level during the UPA administration; importantly, the minister level '2 plus 2' was initiated later for the first time in November 2019. Furthermore, people-to-people interactions need to be strengthened among the general public including the exchange of students in order to broaden the support and understanding of the importance of the Japan-India security relationship. Meanwhile, a better understanding of Japan's new security legislation by both the Japanese and Indian general public would also be important if bilateral security cooperation is to be strengthened. The new security legislation sets the grounds for Tokyo to exercise the right of collective self-defence and allows the SDF to assist foreign militaries under certain conditions. The legislation also enables the SDF personnel to use weapons for protecting UN officials, NGOs, and other PKO troops (called *kaketsuke-keigo*) as well as the UN bases in fulfilling their UN PKO missions. The legislation also enables the SDF to operate more closely with other foreign troops including India. It would be highly beneficial, therefore, for both Japan and India to continue their participations in exercises such as the multinational peacekeeping exercise, Khaan Quest, held annually in Mongolia.

In addition to these unsolved or underdeveloped issues, subsequent governments in both Japan and India need, in a longer-term perspective, to engage more actively in maintaining the present international order based on liberal democratic values. Continuously reaffirming the importance of liberal democratic values in joint statements and declarations would be important, but these measures alone would not be enough. A firm value-oriented diplomacy backed up by concrete substantial measures would be imperative. It needs to be much stronger than the one proposed in 2006.

Conclusion

Prime Minister Manmohan Singh described the Japan-India relationship as being 'at the heart of our Look East policy'. Economic factors have certainly contributed to the deepening of relations between Tokyo and New Delhi during the UPA administration, the most prominent events being the signing of the Japan-India Comprehensive Economic Partnership Agreement (CEPA) and its implementation in August 2011. Equally important were the various developments in the security domain, which had been underdeveloped for the past half-century including the first ten years after the Cold War. These developments took place over the issues related to the emerging challenges in the international and regional security environment and, to a lesser degree, in the national defence of both countries. The steady but continuous engagements by and cooperation between Tokyo and New Delhi in international peace activities such as PKO and HADR also contributed to forming the basis for a stronger strategic relationship. The various underlying factors were also critical for the development of the bilateral relations. The importance of the Japan-India partnership was highlighted by the historic visit by their Imperial Majesties, the Emperor and Empress, and the numerous visits by high-ranking Japanese defence and foreign affairs officials to India during the last two years of the UPA administration. Given the responsibilities of both Tokyo and New Delhi in the international community, further efforts should be made by both sides to overcome the unsolved as well as the underdeveloped issues, and cement the relations into a substantial and long-lasting partnership so that it can function, together with the Japan-U.S. alliance, as public goods for the sake of establishing a peaceful and stable international and regional environment and better serve to ensure the national defence of both countries.

Notes

1. Historically, the commonalities in traditional culture such as Buddhism as well as the various historical events since the mid-19th century have enhanced the rise of mutual respect and affinity among the Japanese and Indian people. These include Japan's rapid developments after the Meiji Restoration and the Second World War

and Japan's indirect contributions to India's independence (i.e., the 1905 victory in the Russo-Japanese War and support for the establishment of the Indian National Army). Indians' high respect for the qualities of the Japanese people, products, and services also played a significant role in developing the relationship.

2. The law was extended twice in 2003 and 2005.

3. Specifically, this includes enhancing Afghanistan's ability to maintain its own security by supporting salaries, training, and literacy education for the National Police; helping reintegrate ex-combatants by providing assistance for vocational training and job creation in local communities; and assisting sustainable and self-reliant development in sectors like agriculture, infrastructure, human resources, education, and healthcare.

4. The SDF have been deployed to Mozambique (1993–95), Rwanda (1994), the Golan Heights (1996–2013), Timor-Leste (2002–04, 2010–12), Afghanistan (2001), Nepal (2007–11), Sudan (2008–11), Haiti (2010–13), and South Sudan (2011–17).

5. These include Egypt (2008–12), Mali (2009–10), Ghana (2011), Kenya (2012–14), South Africa (2013–15), Ethiopia (2014–17), and South Sudan (2014). In March 2014, an SDF officer was sent to the Ethiopian International Peacekeeping Training Center (EIPKTC) as an international consultant for the first time.

6. Since March 2015, Japan also sent two SDF officers to India's Center for UN Peacekeeping (CUNPK) to strengthen ties with New Delhi in PKO activities.

7. Japan's HADR history goes back to 1979, when a medical team manned by volunteer practitioners was sent to support the Cambodian refugees along the Thai border. From 1987 to December 2017, Japan sent relief goods supplies to many parts of the world 523 times, medical teams 57 times, expert teams 48 times, search and rescue teams 20 times, and an infectious diseases response team once. In October 2015, JICA established the Japan Disaster Relief Infectious Disease Response Team to help minimize large-scale outbreaks of infectious diseases overseas based on its Ebola response experience.

8. In 1998, the SDF were dispatched in a HADR mission for the first time to Honduras in the wake of Hurricane Mitch. Following its involvement in Honduras, the SDF have been deployed to places including Turkey (1999), India (2001), Iran (2003–4), Thailand (2004–5), Sumatra (2005), Russia (2005), Pakistan (2005, 2010), Java (2006), West Sumatra (2009), Haiti (2010), New Zealand (2011, 2016), the Philippines (2013), Malaysia (2014), and Nepal (2015). The SDF also sent a liaison officer to U.S. Africa Command (AFRICOM) after the 2014 Ebola outbreak.

9. In 2013, India deployed its C-130 aircraft to the Philippines to deliver relief supplies.

10. The Landing Platform Dock has six helicopters and landing craft that enable New Delhi to deploy relief supplies and manpower faster on debris-littered shores.

11. In August 2015, Russia resubmitted its petition to the United Nations, claiming approximately 1.2 million square kilometers of Arctic sea shelf. This claim goes beyond the rules set in UNCLOS, which allows states to extend their exclusive

economic zones (EEZs) under the condition that they can prove that their continental shelf extends beyond the 200-nm limit.

12. For example, defending Russian interests in the Arctic was newly added as one of the military's tasks in peacetime. In December 2014, the Northern Joint Strategic Command in charge of the Arctic became operational.

13. China's *Xue Long* (Snow Dragon) became the first polar research vessel to complete the Northern Sea Route in 2012. Later in August 2015, five Chinese naval vessels were spotted for the first time sailing in the Bering Sea between the Arctic Ocean and the Pacific.

14. In 2015, Tokyo released its new Arctic policy, which now addresses the Arctic more broadly including global environmental changes, indigenous peoples of the Arctic, science and technology, rule of law and the promotion of international cooperation, Arctic sea routes, natural resource development (mineral and marine living resources), and national security. Likewise, India acknowledges that ice melt in the Arctic has scientific, economic, and geopolitical dimensions, as observed by Science and Technology Minister Harsh Vardhan in 2015. India's engagement in the Arctic began in 1920 when the country signed the Svalbard Treaty.

15. Approximately 83% of China's oil imports transited these areas in 2015.

16. For example, in March 2009 and December 2013, Chinese vessels harassed U.S. ships conducting surveillance in the region. In August 2014, a Chinese fighter allegedly came as close as 30 feet to a U.S. P-8 patrol aircraft. Tensions later escalated in October 2015 when a U.S. Navy destroyer, the USS *Lassen*, sailed within 12 nautical miles (nm) of the Chinese-occupied Subi Reef.

17. China's increasing military presence in the Indian Ocean reflects China's 2015 military strategy, which shifts its naval forces towards 'offshore waters defense and open seas protection'. A *Shang*-class nuclear submarine and a *Song*-class submarine conducted operations there in winter 2013–14 and fall 2014, respectively. A *Song*-class submarine also made a port call in Colombo, Sri Lanka, marking the first time a Chinese submarine entered a port overseas. This was followed by a *Yuan*-class submarine that reportedly was called at a port in Karachi, Pakistan in May 2015.

18. Recently, it has been reported that China plans to build a military base in Jiwani, which is also located in western Pakistan.

19. Later in January 2017, Admiral Harry Harris, commander of U.S. Pacific Command, warned India about China's growing influence in the Indian Ocean region and added that he was also concerned about China's relationship with Pakistan and Bangladesh.

20. Officers from the Maritime Self Defense Force and the Air Self Defense Force were assigned to defence attaché positions to India in 2014 and 2015, respectively.

21. These include Cambodia, Indonesia, Laos, Malaysia, Mongolia, Myanmar, Papua New Guinea, the Philippines, Thailand, Timor-Leste, and Vietnam.

22. The aircraft can cruise at extremely low speeds (approximately 55 miles per hour), take off and land on water within a very short distance, and fly a range of over 2,800 miles.
23. Japan's ODA to China continued at a decreasing rate after 2008. In October 2018, it was reported that Tokyo had decided to terminate its ODA to China.
24. Indian Maritime Security Strategy makes no detailed reference to the South China Sea.
25. In the mid-2000s, Japan and China enjoyed a flow of some 4.17 million people annually, whereas Japan and India had only 150,000 people. Meanwhile, approximately 80,000 Chinese students studied in Japan every year at that time, while the number of Indian students in Japan was only about 400. Furthermore, the number of direct flights between Japan and China totalled 676 a week, whereas the number of weekly direct flights between Japan and India was limited to only 11.
26. The project aims to build three 5-megawatt diesel power plants on South Andaman Island.
27. The Indian Navy has tentative plans to station a number of US-2s on the archipelago.
28. TC-90 aircraft has twice the flight range of current Philippine Navy aircraft.

References

Asia Maritime Transparency Initiative. 2016. 'China's New Spratly Island Defenses. Asia Maritime Transparency Initiative'. Center for Strategic and International Studies, 13 December. Accessed 14 December 2019. https://amti.csis.org/chinas-new-spratly-island-defenses/

Ayyappan, V. 2018. 'DefExpo 2018: Amphibious Aircraft US-2 to Be Made in India'. *Times of India*, 11 April. Accessed 14 December 2019. https://timesofindia.indiatimes.com/business/india-business/defexpo-2018-amphibious-aircraft-us-2-to-be-made-in-india/articleshow/63713866.cms

Bajpai, K. Shankar. 2014. 'Japan, India and the Balance of Power'. *The Hindu*, 27 January. Accessed 14 December 2019. https://www.thehindu.com/opinion/op-ed/japan-india-and-the-balance-of-power/article5620518.ece

Barry, Ellen. 2016. 'As India Collaborates with Japan on Islands, It Looks to Check China'. *New York Times*, 11 March. Accessed 14 December 2019. https://www.nytimes.com/2016/03/12/world/asia/india-japan-china-andaman-nicobar-islands.html

BBC. 2015. 'China Says U.S. Warship's Spratly Islands Passage "Illegal"'. *BBC News*, 27 October. Accessed 14 December 2019. https://www.bbc.com/news/world-asia-china-34647651

Center for Strategic and International Studies (CSIS). 2007. 'The United States, Japan, and India: Toward New Trilateral Cooperation'. U.S.-Japan-India Report, 16

August. Accessed 14 December 2019. https://csis-prod.s3.amazonaws.com/s3fs-public/legacy_files/files/media/csis/pubs/070816_us_j_ireport.pdf

Chotani, Vindu Mai, and Shutaro Sano. 2018. 'Japan's Naval Diplomacy in the Bay of Bengal: In Pursuit of a Sound Peacetime Commitment Strategy in Establishing a Stable Maritime Order'. Institute of National Security Studies of Sri Lanka. Accessed 14 December 2019. http://www.insssl.lk/preview.php?id=188

Economic Times. 2015. 'India Enhancing Security in Andaman & Nicobar: Navy Chief Admiral R. K. Dhowan', *Economic Times*, 3 December. Accessed 14 December 2019. https://economictimes.indiatimes.com/news/defense/india-enhancing-security-in-andaman-nicobar-navy-chief-admiral-r-k-dhowan/articleshow/50033752.cms

Economic Times. 2017. 'China's Forays in Indian Ocean Matter of Concern: U.S. Commander'. *Economic Times*, January 18. Accessed 14 December 2019. https://economictimes.indiatimes.com/news/defense/chinas-forays-in-indian-ocean-matter-of-concern-us-commander/articleshow/56651215.cms

Embassy of India in Beijing. 2018. 'Economic and Trade Relations'. Accessed 14 December 2019. http://indianembassybeijing.in/economic-and-trade-relation.php

Gady, Franz-Stefan. 2016. 'India-Japan Military Aircraft Deal Faces Further Delays'. *The Diplomat*, 15 November. Accessed 14 December 2019. https://thediplomat.com/2016/11/india-japan-military-aircraft-deal-faces-further-delays/

Gentleman, Amelia. 2005. 'Koizumi in India to Strengthen Ties'. *New York Times*, 30 April. Accessed 14 December 2019. https://www.nytimes.com/2005/04/30/world/asia/koizumi-in-india-to-strengthen-ties.html

Gertz, Bill. 2018. 'China Building Military Base in Pakistan'. *Washington Post*, 3 January. Accessed 14 December 2019. https://www.washingtontimes.com/news/2018/jan/3/china-plans-pakistan-military-base-at-jiwani/

Government of Japan (GOJ). 2004. 'National Defense Program Guidelines, FY 2005'. 10 December. Accessed 14 December 2019. http://www.mod.go.jp/e/d_act/d_policy/pdf/national_guidelines.pdf

Government of Japan (GOJ). 2010. 'National Defense Program Guidelines for FY 2011 and beyond'. 17 December. Accessed 14 December 2019. http://www.mod.go.jp/e/d_act/d_policy/pdf/guidelinesFY2011.pdf

Government of Japan (GOJ). 2013a. 'National Security Strategy'. 17 December. Accessed 14 December 2019. https://www.cas.go.jp/jp/siryou/131217anzenhoshou/nss-e.pdf

Government of Japan (GOJ). 2013b. 'National Defense Program Guidelines for FY 2014 and beyond'. 17 December. Accessed 14 December 2019. http://www.mod.go.jp/j/approach/agenda/guideline/2014/pdf/20131217_e2.pdf

Headquarters for Ocean Policy. 2015. 'Japan's Arctic Policy'. 16 October. Accessed 14 December 2019. https://www8.cao.go.jp/ocean/english/arctic/pdf/japans_ap_e.pdf

Horimoto, Takenori. 2015. 'Japan-India Rapprochement and Its Future Issues'. In *Towards the World's Third Great Power: India's Pursuit of Strategic Autonomy*. Iwanami Shoten, Publishers. Accessed 14 December 2019. https://www2.jiia.or.jp/en/pdf/digital_library/japan_s_diplomacy/160411_Takenori_Horimoto.pdf

Hosoya, Yuichi. 2013. 'Japan's Two Strategies for East Asia: The Evolution of Japan's Diplomatic Strategy'. Asia-Pacific Review Vol. 20, Issue 2. Accessed 26 October 2018. DOI: 10.1080/13439006.2013.863825.

INSS. 2000. Institute for National Strategic Studies.. 'The United States and Japan: Advancing towards a Mature Partnership'. INSS Special Report, 11 October. Accessed 14 December 2019. https://spfusa.org/wp-content/uploads/2015/11/ArmitageNyeReport_2000.pdf

Ito, Toru. 2013. '"China Threat" Theory in Indo-Japan Relations'. In India-Japan Relations in Emerging Asia, edited by Takenori Horimoto and Lalima Varma, 113–31. New Delhi: Manohar.

Izuyama, Marie. 2013. 'India, Japan and Maritime Security Cooperation'. In India-Japan Relations in Emerging Asia, edited by Takenori Horimoto and Lalima Varma, 175–200. New Delhi: Manohar.

Japan International Cooperation Agency (JICA). 2015. 'Launch of the Japan Disaster Relief Infectious Disease Response Team'. October 20. Accessed 14 December 2019. https://www.jica.go.jp/english/news/field/2015/151020_01.html

Japan Times. 2016. 'Japan to Train Philippines Naval Pilots to Fly TC-90 Aircraft under Lease Deal'. 22 November. Accessed 14 December 2019. https://www.japantimes.co.jp/news/2016/11/22/national/japan-train-philippine-naval-pilots-fly-tc-90-aircraft-lease-deal/

Khan, Shamshad A. 2015. 'India-Japan Cooperation towards a Rule-Based Order in the Asia-Pacific: Mapping Indian and Japanese Strategic Thinking'. Japan Institute of International Affairs. Accessed 14 December 2019. https://www2.jiia.or.jp/pdf/fellow_report/151218_Shamshad_Khan_JIIA_paper_Final.pdf

Khilnani, Sunil et al. 2012. 'Nonalignment: A Foreign and Strategic Policy for India in the Twenty First Century'. 30 January. Accessed 14 December 2019. http://www.ris.org.in/images/RIS_images/pdf/NonAlignment.pdf

Khurana, G. S. 2004. 'Maritime Security in the Indian Ocean: Convergence Plus Cooperation Equals Resonance'. Strategic Analysis Vol. 28, Issue 3, July–September. Accessed 14 December 2019. https://idsa.in/system/files/strategicanalysis_khurana_0904.pdf

Kramer, Andrew E. 2015. 'Russia's Stakes New Claim to Expanse in the Arctic'. New York Times, 4 August. Accessed 14 December 2019. https://www.nytimes.com/2015/08/05/world/europe/kremlin-stakes-claim-to-arctic-expanse-and-its-resources.html

Ladwig III, Walter, Andrew Erickson, and Justin Mikolay. 2014. 'Diego Garcia and American Security in the Indian Ocean'. In Rebalancing U.S. Forces: Basing and Forward Presence in the Asia Pacific, edited by Andrew Erickson and Carnes Lord, 131–80. Annapolis: Naval Institute Press.

Lakshmi, Rama. 2011. 'India and Afghanistan Sign Security and Trade Pact'. Washington Post, 4 October. Accessed 14 December 2019. https://www.washingtonpost.com/world/asia-pacific/india-and-afghanistan-sign-security-and-trade-pact/2011/10/04/gIQAHLOOLL_story.html?noredirect=on&utm_term=.a7419447cf2a

Mathur, Arpita. 2012. 'India-Japan Relations: Drivers, Trends and Prospects'. RSIS Monograph No. 23. Accessed 14 December 2019. http://www.rsis.edu.sg/wp-content/uploads/2014/07/Monograph2313.pdf

Ministry of Defense of India (MOD of India). 2015. 'Ensuring Secure Seas: Indian Maritime Security Strategy'. 10 October. Accessed 14 December 2019. https://www.indiannavy.nic.in/sites/default/files/Indian_Maritime_Security_Strategy_Document_25Jan16.pdf

Ministry of Defense of Japan (MOD of Japan). 2011. 'Joint Statement of the Security Consultative Committee toward a Deeper and Broader U.S.-Japan Alliance: Building on 50 Years of Partnership'. 21 June. Accessed 14 December 2019.   https://www.mofa.go.jp/region/n-america/us/security/pdfs/joint1106_01.pdf

Ministry of Defense of Japan (MOD of Japan). 2013. 'Defense of Japan'. Accessed 14 December 2019. https://www.mod.go.jp/e/publ/w_paper/2013.html

Ministry of Defense of Japan (MOD of Japan). 2016a. 'Defense of Japan'. Accessed 14 December 2019. http://www.mod.go.jp/e/publ/w_paper/2016.html

Ministry of Defense of Japan (MOD of Japan). 2016b. 'Vientiane Vision: Japan's Defense Cooperation Initiative with ASEAN'. 16 November. Accessed 14 December 2019. http://www.mod.go.jp/e/press/conference/2016/11/161116_1.pdf

Ministry of Defense of Japan (MOD of Japan). 2016c. 'Japan's Defense Capacity Building Assistance'. February. Accessed 14 December 2019. https://www.mofa.go.jp/files/000146830.pdf

Ministry of Defense of Japan (MOD of Japan). 2017. 'Defense of Japan'. Tokyo. Accessed 14 December 2019. https://www.mod.go.jp/e/publ/w_paper/2017.html

Ministry of External Affairs of India (MEA of India). 2013a. 'A Free and Prosperous India: Five Principles of Foreign Policy'. Media Center, 5 November. Accessed 14 December 2019. https://mea.gov.in/articles-in-indian-media.htm?dtl/22430/A+Free+and+Prosperous+India+Five+Principles+of+Foreign+Policy

Ministry of External Affairs of India (MEA of India). 2013b. 'Prime Minister's Address to Japan-India Association, Japan-India Parliamentary Friendship League and International Friendship Exchange Council'. Media Center, 28 May. Assessed 14 December 2019. https://www.mea.gov.in/Speeches-Statements.htm?dtl/21754/Prime+Ministers

Ministry of External Affairs of India (MEA of India). 2015. 'IISS Fullerton Lecture by Dr. S. Jaishankar, Foreign Secretary in Singapore'. Press release, 20 July. Accessed 14 December 2019. https://www.mea.gov.in/Speeches-Statements.htm?dtl/25493/iiss+fullerton+lecture+by+dr+s+jaishankar+foreign+secretary+in+singapore

Ministry of Foreign Affairs of Japan (MOFA of Japan). 2001. 'Japan-India Joint Declaration'. 10 December. Accessed 14 December 2019. https://www.mofa.go.jp/region/asia-paci/india/joint0112.html

Ministry of Foreign Affairs of Japan (MOFA of Japan). 2004. 'Joint Statement: "Central Asia Plus Japan" Dialogue/ Foreign Ministers' Meeting: Relations between Japan and Central Asia as They Enter a New Era'. 28 August. Accessed 14 December 2019. https://www.mofa.go.jp/region/europe/dialogue/joint0408.pdf

Ministry of Foreign Affairs of Japan (MOFA of Japan). 2005. 'Japan Decides to Continue to Dispatch MSDF Vessels to the Indian Ocean in Order to Support International Efforts to Fight against Terrorism (Extension of the Anti-Terrorism Special Measures Law)'. 27 October. Accessed 14 December 2019. https://www.mofa.go.jp/policy/terrorism/measure0610.html

Ministry of Foreign Affairs of Japan (MOFA of Japan). 2006a. 'Joint Statement towards Japan-India Strategic and Global Partnership'. 15 December. Accessed 14 December 2019. https://www.mofa.go.jp/region/asia-paci/india/pdfs/joint0612.pdf

Ministry of Foreign Affairs of Japan (MOFA of Japan). 2006b. 'Speech by Mr. Taro Aso, Minister of Foreign Affairs on the Occasion of the Japan Institute of International Affairs Seminar "Arc of Freedom and Prosperity: Japan's Expanding Diplomatic Horizons"'. 30 November. Accessed 14 December 2019. https://www.mofa.go.jp/announce/fm/aso/speech0611.html

Ministry of Foreign Affairs of Japan (MOFA of Japan). 2006c. 'Japan-China Joint Press Statement'. 8 October. Accessed 14 December 2019. https://www.mofa.go.jp/region/asia-paci/china/joint0610.html

Ministry of Foreign Affairs of Japan (MOFA of Japan). 2007a. 'On the "Arc of Freedom and Prosperity"—An Address by H.E. Mr. Taro Aso, Minister for Foreign Affairs on the Occasion of the 20th Anniversary of the Founding of the Japan Forum on International Relations, Inc'. 12 March. Accessed 14 December 2019. https://www.mofa.go.jp/policy/pillar/address0703.html

Ministry of Foreign Affairs of Japan (MOFA of Japan). 2007b. 'Japan-China Joint Press Statement'. 11 April. Accessed 14 December 2019. https://www.mofa.go.jp/region/asia-paci/china/pv0704/joint.html

Ministry of Foreign Affairs of Japan (MOFA of Japan). 2008a. 'Joint Declaration on Security Cooperation between Japan and India'. 22 October. Accessed 14 December 2019. https://www.mofa.go.jp/region/asia-paci/india/pmv0810/joint_d.html

Ministry of Foreign Affairs of Japan (MOFA of Japan). 2008b. 'Joint Statement between the Government of Japan and the Government of the People's Republic of China on Comprehensive Promotion of a 'Mutually Beneficial Relationship Based on Common Strategic Interests"'. 7 May. Accessed 14 December 2019. https://www.mofa.go.jp/region/asia-paci/china/joint0805.html

Ministry of Foreign Affairs of Japan (MOFA of Japan). 2015a. 'Japan's Assistance in Afghanistan: Towards Self-Reliance'. April. Accessed 14 December 2019. https://www.mofa.go.jp/files/000019264.pdf

Ministry of Foreign Affairs of Japan (MOFA of Japan). 2015b. 'Inaugural U.S.-India-Japan Trilateral Ministerial Dialogue'. Media Note, 30 September. Accessed 14 December 2019. https://www.mofa.go.jp/files/000102078.pdf

Ministry of Foreign Affairs of Japan (MOFA of Japan). 2016. 'Japan's Security Policy'. 6 April. Accessed 14 December 2019. https://www.mofa.go.jp/fp/nsp/page1we_000080.html

Ministry of Foreign Affairs of Japan (MOFA of Japan). 2017. 'Priority Policy for Development Cooperation FY 2017'. April. Accessed 14 December 2019. https://www.mofa.go.jp/files/000259285.pdf

Ministry of Foreign Affairs of Japan (MOFA of Japan). 2019a. 'Japan-India Relations (Basic Data)'. 8 August. Accessed 14 December 2019. https://www.mofa.go.jp/region/asia-paci/india/data.html

Ministry of Foreign Affairs of Japan (MOFA of Japan). 2019b. 'Trends in Chinese Government and Other Vessels in the Waters Surrounding the Senkaku Islands, and Japan's Response—Records of Intrusions of Chinese Government and Other

Vessels into Japan's Territorial Sea'. 9 December. Accessed 14 December 2019. https://www.mofa.go.jp/region/page23e_000021.html

Naval Today. 2018. 'Philippines Receives Final Three TC-90 Aircraft from Japan'. *NavalToday.com*, 26 March. Accessed 14 December 2019. https://navaltoday.com/2018/03/26/philippines-receives-final-three-tc-90-aircraft-from-japan/

NDTV. 2014. 'Threat from Sea on the Rise. Navy Prepared: Admiral RK Dhowan'. *NDTV*, 4 December. Accessed 14 December 2019. https://www.ndtv.com/india-news/threat-from-sea-on-the-rise-navy-prepared-admiral-rk-dhowan-708100

NDTV. 2015. 'India Seeks Increased Participation in Arctic Council'. *NDTV*, 5 May. Accessed 14 December 2019. https://www.ndtv.com/india-news/india-seeks-increased-participation-in-arctic-council-760707

Nippon.com. 2013. 'Behind the New Abe Diplomacy: An Interview with Cabinet Advisor Yachi Shōtarō (Part One)', Nippon.com, 8 August. Accessed 14 December 2019. https://www.nippon.com/en/currents/d00089/

Panda, Ankit. 2013. 'The Nuclear Problem in India-Japan Relations'. *The Diplomat*, 31 October. Accessed 14 December 2019. https://thediplomat.com/2013/10/the-nuclear-problem-in-india-japan-relations/

Pandit, Rajat. 2016. 'To Fight China's Andaman and Nicobar Forays, India Deploys Submarines Hunters'. *Times of India*, 19 January. Accessed 14 December 2019. https://timesofindia.indiatimes.com/india/To-fight-Chinas-Andaman-and-Nicobar-forays-India-deploys-submarine-hunters/articleshow/50632020.cms

Parameswaran, Prashanth. 2015. 'Japan to Join Indian Submarine Race?' *The Diplomat*, 29 January. Accessed 14 December 2019. https://thediplomat.com/2015/01/japan-to-join-indian-submarine-race/

Parmar, Sarabjeet S. 2012. 'Humanitarian Assistance and Disaster Relief (HADR) in India's National Strategy'. Journal of Defense Studies Vol. 6, Issue 1 (January), 91–101. Accessed 14 December 2019. https://idsa.in/system/files/jds_6_1_SarabjeetParmar.pdf

Permanent Mission of India to the United Nations. 2019. 'India and UN Peacekeeping'. Accessed 14 December 2019. https://www.pminewyork.org/pdf/menu/submenu__759614422.pdf

Prime Minister of Japan and His Cabinet (PM&C). 1997. 'Policy Speech by Prime Minister Ryutaro Hashimoto to the 141st Session of the National Diet'. 29 September. Accessed 14 December 2019. https://japan.kantei.go.jp/971006-141diet.html

Prime Minister of Japan and His Cabinet (PM&C). 2014. 'Japan-India Joint Statement: Intensifying the Strategic and Global Partnership'. 25 January. Accessed 14 December 2019. https://japan.kantei.go.jp/96_abe/diplomatic/201401/25india_e.html

Rajagopalan, Rajesh. 2014. 'India Needs to Deftly Deal with Multiple Strategic Partners, including China'. *Economic Times*, 18 September. Accessed 14 December 2019. https://economictimes.indiatimes.com/opinion/et-commentary/india-needs-to-deftly-deal-with-multiple-strategic-partners-and-with-china/printarticle/42743468.cms

Samaranayake, Nilanthi, Catherine Lea and Dmitry Gorenburg. 2014. 'Improving U.S.-India HA/DR Coordination in the Indian Ocean'. CNA Analysis & Solutions,

July. Accessed 14 December 2019. https://www.cna.org/cna_files/pdf/drm-2013-u-004941-final2.pdf

Sano, Shutaro. 2017a. Author's interview with an Indian Commodore (ret.) whose name withheld by request, 14 February.

Sano, Shutaro. 2017b. 'Japan-India Security Cooperation: Building a Solid Foundation amid Uncertainty'. Center for Strategic and International Studies (CSIS) Strategic Japan Working Paper Series. Accessed 14 December 2019. https://csis-prod.s3.amazonaws.com/s3fs-public/170511_Japan_India_3.pdf?epmfEbJcMUP4ZdTvqsYvA2_rej6UWzuO

State Council of the People's Republic of China. 2017. 'Full Text of the Vision for Maritime Cooperation under the Belt and Road Initiative'. 20 June. Accessed 14 December 2019. http://english.gov.cn/archive/publications/2017/06/20/content_281475691873460.htm

Thorne, Devin and Ben Spevack. 2017. 'Harbored Ambitions: How China's Port Investments Are Strategically Reshaping the Indo-Pacific'. C4ADS. Accessed 14 December 2019. https://static1.squarespace.com/static/566ef8b4d8af107232d5358a/t/5ad5e20ef950b777a94b55c3/1523966489456/Harbored+Ambitions.pdf

United Nations. 2018. 'Summary of Contributions to UN Peacekeeping by Country, Mission and Post'. Press release, 31 January. Accessed 14 December 2019. https://peacekeeping.un.org/sites/default/files/msr_31_jan_2018.pdf

U.S. Department of Defense (U.S. DOD). 2016. 'Annual Report to Congress: Military and Security Developments Involving the People's Republic of China'. 26 April. Accessed 14 December 2019. https://dod.defense.gov/Portals/1/Documents/pubs/2016%20China%20Military%20Power%20Report.pdf

U.S. Department of State (U.S. DOS). 2005. 'U.S.-India Disaster Relief Initiative'. Fact Sheet, 18 July. Accessed 14 December 2019. https://2001-2009.state.gov/p/sca/rls/fs/2005/49730.htm

U.S. Department of State (U.S. DOS). 2015. 'U.S. Engagement in the 2015 ASEAN Regional Forum'. Fact Sheet, 6 August. Accessed 14 December 2019. https://2009-2017.state.gov/r/pa/prs/ps/2015/08/245759.htm

U.S. White House. 2002. 'The National Security Strategy of the United States of America'. 17 September. Accessed 14 December 2019. https://2009-2017.state.gov/documents/organization/63562.pdf

Varadarajan, Siddharth. 2006. 'Perils of Three-Way Security Cooperation'. The Hindu, 14 February. Accessed on 14 December 2019. http://svaradarajan.blogspot.com/2006/02/perils-of-three-way-security.html

6

India-Pakistan Relations during the UPA Rule

Isabelle Saint-Mézard

Introduction

At first sight, India-Pakistan relations during the two UPA governments displayed a familiar pattern, where high-level political engagements and brief moments of bonhomie were superseded by worrying tensions, suspended ties, and shattered hopes of peace. In this regard, the UPA governments seemed to reproduce the 'cooperate-and-defect bilateral diplomacy' that often characterized India's approach to Pakistan (Bajpai 2017). However, a closer look at the 2004–2014 decade reveals rather unique features, many of which can be associated with the UPA governments' special approach to this difficult neighbour. Between 2004 and 2008, the first UPA government and Prime Minister Singh himself engaged in multiple channels of communication with their Pakistani counterparts and this led to a real breakthrough. The two countries actually came close to changing the trajectory of their bilateral relations, with major prospects for resolving outstanding issues in the 2004–6 phase. Sustaining talks with Islamabad and exploring avenues for normalizing bilateral ties, while putting clear security preconditions to further progress, thus came to be the hallmark of the first UPA government's approach to Pakistan.

Another feature of the UPA governments' policy towards Pakistan was their deliberate choice to maintain a posture of military restraint in response to cross-border terrorism. This posture was best exemplified in the aftermath of the Mumbai terrorist attack of 26 November 2008, as the Singh government refrained from resorting to the use of force and chose

Isabelle Saint-Mézard, *India-Pakistan Relations during the UPA Rule* In: *Forging New Partnerships, Breaching New Frontiers*. Edited by: Rejaul Karim Laskar, Oxford University Press. © Oxford University Press 2022.
DOI: 10.1093/oso/9780192868060.003.0006

instead to have Pakistan face up to its responsibilities and prosecute the sponsors of the attack. At the same time, because of the trauma of the 26/11 attacks, the policy of the second UPA government towards Pakistan came to be dominated by a sense of disillusionment and the pressing demand that Pakistan delivered justice on the 26/11 case. Significantly though, even in the embittered post-26/11 context, Prime Minister Singh tried to restore some lines of communication with Pakistan, thus choosing a posture of diplomatic perseverance, despite very adverse conditions.

This chapter on India-Pakistan relations during the UPA rule (2004–14) is organized into four sections. Following a brief background on the trajectory of conflict between India and Pakistan (1), the chapter highlights the attempts made by the first UPA government to push multiple formats of negotiations with Pakistan (2). In the next section, it underlines the reluctance of the UPA governments to resort to the use of force in response to Pakistan-based terrorist attacks and their constant preference for a diplomatic approach towards this neighbour (3). In a final section, the chapter assesses India's Pakistan policy under the UPA rule, identifying the main factors hindering the improvement in the bilateral relationship (4).

India-Pakistan Relations: A Trajectory of Conflict and Entrenched Hostility

Pakistan has stood out as a unique and overwhelming factor in Indian foreign policy. The weight of this special neighbour in India's strategic outlook and military posture has been somewhat disproportionate with its actual size. But, admittedly, apart from Pakistan, no other country in the South Asian neighbourhood has displayed such a level of hostility and unfriendliness towards India.

Conventional Wars and Recurring Tensions and Crises

The conflict between India and Pakistan is multi-fold and pre-existed their accession to independence. The roots of their antagonism are to be found in the history of the freedom struggle, the irreconcilable visions, and claims of the Muslim League and the Indian Congress Party, as well as the mass violence and collective trauma of Partition. As independent states, the two neighbours spent most of their existence in a situation of entrenched hostility. They fought three major conventional wars (1947–48, 1965 and 1971) and had recurring phases of tensions and crises. In the process, they accumulated new grievances against each other and found themselves further estranged. The best the two countries could achieve was to come to a relatively lower level of hostility in the 1970s and 1980s.

For both nations, Kashmir has stood out as a central bone of contention, especially as each side has seen this Muslim-majority territory as the litmus test of its national ideology and identity. India has deemed it crucial to integrate this particular territory to vindicate its foundational principles of multiculturalism, pluralism, and secularism. With its self-representation as home for the Muslims of the subcontinent, Pakistan has seen Kashmir as 'the unfinished business of Partition', or to put it differently, as the ultimate step to achieve the construction of the nation. The Kashmir dispute has also been territorial, with India controlling two-third of the ancient princely state and Pakistan one-third. Moreover, in its quest to revise the territorial status quo on Kashmir, Pakistan started to wage a proxy war against India in the late 1980s. It backed anti-India militants, who wreaked havoc in Indian-controlled Kashmir throughout the 1990s and in the rest of India thereafter. This low-intensity conflict against India became Pakistan's favourite modus operandi, as it served its twin goals of challenging India's rule over Jammu and Kashmir and of seeking strategic parity with its far larger rival.

Increasing Tensions and Risks in the 1998–2003 Period

The India-Pakistan rivalry took a turn for the worse in the spring of 1998. In May 1998, the National Democratic Alliance (NDA) government of Prime Minister Vajpayee decided to go for a series of nuclear tests and Pakistan followed suit a few weeks later. The overt nuclearization of the subcontinent entailed a drastic change in the Indo-Pakistan strategic equation. It implied that from then on, war would become a far more dangerous undertaking as it could raise the risk of a potential military escalation up to the nuclear threshold. Aware of the new dangers raised by their respective nuclearization, India and Pakistan initially tried to stabilize their relations. In February 1999, Prime Minister Atal Bihari Vajpayee undertook a ground-breaking bus trip to Lahore and held a historic summit with his Pakistani counterpart, Nawaz Sharif. In their joint declaration, the two Prime Ministers acknowledged that 'the nuclear dimension of the security environment of the two countries add(ed) to their responsibility for avoidance of conflict between the two countries'. As a result, Vajpayee and Sharif admitted that they 'shall intensify their efforts to resolve all issues, including the issue of Jammu and Kashmir' (Vajpayee, Sharif 1999).

However, soon thereafter, Pakistani forces infiltrated the Kargil area in Indian-administered Kashmir, which sparked a brief armed confrontation in the spring of 1999. The so-called Kargil war not only highlighted Pakistan's adventurism and India's self-restraint—as Indian troops 'just' pushed back the Pakistani forces to their side of the Line of Control (LoC)—but it also sent very worrying signals to the international community. Moreover, the two neighbours remained incapable of mending fences, as shown by the failure of the July 2001 Agra Summit between Prime Minister Vajpayee and Pakistan's new strongman, general Musharraf. Relations between India and Pakistan further deteriorated in the context of the post-9/11 attacks on the United States. As a frontline state in the global war on terror, Pakistan was forced to help the U.S. combat Al Qaeda and the Taliban in Afghanistan. At the same time, however, it seemed to give a free hand to anti-Indian terrorist groups. By late 2001, a new outbreak of terrorist attacks struck first Indian Kashmir and, then, the Parliament in New Delhi (on 13 December 2001). In reaction, India proceeded with a mass mobilization of its army along the LoC and international border (IB). Its goal was to push the international community into putting additional pressure on Islamabad so that all terrorist infiltrations into Kashmir came to a stop. The military face-off that subsequently opposed India and Pakistan seemed on the verge of sliding into an open war, with the consequent risks of nuclear use, on two occasions, in December 2001 and in May–June 2002. It took intense mediation from the United States to put an end to the crisis in mid-2002.

The Need for a Peace Process

By 2003, the leadership in Pakistan and India realized that they had reached a stalemate in terms of military options and that they shall go back to the negotiating table (Behera 2016). In April 2003, the Vajpayee government made a peace offer, which president Musharraf accepted. Further progress was achieved by the end of 2003, with the inauguration of a ceasefire in Kashmir. In January 2004, Prime Minister Vajpayee met general Musharraf on the sidelines of the Islamabad Summit conference of SAARC, and, the following month, on 18 February 2004, the Indian and Pakistani Foreign Secretaries started the so-called Composite Dialogue process. This dialogue concept was not exactly new: it was first mooted at the 1997 Male meeting between Prime Minister I.K. Gujral and his Pakistani counterpart, Nawaz Sharif (Dasgupta 2015). Prime Ministers Vajpayee and Sharif tried to launch it again in their 1999 Lahore Summit, but the series of crises between 1998 and 2003 delayed its commencement.

The composite dialogue concept consisted in bringing to the negotiation table a cluster of security issues to be discussed concurrently by different ministries and at different government levels (Dasgupta 2015). The multi-chapter talks were to be led by the two countries' Foreign Secretaries and to cover the eight following issues: the demilitarization of the Siachen Glacier; Sir Creek; the Wullar Barrage/Tulbul Navigation project; Terrorism and drug trafficking; Economic and commercial cooperation; Promotion of friendly exchanges; Peace and security including Confidence Building Measures (CMBs); Jammu and Kashmir. This was a new and accommodative format whereby India and Pakistan agreed to include each other's core concern, i.e. terrorism (under the rubric of peace and security) for the former and Kashmir for the latter. With this innovative approach, it was hoped that a breakthrough in bilateral relations could be eventually achieved, thus putting an end to decades of unsuccessful bilateral parleys.

The First UPA Government's Investment in Multiple Channels of Communication with Pakistan

The UPA government of Prime Minister Singh did not display the combination of military posturing and audacious diplomatic openings that characterized the Vajpayee years. Prime Minister Singh mostly focused on negotiations and, in so doing, pushed three channels of discussions with Pakistan: the composite dialogue, secret backchannel talks, and a high-level political engagement involving the two countries' leaders.

The Composite Dialogue

The UPA government earnestly engaged in the composite dialogue initiated by the previous NDA administration and completed four rounds of negotiations with Pakistan between 2004 and 2008. The most successful outcomes concerned CBMs in the peace and security basket, and more particularly with respect to the facilitation of trade and travel. Progress was especially visible in Kashmir, where divided families were offered a historic opportunity to reconnect. By late 2004 indeed, the two neighbours decided to resume the bus service line between Srinagar and Muzaffarabad. The line increased its frequency from fortnightly to weekly in 2008 (Padder 2012). In the meanwhile, another cross-LoC bus service was initiated between Poonch and Rawalakot in June 2006. During the second half of 2008, triple-entry permits for cross-LoC travel were made available and trade across the LoC was authorized, albeit on a very restricted scale, as only 21 items were allowed to be transacted under barter trade conditions. While the lack of banking facilities and of a telephone line from the Indian side to Pakistan controlled side of Kashmir stood as a major constraint, these steps had a significant symbolic value (Dasgupta 2015).

Beyond Kashmir, other trade and travel exchanges were promoted. In the railways sector, the Samjhauta Express, running between Delhi and Lahore, was resumed in early 2005, and another connection between Munabao (Rajasthan) and Khokhrapar (Sindh) started in 2006. In the road sector, India and Pakistan opened a new bus service from Lahore to Amritsar and resumed the night bus service from Ferozepur and Fazilka to Ludhiana and Chandigarh; they also opened the first overland truck route at the Wagah border crossing in 2007. Finally, air connections were also increased from 12 to 28 flights weekly in 2008. In the cultural field, both countries agreed to host festivals displaying each other's movies in 2006. Pakistan even authorized the legal release of Indian films on its territory in 2008 (Padder 2012). All these measures facilitating people-to-people exchanges generated goodwill on both sides of the border and helped in creating constructive atmospherics. It was hoped that they could contribute to creating peace constituencies in each country.

India and Pakistan also progressed on various security CBMs in the nuclear and conventional fields. In October 2005, they signed an agreement on pre-notification of ballistic missile flight tests. The same year, they also brought into effect a Communication Link between Indian Coast Guards and Pakistan Maritime Security Agency, to better manage the issue of fishermen arrested for straying into each other's waters. In 2006, they launched a Joint Anti-Terrorism Institutional Mechanism to identify and implement counter-terrorism initiatives and investigations in both countries. In 2007, they signed an agreement on Reducing the Risk from Accidents Relating to Nuclear Weapons. Finally, the two neighbours cooperated on various humanitarian issues. In 2005, for instance, in the aftermath of a devastating earthquake in Pakistan-administered Kashmir, the Musharraf government accepted India's offer to help with food and medicine. On a different issue, both sides proceeded to release more than 500 prisoners in repeated instances in 2003, 2004, 2005, 2007, 2008, and 2009.

The Backchannel Talks on Kashmir

The composite dialogue was supplemented by secret backchannel talks. This special format was explored for the first time during the 1999 Lahore Summit, when Prime Ministers Vajpayee and Sharif missioned special emissaries to conduct secret, exploratory talks on Kashmir (Coll 2009), but it could not be pursued because of the cycle of crises that erupted afterwards. The process was eventually revived in 2004 and entrusted to two special envoys, Satinder Lambah, a senior Indian diplomat, and Tariq Aziz, a close aide of Musharraf. Between 2004 and early 2007, Lambah and Aziz held about 20 sessions, with a view to finding new mechanisms to settle the dispute over Kashmir. By late 2006–early 2007, they drafted a non-paper that laid out creative propositions for a settlement of the Kashmir issue. While the full details were not released, the main lines of the document were known to hinge around the following four principles. Firstly, there would be 'no territorial changes' and, instead, the two neighbours would 'soften' the LoC for the free movement of people and goods. Secondly, they would grant greater autonomy and self-governance to both parts of Kashmir. Thirdly, they would gradually demilitarize Kashmir, provided that cross-border terrorism declined. Finally, they would aim at establishing a joint mechanism to supervise 'issues that affected populations on both sides of the LoC' (Coll 2009).

Both Musharraf and Singh publicly hinted at the existence of the backchannel talks. General Musharraf repeatedly touched upon the idea of a settlement in Kashmir, with different proposals, including that of abandoning Pakistan's insistence on a plebiscite in the state, a significant step indeed. But his most serious announcement on the subject came on 5 December 2006, when he articulated his 'four point formula', which more or less corresponded to the four principles laid out in the non-paper (Coll 2009). Prime Minister Singh was slightly more understated. However, he made a meaningful speech on 24 March 2006 in Amritsar, where he spoke of a joint mechanism for socioeconomic cooperation between the two parts of Kashmir (Lambah 2014).

The backchannel talks progressed up until 2006. Such progress and goodwill were made possible by the improving security situation, which was marked by a substantial decline in terrorist infiltrations and ceasefire violations. As seen from the Singh government, general Musharraf seemed to have convinced the Pakistani army of giving the dialogue a chance and of reigning on its terrorist proxies (Coll 2009). Moreover, on the Indian side, Jammu and Kashmir was enjoying a relative normalization of the situation (until 2008): violence was decreasing and the Singh government was making efforts to engage a large spectrum of political stakeholders in the Valley. Overall, there was relative optimism on the Indian side for a few months. This positive outlook transpired in Prime Minister Singh's remarks, when he said in January 2007:

I dream of a day, while retaining our respective national identities, one can have breakfast in Amritsar, lunch in Lahore and dinner in Kabul. That is how my forefathers lived. That is how I want our grandchildren to live. (Singh 2007)

A High-Level Political Dialogue

For the first UPA government, the composite dialogue and backchannel negotiations became a top foreign policy priority. Prime Minister Singh in particular devoted considerable attention to pushing the peace process (he kept the foreign affairs portfolio until 2006, when Pranab Mukherjee became External Affairs Minister). This personal commitment resulted from his conviction that India would not be able to endorse a larger role in world affairs unless it succeeded in stabilizing its neighbourhood in general and its relationship with Pakistan in particular. More to the point, Prime Minister Singh saw the situation through a neoliberal prism and believed that interdependence and the prospects of mutual gains could make India and Pakistan more accommodative to each other's interests. His focus was on geo-economics and he posited that a pacified neighbourhood was required for India to maintain high economic growth. Peace with Pakistan in particular would bring great dividends; it would lessen the huge human and financial cost of protecting the border as well as reopen India's historical connections to Central Asia and Eurasia (Lambah 2014). He thus explained in a statement in 2007:

> I sincerely believe, as I have said so often, that the destiny of the people of South Asia is interlinked. It is not just our past that links us, but our future too. India cannot be a prosperous, dynamic economy and a stable polity if our neighbourhood as a whole is also not economically prosperous and politically stable. Similarly, our neighbours cannot prosper if India does not do so as well. There are enormous opportunities for promoting mutually beneficial cooperation in South Asia. (Singh 2007)

While he invested in negotiations with Pakistan, Prime Minister Singh displayed a rather low-key style, with a clear preference for a quiet diplomacy. In this respect, Kanti Bajpai commented that the UPA government 'was fairly conservative with respect to summits and high-level meetings with Pakistan' and that 'its public diplomacy with Pakistan was almost taciturn even though behind the scene progress was made on Kashmir' (Bajpai 2012). In fact, Prime Minister Singh avoided holding high-level India-Pakistan summits locally. He actually never travelled to Pakistan during his ten-year tenure, while both his predecessor A.B. Vajpayee and successor N. Modi visited Lahore once each. When he interacted with Pakistan's top leaders in India itself, the exchanges were kept rather discreet. Prime Minister Singh's preferred mode of interactions with his Pakistani counterparts proved to be on the sidelines of multilateral meetings (such as the UN general assembly, the Non-Aligned Movement (NAM), and SAARC Summits). These time-limited interactions on neutral grounds (often far away from the subcontinent) presented two advantages: they made it possible to maintain a channel of communication at the highest political level while limiting the media frenzy and high anticipations that accompanied summits held locally, in India or Pakistan.

Quite characteristically, Prime Minister Singh met President Musharraf for the first time in September 2004, on the sidelines of the UN general assembly in New York. On this occasion, both leaders confirmed 'their commitment to continue the bilateral dialogue to restore normalcy and cooperation between India and Pakistan', to implement CBMs, and to explore different options for a negotiated settlement of the Kashmir issue 'in a sincere spirit and purposeful manner' (Joint Statement 2004). Cricket diplomacy also proved to be a useful tool to push parleys and create goodwill on both sides of the border. For instance, Pakistan used the pretext of an India-Pakistan cricket match that was to take place in Delhi to convince the Singh government to invite President Musharraf to come and attend the event. The image of President Musharraf and Prime Minister Singh attending the match next to each other offered a powerful symbol of goodwill, indeed. More importantly, Musharraf stayed in Delhi for three more days to conduct unofficial talks with his Indian hosts. Musharraf's stay in Delhi proved successful and confirmed the optimist mind-set shared by the two states. This was best illustrated by Prime Minister Singh and President Musharraf's comment that the 'peace process was now irreversible' during a joint press conference (Joint statement 2005).

At the same time, Prime Minister Singh and his cabinet ministers kept a watchful eye on any security threat emanating from Pakistan and constantly reminded their Pakistan counterparts of the pre-conditions for dialogue. Their message was that India was willing to address all issues on the agenda and on Kashmir, short of redrawing boundaries, but the prerequisite was that Pakistan fulfilled its commitment to respecting the ceasefire along the LoC and to containing cross-border terrorism. In this respect, a first serious setback happened in July 2006, when a series of bomb blasts struck Mumbai and provoked such a collective chock that the UPA government suspended Foreign Secretary–level dialogue. However, Prime Minister Singh remained committed to his engagement policy and met President Musharraf on the sidelines of the Havana Summit of NAM in September 2006. This meeting allowed the two leaders to reinitiate the dialogue process through the creation of a joint anti-terrorism mechanism (JATM).

However, the two preconditions for dialogue set by the Singh government suffered increasing breaches. Terrorist attacks on Indian soil never really stopped and Delhi felt increasingly exasperated with Pakistan's failure to contain terrorism. Moreover, President Musharraf was confronted with a growing domestic opposition in 2007, which eventually led to his ouster in August 2008. The peace process concomitantly lost momentum in 2007–8.

The UPA Governments' Pakistan Policy in Times of Crisis: Maintaining a Posture of Military Restraint and Persevering with Dialogue

The area where the UPA and NDA governments differed most was in their proclivity to resort to the use of force or at least to threaten the use of it. As observed by Kanti Bajpai, 'the NDA conducted foreign policy on the back of a strong security posture, or, to put it differently, to negotiate from strength—or at least appear to do so' (Bajpai 2012). In contrast, the UPA governments proved unwilling 'to threaten the use of force, even under intense provocation', whether in the form of 'terrorist attacks in metropolitan India' or of LoC violations (Bajpai 2012). Instead, the Singh government remained focused on restoring channels of communication, thus clearly favouring a posture of diplomatic perseverance.

A Reluctance to Threaten the Use of Force

On 26 November 2008, India came under a terrorist attack of an unprecedented scale, as a ten-member terrorist squad launched simultaneous assaults on various high-profile sites in Mumbai and caused the deaths of 166 persons. Indian authorities identified the Pakistan-based Lashkar-e-Toiba (LeT) as the organization responsible for the attacks. As stated by Prime minister Singh himself, the UPA government saw the complex logistics of the assault as proof of the involvement of some official security agencies in Pakistan. The collective trauma and utter sense of betrayal felt in the aftermath of the Mumbai attacks led many to expect a military response, in the form of a limited strike on terror infrastructures in Pakistan or of a military mobilization along the border. Many in the Singh government actually urged military retaliation and both countries put their armed forces on alert. In his account, Shivshankar Menon recollected that he was among those who advocated a military response:

> As foreign secretary, I saw my task as one of assessing the external and other implications and urged both External Affairs Minister Pranab Mukherjee and Prime Minister Manmohan Singh that we should retaliate, and be seen to retaliate, to deter further attacks, for reasons of international credibility and to assuage public sentiment. For me, Pakistan had crossed a line, and that action demanded more than a standard response. My preference was for overt action against LeT headquarters in Muridke or the LeT camps in Pakistan-occupied Kashmir and covert action against their sponsors, the ISI. Mukherjee seemed to agree with me and spoke publicly of all our options being open. (Menon 2016)

However, Prime Minister Singh eventually ruled out a military retaliation against Pakistan. Different factors accounted for his decision, some of which may be mentioned here. First of all, Dr Singh probably had in mind the lessons drawn from the 2002 crisis, including the huge financial burden incurred by the Indian Exchequer (USD2 billion) on this occasion and the limited strategic gains achieved out of this costly and risky operation. Then, India and Pakistan's nuclear arsenals also meant that the military options were limited and that the risk of a military escalation had to be strongly avoided. Finally, there was intense international pressure from the United States and the United Kingdom to prevent a further rise in tensions. While it gave up the military option, the UPA government suspended the composite dialogue and embarked on a relentless diplomatic and media campaign to have Pakistani authorities detain and prosecute the leaders of the LeT and masterminds of the 26/11 attacks. Its objective was to induce the international community to pressure Pakistan to deliver justice. Prime Minister Singh's preference for a diplomatic response certainly enhanced India's image as a responsible power. The problem, however, was that India's demands for justice would never be fully met by Pakistan. This left many in India with the feeling that Pakistan's security establishment was allowed to enjoy a situation of impunity.

Prime Minister Singh's Diplomatic Perseverance

Even after the 26/11 attacks, Prime Minister Singh hoped 'to find a way back to the non-paper' on Kashmir (Coll 2009). With a strengthened majority in the Lower House following the 2009 general election and a renewed mandate as Prime Minister, he felt he had the political capital to pick up the threads of the peace process. An additional incentive was that the new civilian government of President Zardari in Pakistan was also giving positive signals. Prime Minister Singh and his entourage were well aware that the Pakistani army, rather than President Zardari, was the real centre of power with respect to bilateral relations, yet, they wanted to give peace a chance. Prime Minister Singh eventually met his Pakistani counterpart, Yousaf Raza Gilani, in July 2009, on the sidelines of the Summit of NAM in Sharm El-Sheikh. On this occasion, the two leaders decided to mandate their Foreign Secretaries to hold more talks to improve relations.

In his 2009 speech to Parliament (following the Sharm El-Sheikh meeting), Prime Minister Singh explained his belief that India had no other option but to maintain a dialogue with Pakistan, despite all the pitfalls and uncertainties this may entail. In his view, stopping channels of communication with Pakistan would eventually cost India more than maintaining contacts, especially as it would empower those in Pakistan who wanted to disrupt the peace process. Prime Minister Singh further explained:

> I sincerely believe it is our obligation to keep the channels of communication open (…) Unless we talk directly to Pakistan we will have to rely on a third party to do so… Unless you want to go to war with Pakistan,

there is no way, but to go step-by-step... dialogue and engagement are
the best way forward. (Singh 2009)

Singh stayed committed to his engagement policy and met Prime
Minister Gilani again in April 2010, this time on the sidelines of the
SAARC summit in Thimphu. He then promptly invited Gilani to the
2011 world cup cricket semi-final at Mohali. As a result of Singh's determination, the dialogue was slowly resumed in February 2011 and a first
round was held in the summer of that year, followed by another in 2012.
This new dialogue, which was referred to as 'resumed dialogue', rather
than 'composite dialogue', kept the same structure, with its original eight
security baskets on the agenda, and added counter-terrorism, including
the trials of the Mumbai attack perpetrators and humanitarian issues, as
well as cultural exchanges along with the peace and security basket.

However, by mid-2012, the resumed dialogue unravelled in the midst
of growing violence. Prime Minister Singh nevertheless agreed to meet
President Zardari while he was on a private visit to India in April 2012.
The two leaders met again in August 2012 on the sidelines of the NAM
summit in Iran, but no real advance could be envisaged in the absence of
a convincing Pakistani action to curb terrorism. By October 2012, a new
spate of violence along the LoC threatened the military ceasefire that had
held since late 2003. Violence reached a peak in January 2013 with the
killing of two Indian soldiers and the mutilation of one of them, which
sparked outrage. Ceasefire violations continued till mid-2013 and culminated again in early August, with the killing of 19 soldiers in an attack
from Pakistan. As cross-border firings and shelling became more intense
in October, the Singh government made tougher political statements.
The third round of the revived dialogue in 2013 was aborted.

Despite increasingly strained relations, Prime Minister Singh made
it a point to have a meeting with Pakistan's new Prime Minister, Nawaz
Sharif, on the sidelines of the September 2013 UN General Assembly. But
his goal was primarily to reiterate India's grievances regarding ceasefire
violations, Pakistan-based terrorism, and the need for effective action
against the perpetrators of the Mumbai attacks. Singh and Sharif pledged
to reduce violence by ordering regular meetings between the Directors
General of Military Operations (DGMOs) of Indian and Pakistani armies. The DGMOs actually met at Wagah in December 2013 for the

first time in 14 years, but this didn't prevent a new escalation in cross-border firing soon thereafter. In other words, despite the second UPA government's efforts to mitigate the tensions with Pakistan and to prevent a new cycle of crises, bilateral relations eventually froze and both the LoC and IB became the theatre of growing violence. However, the prospect of war remained distant, as the UPA government remained unwilling to resort to a military response.

Assessing the Two UPA Governments' Policy towards Pakistan

The two UPA governments had limited room for manoeuvre for two main reasons. First, the peace process was contingent upon a major parameter on which they had not much influence: the balance of power in Pakistan and the Pakistan military's ingrained hostility towards India. Second, in India itself, Prime Minister Singh's diplomatic perseverance was seen as electorally risky by sections in his own party while it generated impatience and frustration among a growing constituency of hardliners.

The Disappointing Results of the Composite Dialogue

The UPA governments' Pakistan policies present us with a paradox. While Prime Minister Singh invested earnestly in patient and comprehensive negotiations and conducted one of the most promising peace process with Pakistan ever, no historic agreement was signed. Similarly, while India and Pakistan secretly reached a unique scheme for a solution on Kashmir, they failed to translate this major breakthrough into a tangible reality. It would be short-sighted to hold the Singh governments entirely responsible for the disappointing outcomes of the peace process. In fact, the conditions and format of the negotiations had some downside risks that should be taken into account to explain their limited results. With respect to the backchannel talks, for instance, there is no denying that their secrecy helped in exploring new proposals. But the problem with this secrecy was that the larger political circles were kept out of the loop and public opinion remained unprepared for such a major change.

Another problem was that the backchannel talks depended on the involvement of a very limited number of actors, primarily Musharraf and Singh. As Musharraf became confronted with a growing domestic opposition from 2007 on, he could no longer devote his full attention and energy to the talks and this had a direct bearing on their progress (Menon 2016). Then, once Musharraf was evicted, the backchannels talks were abandoned and the settlement solution laid out in the non-paper was cast aside by the civilian and military chiefs alike (Tellis 2017).

Even on the comparatively easier issues of the demilitarization of the Siachen Glacier and on Sir Creek, no agreement could be reached. Similarly, the old dispute over the Wullar Barrage/Tulbul Navigation Project in Indian Kashmir could not be resolved. And while the issue of cross-border terrorism repeatedly derailed the peace process, the JATM proved of little help. Even in the trade area, progress proved to be disappointing, especially as Pakistan never implemented its promise made in late 2011 to grant India the Most Favoured Nation status. In other words, the two sides did have moments of goodwill as part of the peace process, but they continued to harbour intense suspicions against one another, and this certainly limited their ability to progress.

Pakistan's Inner Contradictions

One major obstacle to progress was the internal balance of power in Pakistan. More exactly, the predominance of the army in all matters pertaining to Pakistan's security and foreign policies meant that it had the final say on the decisions regarding relations with India. The dominant role of the army was especially problematic as this institution remained imbued with a 'deeply anti-Indian ethos' (Tellis 2017). Following Musharraf's demise, the new civilian leaders—Asif Ali Zardari from 2008 to 2013 and Nawaz Sharif from 2013 to 2017—sent conciliatory signals towards India. But they were clearly constrained by the army. This was best illustrated by the fact that in the immediate aftermath of the 26/11 attacks, President Zardari offered to help India with the investigation but was stopped by the army in so doing. Similarly, Prime Minister Sharif was interested in improving ties with India but could not do much. The UPA governments were fully aware of the reality of power in Pakistan. Faced with this parameter on which he had no real traction, Prime Minister Singh's approach was to maintain a continuous political engagement in the hope that it may eventually help the civilian leadership to gain greater leverage over the army (Tellis 2017). This calculation was based on the notion that the civilian leadership could be more amenable to a peace process than the army, which was indeed the case as far as Asif Ali Zardari and Nawaz Sharif were concerned.

The army's quasi-monopoly over Pakistan-India relations raised another intractable difficulty, that of its alleged connections with anti-India terrorist groups, such as LeT. These groups repeatedly struck India (India identified the LeT's involvement in the October 2005 bombings in New Delhi, the July 2006 and November 2008 attacks in Mumbai, and the February 2013 attack in Hyderabad, to quote a few). And each of their deadly attacks disrupted the peace process and made it more difficult for the Singh government to pursue its engagement policy with Pakistan. Furthermore, the failure of the Pakistani authorities to prosecute Hafiz Saeed, the founder of LeT and mastermind of the 26/11 assault against Mumbai, was seen in India as proof of Pakistan's sponsoring of terrorism. Indian interests in Afghanistan also came under repeated terrorist attacks. In this country, the attacks were waged by the Haqqani group, which not only had its base in Pakistan but was also known to have close links with Pakistan's military agencies. Thus, the Haqqani group was heavily suspected of serving the interests of the Pakistan army, who was explicitly hostile to India's presence in Afghanistan. According to Ashley Tellis, the Pakistan military should be seen as the main parameter shaping the prospects for a peace process between the countries:

As long as the Pakistani military (or some influential elements within it) continue to actively support and tolerate Islamic fundamentalists, dominate the Pakistani state and perceive India as an adversary, it will set clear limits to every dialogue process. (Tellis 2017)

Finally, Pakistan's internal downward spiral added to the difficulties of the peace process. In 2007, Islamic extremists from the tribal areas started a backlash against the state and spread terrorism in their own country. Insecurity, extremism, and militancy became rampant, yet the Pakistan army remained focused on its rivalry with India and half-heartedly fought these domestic threats. This state of affairs left many an Indian with a sense of frustration and helplessness, as illustrated by these remarks by Shivshankar Menon:

> In light of the condition of Pakistan, it is sometimes argued that we have reached the limits of the outcomes that can be produced by normal state policy, whether of dialogue on all subjects and firmness in substance, or stopping dialogue, or other overt actions. India today lacks the power to solve its Pakistan problem, which largely stems from Pakistan's own condition. The best India can do is to manage the problem. (Menon 2016)

The Constraints of India's Domestic Politics

Prime Minister Singh remained personally committed to the peace process as long as possible. But his Pakistan initiatives increasingly lacked political backing and popular support in India itself, especially after the trauma of the 26/11 attacks. His meeting with Prime Minister Gilani at Sharm El-Sheikh in 2009 sparked anger within the ranks of the political opposition. Singh was accused of having yielded to Pakistan's demands in releasing a joint statement that mentioned Baluchistan and not terrorism.[1] Shivshankar Menon, who held the position of Foreign Secretary, acknowledged that the meeting appeared as hasty and Singh as too accommodating:

> In retrospect, it may be that it was premature to resume dialogue with Pakistan nine months after the Mumbai attack. One problem was the general impression in India that while Pakistan had much to gain by way of international respectability from a dialogue, India did not. (Menon 2016)

Even within his own party, some sections grew worried that Singh's peace approach would be electorally counter-productive with a public opinion largely distrustful of Pakistan and disinclined to support a policy of engagement and concession. The fear of being seen as too soft on Pakistan increased within the Congress party as the 2014 general election came into view. Finally, it should also be underlined that the second UPA government proved far more fragile than its first incarnation during the 2004–9 period. During its second tenure, the UPA government was engulfed in a series of corruption allegations, which absorbed a great deal of its energy. Relations both within the UPA coalition and within the Congress party were strained and Prime Minister Singh became increasingly marginalized. As a result, it became increasingly difficult for him to maintain the engagement policy towards Pakistan.

The Frustration of Indian Hardliners

Domestic politics and electoral concerns were not the only constraints to Prime Minister Singh's engagement policy. He also had to face a large constituency of hardliners, who remained deeply distrustful of Pakistan and who saw his approach as too accommodating and even risky for India's security interests. Not surprisingly, these hawks were to be found primarily in Indian defence and security agencies. For instance, as early as 2006–7, the chiefs of the Indian army came up against progress on the issue of Siachen demilitarization. While traditionally apolitical and loyal to its civilian leaders, the Indian army publicly opposed the prospects of a demilitarization without an authentication of the troops' positions before any withdrawal. On this issue, the military seemed to be driven by the notion that Prime Minister Singh was about to surrender a piece of territory the army had won through great sacrifice (Raghavan 2007).

The opposition also ran among Singh's closest advisers within the Prime Minister Office. The powerful National Security Adviser, M.K. Narayanan (2005 to 2010), made no secret of his diverging views with Dr. Singh's engagement policy towards Pakistan. At a deeper level, this former chief of the intelligence bureau even disagreed with the notion articulated by Dr Singh that India and Pakistan could have a 'shared destiny' (Nambath 2011). This sense of scepticism was deemed to be so pervasive at the top level that, according to the U.S. ambassador in New Delhi, Timothy Roemer, the Prime Minister, was actually quite isolated within his own government by mid-2009.

The hardliner constituency extended beyond the secret corridors of power to the larger strategic community. Retired military officers, former diplomats, and strategic experts regularly challenged the Prime Minister. In 2013, for instance, as Prime Minister Singh was about to meet Nawaz Sharif in New York on the sidelines of the September UN General Assembly, about 40 retired military officers, intelligence and civilian officials released a letter, calling for a stop in bilateral talks 'till Pakistan delivers on containing terror and brings to book the 26/11 perpetrators'. They feared talking to the Pakistani Prime Minister would be seen as a 'sign of appeasement' and 'weakness' (The Hindu, 2013). While the signatories were known for their hawkish position, what was significant was that they felt empowered to come out in the open.[2]

More generally, the hardliners felt that instead of engaging Pakistan, the government should raise the cost on this country for tolerating anti-Indian terrorist groups on its soil. In their view, the most efficient way to force Pakistan to crack down on anti-India terrorists was to show a determination and capability to take a forceful response in the event of a Pakistan-based terrorist attack. To some extent, this vision was shared by a section of the public opinion, which felt increasingly upset by the UPA governments' apparent failure to deter terrorists and their sponsors in Pakistan from attacking India. Interestingly, the perceived need to acquire a punitive capability against Pakistan had been keenly considered in the Indian army. This service had worked on the possibility of a quick, punitive response to a new terrorist attack of a large scale and proposed the Cold Start doctrine in April 2004. This doctrine of limited war lay stress on a quick mobilization capability to launch retaliatory strikes in response to a major Pakistan-based terrorist attack. While the Singh governments never officially acknowledged it, the Cold Start doctrine reflected the Indian army's aspiration to move from its traditionally defensive posture to a more aggressive one, in response to repeated provocations of Pakistani provenance.

Conclusion

As Happymon Jacob, a well-informed observer of India-Pakistan relations, noted retrospectively: 'The period between 2004 and 2007 witnessed hectic diplomatic and political activities leading to one of the best phases of the India–Pakistan relationship' (Jacob, 2016). True to the spirit of the composite dialogue, the two parties agreed to explore each other's core concerns, i.e. terrorism and Kashmir and this led to real—albeit short-lived—progress. On terrorism, there was a relative decline of Pakistan-based terrorist attacks as President Musharraf made efforts to control anti-India militant groups. Then, on Kashmir, the backchannel talks proved to be an effective mechanism and, in early 2007, the two neighbours reached a secret deal that, had it been signed, might have opened a new era, with real prospects for peace in this war-torn region. Concomitantly, the local situation in Kashmir improved up till 2008, as a result of both the optimist atmospherics between India and Pakistan and Prime Minister Singh's efforts at engaging the Kashmiris in Srinagar.

However, the peace process reached a peak in 2007 and then unravelled in the years thereafter. While several factors accounted for this failure, some of the most decisive ones originated from the Pakistani side, which was indicative of the limits of the UPA governments' actions. The first decisive factor was related to Pakistan's internal developments. President Musharraf's domestic difficulties in 2007 and eventual exit in mid-2008 came as a major blow to the peace process, as he was the main driving force behind the resolution package on Kashmir. In many ways, Musharraf was an 'anomaly' in the long line of Pakistani generals who occupied the post of Chief of Army Staff. He indeed proved to be willing to overcome his institution's anti-Indian ethos and to amend Pakistan's sacrosanct stance on Kashmir (Tellis 2017). In this respect, one might be tempted to judge that the Singh government was over-cautious and failed to take advantage of the unique historical opportunity that Musharraf's unorthodox approach offered for the resolution of Kashmir. Admittedly, it is easy to hold such a view with the benefit of time, and one has to remember that, as the architect of the Kargil intrusions in 1999, Musharraf was not seen as a particularly reliable counterpart in India.

The other major decisive factor accounting for the demise of the peace process was the resumption of Pakistan-based terrorist attacks on India from 2008 on. Once Musharraf was ousted from power, cross-border terrorism struck India repeatedly, reaching a peak in lethality with the Mumbai attacks. The reoccurrence of anti-India terrorism from mid-2008 signed the death of the peace process. It goes to the credit of Prime Minister Singh that, in the troubled post-11/08 context, he stuck to a posture of military restraint and diplomatic endurance. At the very least, this approach gave bilateral relations minimal stability despite growing violence on the LoC and IB. However, there is no denying that this approach was difficult to maintain politically and increasingly tested the patience of the Indian public in general and of the Indian hawks in particular.

Notes

1. The reference to Baluchistan was misinterpreted as an acknowledgement of the Indian role in the local insurgency.
2. The signatories included (among others) former Intelligence Bureau Director, Ajit Doval, former Navy Vice-Chief, Vice Admiral (Retd.), K.K. Nayyar, former Chief of the Army Staff, Gen. (Retd.) N.C. Vij, and the former diplomats, M. K. Rasgotra, Kanwal Sibal, and J.C. Sharma.

References

Bajpai K.P. 2012. The UPA's foreign policy, 2004–9. In Saez Lawrence, Singh, Gurharpal. New dimensions of politics in India: The United Progressive Alliance in power. London: Routledge.

Bajpai K.P. 2017. Narendra Modi's Pakistan and China policy: Assertive bilateral diplomacy, active coalition diplomacy. International Affairs, vol. 93, issue 1, 69–91.

Behera N.C. 2016. The Kashmir conflict: Multiple fault lines. Journal of Asian Security and International Affairs. vol. 3, issue 1, March, 41-63.

Coll S. 2009. The back channel: India and Pakistan's secret Kashmir talks. The New Yorker, March 2.

Dasgupta, S. 2015. Kashmir and the India-Pakistan composite dialogue process. RSIS Working Paper, No. 291, 25 p.

Jacob, H. 2016. The Kashmir Uprising and India-Pakistan Relations: A Need for Conflict Resolution, Not Management. Paris: Ifri, Asie.Visions, n° 90, December, 31 p.

Joint Statement. 2004. Meeting between Prime Minister Dr. Manmohan Singh and Pakistan President Mr. Pervez Musharraf. New York, 24 September: https://mea. gov.in/bilateral-documents.htm?dtl/7465/Joint+Statement++Meeting+between+ Prime+Minister+Dr+Manmohan+Singh+and+Pakistan+President+Mr+Pervez+ Musharraf

Joint Statement. 2005. India-Pakistan. New Delhi, 18 April: https://www.mea.gov.in/ Speeches-Statements.htm?dtl/2505/Joint_Statement_IndiaPakistan

Lambah S.K. 2014. A possible outline of a solution. Outlook Magazine. 14 May: https:// www.outlookindia.com/website/story/a-possible-outline-of-a-solution/290718

Menon S. 2016. Choices: Inside the making of India's foreign Policy. Washington D.C.: The Brookings Institution.

Nambath S. 2011. PM isolated on Pakistan. The Hindu. 15 March. https://www.thehindu.com/news/the-india-cables/lsquoPM-isolated-on-Pakistanrsquo/article13675602.ece

Padder, S. 2012. The Composite Dialogue between India and Pakistan: Structure, Process and Agency. Heidelberg: South Asia Institute, Department of Political Science, Heidelberg University, Heidelberg Papers in South Asian and Comparative Politics. No. 65, 21 p.

Raghavan S. 2007. Siachen and civil-military relations. Economic and Political Weekly. Vol. 42, No. 35. 3531–3533 September: https://www.epw.in/journal/2007/35/commentary/siachen-and-civil-military-relations.html

Singh M. 2007. Address of Prime Minister Dr. Manmohan Singh to the Federation of Indian Chambers of Commerce and Industry Annual General Meeting. New Delhi: 8 January. In A. Singh Bhasin. India's Foreign Relations—2007. New Delhi: MEA Geetika Publishers, 1348–1353.

Singh M. 2009. PM's statement in Lok Sabha on the debate on the PM's recent visit's abroad on 29 July, New Delhi: Prime Minister's Office: https://archivepmo.nic.in/drmanmohansingh/speech-details.php?nodeid=777

Tellis A. 2017. Are India-Pakistan peace talks worth a damn? Washington, D.C.: Carnegie Endowment for International Peace, 2 p.

The Hindu. 2013. Don't rush into talks with Pakistan, warn retired officials. 10 August. https://www.thehindu.com/news/national/dont-rush-into-talks-with-pakistan/article5008025.ece

Vajpayee A.B., Sharif M.N. 1999. The Lahore Declaration. 2 February. New Delhi: Ministry of External Affairs,: https://mea.gov.in/in-focus-article.htm?18997/Lahore+Declaration+February+1999

PART III

DIPLOMACY TOWARDS KEY REGIONS

This part examines India's diplomatic outreach towards four key geographic regions of interest to India, namely, South Asia, East and Southeast Asia, Africa, and Central Asia.

7

Quest for a Peaceful, Prosperous, and Friendly Neighbourhood

India's South Asia Policy, 2004–14

Thomas P. Cavanna

Introduction

As the United Progressive Alliance (UPA) assumed leadership in May 2004, India's roaring economy nurtured global ambitions and fuelled a renewed determination to make the country emerge as a great power in the international community. Prime Minister Manmohan Singh set to pursue 'greater engagement' vis-à-vis the United States and China (Roy Chaudhury 2014), engage India's 'extended neighborhood' (Scott 2013, 349), and deepen New Delhi's integration into the world economy (Hall 2016, 276). Yet UPA leaders made clear that they would 'give the highest priority to building closer political, economic, and other ties with [India's] neighbours' (Arndt 2013, 98). This objective stemmed from the conviction that New Delhi and the other countries of South Asia could not 'prosper without the other' (Singh 2006, 695). To be recognized as a great power, India had to demonstrate its ability to handle the region's vast security and economic challenges. Further, ensuring South Asia's stability and development was an absolute prerequisite to enable 'the infrastructures - roads, rail links, energy pipelines, power grids, and water management mechanisms [that would allow] access [to the] markets and resources in Central Asia, the Middle East, and Southeast Asia' (Padukone 2014, 142). Therefore, India would strive 'to reconnect the countries of the subcontinent on the one hand and then reconnect the subcontinent to the larger Asian neighbourhood on the other' (Singh 2005, 353).

Thomas P. Cavanna, *Quest for a Peaceful, Prosperous, and Friendly Neighbourhood* In: *Forging New Partnerships, Breaching New Frontiers.* Edited by: Rejaul Karim Laskar, Oxford University Press. © Oxford University Press 2022.
DOI: 10.1093/oso/9780192868060.003.0007

This chapter investigates how New Delhi defined and conducted its policy towards South Asia (minus Pakistan) during the decade 2004–14. It argues that the UPA advanced a coherent vision that was sensitive to the region's realities. Major obstacles stood in the way, including historical divisions, the limitations of India's power, Pakistan's dangerous policies, and China's skyrocketing rise. Nonetheless, the government of Manmohan Singh navigated adverse circumstances adroitly, steered away from costly strategic blunders, and often promoted New Delhi's regional interests effectively.

The chapter proceeds in six sections. First, it explores the structural challenges that the UPA inherited from the past and examines how it tried to address them. Then, it examines how it attempted to secure India's interests in the context of the war in Afghanistan. Third, the chapter investigates New Delhi's efforts to protect its influence in the Himalayan states of Nepal and Bhutan. Fourth, it describes the notable successes that the UPA achieved in Bangladesh, especially in security cooperation. Fifth, it studies India's rising activism in the Indian Ocean, including in Sri Lanka and the Maldives. Then, the chapter probes New Delhi's efforts to revive the moribund South Asian Association for Regional Cooperation (SAARC).

Addressing Structural Challenges

The UPA inherited structural constraints that were bound to limit its room for manoeuvre in South Asia. First, the region itself was profoundly divided. In fact, the very contours of South Asia had always been hard to capture. A geographic definition remained unsatisfactory given that the Indian plate did not cover Afghanistan or even parts of Pakistan. Religious, ethnic, and linguistic criteria did not help either, given the diversity of local populations. Moreover, the legacy of the British Empire suggested Myanmar's inclusion but not that of Afghanistan (Jaishankar 2013). Most importantly, tensions deepened in recent decades under the effect of the India–Pakistan (nuclear) rivalry, the Afghanistan-Pakistan rivalry, insurgencies, ethno-religious strife, terrorism, scathing poverty, and China's influence.

The second major historical legacy faced by UPA leaders was the uneasy relationship that India had developed with most of its neighbours since 1947. New Delhi often approached the 'Indian subcontinent' with a hegemonic perspective (Destradi 2012a, 57). Prime Minister Jawaharlal Nehru extended treaties of friendship to Bhutan (1949), Nepal (1950), and Sikkim (1950) to bolster New Delhi's influence. Taking this logic further, the Indira and Rajiv Doctrines of the 1970s and 1980s were designed to stem the 'autonomous tendencies' of India's neighbours and to keep extra-regional powers in check. This vision explained New Delhi's intervention in the Bangladeshi war of independence (1971), its absorption of Sikkim (1975), and its intervention in Sri Lanka's civil war (1987-90) (Padukone 2014, 24).

The latter's disastrous outcome prompted a more moderate approach. The Gujral Doctrine (1996) sought to '[walk] more than half the distance' to repair ties with South Asian states—except Pakistan (Khan 2010, 228). New Delhi's rising coalition politics, its need for economic development, and its quest for recognition as a 'responsible actor' entrenched this vision further (Mazumdar 2012, 299). But 'economic dependence', 'cultural similarity', 'national identity' politics, and geopolitical inferiority still incentivized most of India's neighbours to resist India's influence in various ways, including close bonds with its rivals Pakistan and China (Mohan 2004, 238).

Thus, when they came to power, UPA leaders knew that they would have to walk a thin line, especially as India accounted for 75% of South Asia's population, 79% of its GDP, and 83% of its national defence budgets (Destradi 2012a, 58-59). In November 2004, Natwar Singh, the Minister of External Affairs, acknowledged that '[i]t [was] only natural... that [these countries] look[ed] upon India with some degree of apprehension and fear of domination by it. A key objective of our policy is to reassure our neighbours and anchor this assurance in a virtuous web of cross-border, economic and commercial linkages' (Arndt 2013, 99). However, New Delhi also needed to defend its interests actively in a time of upheavals such as growing terrorism, the Afghan war, renewed India-Pakistan tensions, and the stunning rise of China.

Domestic obstacles also loomed on the horizon. India's military was still unable 'to produce weapons of quality' (Cohen 2015, 352) and civil-military relations remained difficult (Staniland and Narang 2015, 211). Moreover, the 600-to-900 officers who populated New Delhi's Ministry of External Affairs could not compete with America's 20,000 diplomats or even China's 4,000 (Ganguly 2015a, 17–18; Staniland and Narang 2015, 210). Politics also caused distortions. The 'intensifying democratic pressures' of the post-Cold War era had made it difficult for most recent Indian governments to behave as 'unified rational actor[s]' (Khilnani 2015, 692–3). Manmohan Singh himself led a minority government heavily dependent on allies (Sridharan 2015, 704). Some of them even pushed for the 'outsourcing of regional foreign policy' to specific Indian states, as illustrated in the case of Tamil Nadu for Sri Lanka or West Bengal for Bangladesh (Cohen 2015, 351). Last, as economic growth dwindled (after 2011) and domestic issues affected his government (allegations of corruption, etc.), Prime Minister Singh saw his own authority decline (Graham 2014). In the end, these difficulties considerably reduced the attention and resources that UPA leaders could dedicate to South Asia.

Addressing the Afghan Conundrum

The Afghan War was one of the UPA's most pressing concerns. New Delhi had welcomed America's Operation Enduring Freedom in October 2001 and endeavoured to support 'a stable and settled Afghanistan, where … the Taliban [would have] given up violence… cut all links with terrorism [and] subscribe[d] to the values of the Afghan Constitution' of January 2004 (Rao 2010, 735). The UPA government expanded these efforts.

India's soaring civilian assistance (mostly grants) helped Afghanistan's infrastructures (42%), its administration (25%), its food supplies (24%), and its health (3%) and education (2%) sectors (Destradi 2014, 105). The bilateral Preferential Trade Agreement of March 2003 offered major benefits as well (Sharma 2011, 111–112). Further, India's construction of a road between Afghanistan and Iran (Hanauer and Chalk 2012, 17) helped circumvent Pakistan, who blocked the transit of Indian goods to Afghanistan. New Delhi's trade with Kabul 'more than [doubled]' in

2006–11 (Mazumdar 2015, 69) and its image among the Afghans improved notably: 74% of positive ratings in 2009 (Dalrymple 2013, 18). UPA leaders cultivated a close relationship with President Hamid Karzai. During his visit to Kabul in August 2005, Prime Minister Singh stayed overnight to express his solidarity with his counterpart (Pant 2012, 7–8). New Delhi regularly advised Karzai to seek ethnic reconciliation and 'avoid isolating' political adversaries. Indian officials feared that Karzai's manoeuvres against his political opponents could prove destabilizing and weaken India's relationship with non-Pashtun leaders (its allies during the Taliban era) (Chandra 2012, 14). Yet the need to protect Afghanistan from the insurgency required bolstering Karzai's authority (Paliwal 2017, 200). Therefore, UPA leaders kept praising 'his courageous leadership' over the years (Karzai and Singh 2010, 732).

India's presence only amounted to 3,600 citizens, ten diplomatic officers, and a few troops (Dalrymple 2013, 11–12; Mazumdar 2015, 78) in the late 2000s. But the Pakistan army, who had long supported the Afghan Taliban to acquire 'strategic depth' on its western flank, repeatedly accused New Delhi of using local assets to stir instability in Baluchistan, Khyber Pakhtunkhwa, and FATA (Tribal Areas) (Paliwal 2017, 10). In August 2008, the Haqqani Network (the Taliban's most violent faction) assaulted the Indian embassy in Kabul (58 dead) with the support of Pakistan's Inter-Services Intelligence. This event fuelled a debate over the merits of an intensified Indian military presence in Afghanistan, which the United States had called for on several occasions (Hanauer and Chalk 2012, 52; _ 2006b). Yet, fearing further turmoil, New Delhi stuck to its civilian approach even as attacks proliferated, including on its embassy in Kabul (October 2009, 17 dead) and its consulate in Jalalabad (August 2013, 9 dead).

UPA leaders also witnessed a preoccupying strategic divergence with the U.S.-led coalition. In December 2008, Manmohan Singh asked '[America] and its partners [to] recognize that they [were] in Afghanistan for the long haul ...' (Paliwal 2017, 249). Moreover, Indian leaders were frustrated with Washington's fear of 'alienating' Pakistan (Abhyankar 2015, 375). New Delhi also had to blunt a U.S. attempt to link the war to a resolution of the Kashmir dispute (Shashank 2014, 94). India even found itself completely isolated during the January 2010 London Conference, as other leaders endorsed talks with the 'good Taliban' and implicitly recognized Pakistan's role as a mediator (Abhyankar 2015, 376).

New Delhi recalibrated its strategy accordingly. Letting the Taliban reclaim power was unthinkable but a dialogue with the factions ready to renounce violence could help avoid diplomatic marginalization and stem Pakistan's influence (Hanauer and Chalk 2012, 15). Most importantly, India signed in October 2011 a *Strategic Partnership Agreement* (SPA) that endorsed 'training, equipping and capacity building programmes' for Afghan National Security Forces (Destradi 2014, 107). According to Manmohan Singh, the SPA demonstrated that New Delhi '[would] stand by the people of Afghanistan … after the withdrawal of international forces', initially scheduled for 2014 (Mullen 2016, 106). As of 2012, India trained 1,000–1,500 Afghan troops and 200 officers annually and provided Kabul with much-needed equipment (helicopters, etc.) (Destradi 2014, 107).

However, New Delhi refused to 'commit troops on the ground' or satisfy Karzai's military 'wish lists' (Miglani 2014). This gap partly stemmed from India's bureaucratic constraints and economic slowdown. India was 'reluctant to proactively seek a defence partnership' (Paliwal 2017, 207–9). Instead, it consolidated its status as Kabul's main market (D'Souza 2013, 190), expanded its financial assistance, whose aggregated amount reached $2 billion in 2012 (Shashank 2014, 88), and encouraged private actors to buttress Afghanistan's potential by investing in local agriculture, manufacturing, telecommunications, and mines (Hajigak iron ore deposit, etc.) (Hanauer and Chalk 2012, 17). In parallel, diplomatic outreach continued. Manmohan Singh kept pushing for an 'Afghan-led, Afghan-owned and Afghan-controlled' peace process (Taneja 2017). He repeatedly advocated for inclusive regional negotiations that would welcome Iran (D'Souza 2013, 202). Indian leaders even engaged China, whose growing involvement could constrain Pakistan's support to the Taliban (Paliwal 2017, 297). At the same time, New Delhi kept criticizing the international community's hasty 'exit strategy', which risked squandering the progress achieved since the fall of the Taliban (_, 2014a).

The Indian debate over whether or not to 'fill the security vacuum' gained steam as the U.S.-led coalition initiated its drawdown (Dalrymple 2013, 27). But UPA leaders were right to resist that temptation. A military intervention would probably only have caused entanglement and more tensions with Pakistan. By keeping its course, New Delhi advanced its interests and contained Islamabad's local influence as effectively as it could.

Protecting the Himalayan Barrier

UPA leaders strived to protect India's northern edge from new challenges. Decades earlier, Prime Minister Nehru had proclaimed that his country could never 'allow [the Himalayan] barrier to be crossed or weakened' (Lama 2010, 116). Yet this very possibility, whose dire consequences had been illustrated by the 1962 Sino-Indian war, seemed to increase in the 21st century as a result of China's rise. Manmohan Singh's government responded with new bases and a troops buildup (Ganguly 2015b, 150). But New Delhi faced growing competition in Nepal and Bhutan.

The Treaty of Peace and Friendship concluded in 1950 had given India large prerogatives over Nepal's foreign policy in exchange for protection and preferential treatment (immigration, business, transit) (Mazumdar 2015, 142). But Kathmandu's monarchy regularly exploited local anti-Indian feelings (Kavitha 2016, 13) and the 'China card' to earn popularity and strategic leverage, respectively (Destradi 2012b, 292). Its attempts to procure Chinese arms led India to impose an economic blockade in spring 1989 (Jaiswal 2016, 98). But the relationship was quickly repaired, and the outbreak in 1996 of a Maoist insurgency with ties to Beijing and Indian insurgents inclined New Delhi to boost its military supplies despite Kathmandu's growing authoritarianism (Destradi 2012a, 108–9).

The UPA denounced King Gyanendra's proclamation of a state of emergency in February 2005 as 'a serious setback to … democracy' and interrupted its arms deliveries. But the monarchy still seemed 'the only institution capable of avoiding [a] descent into anarchy' and of blunting Chinese and Pakistani influence. Therefore, New Delhi maintained its defence training programs and discussed the resumption of arms exports (Destradi 2012b, 295). This leniency was popular in Indian military, political, and business circles, let alone the 10-million strong local Nepalese community (Muni 2012, 317–8). However, New Delhi lost patience with Gyanendra's rigidity (Muni 2012, 324). On 22 April 2006, Foreign Secretary Shyam Saran signalled the break: 'If today or tomorrow the people of Nepal wish to see a different future for themselves, [a] different kind of political arrangements … , that is for the people of Nepal to decide, not for India to decide' (Destradi 2012b, 298). Gyanendra's admission of defeat 48 hours later led to a groundbreaking Comprehensive Peace Agreement (CPA) (Destradi 2012a, 104).

From then onwards, the UPA openly supported Nepal's democratization and search for an 'inclusive system [that would address] the grievances of previously marginalized groups' (Destradi 2012a, 126). But its main objective was to 'strengthen the middle ground of Nepali politics [and prevent it] from turning too far to the left' (Jha 2012, 343). Thus, the Maoists' landslide victory in the April 2008 ballot constituted a hard blow. The decision of Nepal's new Prime Minister, Prachanda, to pay his first state visit to Beijing instead of New Delhi (as tradition dictated) caused consternation in India (Destradi 2012a, 116), a dismay that China's promises of military and infrastructure aid only aggravated (Deol, 2010). Bilateral tensions erupted in May 2009 when Prachanda tried to evict the head of Kathmandu's army, General Katawal, who had opposed the Maoists on numerous occasions (Pandit, 2009). Many observers considered the Prime Minister's move as an 'attempt to cripple the last institution capable of standing up to [him]' (Jha 2012, 340–1). But India swiftly responded by backing a local political resistance that forced Prachanda to resign (Pavitran 2017, 108).

New Delhi subsequently resumed joint military exercises, lifted its arms embargo, and granted Kathmandu duty-free access to its market (Jain 2010, 87; Wagner 2018, 21). As of 2013–4, it accounted for 66% of Nepal's foreign trade (Patel 2017, 75). Yet many locals resented India's unfair water agreements, its mistreatment of expatriated Nepalese workers, and its decision to abandon the monarchy (Nayak 2012, 138–40; Sigdel 2018, 14). Additionally, Kathmandu criticized New Delhi's unwillingness to revise the 1950 friendship treaty (Bagchi 2014) and its interference during the negotiation of Nepal's new Constitution (Kumar 2016). Tensions also arose as Kathmandu became more reluctant to stem 'the flow of terrorists, fake currency, and criminals across the border' and as it increasingly repressed its Tibetan refugees to please China (Kumar 2011, 74; Muni 2015, 404). Despite the UPA's concerns, Beijing continued to expand its local influence, as shown by the extension of the Tibet railway line (decided in January 2012) (Singh 2016, 114), soaring bilateral military assistance (Wolf 2018, 7), and the fact that China overtook India as Nepal's largest investor in 2013 (Pant 2015).

New Delhi's relationship with Bhutan displayed similar patterns. The 1949 Friendship Treaty had shielded the small Himalayan state from Chinese ambitions and opened the flows of bilateral assistance (Sikri 2009, 87). But it had also 'nipped in the bud [Bhutan's] aspirations to carve out its own' foreign policy. In February 2007, India signed a revised treaty that gave more leeway to Thimphu (Malik and Sheikh 2016, 46–47). The relationship also improved after Bhutan became a constitutional democracy and signed a Free Trade Agreement with New Delhi. By then, India weighed for about 74% and 95% of its neighbour's imports and exports, respectively (Kumar 2011, 78), let alone substantial investments (hydroelectricity, etc.) (Bisht 2010, 350–1).

However, New Delhi's reach gradually declined. From the mid-2000s onwards, episodic Sino-Bhutanese border talks left Indian leaders 'livid in anger' (Fernandez, 2005). New Delhi worried that a deal could expose the Siliguri Corridor that linked India's mainland to its isolated northeastern states (Bisht 2010, 351). Its anxiety deepened as Beijing developed its local economic presence and evoked a normalization with Thimphu 'without India's knowledge' in June 2012 (Saklani and Tortajada 2016). Many saw the interruption of Indian subsidies of cooking gas and kerosene right before Bhutan's July 2013 elections as a sanction (Malik and Sheikh, 48). Yet this move strained the bilateral relationship without derailing China's influence.

At the end of the UPA rule, India still capitalized on huge geographic advantages, i.e. the fact that Nepal and Bhutan were landlocked and that the Himalayan barrier complicated their access to China. However, despite some missteps, there was little that UPA leaders could do to thwart Beijing's economic might, not to mention Kathmandu and Thimpu's structural drive for autonomy.

Restoring the Relationship with Bangladesh

The UPA's successful policy vis-à-vis Bangladesh sharply departed from the results of previous Indian governments. The honeymoon that followed Dhaka's independence had abruptly ended after Mujibur Rahman's assassination in 1975 during a military coup and the local rise of an Islamic ideology (Jain 2010, 91). The relationship had declined further after Bangladesh operated a rapprochement with Pakistan and China, complained about unfair water sharing, and mistreated its massive Hindu community (Datta and Srinivasan 2015, 391). However, New Delhi's chief priority in the following years was to counter the insurgents and terrorists (Jamat-ul-Mujahideen, etc.) who used its neighbour's territory to attack India—sometimes with Islamabad's support (Pant 2011, 90–91).

This preoccupation still prevailed under the UPA. Bangladesh's instability worsened during the rule of Khaleda Zia's BNP (Bangladesh Nationalist Party), with 15,000 victims of 'killings, rapes, torture, arson... land-grab and damage to property' in 2001–6 (Destradi 2012a, 134–5). At that point, the country reportedly counted 50,000 Islamists, some of them nurtured by national political forces (Pant 2011, 87). In August 2006, Foreign Secretary Shyam Saran tried to convince Prime Minister Zia to crack down on local ISI-sponsored camps (Jain 2010, 94). But these efforts remained fruitless until the BNP government fell after attempts to rig the 2006 Parliamentary elections.

The dialogue improved under Fakhruddin Ahmed's caretaker government. However, the real strides took place after the election of the Awami League's Sheikh Hasina (Mujibur Rahman's daughter) in December 2008. Despite an unsuccessful mutiny fomented by paramilitary forces (with the complicity of some BNP members) in February 2009 (Pant 2016, 94), the two governments seized 'a historic opportunity to write a new chapter in [the India-Bangladesh] relationship' (_ 2010, 756). Dhaka cracked down on insurgent and terrorist leaders (United Liberation Front of Assam in 2009, Jamaat-ul-Mujahideen in 2010) (Mazumdar 2015, 98; Pant 2011, 91). India and Bangladesh bolstered their defence ties (Wagner 2018, 19). During her visit to New Delhi in January 2010, Sheikh Hasina and Manmohan Singh signed a Memorandum of Understanding on the bilateral relationship (Pattanaik 2015, 220). Finally, thanks to New Delhi's concessions, trade between the two countries climbed from $1 billion to $6.6 billion in 2001–14 (Datta and Srinivasan 2015, 393; Pant, 2016, p. 103), although Dhaka's deficit remained a salient issue (Pant 2011, 90).

The picture was mixed in other domains. The management of the 54 rivers crossing the border remained a 'highly emotive' topic in Bangladesh (Datta and Srinivasan 2015, 389). New Delhi and Dhaka found an agreement on the Teesta River in September 2011 but the regional government of West Bengal, concerned about diminishing water volumes, prevented its ratification (Gokarn and Sajjanhar 2014, 21). Connectivity also remained suboptimal. Hoping to access its isolated northeastern states via Bangladesh, New Delhi extended a $1 billion credit to its neighbour in August 2010 (Schaffer and Schaffer 2016, 277). Yet, worried about its national sovereignty, Dhaka refused to sign a transit agreement (Datta and Srinivasan 2015, 390). Illegal immigration also fuelled tensions (Sullivan, 2007). While New Delhi strived to fight terrorism, smuggling, and intercommunal tensions, Bangladeshi leaders criticized its construction of a fence and the heavy-handed behaviour of its Border Security Forces. The border itself remained disputed. In September 2011, the two countries signed a protocol to their 1974 Land Boundary Agreement (LBA). However, Assamese and West Bengali political parties opposed it due to fear of territorial losses (Datta and Srinivasan 2015, 389). Finally, China's trade with Dhaka, which overtook New Delhi's in 2004, kept growing at a fast pace (Kashem 2016, 21).

However, compared to the low point reached in the early 2000s, the improvement of India-Bangladesh relations under the UPA rule was no less than dramatic. It also enabled major breakthroughs (like the LBA's ratification) in the following years.

Laying Claim on the Indian Ocean

Like their predecessors, UPA leaders conceived their maritime ambitions unambiguously: the Indian Ocean 'must be, and must be seen to be, "India's ocean" ' (Brewster 2018, 18). This agenda was designed to address the country's skyrocketing dependency on oil and gas from the Persian Gulf (Hornat 2016, 431–2), 'establish a forward defense perimeter', and facilitate India's ascent as a great power (Brewster 2018, 19–20).

Taking those ambitions to new heights, Manmohan Singh's government endorsed the April 2004 Maritime Doctrine, which stated that India's navy could potentially assume 'control of the choke points [and use them as] bargaining chip in the international power game' (Holmes 2011, 159). The 2007 Maritime Military Strategy confirmed 'a shift ... from a small coastal-hugging passive brown-water fleet to a larger ocean-going active blue water fleet capable of power projection' (Scott 2015, 468). At that point, New Delhi planned to possess three aircraft carriers, 60 'major combatants', and 400 aircraft by 2022 (Holmes 2011, 164).

This dynamic largely derived from concerns about Beijing's attempt to 'strategically encircle' India (Pant 2016, 185). Predicting a decline of America's regional commitment and an increase in the 'disparity' between the Chinese and Indian economies, the UPA made overtures to Beijing (Chaudhuri 2018, 56–59), even offering 'to keep open vital sea lanes between the Middle East and Asia' (Lamont and Dyer, 2010). Yet, China consistently declined these overtures. New Delhi's anxiety grew further in 2008 when Beijing mounted anti-piracy efforts in the Horn of Africa, produced an unprecedently ambitious White Paper (Chaudhuri 2018, 57–61), and developed its influence in Sri Lanka and the Maldives.

Following its disastrous intervention in Sri Lanka's civil war in the late 1980s, India had adopted a hands-off approach in the process that prompted the 2002 ceasefire between Colombo and the Tamil Tigers (LTTE) (Mazumdar 2012, 287). Yet the conflict resumed soon after the UPA's return to power. New Delhi encouraged Sri Lanka to seek a diplomatic solution and to minimize civilian casualties. This stance was partly driven by domestic politics: South India counted 50 million ethnic Tamils (Mazumdar 2015, 109) and Tamil Nadu's DMK (Dravida Munnetra Kazhagam) was the government's third largest party during the UPA's first mandate (DeVotta 2010, 48).

However, throughout those years, India trained Colombo's security forces, offered 'non-lethal weapons [and] ships' (ICG 2011, 4), and provided intelligence on LTTE's logistical lines (Suryanarayan 2015, 418). Several motives explained this ambivalence. First, the UPA quickly concluded that the Tamil Tigers were 'the intransigent party … as well as a threat' (Sridharan 2016, 63). Second, Colombo's chances of victory became more obvious over time (ICG 2011, 4). Third, Indian leaders believed Sri Lanka's promises about a future devolution of power (ICG 2011, 6). Most importantly, New Delhi feared that Colombo would seek assistance elsewhere, as National Security Advisor M.K. Narayanan recognized in 2007: 'We are the big power in this region […] We strongly believe that whatever requirements the Sri Lankan government has, they should come to us and we will give them what we think is necessary. We do not favour them going to China or Pakistan or any other country'

(ICG 2011, 15). Yet, worried about human rights violations and the co-hesion of the UPA coalition, Manmohan Singh stuck to his promise that India would not supply Colombo with 'lethal offensive military hard-ware' (_ 2006c).

Following the end of the conflict, UPA leaders set to enhance bilateral ties. India was Sri Lanka's main commercial partner (Mazumdar 2015, 119) and investor ($160 million in 2012) (Sridharan 2016, 65). Its finan-cial and development assistance reached $1.5 billion in 2009–10 (ICG 2011, 2). Further, the two countries bolstered military cooperation, which comprised an annual defence dialogue and joint naval exercises (Wagner 2018, 22–23). Yet despite New Delhi's insistence on 'the urgent and imperative need for... genuine national reconciliation', Mahinda Rajapaksa, reelected president of Sri Lanka in a landslide victory in January 2010, refused to make genuine concessions (Krishna 2011b, 941; Behuria 2018, 169). In March 2012, India supported a UN Human Rights Commission resolution to investigate past atrocities. But these pressures incited Rajapaksa to get closer to China (Mazumdar 2015, 126; Sridharan 2016, 65). Beijing had already increased its influence in previous years by exploiting India's inability to deliver offensive weapons and U.S. sanctions against Colombo's human rights violations (_, 26 April 2009). In fact, its booming assistance had played a key role in the LTTE's demise. China's economic clout was just as impressive. As of 2009, Beijing emerged as Sri Lanka's largest aid donor ($1.2 billion committed) and invested in major projects, including in the port of Hambantota, in which Colombo had offered New Delhi to invest a few years earlier (ICG 2011, 18–19). Worse, China's skyrocketing trade with Sri Lanka would overtake India's by 2016 (Behuria 2018, 174).

Similar challenges surfaced in the Maldives, with whom New Delhi had maintained close ties since Nov. 1988, the date of its intervention to pre-vent a coup against the autocratic President Maumoon Abdul Gayoom (Mazumdar 2015, 168). The two countries developed their bilateral eco-nomic relationship and their cooperation against global warming (Bussa 2017, 94; Kumar 2012, 104). Moreover, defence ties expanded to encom-pass Male's partial integration into India's 'Southern Naval Command' and joint efforts against 'piracy, maritime security and terrorism' (Poplin 2013, 4). UPA leaders also regularly expressed their commitment to 'a deeper and stronger partnership' (Krishna 2011a, 766).

However, China, which opened its first local embassy in 2011, made growing strides during those years. UPA leaders were relieved to see the winner of the November 2013 presidential elections, Abdulla Yameen Abdul Gayoom, choose New Delhi for his first state visit (Gupta 2014, 2). But Beijing kept increasing its economic reach, as illustrated by Male's cancellation of a contract awarded to an Indian company to develop the country's main airport—and which would later be awarded to a Chinese competitor (Robinson, 2012). Despite the Maldivian government's reassurances, New Delhi grew increasingly concerned about China's local influence (Philip 2013).

Those developments unfolded as Sino-Indian tensions worsened. In 2013, the UPA started presenting itself as a 'net security provider' (Chaudhuri 2018, 56–57) for the region. This reorientation was encouraged by the United States, which saw India as the linchpin of its 'pivot-rebalance' towards the Asia-Pacific (Hornat 2016, 435). New Delhi accelerated its naval buildup and extended its diplomatic engagement. In 2013–4, it convinced the Maldives, Seychelles, Sri Lanka, and Mauritius to join a Maritime Security Cooperation Framework for 'counter-terrorism and anti-piracy, as well as intelligence sharing on illegal maritime activities' (_ 2014b, ii). It also tried to develop the IONS (Indian Ocean Naval Symposium), created in 2008, which excludes Beijing (Hornat 2016, 433).

Yet this activism happened after 'long delays and cost escalations'. As of 2014, 60% of India's vessels were reportedly 'approaching obsolescence' (_ 2014b, i). More broadly, facing financial limitations, domestic problems, other commitments across the world, and ever-pervasive threats on land, 'the top political leadership never had the time or inclination to lay out a clear set of goals in regard to the Indian Ocean' (Mohan 2015, 2). Meanwhile, the announcement of the 'Maritime Silk Road' in late 2013 suggested that China was now playing in a league of its own.

Reviving Regional Cooperation through SAARC

India's efforts to develop the South Asian Association for Regional Cooperation during the UPA years encountered the same obstacles as in the past. Since its creation in 1985, SAARC had always been a weak institution, eluding contentious issues and muddling through the tensions that divided its members (Chatterjee Miller and Gopalaswamy 2016). Although New Delhi adopted a more lenient stance in the post-Cold War era, it still chafed at its neighbours' constant efforts to 'multilateraliz[e] what were fundamentally … bilateral issues' (Padukone 2014, 83). As of the mid-2000s, intra-regional commerce stood at a paltry 4.7%, far behind the 26% reached by ASEAN (the Association of Southeast Asian Nations) (Dubey 2010, 55).

The UPA tried to advance a new vision. Prime Minister Singh expressed his regret 'that regional … cooperation … ha[d] fallen far short of … expectations and the dreams of [the] founding fathers'. As he explained, South Asian states could not 'be the crossroads of Asia [and] remain disconnected within [their] own region' (_ 2005b, 352). India regularly underscored its determination 'to accept asymmetrical responsibilities, including opening up her markets … without insisting on reciprocity' (Sidhu and Sandhu 2014, 6).

Yet the UPA never managed to break the standstill. As early as 2005, Foreign Secretary Shyam Saran criticized attempts to 'seek association with countries outside the region … in a barely disguised effort to "counterbalance" India' (Saran 2005). A few months later, joint efforts by Pakistan, Bangladesh, and Nepal forced New Delhi to accept Beijing's obtention of an observer status, a blow only partially compensated by Japan's obtention of a similar status (Bussa 2017, 134). In the following years, India struggled to resist their lobbying for China's accession as full member (Madan 2014, 11–12). But New Delhi's rivalry with Pakistan and lingering mistrust with other neighbours sufficed to hamper SAARC's progress anyway (Mohan 2016). Dismal infrastructures, persistent tariffs, and the small size of most local economies compounded those difficulties, which torpedoed the implementation of the Free Trade Area agreement negotiated in 2006 (Kumar 2010, 103). When the UPA left power, SAARC accounted for barely 5.6% of India's exports and 0.5% of its imports (Chowdhury 2014). New Delhi's interest in alternative bodies, like the Bay of Bengal Initiative for Multi Sectoral Technical and Economic Cooperation (BIMSTEC), met equally disappointing results (_, March 31, 2015). Most regional states 'ha[d still] not even accepted the goal of regional economic integration' (Dubey 2010, 60).

Conclusion

The UPA era was characterized by growing expectations about New Delhi's rise, which dictated looking beyond South Asia, its traditional sphere of influence. However, India could not thrive globally without ensuring stability, building economic connectivity, and curbing the influence of great powers in its own neighbourhood. While these objectives were not new, Manmohan Singh's government contributed to important evolutions. First, using economic and diplomatic engagement, New Delhi broke with many (albeit not all) of the overbearing policies that strained relations with its South Asian neighbours in the past. Second, it carefully calibrated its policy vis-à-vis the Afghan War.

Ultimately, promises did not fully materialize, largely because of Islamabad's incendiary policies, mistrust with other neighbours, India's financial limitations, its political and bureaucratic constraints, and China's skyrocketing power. Yet UPA leaders demonstrated a sophisticated understanding of South Asia's history and deftly navigated its complex geopolitical environment. They often made the most of limited resources and adverse circumstances, steered away from a potentially catastrophic conflict with Pakistan, and started to position India as a more inclusive power, a security provider, and a major economic partner. All things considered, these were no small achievements.

References

Abhyankar, Rajendra M. (2015), 'Afghanistan after the 2014 U.S. Drawdown: The Transformation of India's Policy', *Asian Survey*, Vol. 55, Issue 2 (2015): 371–97.

Arndt, Michael (2013), *India's Foreign Policy and Regional Multilateralism* (London: Palgrave Macmillan, 2013).

Bagchi, Indrani (2014), 'India Ready to Revise 1950 Friendship Treaty with Nepal', *The Times of India*, 4 Aug. 2014, https://timesofindia.indiatimes.com/india/India-ready-to-revise-1950-friendship-treaty-with-Nepal/articleshow/39577338.cms

Behuria, A.K. (2018), 'How Sri Lanka Walked into a Debt Trap, and the Way Out', *Strategic Analysis*, Vol. 42, Issue 2 (2018): 168–78.

Bisht, Mehda (2010), 'India–Bhutan Relations: From Developmental Cooperation to Strategic Partnership', *Strategic Analysis*, Vol. 34, Issue 3 (2010): 350–3.

Brewster, David (2018), 'A Contest of Status and Legitimacy in the Indian Ocean', in ed. David Brewster, *India and China at Sea: Competition for Naval Dominance in the Indian Ocean* (New Delhi: Oxford University Press, 2018), pp. 10–38.

Bussa, Laxminarayana (2017), *India-Maldives Relations* (New Delhi: Avni Publications, 2017).

Chandra, Vishal (2012), 'Afghanistan: Likely Scenarios and India's Options', in eds. Ruhel Dahiya and Ashok K. Behuria, *India's Neighborhood: Challenges in the Next Two Decades* (New Delhi: Institute for Defence Studies and Analyses, Pentagon Press, 2012), pp. 1–18.

Chatterjee Miller, Manjari and Bharath Gopalaswamy (2016), 'SAARC Is Dead; Long Live SAARC', *The Diplomat*, 5 Nov. 2016, https://thediplomat.com/2016/11/saarc-is-dead-long-live-saarc/

Chaudhuri, Pramit Pal (2018), 'The China Factor in Indian Ocean Policy of the Modi and Singh Government', in ed. David Brewster, *India and China at Sea: Competition for Naval Dominance in the Indian Ocean* (New Delhi: Oxford University Press, 2018), pp. 56–74.

Chowdhury, Jhinuk (2014), 'Is There Any Hope for SAARC?', *The Diplomat*, 8 Dec. 2014, https://thediplomat.com/2014/12/is-there-any-hope-for-saarc/

Cohen, Stephen P. (2015), 'India and the Region', in eds. David M. Malone, C. Raja Mohan and Srinath Raghavan, *The Oxford Handbook of Indian Foreign Policy* (New York: Oxford University Press, 2015), pp. 341–355.

D'Souza, Shanthie Mariet (2013), 'India's Evolving Policy Contours towards Post-2014 Afghanistan', *Journal of South Asian Development*, Vol. 8, Issue 2 (2013): 185–207.

Dalrymple, William (2013), *A Deadly Triangle: Afghanistan, Pakistan, and India* (New York: Brookings Institution Press, 2013).

Datta, Sreeradha and Krishnan Srinivasan (2015), 'Bangladesh', in eds. David M. Malone, C. Raja Mohan and Srinath Raghavan, *The Oxford Handbook of Indian Foreign Policy* (New York: Oxford University Press, 2015), pp. 384–397.

Deol, Jivan (2010), 'How Nepal Sums Up the India-China Story', *Financial Express (India)*, 8 Jan. 2010, https://www.financialexpress.com/archive/hownepalsumsup theindiachinastory/564675/

Destradi, Sandra (2012a), *Indian Foreign and Security Policy in South Asia: Regional Power Strategies* (Milton Park, Abingdon, Oxon, New York: Routledge, 2012).

Destradi, Sandra (2012b), 'India as a Democracy Promoter? New Delhi's Involvement in Nepal's Return to Democracy', *Democratization*, Vol. 19, Issue 2 (2012): 286–311.

Destradi, Sandra (2014), 'India: A Reluctant Partner for Afghanistan', *The Washington Quarterly*, Vol. 37, Issue 2 (2014): 103–117.

DeVotta, Neil (2010), 'When Individuals, States, and Systems Collide: India's Foreign Policy towards Sri Lanka', in ed. Sumit Ganguly, *India's Foreign Policy: Retrospect and Prospect* (New Delhi: Oxford University Press, 2010), pp. 32–61.

Dubey, Muchkund (2010), 'Regional Economic Integration in South Asia: The Development of Institutions and the Role of Politics', in eds. Rafiq Dossani, Daniel C. Schneider and Vikram Sood, *Does South Asia Exist? Prospects for Regional Integration* (Stanford, CA: Walter H. Shorenstein Asia Pacific Research Center; Washington D.C.: Brookings Institution, 2010), pp. 53–84.

Economic Times (2009), 'India Upset with China over Sri Lanka Crisis', *India Times*, 26 Apr. 2009, https://economictimes.indiatimes.com/news/politics-and-nation/india-upset-with-china-over-sri-lanka-crisis/articleshow/4450765.cms?from=mdr

Fernandez, Percy (2005), 'China Inching Closer to India through Bhutan', *The Times of India*, 2 Aug. 2005, https://timesofindia.indiatimes.com/india/China-inching-closer-to-India-through-Bhutan/articleshow/1187893.cms

Ganguly, Sumit (2015a), *Indian Foreign Policy* (New Delhi: Oxford University Press, 2015).

Ganguly, Sumit (2015b), 'India's National Security', in eds. David M. Malone, C. Raja Mohan and Srinath Raghavan, *The Oxford Handbook of Indian Foreign Policy* (New York: Oxford University Press, 2015), pp. 145–159.

Gokarn, Subir and Anuradha Sajjanhar (2014), 'Turning Water Challenges into Opportunities', in eds. 'Reinvigorating SAARC: Opportunities and Challenges', *Brookings Institution*, Nov. 2014, pp. 21–22, https://www.brookings.edu/wp-content/uploads/2014/11/saarc_briefing-book.pdf

Graham, Sarah (2014), 'Manmohan Singh's Legacy (Part 2): Foreign Policy', *The Interpreter*, 19 May 2014, https://www.lowyinstitute.org/the-interpreter/manmohan-singhs-legacy-part-2-foreign-policy

Gupta, Arvind (2014), 'India and Maldives: Ties Must Be Consolidated', Institute for Defense Studies and Analyses (IDSA), 13 Jan. 2014, pp. 1–5, https://idsa.in/system/files/PB_India-Maldives_agupta.pdf

Hall, Ian (2016), 'Multialignment and Indian Foreign Policy under Narendra Modi', *The Commonwealth Journal of International Affairs*, Vol. 15, Issue 3 (2016): 271–86.

Hanauer, Larry and Peter Chalk (2012), 'India's and Pakistan's Strategies in Afghanistan: Implications for the United States and the Region', *Rand Corporation*, 2012, pp. 1–72, https://www.rand.org/content/dam/rand/pubs/occasional_papers/2012/RAND_OP387.pdf

Holmes, James R. (2011), 'Looking South: Indian Ocean', in ed. David Scott, *Handbook of India's International Relations* (London, New York: Routledge, 2011), pp. 156–166.

Hornat, Jan (2016), 'The Power Triangle in the Indian Ocean: China, India and the United States', *Cambridge Review of International Affairs*, Vol. 29, Issue 2 (2016): 425–43.

Jain, B.M. (2010), *India in the New South Asia: Strategic, Military, and Economic Concerns in the Age of Nuclear Diplomacy* (London: Tauris Academic Studies, 2010).

Jaishankar, Dhruva (2013), 'Does "South Asia" Exist?', *Foreign Policy*, 26 Nov. 2013, https://foreignpolicy.com/2013/11/26/does-south-asia-exist/

Jaiswal, Pramod (2016), 'Nepal between India and China: Demystifying Big Powers Interplay', in eds. Jaiswal, Pramod and Kochhar, Geeta, *India-China-Nepal: Decoding Trilateralism* (New Delhi: G.B. Books, 2016), pp. 81–106.

Jha, Prashant (2012), 'A Nepali Perspective on International Involvement in Nepal', in eds. Sebastian von Einsiedel, David M. Malone, and Suman Pradahn, *Nepal in Transition: from People's War to Fragile Peace* (New York: Cambridge University Press, 2012), pp. 332–360.

Karzai, Hamid and Manmohan Singh (2010), 'Statements to the Press by Prime Minister Dr. Manmohan Singh and Afghan President Hamid Karzai', New Delhi, 26 Apr. 2010, in ed. Avtar Singh Bhasin, *India's Foreign Relations – 2010 Documents* (New Delhi: Geetika Publishers, in cooperation with the Public Diplomacy Division of the Ministry of External Affairs, 2011), pp. 731–733, http://www.mea.gov.in/Images/pdf/Indias_Foreign_Relations_2010.pdf

Kashem, Md. Abdul (2016), 'Recent Issues in Bangladesh-India Relations: A Bangladeshi Perspective', *Space and Culture*, Vol. 4, No. 1 (Jun. 2016): 19–24.

Kavitha, K.K. (2016), 'The Changing Paradigm of India-Nepal Relations: Problems and Prospects', *Journal of Research in Business and Management*, Vol. 4, Issue 5 (2016): 10–15.

Keenan, Alan and K. Mudiyanse (pseudonym) (2011), 'India and Sri Lanka after the LTTE', *International Crisis Group*, Asia Report 206, 23 Jun. 2011, https://www.files. ethz.ch/isn/130395/206%20India%20and%20Sri%20Lanka%20after%20the%20 LTTE.pdf

Khan, Feroz Hassan (2010), 'Security Impediments to Regionalism in South Asia', in eds. Rafiq Dossani, Daniel C. Schneider and Vikram Sood, *Does South Asia Exist? Prospects for Regional Integration* (Stanford, CA: Walter H. Shorenstein Asia Pacific Research Center; Washington DC: Brookings Institution, 2010), pp. 227–250.

Khilnani, Sunil (2015), 'India's Rise: The Search for Wealth and Power in the Twenty-First Century', in eds. David M. Malone, C. Raja Mohan and Srinath Raghavan, *The Oxford Handbook of Indian Foreign Policy* (New York: Oxford University Press, 2015), pp. 681–698.

Krishna, S.M. (2011a), 'Remarks by External Affairs Minister S.M. Krishna at Joint Press Conference at Male', 28 Jul. 2011, in ed. Avtar Singh Bhasin, *India's Foreign Relations – 2011 Documents* (New Delhi: Geetika Publishers, in co-operation with the Public Diplomacy Division of the Ministry of External Affairs, 2011), pp. 765–766, http://www.mea.gov.in/Images/pdf/India-foreign-relation-2011.pdf

Krishna, S.M. (2011b), Statement (Excerpts) by External Affairs Minister S.M. Krishna in the Lok Sabha on 'The Steps Taken by GOI for Relief and Resettlement of Tamils in Sri Lanka', New Delhi, 26 Aug. 2011, in ed. Avtar Singh Bhasin, *India's Foreign Relations – 2011 Documents* (New Delhi: Geetika Publishers, in cooperation with the Public Diplomacy Division of the Ministry of External Affairs, 2011), pp. 940–945, http://www.mea.gov.in/Images/pdf/India-foreign-relation-2011.pdf

Kumar, Anand (2012), 'Maldives: Harmonising Efforts to Mitigate Adverse Impacts of Climate Change and Achieve Growth', in eds. Ruhel Dahiya and Ashok K. Behuria, *India's Neighborhood: Challenges in the Next Two Decades* (New Delhi: Institute for Defence Studies and Analyses, Pentagon Press, 2012), pp. 95–109.

Kumar, Rajiv (2010), 'Is a Successful SAARC Imperative for India?', in eds. Rafiq Dossani, Daniel C. Schneider and Vikram Sood, *Does South Asia Exist? Prospects for Regional Integration* (Stanford, CA: Walter H. Shorenstein Asia Pacific Research Center; Washington DC: Brookings Institution, 2010), pp. 99–114.

Kumar, Satish (2011), 'India and the Himalayan States', ed. David Scott, *Handbook of India's International Relations* (London, New York: Routledge, 2011), pp. 70–82.

Kumar, Sumit (2016), 'A Turnaround in India-Nepal Relations', *The Diplomat*, 8 Mar. 2016, https://thediplomat.com/2016/03/a-turnaround-in-india-nepal-relations/

Lama, Mahendra P. (2010), 'Bhutan, Nepal, and SAARC: Harnessing Old Resources with New Instruments', in eds. Rafiq Dossani, Daniel C. Schneider and Vikram Sood, *Does South Asia Exist? Prospects for Regional Integration* (Stanford, CA: Walter H. Shorenstein Asia Pacific Research Center; Washington D.C.: Brookings Institution, 2010), pp. 115–150.

Lamont, James and Geoff Dyer (2010), 'India Offers to Protect China Oil Shipments', *Financial Times*, 17 Feb. 2010, https://www.ft.com/content/6788f896-1be8-11df-a5e1-00144feab49a

Madan, Tanvi (2014), 'A Role for China in SAARC', in eds. 'Reinvigorating SAARC: Opportunities and Challenges', *Brookings Institution*, Nov. 2014, pp. 11–12, https://www.brookings.edu/wp-content/uploads/2014/11/saarc_briefing-book.pdf

Malik, Arif Hussain and Nazir Ahmad Sheikh (2016), 'Changing Dynamics of Indo-Bhutan Relations: Implications for India', *International Journal of Political Science and Development*, Vol. 4, Issue 2 (Feb. 2016): 44–53.

Mazumdar, Arijit (2012), 'India's South Asia Policy in the Twenty-First Century: New Approach, Old Strategy', *Contemporary politics*, Vol. 3, Issue 3 (Sept. 2012): 286–302.

Mazumdar, Arijit (2015), *Indian Foreign Policy in Transition: Relations with South Asia* (Abingdon, Oxon, NY: Routledge, 2015).

Miglani, Sanjeev (2014), 'India Turns to Russia to Help Supply Arms to Afghan Forces', *Reuters*, 30 Apr. 2014, https://www.reuters.com/article/us-india-afghanistan-arms/india-turns-to-russia-to-help-supply-arms-to-afghan-forces-idUSBREA3T0J320140430

Mohan, C. Raja (2004), *Crossing the Rubicon: The Shaping of India's New Foreign Policy* (New York: Palgrave Macmillan, 2004).

Mohan, C. Raja (2015), 'Modi and the Indian Ocean: Restoring India's Sphere of Influence', *ISAS Insights*, No. 277, 20 Mar. 2015, pp. 1–7, https://www.files.ethz.ch/isn/189804/ISAS_Insights_No._277_-_Modi_and_the_Indian_Ocean_20032015163047.pdf

Mohan, C. Raja (2016), 'Raja Mandala: SAARC Minus One', *The Indian Express*, 29 Sep. 2016, https://indianexpress.com/article/opinion/columns/saarc-islamabad-summit-india-pakistan-regional-cooperation-3055070/

Mullen, Rani D. (2016), 'India-Afghanistan Relations', in ed. Ganguly, Sumit, *Engaging the World: Indian Foreign Policy since 1947* (New Delhi: Oxford University Press, 2016), pp. 105–132.

Muni, S.D. (2012), 'Bringing the Maoists Down from the Hills: India's Role', in eds. SebastianVon Einsiedel, David M. Malone and Suman Pradahn, *Nepal in Transition: from People's War to Fragile Peace* (New York: Cambridge University Press, 2012), pp. 313–331.

Muni, S.D. (2015), 'India's Nepal Policy', in eds. David M. Malone, C. Raja Mohan and Srinath Raghavan, *The Oxford Handbook of Indian Foreign Policy* (New York: Oxford University Press, 2015), pp. 398–411.

Nayak, Nihar (2012), 'Nepal: Issues and Concerns in India-Nepal Relations', in eds. Ruhel Dahiya and Ashok K. Behuria, *India's Neighborhood: Challenges in the Next Two Decades* (New Delhi: Institute for Defence Studies and Analyses, Pentagon Press, 2012), pp. 137–162.

Padukone, Neil (2014), *Beyond South Asia: India's Strategic Evolution and the Reintegration of the Subcontinent* (New York: Bloomsbury Academic, 2014).

Paliwal, Avinash (2017), *My Enemy's Enemy: India in Afghanistan from the Soviet Invasion to the U.S. Withdrawal* (London: Hurst & Company, 2017).

Pandit, Rajat (2009), 'China Inroads into Nepal Army Gives India the Jitters', *The Times of India*, 7 May 2009, https://timesofindia.indiatimes.com/india/

China-inroads-into-Nepal-army-gives-India-the-jitters/articleshow/4489697. cms

Pant, Harsh V. (2011), 'India's Relations with Bangladesh', in ed. David Scott, *Handbook of India's International Relations* (London, New York: Routledge, 2011), pp. 83–94.

Pant, Harsh V. (2012), *India's Changing Afghanistan Policy: Regional and Global Implications* (Carlisle, PA: Strategic Studies Institute, U.S. Army War College, 2012), http://ssi.armywarcollege.edu/pdffiles/pub1141.pdf

Pant, Harsh V. (2015), 'Turmoil in India-Nepal Ties as China Moves In', *The Diplomat*, 3 Nov. 2015, https://thediplomat.com/2015/11/turmoil-in-india-nepal-ties-as-china-moves-in/

Pant, Harsh V. (2016), *Indian Foreign Policy: An Overview* (Manchester: Manchester University Press, 2016).

Patel, Sneha (2017), 'A New Journey in the New Context: Nepal-India Relations', *IOSR Journal of Humanities and Social Science*, Vol. 22, Issue 9 (Sep. 2017): 73–79.

Pattanaik, Smruti (2015), 'India-Bangladesh Relations: Moving towards Greater Synergy', *Indian Foreign Affairs Journal*, Vol. 10, Issue 3 (Jul.–Sep. 2015): 203–254.

Pavitran K.S. (2017), 'Faultlines in India's Neighborhood Policy and Nepal's Quest for Identity', in ed. Vinodan, C., *India's Foreign Policy and Diplomacy: Emerging Scenario and Challenges* (New Delhi: New Century Publications, 2017), pp. 103–115.

Poplin, Cody M. (2013), 'India-Maldives Brief', *Center for Policy Research*, 16 May 2013 (updated on 2 Dec. 2014), https://cprindia.org/briefsreports/india-maldives-brief/.

Rao, Nirupama (2010), 'Speech by Foreign Secretary Mrs. Nirupama Rao on Afghanistan-India-Pakistan Trialogue Organised by Delhi Policy Group', New Delhi, 13 Jun. 2010, in ed. Avtar Singh Bhasin, *India's Foreign Relations – 2010 Documents* (New Delhi: Geetika Publishers, in cooperation with the Public Diplomacy Division of the Ministry of External Affairs, 2011), pp. 734–740, http://www.mea.gov.in/Images/pdf/Indias_Foreign_Relations_2010.pdf

Robinson, J.J. (2012), 'Maldives Cancels GMR's $511 Million Airport Project', *Reuters*, 28 Nov. 2012, https://www.reuters.com/article/maldives-india-gmr/maldives-cancels-gmrs-511-million-airport-project-idINDEE8AR01Z20121128

Roy Chaudhury, Dipana (2014), 'India's Foreign Policy: With Landmark Deals, Manmohan Singh Government Promised Much, Delivered Little', *The Economic Times*, 23 Feb. 2014, https://economictimes.indiatimes.com/news/politics-and-nation/indias-foreign-policy-with-landmark-deals-manmohan-singh-government-promised-much-delivered-little/articleshow/30864051.cms

Saklani, Udisha and Cecilia Tortajada (2016), 'The China Factor in India–Bhutan Relations', *East Asia Forum*, 15 Oct. 2016, http://www.eastasiaforum.org/2016/10/15/the-china-factor-in-india-bhutan-relations/

Saran, Shyam (2005), 'Foreign Secretary Mr. Shyam Saran's Speech on "India and Its Neighbours" at the India International Centre (IIC)', New Delhi, 14 Feb. 2005, in ed. Avtar Singh Bhasin, *India's Foreign Relations, 2005 Documents* (New Delhi: Geetika Publishers, in cooperation with the Public Diplomacy Division of the Ministry of External Affairs, 2005), pp. 331–336, https://mea.gov.in/Uploads/PublicationDocs/186_foreign-relations-2005.pdf

Schaffer, Teresita C. and Howard B. Schaffer (2016), *India at the Global High Table: The Quest for Regional Primacy and Strategic Autonomy* (Washington D.C.: Brookings Institution Press, 2016).

Scott, David (2013), 'India's "Extended Neighborhood" Concept: Power Projection for a Rising power', in eds. Kanti P. Bajpai, Harsh V. Pant, *India's Foreign Policy: A Reader* (New Delhi: Oxford University Press, 2013), pp. 349–388.

Scott, David (2015), 'The Indian Ocean as India's Ocean', in eds. David M. Malone, C. Raja Mohan and Srinath Raghavan, *The Oxford Handbook of Indian Foreign Policy* (New York: Oxford University Press, 2015), pp. 466–480.

Sharma, Raghav (2011), 'India's Relations with Afghanistan', in ed. David Scott, *Handbook of India's International Relations* (London, New York: Routledge, 2011), pp. 107–117.

Shashank, Joshi (2014), 'India's Role in a Changing Afghanistan', *The Washington Quarterly*, Vol. 37, Issue 2 (2014): 87–102.

Sidhu, W.P.S. and Rohan Sandhu (2014), 'Reinvigorating SAARC', in eds. _, 'Reinvigorating SAARC: Opportunities and Challenges', *Brookings Institution*, Nov. 2014, pp. 5–7, https://www.brookings.edu/wp-content/uploads/2014/11/saarc_briefing-book.pdf

Sigdel, Anil (2018), 'China's Growing Footprint in Nepal: Challenges and Opportunities for India', *Observer Research Foundation*, Issue 260 (Oct. 2018), pp. 1–12, https://www.orfonline.org/research/chinas-growing-footprint-in-nepal-challenges-and-opportunities-for-india/

Sikri, Rajiv (2009), *Challenge and Strategy: Rethinking India's Foreign Policy* (New Delhi: SAGE Publications; Thousand Oaks, CA: Sage, 2009).

Singh, Bawa (2016), 'Changing Dynamics of Strategic Relationship between China and Nepal: Theorizing India's Concerns' in eds. Jaiswal, Pramod and Kochhar, Geeta, *India-China-Nepal: Decoding Trilateralism* (New Delhi: G.B. Books, 2016), pp. 107–118.

Singh, Manmohan (2005), Statement by Prime Minister Dr. Manmohan Singh at the 13th SAARC Summit, Dhaka, 12 Nov. 2005, in ed. Avtar Singh Bhasin, *India's Foreign Relations, 2005 Documents* (New Delhi: Geetika Publishers, in cooperation with the External Publicity Division of the Ministry of External Affairs, 2005), pp. 350–355, https://mea.gov.in/Uploads/PublicationDocs/186_foreign-relations-2005.pdf

Singh, Manmohan (2006), Prime Minister Dr. Manmohan Singh, 'Speech at the Banquet in Honour of Bangladesh Prime Minister Begum Khaleda Zia', New Delhi, 21 Mar. 2006, in ed. Avtar Singh Bhasin, *India's Foreign Relations, Documents 2006* (New Delhi: Geetika Publishers, in cooperation with the Public Diplomacy Division of the Ministry of External Affairs, 2007), pp. 694–695, http://www.mea.gov.in/images/pdf/main_2006.pdf

Singh, Manmohan and Sheikh Hasina (2010), 'Joint Communiqué issued on the Occasion of the Visit to India of Her Excellency Sheikh Hasina, Prime Minister of Bangladesh', New Delhi, 12 Jan. 2010, in ed. Avtar Singh Bhasin, *India's Foreign Relations – 2010 Documents* (New Delhi: Geetika Publishers, in cooperation with the Public Diplomacy Division of the Ministry of External Affairs, 2011), pp. 755–762, http://www.mea.gov.in/Images/pdf/Indias_Foreign_Relations_2010.pdf

Sridharan, Eswaran (2015), 'Rising or Constrained Power', in eds. David M. Malone, C. Raja Mohan and Srinath Raghavan, *The Oxford Handbook of Indian Foreign Policy* (New York: Oxford University Press, 2015), pp. 699–712.

Sridharan, Eswaran (2016), 'Indo-Sri Lanka Relations: Geopolitics, Domestic Politics, or Something More complex?' in ed. Ganguly, Sumit, *Engaging the World: Indian Foreign Policy since 1947* (New Delhi: Oxford University Press, 2016), pp. 49–75.

Staniland, Paul and Vipin Narang (2015), 'State and Politics', in eds. David M. Malone, C. Raja Mohan and Srinath Raghavan, *The Oxford Handbook of Indian Foreign Policy* (New York: Oxford University Press, 2015), pp. 205–218.

Strategic Comments (2014b), 'Challenges for India's New Naval Chief', *Strategic Comments*, Vol. 20, Issue 4 (2014): i–ii.

Sullivan, Tim (2007), 'India Seals Itself Off from Bangladesh', *Associated Press*, 25 Jun. 2007, https://oklahoman.com/article/3070306/india-seals-itself-off-from-bangladesh?

Suryanarayan, V. (2015), 'India-Sri Lanka Equation: Geography as Opportunity', in eds. David M. Malone, C. Raja Mohan and Srinath Raghavan, *The Oxford Handbook of Indian Foreign Policy* (New York: Oxford University Press, 2015), pp. 412–423.

Taneja, Kabir (2017), 'India and the Afghan Taliban: Can New Delhi Contribute to an Afghan Political Solution', *The Diplomat*, 30 Nov. 2017, https://thediplomat.com/2017/11/india-and-the-afghan-taliban/

The Hindu (2015), 'BIMSTEC Is Unlikely to Move Forward', *The Hindu*, 31 Mar. 2015, https://www.thehindu.com/news/cities/kolkata/bimstec-is-unlikely-to-move-forward/article7051952.ece

The Times of India (2006b), 'Pak to US: Limit Indian Troops in Afghanistan', *The Times of India*, 12 Jun. 2006, https://timesofindia.indiatimes.com/india/Pak-to-US-Limit-Indian-troops-in-Afghanistan/articleshow/1636909.cms

The Times of India (2006c), 'Center Not to Provide Lethal Weapons to Sri Lanka', *The Times of India*, 18 Nov. 2006, https://timesofindia.indiatimes.com/india/Centre-not-to-provide-lethal-weapons-to-Sri-Lanka-PM/articleshow/465556.cms

The Times of India (2014a), 'India Rejects "Exit" Strategy for Afghanistan', 16 Jan. 2014, *The Times of India*, https://timesofindia.indiatimes.com/india/India-rejects-exit-strategy-for-Afghanistan/articleshow/28898763.cms

Thomas Philip, Joji (2013), 'Intelligence Agencies Fear China Is Trying to Encircle India via Tech Deals with Neighboring Nations', *The Economic Times*, 23 Jan. 2013, https://economictimes.indiatimes.com/news/company/corporate-trends/intelligence-agencies-fear-china-is-trying-to-encircle-india-via-tech-deals-with-neighbouring-nations/articleshow/18139596.cms

Wagner, Christian, (2018) 'India's Bilateral Security Relations in South Asia', *Strategic Analysis*, Vol. 42, Issue 1 (2018): 15–28.

Wolf, Siegfried O. (2018), 'Growing Nepal-China Security Cooperation and Its Ramifications for India', *South Asia Democratic Forum*, Issue 35, 10 Jan. 2018, pp. 1–11, https://www.sadf.eu/wp-content/uploads/2018/01/35FOCUS.N.35.Wolf_.pdf

8

India's 'Look East' Policy during the UPA Era

John D. Ciorciari

Introduction

For nearly two decades, India has pursued a 'Look East' policy, reflecting the critical role of Southeast Asia, East Asia, and the Pacific to India's security and prosperity. Launched informally by Prime Minister Narasimha Rao in 1991, the Look East policy initially focused on boosting economic engagement with Southeast Asia. By the time the United Progressive Alliance (UPA) government took office, the policy had broadened in geographic and thematic scope, extending to East Asia and encompassing a more prominent security pillar. India enjoyed rising eastbound trade, engaged in security cooperation with several Southeast Asian partners, and participated more actively in regional diplomacy organized around the Association of Southeast Asian Nations (ASEAN). Nevertheless, in most respects, India remained an external power looking into the extant Asia-Pacific regional order.

The UPA government changed that. It capitalized on India's rising capabilities, as well as uncertainty surrounding China's rise and waning U.S. primacy, to secure a pivotal position for India within an expanded regional order. After a breakthrough in relations with Washington, India emerged as a key node in a new maritime security framework organized with its fellow 'Quad' countries of Australia, Japan, and the United States. Diplomatically, India's overtures to the east translated into membership in the East Asia Summit (EAS) and a host of plurilateral forums that brought New Delhi more fully into the tent defined by Asia's regional institutional architecture. Despite ambivalence about further economic

John D. Ciorciari, *India's 'Look East' Policy during the UPA Era* In: *Forging New Partnerships, Breaching New Frontiers*. Edited by: Rejaul Karim Laskar, Oxford University Press. © Oxford University Press 2022.
DOI: 10.1093/oso/9780192868060.003.0008

liberalization, the UPA government advanced its trade and investment links in East and Southeast Asia significantly. In ideational terms, India retained a relatively autonomous voice—sometimes to the consternation of its partners, but in a manner that preserved a strong degree of diplomatic autonomy and corresponding capacity to exert influence as a 'swing state' on certain divisive issues.

The first section of this chapter reviews the origins of the Look East policy, and the second offers an overview of its early evolution. The third and principal section discusses the policy's development between 2004 and 2014. It examines the expansion of India's maritime security role, inclusion in key clubs and organizations defining the regional order, key bilateral ties with partners including the United States and Japan, and initiatives to strengthen connectivity with Southeast Asia. The third section also discusses India's positions on economic and political liberalization and regional responses to the UPA's approach to the Look East policy. The analysis illustrates how the UPA government positioned itself as a key player in the emergent Indo-Pacific order by redefining India's role in the regional security arena, securing a more prominent place within Asia's multilateral institutional framework, and raising its relevance in the economic domain. Although the term 'Indo-Pacific' did not come into widespread use until 2016, this chapter argues that the foundations for this re-conception of the regional order were laid largely during the UPA period.

Origins of the 'Look East' Policy

The Look East policy emerged in 1991 as the Rao government adjusted strategically to the end of the Cold War, embarked on a bold strategy of economic liberalization, and sought in both contexts to strengthen co-operation with the states of Southeast Asia. For decades, India's relations in the region had been marked by unfulfilled promise. Early Indian diplomatic initiatives had looked east. In the late 1940s, Indian leaders sought to spearhead a pan-Asian anti-colonial movement through the 1947 Asian Relations Conference and an ensuing diplomatic conference to promote Indonesian independence. India also supported Vietnam's independence and the emergence of the People's Republic of China.

Most notably, India played a central role at the Afro-Asian Conference in Bandung, which subsequently spawned the Non-Aligned Movement with Jawaharlal Nehru as a founding father.

Nevertheless, Cold War divisions and associated economic cleavages conspired against closer links to East and Southeast Asia. Sino-Indian rivalry undermined the pan-Asian project, particularly after the 1962 war and Indo-Pakistani wars of 1965 and 1971. India's tilt towards Moscow also estranged New Delhi politically from the five Westward-leaning states that formed the Association of Southeast Asian Nations (ASEAN) in 1967—Indonesia, Thailand, Malaysia, Singapore, and the Philippines. The nadir came after India's 1971 Friendship Treaty with the Soviet Union and the 1979 Vietnamese invasion of Cambodia. India became the sole non-communist state to recognize the Vietnam-backed regime in Phnom Penh, isolating New Delhi further from China, Japan, and the ASEAN states—all of which aligned against Moscow and Hanoi.

Economic links were also weak. Tense relations with Bangladesh and the insularity of the Burmese military regime impeded overland linkage to mainland Southeast Asia, and India's autarkic development model limited its economic appeal to the more dynamic maritime ASEAN economies. Moreover, the same colonial legacies that drove India's early pan-Asian initiatives impeded cooperation in some respects, as Indian and Southeast Asian leaders often focused more on engagement with Western metropoles than with one another.

The end of the Cold War brought about dramatic shifts in Indian foreign policy. The collapse of the Soviet Union meant the loss of an important source of arms, trade, aid, and political protection. The 1990–91 Gulf War also contributed to an economic crisis, as remittances from the Persian Gulf plunged, trade slumped, oil prices spiked, and Iraq defaulted on large debt payments to New Delhi. A bailout from the International Monetary Fund helped stem the crisis, but political instability and unrest in Northeast India and Jammu and Kashmir shook the state. When the Rao government took office in June 1991, it moved quickly to launch a liberalization program that would boost trade and attract much-needed foreign investment.

Rao's turn to Southeast Asia was driven both by economic and strategic imperatives. The crisis in the Gulf had shown the perils of dependency on Middle Eastern oil and gas, encouraging Indian outreach to producers such as Myanmar, Brunei, and Indonesia. By the early 1990s, the 'tiger' economies of Southeast Asia were racing ahead, and states like Thailand, Malaysia, and Singapore offered promising trade and investment partners and gateways to global markets. Strategically, looking east offered a way to address underdevelopment and unrest in Northeast India and to counter rising Chinese influence, particularly in Myanmar. It was also a means to connect to the Western-led institutional and security order in East Asia and thus to adapt to new realities after the loss of significant Soviet support.

Early Evolution of the Policy

The Look East policy was not formally announced through an official statement or white paper, and it did not amount to a clearly articulated strategic plan. Rather, journalists and scholars began applying the label to depict India's increased attention to Southeast Asia (see, e.g., Tasker 1993). The Rao government focused primarily on boosting trade and investment. In a 1993 speech in Singapore, Rao highlighted India's economic openness and said: 'The Asia-Pacific would be the springboard for our leap into the global market place' (Rao 1994, 31). To facilitate economic engagement, India plugged into ASEAN's multilateral diplomatic framework. In 1992, India and ASEAN established a Sectoral Dialogue Partnership on trade, tourism, and investment before graduating to a Full Dialogue Partnership at the ministerial level, which enabled Indian participation at ASEAN's annual Post Ministerial Conference. Together, they outlined a vision for enhanced cooperation in fields including science and technology, infrastructure, and human resource development. Security links also developed, albeit more embryonically. India began hosting biennial *Milan* naval exercises in the Andaman and Nicobar Islands in 1995 with Indonesia, Singapore, Thailand, and Sri Lanka. By 1996, the Indian Ministry of External Affairs had adopted the 'Look East' label, giving the policy a more official imprimatur (Indian Ministry of External Affairs 1996, 17).

The first phase of India's Look East policy continued after Rao and the Congress Party left office, through a series of short-lived governments beginning in 1996 and the longer incumbency of Atal Bihari Vajpayee of the conservative Bharatiya Janata Party from 1998 to 2004. Promoting trade and investment remained priorities. To promote links to its near abroad, India endorsed BIMSTEC, a regional initiative launched by Thailand in 1997 to foster cooperation between Bangladesh, India, Myanmar, Sri Lanka, and Thailand. By 2004, when the UPA government took office, India had sponsored Nepal and Bhutan for membership, and the acronym had evolved to signify the Bay of Bengal Initiative for Multi-Sectoral, Technical, and Economic Cooperation. The establishment of the Mekong-Ganga Cooperation forum in 2000 similarly aimed to connect India to the states of mainland Southeast Asia, including Laos, Cambodia, and Vietnam.

India also pressed to advance economic and diplomatic ties to the ASEAN region more broadly, and that effort paid dividends. India's annual two-way trade with Southeast Asian partners climbed from less than $3 billion in 1991 to over $12 billion by 2003, led by its trade with Singapore and Malaysia (ASEAN 2012). In 2002, India became only the fourth state to engage in an ASEAN Summit Level Partnership, following China, Japan, and South Korea. In 2003, at the second ASEAN-India Summit, the two sides inked a Framework Agreement on Comprehensive Economic Cooperation, paving the way towards an envisaged free trade deal. At the same time, India and China became the first two countries outside of Southeast Asia to sign the 1976 Treaty of Amity and Cooperation—the statement of ASEAN's bedrock principles. India's signature constituted an important commitment to the region by acknowledging the established rules of the road in Southeast Asia.

India's security ties to the east also grew, albeit modestly. In 1996, India received an important acknowledgement as a regional security actor when it was invited to join the ASEAN Regional Forum (ARF), created a few years prior to foster regional security cooperation. The U.S. government and others were initially wary of Indian membership, fearing it would complicate diplomacy, saddle the ARF with the intractable Indo-Pakistani feud, and dilute the forum's focus on Asia-Pacific security issues. However, ASEAN members came to view India as an important counterweight to China and issued the invitation without seeking U.S. approval (Ba 2009, 182). After the 9/11 attacks and the December 2001 attack on India's Parliament House by extremists linked to Pakistan, the Vajpayee government pursued stronger counter-terrorism cooperation in Southeast Asia, inking a joint declaration with ASEAN on that front in 2003 (Acharya 2006, 314).

By 2003, India thus had begun expanding the Look East policy beyond its initial focus on trade and investment in the ASEAN region. Minister of External Affairs Yashwant Sinha called this 'Phase 2' of the Look East policy, which entailed 'an expanded definition of "East" extending from Australia to China and East Asia with ASEAN at its core' and 'a shift in focus from exclusively economic issues to economic and security issues' (Sinha 2003). The path was thus paved for the UPA initiatives to follow.

The UPA Looks East, 2004–14

The UPA period saw the Look East policy take a clearer strategic form, including a much more prominent defence element, stronger partnerships with the United States and Japan, and deeper investment in regional markets and diplomatic institutions. A changing configuration of power in Asia and the Pacific created an opening for India to play a more pivotal role. India's rising economic and military capabilities made it an appealing partner to governments concerned about China's surging regional influence, uncertain about the durability of America's strategic commitment to Asia, and keen to hedge or diversify in their foreign relations. At the same time, India's dual identity as a democracy and champion for developing country interests made it a palatable partner to both ASEAN members and wealthy democracies such as Australia, Japan, and the United States.

Strong demand for India to play a larger regional role did not render the process automatic. To seize the opportunity, the UPA government had to make proactive choices, some of which were highly controversial and bore substantial costs. The UPA's decisions to accelerate rapprochement with the United States, conclude a landmark civil nuclear agreement, and embed India in close security collaboration with the United States and Japan brought domestic blowback, elicited anger from Beijing, and called into question India's longstanding commitments to autonomy, non-alignment, and respect for Westphalian sovereignty. India's continued engagement in regional trade initiatives also threatened to pry open the door to further infusion of foreign capital and competition, threatening long-protected sectors of the Indian economy and taking the country further down a much-debated path to liberalization. The Singh government's aims were to capitalize on India's opportunity for a much more substantial strategic, diplomatic and economic role in the region without forfeiting too much autonomy, opening too quickly, or losing its appeal as a partner to less democratic Asian neighbours. To a large extent, it succeeded.

Indo-U.S. Rapprochement and Indian Naval Outreach

The most dramatic changes came in the security arena. The UPA government conceived of the Look East policy through the prism of a modern incarnation of Kautilya's ancient *Mandala* concept. In a May 2007 speech, Foreign Secretary Shivshankar Menon outlined the UPA's approach, noting the changes in the international security order to justify a re-interpretation of India's longstanding policy of non-alignment. Menon described India's security as lying within 'a neighborhood of widening concentric circles'—a layered view towards the Pacific extending from 'Sri Lanka in South Asia to ASEAN and further East to Japan'. He noted that despite its multidirectional vulnerabilities, 'Geography gives India a unique position in the geo-politics of the Asian continent' in an era witnessing 'a major realignment of forces'—a nod to India's potential to serve as a pivotal actor in establishing a new equilibrium among the great powers. To promote stability, he called on Asian countries to 'construct an open security order', pointing to the ARF and thus to a regional se-curity framework in which India would play a pivotal role (Menon 2007).

For the UPA government, the principal gatekeeper towards an ex-panded regional security role was the United States. A frosty relation-ship during the Cold War, renewed tensions over India's nuclear program after the 1998 Pokhran tests, and the confounding role of Pakistan all had limited security ties greatly before the 9/11 attacks and rising concerns about China began to provide a thaw. Vajpayee had even described the United States and India as 'natural allies' (Vajpayee 2000)—an assertion that was indicative of rapprochement, even if it was hyperbolic.

Although Singh's Congress Party was identified strongly with India's tradition of non-alignment, the UPA government continued to pursue a closer partnership with the United States. In 2005, Singh and U.S. President George W. Bush announced plans for a landmark civil nuclear agreement, which would have tremendous practical and symbolic significance. The talks offered India potential recognition as a legitimate member of the nuclear club after years of ostracism and, by extension, signalled the U.S. recognition of India as a major power and prospective strategic partner. Defence links strengthened with the 2005 'New Framework for India-U.S. Defense', which envisaged maritime security cooperation, shared defence technology, and other collaboration.

The UPA government's growing defence ties to Washington were crucial to the evolution of the Look East policy, facilitating India's defence and diplomatic cooperation with other U.S. security partners in the Pacific. For India, Chinese ports around the Bay of Bengal, ostensibly for commercial reasons, were a potential 'string of pearls' encircling India from the Malacca Strait to the Red Sea and the Persian Gulf. Piracy was also a continuing nuisance. The UPA government responded partly through self-help remedies, shifting naval capabilities from the Western Command based in Mumbai—historically seen as the 'sword arm' of the Indian Navy—to the Eastern Command headquartered at Visakhapatnam and facing the Bay of Bengal (Singh 2011, 244–45). Enhanced naval partnerships were also a major focus. In 2004, the Indian Navy thus created a directorate of foreign cooperation, and the Ministry of Defence began to feature progress on external defence partnerships in its annual reports (Naidu 2013, 67).

India's appeal to maritime security partners in Asia and the Pacific waxed as the UPA government reinvested in naval capabilities and shifted more of them eastward. Among the key indicators were the relocation and expansion of annual Indo-U.S. *Malabar* joint naval exercises. Since their inception in 1992, the *Malabar* exercises had been bilateral and conducted in the Arabian Sea, reflecting the two states' shared strategic priority on the approaches to the Red Sea and the Persian Gulf. In 2007, India participated in unprecedented *Malabar* exercises with Japan and the United States off the Japanese island of Okinawa. Several months later, *Malabar* expanded to include Australia and Singapore as well, moving east of the Subcontinent to the Bay of Bengal. Both the composition and location of the exercises reflected an added emphasis on security in the Look East Policy as India and its *Malabar* partners grew increasingly concerned about Chinese naval ambitions in Myanmar, Bangladesh, Sri Lanka, and around the vital Malacca Strait.

These steps were not costless. Domestically, critics on the left flayed the Singh government for drifting too close to the United States and compromising India's autonomy and tradition of non-alignment. For a time, the UPA government wavered on whether to expand the *Malabar* exercises and shift them eastward in 2007, considering postponement or cancellation before the Indian Navy insisted on keeping the agreed schedule. Singh also confronted stiff opposition in Parliament and had to win a vote of confidence to bring the 2008 Indo-U.S. civil nuclear deal to fruition. Nevertheless, Singh succeeded in reorienting India as a major strategic partner of the United States.

Indo-U.S. rapprochement helped enable the rapid development of India's ties to Japan, which are not bedevilled by the historical legacy that has troubled Japan's relations with many other Asian neighbours. Japanese officials were keen to build upon shared strategic interests, economic complementarities, and common democratic values. During the UPA period, Japan emerged in many ways as India's most important Asian partner, providing extensive investment, deepening trade, and signing a Joint Declaration on Security Cooperation in 2008 during Singh's visit to Tokyo.

Naval ties also strengthened with several ASEAN members, building on the *Milan* exercises that dated back to the early 1990s. Shared concerns about Chinese encroachment in the South China Sea were partly responsible for that cooperation but shared concerns about piracy and disaster relief also played roles. In that regard, the Indian Navy won plaudits for its deployment to participate in relief and reconstruction efforts after the devastating tsunami of December 2004. India also joined a regional agreement to combat piracy in 2006—a means both to address an important ongoing security concern and to foster closer maritime cooperation with ASEAN partners in a manner not directed at China, which also participated.

Invitations to an Expanding Regional Order: The EAS and the Quad

As Indian security ties strengthened to the United States, Japan, and ASEAN states, the UPA government also secured two very different invitations to play larger roles in the regional order in Asia and the Pacific. One enabled India to join the EAS in 2005, and the other included India in the Quadrilateral Security Dialogue with Australia, Japan, and the United States. Although the EAS and the Quad initiative suggested very different models for regional order, India's invitation to each forum was motivated largely by concerns about China. Both the expanded EAS and the Quad envisioned India playing a crucial role within a region stretching from the Subcontinent to the Western Pacific. It was through these initiatives that the shoots of a new 'Indo-Pacific' order became apparent.

India's inclusion in the EAS was a watershed in its relationship to the regional institutional architecture. Since the early 1990s, some Asian governments had pushed to build institutions that would put East Asia more clearly in the driver's seat and counterbalance the U.S. influence in the region. That effort dated back to stalled proposals for an East Asia Economic Group and Asian Monetary Fund in the 1990s and the subsequent creation of ASEAN Plus Three (APT) including the ASEAN states, China, South Korea, and Japan. At the 2004 APT meeting, Malaysian Prime Minister Abdullah Badawi revived the push for an Asian-only forum by proposing an EAS that would exclude the United States and thus act as a potential counterweight to the ARF and APEC. Whether India would be treated as an insider or outsider in this equation would have important implications for the EAS and the regional institutional order. The question of Indian membership thus became a key point of controversy.

Chinese Premier Wen Jiabao swiftly backed Malaysia's vision for an EAS, keen to develop a relatively exclusive regional forum in which China could exercise leadership. Other governments worried that such a forum would deepen regional divisions and contribute to an unwanted Chinese sphere of influence. Japan, Indonesia, Singapore, and Vietnam thus led a campaign to include India, Australia, and New Zealand—a campaign Chinese officials saw as a thinly veiled effort to constrain Beijing. Chinese state media referred to India, Australia, and New Zealand as 'outsiders' and accused Tokyo in particular of 'trying to drag countries outside this region' into the EAS (Malik 2006, 208). In official negotiations, India's role was particularly sensitive given its size and its tense bilateral relationship with China (Naidu 2005, 716).

For the UPA government, the debate amounted to an intergovern-mental referendum on India's place in the evolving regional order. Chinese diplomats fanned out across Southeast Asia to lobby for re-stricting the EAS to APT participants but found little support beyond Kuala Lumpur. Other ASEAN members welcomed India and New Zealand and supported Australia's bid to join if it acceded to the Treaty of Amity and Cooperation, which it did (Malik 2006, 208). India's inclusion in the EAS was a clear indication of the rising recognition of its poten-tial role in facilitating a desirable balance of influence among the major powers in Asia and the Pacific. India received a modest further acknow-ledgement the following year when it was invited to join the Asia-Europe Meeting (ASEM).

India did remain an outsider with respect to some regional forums. After failing to block India's inclusion in the EAS, China pressed for a two-tiered structure in which ASEAN + 3 participants would function as core EAS members and India, Australia, and New Zealand would have secondary status. Malaysia welcomed that concept and embedded it by describing ASEAN + 3 rather than the EAS as the vehicle for developing an East Asian Community—the longstanding lodestar for multilateral diplomacy in the region. In the years following, ASEAN + 3 saw some of the most concrete and substantial initiatives in regional economic co-operation, such as the Chiang Mai Initiative Multilateralization, whereby participants developed a reserve pool to provide emergency finan-cial support. India also remained outside of the Asia-Pacific Economic Cooperation (APEC) forum, which despite losing ground to ASEAN + 3 remained an important component of the overall regional economic architecture.

In 2007, the UPA government was invited into a very different club, implying a distinct approach to reforming the regional order. In early 2007, Japanese Prime Minister Shinzo Abe proposed a Quadrilateral Security Dialogue in which India would join a series of trilateral meetings between Australia, Japan, and the United States convened since 2002. The initiative was part of Japan's campaign for values-based diplomacy, led by Foreign Minister Taro Aso, who emphasized India's role as a fellow democracy crucial to achieving Japan's vision for an 'Arc of Freedom and Prosperity' (Aso 2007). The Bush administration signalled its view of India as a key part of the evolving regional order, notably referring to India as an 'Asian' power rather than merely a South Asian power (Naidu 2013, 69). As in Tokyo, proponents of the Quad initiative in Washington characterized it as a concert of democracies, if not also an alliance—a potential Asian analogue to NATO.

India's participation in the Quadrilateral Security Dialogue, alongside its burgeoning security links to the Quad countries, brought stern criticism from Beijing. Even before the first Quad meeting in Manila in November 2007, China issued a demarche to the participating governments, demanding information and implicitly protesting against an initiative it regarded as part of a broader effort at containment. Although Singh and Foreign Secretary Shivshankar Menon downplayed the extent to which these initiatives were directed at China, most ASEAN members also saw the initiative as an effort to balance against Beijing. Southeast Asian governments generally were concerned that the Quad would deepen regional divisions and pressure them to choose sides. At home, Singh took political fire from coalition members on his left.

Although India participated in the 2007 meeting of the Quad, Singh insisted that it did not amount to an incipient alliance and downplayed the notion that India had joined a league of assertive democracy promoters. India's appeal as a partner to many ASEAN members rested partly on New Delhi's track record of non-interference in its Southeast Asian neighbours' domestic political affairs. Although the abuses of the Myanmar junta sometimes tested India's respect for sovereign prerogative, its general adherence to the non-interference norm was an implicit expectation of ASEAN members facilitating a greater Indian role in the regional order.

The Quad initiative stalled in 2008 when Australia withdrew under pressure from Beijing and was not resurrected until 2017, well after the end of the UPA era. However, India's strategic engagement with Japan and the United States continued. In Tokyo, despite a revolving door of prime ministers before Abe's eventual return, India continued to factor centrally in Japanese foreign policy. In Washington, shortly after taking office in 2009, U.S. President Barack Obama called India and the United States 'natural allies' (White House 2009), signalling that his administration would remain committed to the Indo-U.S. strategic partnership.

Solidifying Key Bilateral Partnerships

For the UPA government, the period after the conclusion of the Indo-U.S. civil nuclear deal saw India's key bilateral relationship with Japan continue to strengthen. India became the largest destination for Japanese development assistance and investment in major infrastructure projects, such as the transportation corridors between Delhi, Mumbai, and Kolkata and between Bangalore and Chennai. Bilateral trade and investment surged, and in 2011 Japan and India signed a Comprehensive Economic Partnership Agreement. Abe's return as Prime Minister in late 2012 gave the relationship an added boost, culminating in the first visit of the Emperor and Empress to India and an exchange of visits by Abe and Singh.

Indo-U.S. relations during the Obama presidency and Singh's second term were more turbulent but arguably settled into a more sustainable dynamic. The hopes and expectations for the partnership cultivated during Singh's first term and embedded in the rhetoric on 'natural allies' were unrealistic given the domestic constraints in each country and divergence in certain of their strategic interests (see Lalwani and Byrne 2019). For the UPA government, stronger Indo-U.S. relations were at times a double-edged sword. They gave New Delhi leverage and access to U.S.-led security structures and institutions but raised risks to India's cherished autonomy. When U.S. Defense Secretary Leon Panetta visited New Delhi in 2012 and described India as the linchpin of the U.S. rebalance to Asia, the Singh government was therefore uncomfortable (Naidu 2013, 70). Indian strategists were keen to preserve the independence and the influence that flows from India's role as a 'swing state' on certain key international issues—not simply to be a reliable cornerstone in a U.S.-led regional order.

Other issues strained Indo-U.S. relations as well. U.S. officials were disappointed by an Indian law on civil nuclear liability that they saw as disfavouring American firms, as well as Indian purchases of defence hardware from other suppliers. American policymakers also criticized India's perceived ambivalence on pursuing deeper ties during Singh's second term, especially after a series of domestic corruption allegations weakened the UPA government (Tellis 2018). Indian officials complained about the pace of technology transfer. A diplomatic row erupted in 2013 over the arrest in New York of Indian diplomat Devyani Khobragade, who was charged with visa fraud and detained before being sent home. Policy differences with respect to Iran and Afghanistan continued as irritants.

Nevertheless, India and the United States continued to engage through a Strategic Dialogue, and the Obama administration welcomed the Look East policy explicitly, treating India as a vital factor in the regional order (see, e.g., Donilon 2012). In 2013, Singh and Obama celebrated what they described as a 'comprehensive global strategic partnership, both in name and substance' (White House 2013).

In both the United States and Japan, partnership with India came to be seen as a strategic necessity. The UPA government thus managed to secure significant benefits at a relatively modest cost and to consolidate a pair of bilateral relationships that welded India into the security framework defining one crucial aspect of the Indo-Pacific order.

Engaging in the Near Abroad

While India's partnerships with Japan and the United States became major spokes embedding it within the regional security architecture, the UPA government's Look East policy also involved a range of bilateral and multilateral ventures with its nearer neighbours. Economics provided the primary initial impetus for the Look East policy and continued to feature prominently in the UPA government's approach, punctuated by the conclusion of the ASEAN-India free trade agreement (FTA) in 2009. Bilateral trade deals with Singapore, Thailand, and Malaysia and new bilateral investment treaties with China, Bangladesh, Myanmar, and Brunei were also signed during the UPA period.

The Singh government continued its predecessors' investment in BIMSTEC as an institutional bridge between South and Southeast Asia and a way to get around the paralyzing effect of the Indo-Pakistani dispute within the South Asian Association for Regional Cooperation (SAARC) (Narine 2018, 232). India also invested heavily in its relationship with ASEAN. One major emphasis was infrastructure connectivity. The push for connectivity was aimed partly at addressing long-term underdevelopment and insecurity in India's isolated northeastern provinces. It also pertained directly to the UPA government's strategic concerns regarding the rise of China. Rajiv Sikri, who served as Secretary in India's Ministry of External Affairs and as a lead diplomat within Asia, explains:

> Myanmar, Thailand, Laos, Cambodia and Vietnam are being hard-wired with China and inexorably sucked into China's economic whirlpool. These mushrooming linkages are creating new long-term political linkages and economic interdependencies among Asian countries. Unfortunately, these leave out India, thereby creating a situation where India could remain strategically and economically boxed up in the South Asian region, mired in dealings with its fractious neighbors. (Sikri 2009, 134)

India liberalized the civil aviation sector, enabling much more frequent and affordable transit to the ASEAN region by air. India and Myanmar built new cross-border road linkages—an initiative highlighted by the first two editions of the ASEAN-India Car Rally in 2004 and 2012, first Assam to Indonesia and then back. More challenging was the establishment of strong rail linkages to Southeast Asia. The Singh government set an eventual aim of linking New Delhi to Hanoi by rail via Myanmar, Thailand, and Cambodia, and by 2014 some parts were completed.

More controversially, the UPA government waded into the South China Sea by sailing vessels through disputed waters, boosting security cooperation with littoral states including Vietnam and the Philippines, and advocating diplomatically for the freedom of navigation while seeking studiously to avoid taking sides. Bilateral SIMBEX exercises between Singapore and India in the South China Sea began in 2005, and Indian companies also invested in the exploration of the seabed in the South China Sea, particularly in concert with Vietnam.

The South China Sea issue in particular attracted ire from China, as did India's broader security reorientation. Sino-Indian friction also continued in the disputed areas of Arunachal Pradesh and Jammu and Kashmir. The Singh government nevertheless sought to manage tension with Beijing, largely by encouraging commerce between the two Asian giants. At the BRICS Summit meetings in 2011 and 2012, India and China resumed defence ties, pledged to pursue greatly expanded trade, and agreed to cooperate on new multilateral initiatives with their fellow BRICS nations. Although stand-offs in the Himalayas rekindled tension late in Singh's second term, the overall economic trajectory of the relationship was positive during the UPA period.

The economist thrust of the Look East policy yielded clear benefits in investment and trade. Weak investment had long plagued India during the years of the 'licence raj' and even after Rao's liberalizations. In 2004, foreign direct investment (FDI) inflows stood at just $5 billion. By 2014, India was one of the largest destinations for FDI in the developing world, second only to China in that category and attracting $34 billion of inflows. A sizable share of that investment came from Asian partners including Japan, China, South Korea, and Singapore (Reserve Bank of India 2019).

Trade also rose. Between 2004 and 2014, India's two-way trade with the ASEAN region grew from $17 billion to $81 billion, trade with China jumped from $10 billion to $71 billion (albeit with a $38 billion deficit), and trade with Japan rose from $5 billion to roughly $16 billion. Still, these gains should not be overstated. Other major economies also saw sharp increases in regional trade, and India's overall share of trade with ASEAN, China, and Japan remained small—particularly in the case of Japan. India's economy grew briskly, but its lag in trade limited its effective weight in the regional economy.

Ambivalence on Economic Opening

India's capacity to boost trade with Asian partners was constrained by its enduring ambivalence about trade liberalization and reluctance to open long-protected industries to more robust foreign competition. Trade and investment liberalization remained subjects of much debate within the UPA's governing coalition; among technocrats in key economic policy institutions such as the Bank of India, Commerce Ministry, and Ministry of Finance; and in the broader domestic political environment.

During the Doha Round of World Trade Organization talks, India focused on what Commerce Minister Kamal Nath called the 'development deficit' in the outcomes of the preceding Uruguay Round—including intellectual property protections and lingering agricultural tariffs benefitting rich countries (Nath 2005). India also pushed for 'proportionality', whereby developed countries would concede less than developed economies. While India's stance won plaudits from many capitals in the Global South, many proponents of free trade came to view India as a key impediment. That reputation had repercussions for the Look East policy. Perhaps most notably, it undermined India's longstanding bid to join APEC, as some members feared that India had done too little to liberalize its economy and would obstruct progress towards freer regional trade.

Ambivalence about further market opening and reform also explains why India did not join talks for a Trans-Pacific Partnership (TPP), the most ambitious regional trade initiative launched during the period of UPA rule. India nevertheless did participate in negotiations over a Regional Comprehensive Economic Partnership (RCEP), a less demanding arrangement that would require fewer concessions. India emerged in the RCEP talks as a key factor, largely due to its reservations about lowering trade barriers. India's participation in the regional trade order during the UPA period thus had a partial, hesitant quality—one that would be manifest several years later in its 2019 decision to pull out of the RCEP.

Ideational Positioning

In the arena of values diplomacy, UPA leaders largely adhered to India's tradition of respect for national sovereignty. This represented an important element of their overall aim to preserve diplomatic autonomy in a period when the Bush and Abe administrations put a high priority on democracy promotion. Although the Singh government voiced support for democratic principles at a general level, specific applications of those principles to its Asian neighbours were much less comfortable, rubbing up against the *Panchsheel* principles that had long animated its diplomacy in the Global South. The regional context became more accommodating with the advent of Obama's 'pivot' and 'rebalance' to Asia, which among other elements, put added emphasis on seeking to engage with erstwhile adversaries, including Myanmar.

The UPA government took a pragmatic line towards the human rights abuses and humanitarian crises in Myanmar. Although India had once offered staunch diplomatic support for Burma's National League for Democracy and Aung San Suu Kyi (who had lived and studied in India), its policy had shifted in the 1990s as concerns about Chinese influence in Myanmar mounted. By the time Singh took office, India had embraced ASEAN's policy of 'constructive engagement', and Singh made clear his intention to maintain that path. In October 2004, shortly after moderate prime minister General Khin Nyunt was purged in favour of perceived hardliner General Than Shwe, Singh hosted Than Shwe in New Delhi— the first such visit by a Burmese head of state in more than two decades (Holliday 2005, 409).

During the 2007 Saffron Revolution, during which Myanmar's security forces stamped out demands for reform led by the Buddhist clergy, Indian officials maintained a studious silence for weeks before an External Ministry spokesman expressed that India was 'concerned at and closely monitoring the situation in Myanmar' and hoped that all sides would 'resolve their issues peacefully through dialogue' (*Times of India* 2007). The following year, when Cyclone Nargis ravaged Myanmar and the ruling junta failed to address dire public needs, India resisted Western diplomatic efforts to justify humanitarian intervention under the rubric of the Responsibility to Protect (Junk 2016, 91). Instead, the UPA government took a low-key, closed-door diplomatic approach and offered the Myanmar junta humanitarian aid without condemnation (Indian Ministry of External Affairs 2008). As a consequence, India was able to provide relief quickly, while the Myanmar junta initially blocked Western aid delivery (Jaganathan and Kurtz 2014, 471).

Myanmar's gradual opening helped ease the pressure on New Delhi to take a harder line. In particular, the United States opening to Myanmar, which began at the end of the Bush administration and accelerated under Barack Obama, thus relieved an irritant in India's relations with the West by bringing Indian and the U.S. approaches into closer alignment. The same was true elsewhere in Southeast Asia, as in Vietnam, where the U.S. pressure on human rights and democracy was tempered by a growing strategic cooperation with Hanoi as a check on Chinese influence.

Similarly, the UPA government maintained India's policy of non-interference on human rights abuses in Tibet. When protests arose in Tibet in 2008 and were harshly repressed, they voiced their 'distress' while reaffirming that the matter was an internal Chinese affair (*The Hindu* 2008). Moreover, Indian authorities arrested Tibetan exiles in India who planned to march in protest to China during the 2008 summer

Olympic Games in Beijing. In 2014, days before the UPA's end in office, India offered a subdued response to the Thai military coup, with an MEA statement expressing only 'hope that the people of Thailand resolve the political situation peacefully through dialogue and uphold the rule of law' (Embassy of India in Bangkok 2014). India did cancel a joint exercise with the Thai army, which was significant given its general commitment to non-interference, but otherwise, its response amounted to business as usual, contrasting with vocal criticism from Washington and subtler critiques from Tokyo.

The UPA government's non-interference policy brought substantial criticism at home and abroad. As Indian officials welcomed the Myanmar junta's re-engagement in 2010, parliamentarian Shashi Tharoor argued: 'It is a policy that is governed by the head rather than the heart, but in the process India is losing a little bit of its soul' (Tharoor 2010). Nobel laureate Amartya Sen expressed his sense of heartbreak that India's democratic leaders would help in 'welcoming the butchers from Myanmar' as part of a 'narrowly defined national interest' (Garton Ash 2010). Although India did support resolutions condemning abuses at the end of the Sri Lankan civil war, international human rights and democracy advocates continued to view India as a 'chronic fence-sitter' in international forums (Ganguly 2013). Others faulted its 'sovereignty hawks' for an outmoded approach to foreign policy (Ganguly and Sridharan 2013) or chided India for its reluctance to mount an ideational counteroffensive to China. Nevertheless, it had the intended benefit to India of keeping all diplomatic doors open.

Conclusion

By some accounts, the Look East policy evolved during the UPA years into 'one of the most successful foreign policy initiatives that India has undertaken' (Naidu 2013, 55). Importantly, while India was looking east, many East and Southeast Asian governments were looking west, keen to engage New Delhi. The Singh government was able to translate that eagerness into a much more central position in regional security affairs, anchored in its bilateral ties to Washington and Tokyo but supplemented by links to several ASEAN states. In fact, the security elements of the Look

East policy arguably came to surpass the economic aspects of the policy in prominence. India also gained a seat at the table of the EAS, participated in the RCEP negotiations, and otherwise became more enmeshed in a multilateral institutional architecture that shifted its boundary west in concert with India's gaze east. Ideationally, the UPA government sought to stay out of a corner, preserving its autonomy and ability to engage on favourable terms with its key democratic partners and with the many non-democratic states of Southeast Asia.

Overall, the UPA government's Look East policy put the pieces in place for India's major role in what would later be labelled the Indo-Pacific order. In the years since 2014, the Japanese, U.S., Australian, and Indian governments have set forth Indo-Pacific concepts and strategies that built on the Quad initiative of 2007. The Quad architecture gives India considerable weight as a crucial pillar in a balance-of-power arrangement more or less explicitly intended to counter a rising China. However, India's consistent outreach to ASEAN and accession to the EAS, among other UPA diplomatic initiatives, also has given India great importance within ASEAN's Indo-Pacific Outlook, championed by Indonesia but supported broadly in Southeast Asia. That model prioritizes economic linkages, diversification, and multilateral diplomacy to dull the edges of conflictual great-power politics. The UPA's Look East policy thus left India reasonably well positioned to adapt and maintain centrality in a fluid regional environment.

References

Acharya, Arabinda. 2006. 'India and Southeast Asia in the Age of Terror: Building Partnerships for Peace', *Contemporary Southeast Asia* 28(2), 297–321.

ASEAN. 2012. *ASEAN-India Dialogue Relations*. Jakarta: Association of Southeast Asian Nations. June.

Aso, Taro. 2007. Address on the 'Arc of Freedom and Prosperity', Tokyo, March 12.

Ba, Alice D. 2009. *(Re)Negotiating East and Southeast Asia: Region, Regionalism, and the Association of Southeast Asian Nations*. Stanford, CA: Stanford University Press.

Donilon, Tom. 2012. 'President Obama's Asia Policy and Upcoming Trip to Asia', The White House, Washington, DC, November 15.

Embassy of India in Bangkok. 2014. 'Official Spokesperson's Response to a Media Inquiry on the Situation in Thailand', press release, May 21.

Ganguly, Meenakshi. 2013. 'Can India Be an International Human Rights Leader?', *openDemocracy*, June 21.

Ganguly, Sumit and Eswaran Sridharan. 2013. 'The End of India's Sovereignty Hawks?' *Foreign Policy,* November 7.

Garton Ash, Timothy. 2010. 'Step Up, India', *Los Angeles Times.* November 18.

Holliday, Ian. 2005. 'Japan and the Myanmar Stalemate: Regional Power and Resolution of a Regional Problem', *Japanese Journal of Political Science* 6(3), 393–410.

Indian Ministry of External Affairs. 1996. *Annual Report 1995–96.* New Delhi: Ministry of External Affairs.

Indian Ministry of External Affairs. 2008. 'On India's assistance for the cyclone in Myanmar', press release, May 12.

Janganathan, Madhan Mohan and Gerrit Kurtz. 2014. Singing the tune of sovereignty? India and the responsibility to protect. *Conflict, Security & Development* 14(4), 461–87.

Junk, Julian. 2016. 'Testing Boundaries: Cyclone Nargis in Myanmar and the Scope of R2P', *Global Society* 30(1), 78–93.

Lalwani, Sameer and Heather Byrne. 2019. 'Great Expectations: Asking Too Much of the US-India Strategic Partnership', *Washington Quarterly* 42(3), 41–64.

Malik, Mohan. 2006. 'The East Asia Summit', *Australian Journal of International Affairs* 60(2), 207–11.

Menon, Shivshankar. 2007. Speech by Foreign Secretary Shri Shivshankar Menon on 'India and International Security' at the International Institute of Strategic Studies. London, May 3, 2007.

Naidu, G.V.C. 2005. 'India and the East Asia Summit', *Strategic Analysis* 29(4), 711–16.

Naidu, G.V.C. 2013. 'India and East Asia: The Look East Policy', *Perceptions* 18(1), 53–74.

Narine, Shaun. 2018. *The New ASEAN in Asia Pacific and Beyond.* Boulder, CO: Lynne Rienner.

Nath, Kamal. 2005. Statement at the Ministerial Conference, Sixth Session, Hong Kong, New Delhi: Ministry of Commerce and Industry, December 14.

Rao, P.V. Narasimha. 1994. *India and the Asia-Pacific: Forging a New Relationship.* Singapore: Institute of Southeast Asian Studies.

Reserve Bank of India. 2019. *Annual Report 2018–19.* Mumbai: RBI.

Sikri, Rajiv. 2009. 'India's "Look East" Policy', *Asia-Pacific Review* 16(1), 131–45.

Singh, Swaran. 2011. 'China's Forays into the Indian Ocean: Strategic Implications for India', *Journal of the Indian Ocean Region* 7(2), 235–48.

Sinha, Yashwant. 2003. Remarks by Shri Yashwant Sinha, External Affairs Minister of India, at the Plenary Session Second India—ASEAN Business Summit, New Delhi, September 4.

Tasker, Rodney. 1993. 'Rao's Look-East Policy: India Befriends Thailand for Trade and Investment', *Far Eastern Economic Review* 156(16), 16.

Tellis, Ashley. 2018. 'Narendra Modi and U.S.-India Relations', in Bibek Debroy, Anirban Ganguly, and Kishore Desai, eds., *Making of New India: Transformation Under Modi Government*, New Delhi: Wisdon Tree.

Tharoor, Shashi. 2010. 'Knight of the Generals?' *The Times of India.* November 10.

The Hindu. 2008. 'Tibet: India expresses distress, urges dialogue'. March 16.

Times of India. 2007. 'Political reform in Myanmar should be broad-based, says India'. September 26.

Vajpayee, Atal Bihari. 2000. Address at the Asia Society. New York, September 7.

White House. 2009. Remarks by President Obama and Prime Minister Singh of India in Joint Press Conference. Washington, DC, November 24.

White House. 2013. U.S.-India Joint Statement. Washington, DC, September 27.

9

India-Africa Relations under the UPA Governments

Barnaby Dye and Ricardo Soares de Oliveira

Introduction

During the first decade of the 21st century, India-Africa relations accelerated rapidly. Whilst not always at the forefront of India's foreign policy focus, economic ties, diplomatic engagements, and development cooperation grew to new heights. Trade stood at U.S.$7.2 billion in 2001 and rose to U.S.$78 billion[1] by the end of the UPA government in 2014,[2] although 79% of this went to Mauritius partly because of a double taxation agreement.[3] From 2002 to 2005 India led Greenfield Foreign Direct Investment into Africa whilst development cooperation with the continent grew from $350 million in 2006 to $1.5 billion in 2009 and $5 billion by 2011.[4] This launched India into the upper echelons of Africa's international partners, standing as the fourth largest export destination and fifth largest source of imports by 2015.[5] The commodity boom of the 2000s and India's increasing hunger for raw imports were important factors pushing this trend, as were an increasingly globalized set of Indian-owned companies vying for international profit-making opportunities.

The UPA government introduced a number of flagship initiatives that recognized and advanced these growing links, including the India-Africa Forum, and large-scale development-cooperation programmes around education and healthcare. Meanwhile investment grew, with the expansion of a subsidized Lines of Credit (LoC) scheme which had extended U.S.$6.28 billion by 2014.[6] The UPA government heralded these initiatives with much fanfare, using the grand rhetoric of South-South Cooperation: India would be the brother to Africa, the equal

Barnaby Dye and Ricardo Soares de Oliveira, *India-Africa Relations under the UPA Governments* In: *Forging New Partnerships, Breaching New Frontiers.* Edited by: Rejaul Karim Laskar, Oxford University Press. © Oxford University Press 2022. DOI: 10.1093/oso/9780192868060.003.0009 development partner generating win-win, mutually beneficial partner-ships.[7] Has this rhetoric matched actions? And how responsible was the UPA government for the booming India-Africa relationship?

This chapter starts by situating this 2004–14 era historically. It then provides an overview of India's links with Africa from pre-colonial times to the 21st century, but with a particular focus on the 1990s when modern-day relations with the continent were formed. The chapter then provides an overview of India-Africa ties under the 2004–14 UPA admin-istration and proceeds to analyse key trends in that era in relation to the important role of the private sector. It also examines if and to what extent official rhetoric matched action on the ground. The chapter concludes by arguing that significant opportunities do remain for a qualitative shift in India-Africa relations. With a large and often well-integrated diaspora, India has an unparalleled network to tap into and the country's levels of education, technology, agriculture, and healthcare could offer important solutions to unlock the continent's economic potential.

The chapter makes three arguments about India-Africa relations during the UPA government. The first emphasizes the role of the Indian private sector as a central actor driving India-Africa ties. Indeed, it dem-onstrates how this group often acted independently of the UPA admin-istration, whether through establishing projects on the continent or building relations with African states. Relatedly, we show that although the UPA government upgraded India-Africa relations, the government was often not as central to increasing ties as it portrayed itself. Even in areas where there were deliberate state-led efforts, such as in oil, a mix-ture of bureaucratic limitations, fractures amongst the government, and the *de facto* lesser diplomatic status of Africa in Indian global ambitions meant that the state was not always the lead actor in this arena.

Partly as a consequence, India-Africa ties were marked by contrasts between rhetoric and reality. Despite the pervasive discourse of the Non-Aligned Movement emphasizing win-win, South-South Cooperation be-tween equals, the drivers for India's interest in the continent lay more in fear of other Asian states, and especially China, gaining ground across the world and in the Indian Ocean especially, and in a desire to secure natural resources. Additionally, Indian trade with the continent tended to exchange raw African commodities for relatively high-value services and manufactured goods like automobiles and pharmaceutical products.

Partly as a consequence, engagements tended to reinforce the established pattern of Africa's relations that contributes to Africa's experience of economic progress without industrialization. With the private sector as the most organized and active group of agents, India-Africa relations under the UPA administration reached new heights but essentially followed the established trajectory.

Historical Background to the UPA's India-Africa Relations

Although maritime relations between South Asia and East Africa long predate western colonialism in both regions, many contemporary patterns of interaction are connected to this era.[8] Some analysts trace the roots of modern Indian-African relations to Mahatma Gandhi's time in South Africa, where he campaigned for the rights of the Indian community.[9] Others see ties stemming from India's first Prime Minister Jawaharlal Nehru and his mission to place newly independent India outside the Cold War's binary of capitalist West versus communist East.[10] The solution was the Non-Aligned Movement (NAM), a coalition of developing countries that would band together to protect their international freedom. The NAM was the bedrock for India's relations with newly independent countries in Africa, given that many prominent independence leaders on the continent, including Ghana's Kwame Nkrumah, Tanzania's Julius Nyerere, and Zambia's Kenneth Kaunda, also championed the NAM and its principles of South-South solidarity. Practically, this era started a number of development cooperation projects, formalized under India's International Technical and Economic Cooperation (ITEC) scheme from 1964. ITEC offers scholarships for Africans to study in India, funds technical training programmes directly, and provides grants for the construction of training centres and other projects on request. Whilst significant in setting the framework for future interactions, India-Africa ties during the immediate post-independence period were limited to a small volume of development cooperation and a degree of mutual diplomatic support. Economic engagement was further reduced during Prime Minister Indira Gandhi's isolation period in the 1970s. Although India's economy started changing in the 1980s, the legacy of this diminished rapport endured throughout the decade, with Africa-India trade standing at a meagre of $967,000 in 1990.[11]

It has become customary to couch the recent boom in India-Africa relations in terms of a longer historical trajectory but there was, in fact, nothing inevitable about what unfolded in the 21st Century. Indeed, the use of such historical claims is commonplace amongst other emerging powers, such as China and Brazil, in justifying and promoting their growing ties with Africa. For all involved, this history is used as part of a strenuous effort to distinguish themselves from the western presence on the continent. In this regard, India is one of the several states in the developing world in which 'independence in foreign policy was [equated with] maintaining political distance from the West'.[12] In the case of the UPA government, the NAM rhetoric remained central (this had been far less the case with the BJP governments from 1998 to 2004, and arguably again since 2014), although this did not always match Indian policy, as discussed below.

The boom in India-Africa ties more directly stems from India's economic liberalization in the 1990s, overseen by Congress-Party Prime Minister P. V. Narasimha Rao and (future PM) Manmohan Singh as Finance Minister. This decade cemented a decisive domestic policy shift, underway since the mid-1980s, from an interventionist, regulated 'Licence Raj', to a more market-based economy.[13] This apparent reinvention of India[14] also reduced controls on international trade and currency, removing barriers for Indian firms' internationalization. For example, a $2million cap on removing currency was raised in 2002 to $100 million a year.[15] It also involved a rapprochement with India's large global diaspora, who were encouraged to build ties with the country and identify as Indian when before they had not. With this change, many firms from what Taylor calls India's rentier class of large, family-owned conglomerates[16] established or expanded operations in Africa from the 1990s.

Mirroring this large degree of private sector activity, India's business federations also played an important role in driving greater India-Africa ties during this period. The country has two major groupings with regards to the Africa relationship, the Federation of Indian Chambers of Commerce & Industry (FICCI), tending to represent established, family firms, and the Confederation of Indian Industry (CII), representing newer market entrants.[17] According to Sinha,[18] both played a crucial role in India's internationalization to Africa and elsewhere through increasing awareness of opportunities and facilitating business negotiations. Moreover, both FICCI and CII led lobbying efforts to increase government support for internationalizing to Africa.[19] This resulted in 'Focus Africa', a program launched in 2002 that provided a dedicated fund for the federations to undertake business promotion activities, including conferences, international business delegations, and trade fairs. More significantly, 2003 saw the start of ExIm Bank lending to Africa with the launch of the India Development Economic Assistance Scheme (IDEAS) that subsidized credit in-line with World Bank rules.[20] This represented the first substantive activity in this area as previously, between 1966 and 2003, India had lent only U.S.$1.816 million.[21] This was important as it increased the availability and ease of access to such government-brokered credit for developing countries, as previously, the State Bank of India's limited resources and regulations slowed down the availability of funds.

India-Africa Relations 2004–14: Upgrading, Continuity and the Contrasts between Rhetoric and Reality

Drivers for Increased Ties

The incoming UPA government in 2004 inherited this upwards trajectory in relations with the African continent and continued to support the underlying economic and cooperation policies enabling this trend. However, the UPA administration also undertook an upgrading of these ties. There were two key drivers for this. The first stemmed from concerns about China's dramatic push in diplomatic, economic, and development-cooperation activity. During the UPA, the extent of China's booming relations with Africa became clear, as demonstrated by the 2006 Forum on China-Africa Cooperation (FOCAC), whose event in Beijing brought together top leaders from almost all African countries and set out the framework for diplomatic, economic and development ties.[22] On top of China's rise, Indian officials saw Japan's concerted effort at building relations with the continent. Collectively, this worried diplomats and politicians, who tended to see 'Africa' as a natural partner for India, given the diaspora links and common Indian Ocean territory.

The second driver was India's quest for energy resources. From 2005, the Indian state became increasingly concerned about the need to diversify the country's oil supplies, particularly given the country's increasing demand for oil, its dwindling domestic supplies, and reliance on a relatively small number of Middle Eastern states, particularly Saudi Arabia.[23] Older established drivers also continued to play a role in the UPA's thinking. India has long courted African votes in multi-lateral global governance fora, such as the World Trade Organization, United Nations, and Climate negotiations, given the continent tends to vote as a bloc. Gaining Africa's 54 would boost the opportunity for India to achieve long-standing foreign policy objectives such as the securing of a permanent UN Security Council seat or reform of global trade. The UPA administration also wanted to support the internationalization of Indian corporations. Given Africa's strong economic growth, population increase, and emerging middle class, the continent represented an increasingly important market opportunity for Indian goods. Additionally, Africa has long been an important source for a number of strategic commodities for India, including diamonds, phosphates, and copper.[24]

Key Instruments

India-Africa Forum Summits

Thus, the UPA government markedly increased Africa-related activity, although their often frantic actions rarely achieved the sum of their parts. This upgrading is best demonstrated by the India-Africa Forum Summits, regular meetings of African and Indian political leaders. Like FOCAC, it was planned to happen every three years and bring governments together to facilitate a coordinated approach for diplomacy, economic relations, and development cooperation. However, rather than China's all-encompassing events, the summits used the African Union's Banjul Formula, that rotated invitations between 15 selected countries. The first of these smaller-scale India-Africa Forum Summits was held in Delhi in 2008, followed by another in 2011, hosted by the African Union's Headquarters in Addis Ababa, Ethiopia. Despite the lower-level of diplomatic spectacle, the Forums did represent an upgrading of India-Africa ties by the UPA administration, not least by setting expectations of increased ties including spending pledges on Lines of Credit (over \$5 billion each in 2008 and 2011[25]), on development cooperation and multilateral engagement.

ExIm Bank Lines of Credit (LoCs)
In line with this scaled-up relationship, and responding to the interests of African states, the subsidized ExIm-Bank IDEAS scheme expanded. For instance, by 2008, the ExIm Bank had extended \$5billion of credit through the LoCs scheme. LoCs also became increasingly ambitious. Between 2004 and 2008, they had primarily supported trade, but from 2008, infrastructure projects were the main recipient.[26] Between 2005 and 2014, power projects received the most finance, reputedly 28.5% of loans,[27] followed by railways and agriculture.[28] The summits themselves provided a venue for state-to-state agreements on LoCs, as demonstrated by a deal to construct Jubilee House, the Ghanaian Presidential Office,[29] and the announcement of railway investment in Ethiopia.[30] Indeed, the forums attempted to instigate more focus. Ethiopia received particular attention: 607 LoCs backed irrigation for sugar plantations, sugar processing facilities, and 607 MW of biogas energy plants to process the sugar-plant waste, reportedly employing a collective total of 162,000 people.[31] Additionally, the ExIm bank approved a U.S.\$300million loan for the Addis-Djibouti railway.[32] Furthermore, a U.S.\$1billion oil-for-credit deal was generically offered to West African petro-states in 2005,[33] a model imitating China's so-called Angola model that promised infrastructure finance in exchange for commodities. One author[34] demonstrates that the expansion of infrastructure construction in Africa included dam building, with Indian firms and ExIm-Bank finance engaged in six schemes. This allowed a number of Indian infrastructure companies to expand to Africa for the first time, from larger firms like Shapoorji Pallonji to newcomers like Angelique International.

Development Cooperation
India also built stronger relations with Africa by scaling up its development cooperation. Technical cooperation through ITEC grew,[35] with grants increasing from U.S.\$4–10million in 1997/1998 to U.S.\$71.62million in 2003/2004 and U.S.\$125.81million in 2006/2007,[36] and the number of scholarships increased.[37] The forum summits also

provided impetus to initiate new schemes. At the 2008 event, for example, India announced the U.S.$1 billion Pan-African e-Network scheme.[38] It envisaged two networks connecting universities and hospitals respectively in India and selected African countries with the aim of providing support and capacity-building and teaching.[39] The Forum also granted a free trade/zero-tariff agreement to the Africa's poorest 34 states and expanded the ITEC programme which included doubling scholarships and increasing technical training to 5000 places by 2009/2010.[40] Additionally, the Forum launched a 'V-VIP' network of secure phone lines between African heads of States and India.[41] The Ministry of External Affairs handled both the line of credit IDEAS scheme and the development cooperation. In order to increase its capacity to deal with the greater activity in both these area (to assess incoming requests, approve government funds, and monitor projects), the UPA administration created the Development Partnership Administration under the MEA in 2013. Additionally, the UPA began increasing recruitment of diplomats around the same time.[42] This was also a significant move given that since the 1980s, such recruitment had been scaled back, causing capacity constraints in MEA discussed below. Therefore, the UPA administration, somewhat belatedly, also began improving the institutional structure to support the upgrade in development cooperation with Africa.

Energy

Given the importance of India's quest for energy resources in driving the increase in India-Africa relations, the UPA's tenure saw growing efforts to secure international deals for the state-owned oil company ONGC. The Began Report of 2006 identified the importance of increasing and diversifying India's imports of oil from a narrow group of Middle Eastern states-mainly Saudi Arabia. The importance ascribed to this goal led to an Integrated Energy Policy[43] and Energy Coordination Committee[44] that attempted to geographically diversify the country's supplies and support OVL's (the international arm of India's National Oil Company, ONGC) acquisition of petroleum supplies.[45] During the 2000s, a number of oil supplies were being discovered across Africa, whilst known reservoirs were expanded. With the additional benefit of the low-sulphur content oil, the continent became an attractive area for India to solve its energy needs. The most notable deal done on the continent involved the government of Sudan, where OVL, the international arm of the state-owned firm ONGC bought out Canadian firm Talisman's 25% share in the Greater Nile Petroleum Operating Company.[46] To secure this strategic resource, the Indian government supported other activities in the country, providing a U.S.$50 million LoC for infrastructure, education and training, and agriculture projects whilst the state-owned OVL agreed to build a pipeline to the red sea. Beri[47] estimates the total investment in the country at U.S.$2 billion.

Re-engaging the Diaspora

An important asset for India vis-à-vis Africa is the presence of a large Indian diaspora there. Particularly concentrated in East Africa and countries like Kenya and Tanzania, as well as in South Africa and Ghana, this community frequently traces its modern history back to colonial times. Given this longstanding presence, the Indian diaspora is often well integrated into these countries' private sectors and own prominent companies in East Africa and elsewhere. These include the Motisun Group in Tanzania and Nakumatt supermarkets in East Africa, to name but a few.[48] Interviews conducted by the authors[49] show that the diaspora became not only an important source for knowledge about business opportunities on the continent but also an increasing site of demand for Indian products. After the 1990s liberalizing of Indian trade, this group was able to take advantage of continuing links to India to expand the trade of Indian products that are competitive in Africa such as automobiles and fertilizer. In the early post-colonial years, diaspora was implicitly perceived by Delhi, especially in the African context, as at best irrelevant, and at worst, a reactionary element that could trouble bilateral relations. This had been the case in East Africa in particular, where Indian-origin communities were targeted in the 1960s and 1970s. After a long period of disengagement, however, deliberate attempts by the state to better include this group—now increasingly perceived as a major global asset—started in 1999.[50] The UPA administration deepened this reengagement. They established the Ministry of Overseas Indian Affairs in 2004, and in 2006 created the 'Overseas Citizenship of India' status for the diaspora, effectively a half-way house to full citizenship.[51] This enhanced the degree to which people of Indian origin identified with the country, as well as giving them easier access for travel and business in India. Overall then, the Congress-led UPA government did therefore expand India-Africa ties, whether through development cooperation efforts or energy diplomacy. However, our analysis suggests that the government's action in pushing India-Africa relations forward was often sporadic and limited, particularly in contrast to the resources and spectacle of China's Africa focus. The section below deepens this analysis, demonstrating structural constraints that hampered the furthering of India-Africa relations. This created contradictions between the rhetoric of brotherhood and assertions of the importance of Africa for India, on the one hand, and the limited action on the ground, on the other, as well as between the narrative of state-led cooperation and stronger agency and initiative of a relatively independent Indian private sector.

The Rhetoric versus the Reality in India-Africa Relations

An overt feature of India's Africa ties under the UPA was the official rhetorical use of South-South Cooperation. With roots in the Non-Aligned Movement era immediately post-independence, this discourse espouses the principles of solidarity and equality in foreign relations between developing countries. Each of the India-Africa Summits has re-affirmed this framing of the relationship, the supposed brotherhood shared by Africa— too often painted uniformly—and India. Arguably, this has influenced elements of India's approach to Africa. Certainly on a multi-lateral level, as Hurrell, Sengupta, and Narlikar[52] show, these principles have framed India's actions in trade and climate change negotiations during the UPA's tenure, as they have stood up for other developing-country interests, including on positions that are not to India's direct economic advantage. The framing of South-South Cooperation is also used to justify the lack of conditionality in India's development activity. For instance, under the UPA, the subsidized ExIm Bank credit only requires around 75% of the value of the loan to go to Indian exports without focusing on its developmental impact[53] or the rigour of its technical project appraisal.[54] In this sense, India followed the roadmap of other emerging powers, framing its relations as one of mutual benefit between equals whilst pursuing a set of development cooperation activities alongside the extension of government loans to support domestic companies' internationalization.

However, this proclamation of India's unique, mutually beneficial friendship with Africa contrasts with evidence of what occurred during UPA's decade of administration. For a start, the pattern of investment and trade tended to replicate the existing structural tendencies of Africa's international relations: Chakrabarty shows that primary commodities, primarily petroleum and minerals products, were exchanged for manufactured products and services from India.[55] This is reflected in the concentration of trade with Nigeria, Algeria, Angola, and South Africa,[56] four of the largest, resource-rich economies in Africa, a pattern similar to that long established between Africa and Europe. Given the additional value of the manufactured goods, this exchange keeps Africa in a long-established, and structurally weaker, international economic position. Whilst not new to the UPA period, this begs the question of who benefits. With India's economic cooperation with Africa not supporting a structural transformation away from primary commodity extraction to industrialization or the technological service sector, wider societal benefits are questionable.

Such trade does, however, tend to benefit the established political-economic elite of those countries trading minerals and petroleum on the continent, with most African states' main income source and key businesses oriented around resource extraction. Additionally, as with many large development projects, the ExIm Bank loans for infrastructure and agriculture typically entail trade-offs, with those displaced losing land, communities, and livelihoods. For instance, Dye[57] argues that the Nyabarongo Dam in Rwanda had significant negative impacts on its local community alongside some positives, with the project's main service—electricity—going to those who can afford it. Rahmato[58] additionally shows the negative consequences of large Indian sugar plantations in Ethiopia, given their displacement of farmers without compensation. Whilst responsibility for such outcomes significantly rests on the recipient African governments, such cases at least complicate the idea of enhanced India-Africa ties as singularly positive.

Rhetoric also did not match the state's degree of diplomatic intensity. During the UPA administration, few visits to the continent were made by the Indian Prime Minister and President, with those that took place usually pertaining to international summits rather than multi-country state visits.[59] This feature is particularly clear in contrast to Brazilian President Lula's contemporaneous 29 trips between 2003 and 2010 or top-ranking Chinese officials' regular travel to the continent. Ultimately this lower level of diplomatic activity reflects the lesser status of ties with Africa, and arguably the UPA's limited foreign policy action more widely. The Indian diplomatic service has consistently seen relations with the United States, with the neighbourhood (Pakistan, Nepal, Afghanistan, Bangladesh, and Sri Lanka), with China and with Russia, and to a lesser extent the UK and Europe. This partly stems from their importance to India in military security, especially given past wars with China and the ongoing hostile rivalry with Pakistan. These militarily powerful and prox-imate countries remained the primary foreign-policy focus. Africa's lower strategic relevance is also reflected in trade ties. As a continent, trade has risen to a significant level, from 6% in 2004 to 10% in 2014.[60] However, important individual countries in Africa may be, the continent as a whole is out-ranked by India's other economic partners, such as China, which accounts for 15.8% of India's imports and (combined with Hong Kong) 8.2% of exports, or the United States, which alone takes 5% of imports 15% of exports.[61] Consequently, India's diplomatic service, and arguably the UPA political leadership, stuck to the established and justifiable focus on long-established strategically important countries.

This point is further evidenced by the degree of state-led activity in Afghanistan. The rupture of the NATO-led invasion in 2001 created an opportunity to disrupt the Pakistani military's influence in Afghanistan. The UPA administration took India's pre-existing charm offensive to new heights, with Prime Minister Manmohan Singh laying the foundation for the U.S.$75 million ExIm Bank-financed national parliament and an-nouncing a series of other initiatives covering health, the power sector, and education.[62] A U.S.$290-million flagship project for this initiative was the symbolically named India-Afghan Friendship Dam (the recon-structed and expanded Salma Dam). In contrast to infrastructure pro-jects in Africa, this Afghanistan drive comes primarily from state-to-state dialogue, as demonstrated by successive Prime Ministers visiting the site and announcing its commissioning. In contrast, Kabu 16 in Burundi (20 MW) and Nyabarongo Dam in Rwanda (28 MW) are similar sizes to the Afghan-Friendship Dam but had no high-level political engagement from

India. Rather than a state-led engagement, both African dams stemmed from the initiative of a private company, Angelique International.[63] Again this suggests that ties with countries in Africa are, on the whole, not given the same level of significance and do not receive the same level of Indian government-brokered support.

Perhaps the only area where such concerted action is evident to some extent is in the petroleum field, discussed above. Nonetheless, it is important to recognize, as we discuss below, that coordination between different parts of the Indian state remained an issue even in this energy arena, and that ONGC, in particular, remained somewhat mired in bureaucratic inertia. However, even this modest degree of state direction and strategy was not replicated elsewhere. Despite other potentially strategic interests in other African raw commodities, evidence of state-led engagement is limited. For instance, India is the world's largest diamond processor, cutting and polishing 90% of those in the world. 80% of that supply comes from African countries, including South Africa and Botswana.[64] However, with the exception of South Africa, where ties have been consistently emphasized, for instance, through the India-Brazil-South Africa multi-lateral group, there does not appear to have been any substantive strategic state-to-state effort to secure more wide-ranging diplomatic and trade ties.

There are a number of long-standing structural issues behind this relative absence of the state that go beyond the UPA's tenure. The first of these is the resistance to spending on international development cooperation and diplomacy within India's Lok Shaba (lower house of India's parliament). Given the country's own levels of poverty and given a desire amongst parliamentarians to hand out projects to their constituents, governments have found it difficult to increase spending on international goals. This affects the MEA's budget, and thereby the number of diplomats, embassies, and the amount of activity the Foreign Service can undertake. It also caps the degree of subsidized lending possible through the ExIm bank and scale of development cooperation projects. Consequently, India's diplomatic service is far smaller than other emerging powers. In 2011, India had 750 diplomats compared to China's 6000[65] and only 29[66] embassies in Africa compared to 53 Chinese[67] and 34 Brazilian.[68] Moreover, the newly created Development Partnership Administration mentioned above had just 20 officials with diplomatic ranking.[69] This relatively thin presence on the ground and dearth of human resources are important constraints. For the other emerging powers in Africa,[70] embassies have played a vital role in advancing investment opportunities[71] and in connecting companies from their own countries.[72]

The process of strengthening relations with Africa during the UPA administration was further dented by a longstanding policy of recognizing as Indian companies only those that are resident in India for tax purposes. This has excluded a number of more internationalized firms that split operations between different jurisdictions, particularly for international activities. For instance, ArcelorMittal—the product of Indian Mittal Steel taking over Spanish Arcelor—has major steel investments across Europe but has also operated for decades in South Africa. Despite being owned by Indian national Lakshmi Mittal, the fact that its headquarters are in Luxembourg means that the government does not consider it 'Indian'. Similarly, parts of the conglomerate Tata are registered in overseas jurisdictions and consequently receive little state support.

Another important factor undermining the UPA government in building ties with the continent were divisions within the government. This is partly reflected in the lack of integration between the key ministries, whereby parts of the civil service tend to remain relatively isolated from one another.[73] Such splits are also evident within departments, as for instance, the Ministry of Foreign affairs has not sought to connect the subsidized ExIm credit and the ITEC development cooperation although they oversee both programmes.[74] This limitation was worsened by splits amongst the political leadership. A prominent example here was the dispute between Petroleum Minister Mani Shankar Aiyar (2004–6), who publicly fell out with the head of ONGC, Subir Raha, hampering the ability of India to secure international deals.[75] Aiyar's period in office saw a very activist international energy policy agenda, and in many ways, it represented the peak of the government's interest in this area but its results were limited. Aiyar's replacement for the next five years, the seasoned Mumbai Congress Party politician Murli Deora, represented a return to a more traditional, lower profile role for the Ministry. Throughout, private sector voices complained of continuing 'political/bureaucratic management of what are essentially business concerns' as a major factor in the lagging competitiveness of Indian oil investments abroad.[76]

The degree of messiness in attempts to build India's presence in Africa's (and especially the Gulf of Guinea's) oil fields contrasts with the more concerted effort in Russia. Here both governments are interested in pursuing ties in order to achieve greater diversification of trade. Aided by annual summits from 1999 and building on long-standing relations, India and Russia have brokered increased ties in energy through state-led firms. In 2005, ONGC acquired Imperial Energy for U.S.$2.6 billion[77] and collaborated with Russian government-owned Gazprom and Rosneft in Siberia. Such engagement expanded with the 2010 intergovernmental agreement on oil and gas cooperation. Again this underlines that in spite of the rhetoric, The UPA administration decided that ties with countries in Africa were less geopolitically important and that the region is not given the same priority or degree of state backing as other geopolitical regions deemed more central to India's national interest.

The Corporate Lead

Overall, the structural budgetary limitations for conducting diplomacy and development cooperation, combined with a longer-standing interest in other international relationships, limited government leadership in the 21st century drive for enhanced ties with countries in Africa. Given this absence of the state, both before, during, and after the UPA administration, India's private sector played a key role in pushing forward economic engagements with the continent. For example, in mining, ArcelorMittal expanded operations in its long-held South African mines and in 2005 signed an agreement to start iron-ore operations in Liberia and started another, ultimately failed, project in Senegal.[78] Elsewhere, Vedanta took up operations in Zambia's Konkola mine in 2004, which accounted for 65% of the country's copper production by 2012.[79] Meanwhile, Reliance expanded Africa's operations in oil marketing from 2007 through a 76% stake in the Gulf Africa Petroleum Corporation (GAPCO). Tata began operations on the continent in 1977 but scaled up its businesses from the 1990s, investing U.S.$145 million[80] including the purchase of Ferrochrome in South Africa[81] and through the Taj Hotels chain.[82] Additionally, a number of large, competitive Indian firms have expanded exports to Africa. Examples here include Ashok Leyland[83] and Mahindra[84] in automobiles and Jain Irrigation, Kirloskar Pumps,[85] and the state-owned ISCO Fertiliser Company[86] in agriculture. Indian private-sector hospitals and universities also expanded to Africa. The Mahatma Gandhi University, for example, built a campus in Rwanda in 2014 whilst T. John College started operating three campuses in Mauritius in 2015.

Although state-to-state relations provide background stability to enable such private sector activity, and whilst aforementioned changes in the government of India's trade and export policy in 1990s opened the possibility for such opportunities, what is important about private-sector activity in Africa was the degree to which the initiative to identify, invest and secure deals happened independently. For example, Cheru and Modi's edited volume documents several large Indian private-sector agricultural projects in Ethiopia.[87] Another prominent example is the deal Mittal Energy-OVL (the latter a subsidiary of a state-owned firm) secured in Nigeria two exploration blocks in 2005. In exchange, and without pledges from the state and ExIm Bank, they signed a deal with the Nigerian state to develop U.S.$6 billion of infrastructure, including an oil refinery, an east-west railway, and a 2000 MW power plant.[88] The centrality of private-sector actors is also evident in the way in which the state-subsidized ExIm Bank-IDEAS loan scheme was initiated. Dye[89] demonstrates in the case of Nyabarongo Dam in Rwanda, how an Indian firm, Angelique international, initiated this project and, along with Saxena,[90] shows that this was the widespread modality for ExIm Bank loans: Compensating for the absence of State-State dialogue, Indian firms took advantage of the subsidized loan to offer themselves to governments in Africa, stating that the host country could apply for this credit scheme.

The Key Role of Business Federations

A key actor forging greater economic links between India and Africa has been India's private sector federations. The two leading groups, FICCI and CII, played a prominent role in lobbying the government to fund trade missions and conferences, resulting in the 2002 Focus Africa fund. Using this money, FICCI has subsequently convened numerous trade missions to Africa, each one focused on different sectors such as pharmaceuticals or agriculture. Their flagship event is called 'Namaskar Africa' and has a rotating focus. CII has played a similar role, organizing trade missions and hosting the well-attended annual India-Africa Conclave in partnership with the Indian ExIm Bank which had involved 800 delegates from 25 countries by 2012.[91] These events have been well attended every year by politicians from Africa, including at senior levels, with the 2009 meeting hosting Rwanda's President Paul Kagame, for instance. Compared to the government agencies, these private sector operators had a far greater, and more consistent, presence continually engaging with politicians in Africa and visiting the continent at least as regularly as the Indian government officials. Indeed, they are often the main agents organizing the trade fairs and investment exhibition events conducted by Indian embassies in Africa.[92] Overall, the degree of consistent activity suggests that FICCI and CII had a cohesive (if entirely business-focused) idea of what India-Africa relations could become and a detailed attention to promoting Indian commercial interests in the sectors where they have competitive advantages.

Conclusion

In coming to grips with India's policy towards Africa, some analysts have posited the emergence of a 'Delhi consensus' during the years of UPA rule. According to this view, India, especially in the context of East Africa,[93] pushed an Africa policy that was 'softer' than China's, with much activity originating beyond the state in the private sector and diaspora actions, leading to a more horizontal integration into African economies, utilizing local firms, labour, and supply chains rather than relying solely on imports. This would imply an approach to development cooperation that is more bottom-up, taking in African countries' demands, engaging diaspora in recipient economies, and with a focus on areas such as health and education, arguably to a greater extent than others.

Whilst this view captures some of the realities on the ground (and the considerable differences between India and China's approaches to Africa, the latter tightly led by a state under Communist Party rule), this chapter sees Africa-India relations in the way they materialized in 2004–14, as lacking in strong cohesion and not being the product of a joined-up agenda under UPA. We have argued that despite an important upgrading of ties and the assertion of a rhetoric marked by strong continuities

with NAM-era South-South Cooperation, Africa was not a major foreign policy priority for the UPA government (this is entirely consistent
with the status of Africa in the foreign policies of India, both pre-2004
and post-2014). State action on the continent was somewhat sporadic,
despite a number of high-level diplomatic attempts best illustrated by
Petroleum Minister Mani Shankar Aiyar's relatively brief period in office.
Notwithstanding action regarding oil investment, summit activity, and
development cooperation, the Africa policy that emerged was less sustained and vigorous than the rhetoric deployed around it. Further to this,
the pattern of trade that transpired during this period—Africa exporting
to India primary resources, with India exporting to Africa agricultural
products, automobiles, pharmaceuticals, etc.—is not significantly different from pre-existing trade patterns between Africa and the rest of the
world, and especially the West. Structural patterns that existed before the
UPA regime, therefore, persisted into the 2004–14 era.

However, it is undeniable that the decade under UPA rule did see an
important upgrading of India-Africa relations, in continuity with the upwards trajectory initiated in the 1990s, and that this approach was different from both the Beijing approach and the Washington consensus.
The key initiative and key agency in getting deals implemented resided
with private companies, with diaspora playing a vital, ground-up role that
is absent in the Africa policies of other major players on the continent.
More generally, the potential for India in Africa remains strong: India can
provide Africa with cheaper but good standard services in health, education, and pharmaceuticals, and will likely remain an important partner
for the continent's development.

Notes

1. Others put this a $71 billion (Viswanathan 2015; Wagner 2019).
2. Afreximbank and ExIm India (2018). Having been $967,000 in 1990.
3. Chakrabarty (2017).
4. Taylor (2016).
5. Eurostat (online data code: Comext data code: DS-018995).
6. Singhal and Qadri (2014).
7. E.g. Manmohan Singh's speech to a Joint Assembly of the Nigeria National
   Assembly, 15th October, 2007.

8. Of several historical works emphasizing longstanding connections across the Indian Ocean see e.g. Bose (2009) and especially Metcalf (2007).
9. Interviews, former senior MEA official; senior official ORF (2016); Dubey (2016); Dubey and Biswas (2016).
10. Mawdsley and McCann (2011); Mawdsley (2011).
11. Viswanathan (2015).
12. Mohan (2002), 33.
13. Price (2011); Corbridge and Harriss (2000); D'Costa (2010).
14. Corbridge and Harriss (2000); Bajpai (2011); Vanaik (2011); D'Costa (2010); Corbridge and Harriss (2000); Also part of a desire to increase their international profile (Adeney and Wyatt 2010, 216).
15. Price (2011).
16. Taylor (2016).
17. Sinha (2011).
18. Sinha (2011).
19. Interview, Senior Official, Business Federation, 2016.
20. Although a global programme, typically 60% goes to Africa.
21. Saxena (2016).
22. Alden, Large, and Soares de Oliveira (2008); Bräutigam (2011).
23. Soares de Oliveira (2008).
24. Carmody (2013), 74.
25. Wagner (2019).
26. Saxena (2016); Singhal and Qadri (2014); Interview, Officials, ExIm Bank, 2016.
27. Interview, Official, MEA, 2016.
28. Saxena (2016); energy and transport accounting for 50% of loans.
29. Interviews, S&P, MEA Official, 2019.
30. Carmody (2011).
31. Singhal and Qadri (2014).
32. Jalata (2014). Although this went unused and was later repurposed for a transmission line.
33. Frynas and Paulo (2007, 232). Although lines of credit were actually negotiated separately with individual countries.
34. Dye (2018) details discussion, particularly in chapter 2.
35. Carmody (2011).
36. Figures from the not-published MEA database analysed during 2016 fieldwork.
37. Interview, Senior Researcher, 2016.
38. Price (2011).
39. E.g. Deals now exist with the Apollo Hospital group for tele-consulting in 16 countries, with the infrastructure provided by Airtel. At https://www.lusakati mes.com/2016/07/15/airtel-africa-apollo-hospitals-brings-expert-healthcare-africa/.
40. Viswanathan (2015).
41. Cheru and Obi (2011); Carmody (2013); Carmody (2011).

42. Interviews with former senior diplomats, Delhi, 2020.

43. Beri and Institute for Defence Studies and Analyses (2015).

44. Taylor (2016).

45. Sharma and Mahajan (2007).

46. With Petronas (Malaysian) 30%; CNPC (Chinese) 40% (Patey 2011; Verma 2017; Patey 2014).

47. Biswas (2015).

48. McCann (2011) is a discussion of the role of diaspora in India-Africa relations centred on Kenya

49. Interviews, Senior Officials, BHEL, Shapoorji Pallonji, 2016, 2019.

50. Wagner (2019). E.g. Through the creation of a commission on the diaspora.

51. Wagner (2019).

52. Hurrell and Sengupta (2012); Hurrell and Narlikar (2006); Narlikar (2013).

53. Dye (2018).

54. Saxena (2016).

55. Chakrabarty (2017).

56. Carmody (2011); Chakrabarty (2017); Vines (2010).

57. Dye (2016).

58. Rahmato (2013).

59. 2004 Mauritius, 06 SA, 07 Nigeria/SA (IBSA(/Uganda (Commonwealth Heads of State), 2009 Egypt (NAM summit), Ethiopia (Forum) Tanzania, SA (BRICS). (MEA, Database of Incoming Visits https://www.mea.gov.in/incoming-visits. htm?1/incoming_visits).

60. Afreximbank and ExIm India (2018); Eurostat (online data code: Comext data code: DS-018995); Chen and Nord.

61. Data from ExImAtlasIndia (https://www.eximatlasindia.com/); Telling in 2009 India's trade with Africa stood at 39 billion, not China's 109 billion (Cheru and Obi 2011).

62. D'Souza (2007).

63. Dye (2016, 2018).

64. Carmody (2011).

65. Taylor, van der Merwe, and Dodd (2016); Dubey and Biswas (2016).

66. Out of 54 countries.

67. Taylor (2016).

68. Stolte (2015).

69. Taylor (2016).

70. For Brazil, see Dye and Alencastro (2020) and Dye (2021), For China Gill and Reilly (2007); Pehnelt (2011).

71. Although, given the volume of private firms, embassies have not controlled activity nor are they fully knowledgeable, especially in agriculture. See Gu et al. (2016).

72. Dye (2018, chap. 2).

73. Lucey, Makokera, and Schoeman (2015).

74. Singhal and Qadri (2014).
75. Interviews with Mani Shankar Aiyar and Ambassador Talmiz Ahmad, Aiyar's adviser during his tenure has Petroleum Minister, Delhi, August 2009.
76. Interview with Vikram Mehta, Chairman of Shell India, Mumbai, September 2009. See also Soares de Oliveira (2008).
77. Foshko (2011), 44.
78. *Reuters* (2013).
79. Carmody (2011).
80. Taylor, van der Merwe, and Dodd (2016, 2).
81. Viswanathan (2015).
82. Interview, Senior Civil Servant, 2016.
83. Adisu, Sharkey, and Okoroafo (2013).
84. Interview, Senior Researcher, ORF, 2016.
85. Interviews, Senior Official, Business Federation; Senior Researcher, ORF, 2016.
86. Interview, Former Senior Official, MEA, 2016.
87. Cheru and Modi (2013). E.g. Kortori flower cultivation plantation.
88. This eventually fell through when one block was found to not have oil (Lucey, Makokera, and Schoeman 2015; Verma 2017).
89. Dye (2018).
90. Saxena (2016).
91. Saran (2012). The first 2005 meeting saw 160 delegates discussing 70 projects worth U.S.$5 billion whilst the second expanded to 300 delegates discussing $17 billion worth of projects with governments making specific investment requests Naidu (2008, 121–2).
92. Interviews, former senior MEA official, 2016; MEA official, 2019.
93. Narlikar (2010a, 2010b, 2013).

References

Adeney, Katharine, and Andrew Wyatt. 2010. *Contemporary India*. Contemporary States and Societies Houndsmills. Basingstoke, Hampshire; New York: Palgrave Macmillan.
Adisu, Kinfu, Thomas Sharkey, and Sam Okoroafo. 2013. 'Analyzing Indian Policies and Firm Strategies in Africa.' *Journal of Management Research* 5, no. 3. At http://www.macrothink.org/journal/index.php/jmr/article/view/3499,   accessed December 4, 2017.
Afreximbank, and ExIm India. 2018. *Deepening South-South Collaboration: An Analysis of Africa and India's Trade and Investment*. Cairo: Afreximbank and Exim India.
Alden, Chris, Daniel Large, and Ricardo Soares de Oliveira. 2008. 'Introduction: China Returns to Africa.' In Chris Alden, Daniel Large, and Ricardo Soares de Oliveira, eds. *China Returns to Africa: A Rising Power and a Continent Embrace*. London: Hurst.

Bajpai, Kanti. 2011. 'India and the World.' In Niraja Gopal Jayal and Pratap Bhanu Mehta, eds. *The Oxford Companion to Politics in India*, Student edition/with a new preface. New Delhi: Oxford University Press.

Beri, Ruchita, and Institute for Defence Studies and Analyses, eds. 2015. *India and Africa: Common Security Challenges for the Next Decade*. New Delhi: Pentagon Press in association with Institute for Defence Studies & Analyses.

Biswas, Aparajita. 2015. 'India's Energy Security Issues and African Oil.' In Ruchita Beri and Institute for Defence Studies and Analyses, eds. *India and Africa: Common Security Challenges for the Next Decade*. New Delhi: Pentagon Press in association with Institute for Defence Studies & Analyses.

Bose S. 2009. *A Hundred Horizons: The Indian Ocean in the Age of Global Empire*. Cambridge, MA: Harvard University Press.

Bräutigam, Deborah. 2011. *The Dragon's Gift: The Real Story of China in Africa*. 1st publ. in pbk. Oxford: Oxford University Press.

Carmody, Pádraig Risteard. 2011. 'India and the "Asian Drivers" in Africa.' In Emma Mawdsley and Gerard McCann, eds. *India in Africa: Changing Geographies of Power*. Cape Town: Pambazuka Press.

———. 2013. *The Rise of the BRICS in Africa: The Geopolitics of South-South Relations*. London; New York: Zed Books.

Chakrabarty, Malancha. 2017. 'Indian Investments in Africa: Scale, Trends, and Policy Recommendations.' ORF Working Paper New Delhi: Observer Research Foundation. At https://www.orfonline.org/wp-content/uploads/2017/05/ORF_WorkingPaper_IndiaInAfrica.pdf.

Chen, Wenjie, and Roger Nord. 2018. 'Reassessing Africa's Global Partnerships. Approaches for Engaging the New World Order.' In The Brookings Institution and Brahima S. Coulibaly, eds. *Foresight Africa: Top Priorities for the Continent in 2018*. Washington DC: The Brookings Institution.

Cheru, Fantu, and Cyril I. Obi. 2011. 'India-Africa Relations in the 21st Century: Genuine Partnership or a Marriage of Convenience?' In Emma Mawdsley and Gerard McCann, eds. *India in Africa: Changing Geographies of Power*. Cape Town: Pambazuka Press.

Cheru, Fantu, and Renu Modi, eds. 2013. *Agricultural Development and Food Security in Africa: The Impact of Chinese, Indian and Brazilian Investments* (Africa Now). London: Zed Books.

Corbridge, Stuart, and John Harriss. 2000. *Reinventing India: Liberalization, Hindu Nationalism, and Popular Democracy*. Cambridge, UK; Malden, MA: Polity; Blackwell Publishers.

D'Costa, Anthony P., ed. 2010. *A New India? Critical Reflections in the Long Twentieth Century*. India and Asia in the Global Economy London; New York, NY: Anthem Press.

D'Souza, Shanthie Mariet. 2007. 'India's Aid to Afghanistan: Challenges and Prospects.' *Strategic Analysis* 31, no. 5: 833–42.

Dubey, Ajay Kumar. 2016. 'India-Africa Relations: Historical Goodwill and a Vision for the Future.' In Ajay Kumar Dubey and Aparajita Biswas, eds. *India and Africa's Partnership: A Vision for a New Future*. India Studies in Business and Economics New Delhi: Springer.

Dubey, Ajay Kumar, and Aparajita Biswas, eds. 2016. *India and Africa's Partnership: A Vision for a New Future*. India Studies in Business and Economics New Delhi: Springer.

Dye, Barnaby Joseph. 2016. 'The Return of "High Modernism"? Exploring the Changing Development Paradigm through a Rwandan Case Study of Dam Construction.' *Journal of Eastern African Studies* 10, no. 2: 303–24.

———. 2018. *The Politics of Dam Resurgence: High Modernist Statebuilding and the Emerging Powers in Africa*. Oxford: University of Oxford.

Dye, Barnaby Joseph. 2021 Brazil's Boom and Bust in Tanzania: A Case Study of Naivety? In M Alencastro and P Seabra, eds. Brazil-Africa Relations in the 21st Century. Switzerland: Springer International Publishing.

Dye, Barnaby Joseph, and Mathias Alencastro. 2020. 'Debunking Brazilian Exceptionalism in Its Africa Relations: Evidence from Rwanda and Tanzania.' *Global Society* 34, no. 4: 166-186.

Eurostat (online data code: Comext data code: DS-018995). 'EU Trade since 1988 by SITC (DS-018995).' At https://ec.europa.eu/eurostat/statistics-explained/index. php?title=Africa-EU_-_international_trade_in_goods_statistics.

Foshko, Katherine. 2011. *Re-Energising the India-Russia Relationship: Opportunities and Challenges for the 21st Century*. Gateway House Research Paper Mumbai: Gateway House.

Frynas, Jedrzej George, and Manuel Paulo. 2007. 'A New Scramble for African Oil? Historical, Political, and Business Perspectives.' *African Affairs* 106, no. 423: 229–51.

Gerrard, McCann. 2011. Diaspora, political economy and India's relations with Kenya. In E Mawdsley and G McCann, eds. *India in Africa: Changing Geographies of Power*. Cape Town: Pambazuka Press.

Gill, Bates, and James Reilly. 2007. 'The Tenuous Hold of China Inc. in Africa.' *The Washington Quarterly* 30, no. 3: 37–52.

Gu, Jing, Chuanhong Zhang, Alcides Vaz, and Langton Mukwereza. 2016. 'Chinese State Capitalism? Rethinking the Role of the State and Business in Chinese Development Cooperation in Africa.' *World Development* 81: 24–34.

Hurrell, Andrew, and Amrita Narlikar. 2006. 'A New Politics of Confrontation? Brazil and India in Multilateral Trade Negotiations.' *Global Society* 20, no. 4: 415–33.

Hurrell, Andrew, and Sandeep Sengupta. 2012. 'Emerging Powers, North-South Relations and Global Climate Politics.' *International Affairs* 88, no. 3: 463–84.

Jalata, Gedion G. 2014. 'Development Assistance from the South: Comparative Analysis of Chinese and Indian to Ethiopia.' *Chinese Studies* 03, no. 01: 24–39.

Lucey, Amanda, Catherine Grant Makokera, and Mark Schoeman. 2015. 'India-Africa Relations: The Role of the Private Sector. From Mombasa to Mumbai: How Can Trade between India and Africa Be Improved?' Fahamu Emerging Powers Project ISS Pretoria: Institute for Security Studies. At https://issafrica.org/resea rch/papers/india-africa-relations-the-role-of-the-private-sector.

Mawdsley, Emma. 2011. 'The Rhetorics and Rituals of "South-South" Development Cooperation: Notes on India an Africa.' In Emma Mawdsley and Gerard McCann, eds. *India in Africa: Changing Geographies of Power*. Cape Town: Pambazuka Press.

Mawdsley, Emma, and Gerard McCann, eds. 2011. *India in Africa: Changing Geographies of Power*. Cape Town: Pambazuka Press.

Metcalf, Thomas R. 2008. *Imperial Connections: India in the Indian Ocean Arena, 1860 - 1920*. Berkley, CA: University of California Press.

Mohan, Raja C. 2005. *Crossing the Rubicon: The Shaping of India's New Foreign Policy*. New Delhi; New York: Penguin Books.

Naidu, Sanusha. 2008. 'India's Growing African Strategy.' *Review of African Political Economy* 35, no. 115: 116–28.

Narlikar, Amrita. 2010a. *New Powers: How to Become One and How to Manage Them*. London. Hurst.

———. 2010b. 'India's Rise to Power: Where Does East Africa Fit in?' *Review of African Political Economy* 37, no. 126: 451–64.

———. 2013. 'India Rising: Responsible to Whom?' *International Affairs* 89, no. 3: 595–614.

Patey, Luke A. 2011. 'Fragile Fortunes: India's Oil Venture into War-Torn Sudan.' In Emma Mawdsley and Gerard McCann, eds. *India in Africa: Changing Geographies of Power* Cape Town: Pambazuka Press.

———. 2014. *The New Kings of Crude: China, India, and the Global Struggle for Oil in Sudan and South Sudan*. London, United Kingdom: Hurst & Company.

Pehnelt, Gernot. 2011. 'The Political Economy of China's Aid Policy in Africa.' In Andreas Freytag, ed. *Securing the Global Economy: G8 Global Governance for a Post-Crisis World*. Global Finance Series Farnham, Surrey, England; Burlington, VT: Ashgate.

Price, Gareth. 2011. 'For the Global Good: India's Developing International Role.' A Chatham House Report. St James' Square, London: Chatham House.

Rahmato, D. 2013. 'Up for Grabs: The Case of Large Indian Investments in Ethiopian Agriculture.' In Fantu Cheru and Renu Modi, eds. *Agricultural Development and Food Security in Africa: The Impact of Chinese, Indian and Brazilian Investments* Africa Now London: Zed Books.

Reuters. 2013. 'Senegal Wins Court Case against Arcelor Mittal—Government.' *Reuters*, September 10. At https://www.reuters.com/article/senegal-arcelormittal/senegal-wins-court-case-against-arcelor-mittal-government-idUSL5N0H64EZ2 0130910.

Saran, (Ambassador) Shyam. 2012. 'India and Africa: Development Partnership.' Discussion Paper 180. New Delhi: Research and Information System for Developing Countries.

Saxena, Prabodh. 2016. 'India's Credit Lines: Instrument of Economic Diplomacy.' In Sachin Chaturvedi and Anthea Mulakala, eds. *India's Approach to Development Cooperation*, 1st Edition Routledge Contemporary South Asia Series 113. London; New York: Routledge Taylor & Francis.

Sharma, Devika, and Deepti Mahajan. 2007. 'Energising Ties: The Politics of Oil.' *South African Journal of International Affairs* 14, no. 2: 37–52.

Sinha, Aseema. 2011. 'Business and Politics.' In Niraja Gopal Jayal and Pratap Bhanu Mehta, eds. *The Oxford Companion to Politics in India*, Student edition/with a new preface. New Delhi: Oxford University Press.

Singhal, Rajrishi, and Asgar Qadri. 2014. 'Development and Diplomacy Through Lines of Credit: Achievements and Lessons Learnt.' Occasional Paper 53. New Delhi: Observer Research Foundation (ORF).

Soares de Oliveira, Ricardo. 2008. 'India's Rise and the Global Politics of Energy Supply: Challenges for the Next Decade.' The 11th Vasant J. Sheth Memorial Lecture.

Stolte, Christina. 2015. *Brazil's Africa Strategy: Role Conception and the Drive for International Status*. New York: Palgrave Macmillan.

Taylor, Ian. 2016. 'India's Economic Diplomacy in Africa.' In Ajay Kumar Dubey and Aparajita Biswas, eds. *India and Africa's Partnership*. New Delhi: Springer India. At http://link.springer.com/10.1007/978-81-322-2619-2_6, accessed December 4, 2017.

Taylor, Ian, Justin van der Merwe, and Nicole Dodd. 2016. 'Nehru's Neoliberals: Draining or Aiding Africa?' In Justin van der Merwe, Ian Taylor, and Alexandra Arkhangelskaya, eds. *Emerging Powers in Africa*. Cham: Springer International Publishing. At http://link.springer.com/10.1007/978-3-319-40736-4_6, accessed November 16, 2017.

Vanaik, Achim. 2011. 'India's Foreign Policy since the End of the Cold War: Domestic Determinants?' In Sanjay Ruparelia, Sanjay Reddy, John Harriss, and Stuart Corbridge, eds. *Understanding India's New Political Economy: A Great Transformation?* Abingdon, Oxon; New York: Routledge.

Verma, Rajneesh. 2017. *India and China in Africa: A Comparative Perspective of the Oil Industry*. New York: Routledge. At http://www.tandfebooks.com/isbn/978131 5650685, accessed July 7, 2018.

Vines, Alex. 2010. 'India's Africa Engagement: Prospects for the 2011 India–Africa Forum.' Programme Paper AFP 2010/01. St James' Square, London: Chatham House.

Viswanathan, H.S.S. 2015. 'India-Africa Relations: Nurturing and Enduring Partnership.' In Abhijnan Rej, Tanoubi Ngangom, and Observer Research Foundation, eds. *Common Futures: India and Africa in Partnership*. New Delhi: Observer Research Foundation.

Wagner, Christian. 2019. 'India's Africa Policy.' *SWP Research Paper*. At https://www.swp-berlin.org/10.18449/2019RP09/, accessed November 29, 2019.

10

Quest for Energy, Connectivity, and Security

India-Central Asia Relations during the UPA Rule

Bhavna Dave

Introduction

India and Central Asia have enjoyed close cultural and religious connections for centuries. The shared ties were further reinforced by the mutual interest and goodwill generated by Indo-Soviet friendship. Yet despite centuries-old cultural-spiritual links and the assumed affinity between their peoples, Central Asia has remained a remote region in India's extended neighbourhood, remaining near and yet quite far. The potential of India's enormous cultural capital remains unrealized due to the profound geographical disadvantage of the lack of easy access routes to the region. India was practically invisible as a strategic or diplomatic actor at least until the mid-2000s. In contrast, China, with the geopolitical advantage of a 3200-km long border that it shares with Kazakhstan, Kyrgyzstan, and Tajikistan, has made enormous strides in establishing itself as the most prominent economic actor in the Central Asian region, enhanced its role in security provision, and bolstered its public diplomacy to muster 'soft power' and promote its developmental model. As a strategic-late mover, India is just about carving a niche for itself in a region that has been incorporated within China's Silk Road Economic Belt (SREB), linking China with the Middle East, Europe, and Africa.

After nearly two decades of 'discursive activity that exceeded the reality of bilateral relationship' (Peyrouse and Laruelle 2011), a gradual shift in India's policy towards the Central Asian region became discernible under

Bhavna Dave, *Quest for Energy, Connectivity, and Security* In: *Forging New Partnerships, Breaching New Frontiers*. Edited by: Rejaul Karim Laskar, Oxford University Press. © Oxford University Press 2022.
DOI: 10.1093/oso/9780192868060.003.0010

the second term of the UPA as the Manmohan Singh government began looking to Central Asia for India's growing energy needs to sustain its burgeoning economic growth and devise solutions to the lack of transport connectivity that had continued to stymie the development of economic ties with the region.

The adoption in 2012 of 'Connect Central Asia' Policy, a much-belated act, nonetheless denoted India's first comprehensive attempt to develop a strategy for the region. It marked a departure from the complacency, lethargy, and lofty iterations of cultural ties that had marred the formulation of an appropriate response to the transformations occurring in the Central Asian states and the rapid shifts in regional geopolitics. It sought to articulate a broader vision of the region by prioritizing the establishment of transport connectivity, investments in energy and acknowledging that these would require building on India's existing partnerships with various regional actors and engaging actively with the emerging multilateral organizations.

The launch of the Connect Central Asia Policy in 2012 also reflected a shift in India's strategic approach to Afghanistan in light of the changed context with the departure of NATO troops in 2014 and scaling down of the U.S. engagement in Afghanistan and the Eurasian region. The concept of a 'Greater Central Asia' promoted by the U.S. centred on the establishment of a New Silk Road (NSR) for forging transport and trade linkages as well as people-to-people contacts between Central Asia and South Asia through Afghanistan in which India potentially had a vital role. However, by 2013, this idea had fizzled out due to the lack of a strategic vision and financial investments. At the same time, during the visit to Astana in October 2013, Xi Jinping launched China's SREB Initiative, which became an integral element of what later was presented as the Belt and Road Initiative (BRI).

India's decision in 2011 to seek membership of the Shanghai Cooperation Organization (SCO), which it had joined as an observer in 2005 with a lukewarm participation (Raman 2006), was an important precursor to the launch of the Connect Central Asia Policy, marking a shift to engaging with multilateral organizations in the region, instead of the earlier focus on bilateral ties and relying on Russia for advancing its objectives.

This chapter will identify the processes shaping India's diplomacy towards Central Asia during the UPA rule, leading to the adoption of Connect Central Asia Policy and its ensuing realization. It will analyse the policies and measures adopted by the UPA in four key areas: (i) connectivity; (ii) energy partnerships; (iii) strategic engagement; and (iv) multilateral cooperation. The analysis of the aforementioned areas details how India's Central Asia policy has evolved through adjustment to a number of important geopolitical shifts in the region: the all-round dominance of China, the growing Sino-Russian partnership in regional multilateral fora such as the SCO, India's limited strategic engagement with the United States in the creation of a 'Greater Central Asia' incorporating Afghanistan with Central and South Asia, its turn to Iran for the solution to the problem of connectivity with Central Asia, and the continuing rivalry with Pakistan whose efforts to establish close links with Central Asia received a boost by its partnership with China in the construction of the China Pakistan Economic Corridor (CPEC), connecting China's Xinjiang region to the China-built Gwadar port in the Arabian Sea. In conclusion, the chapter notes that being at a geographical disadvantage that turned it into a late mover to the region, India, during the UPA period, has had to carve out its options through an enhanced multilateral cooperation with a range of actors and institutions in its extended neighbourhood and build on the niches where it possessed a distinct edge.

Evolution of India's Policy towards Central Asia

Prime Minister Narasimha Rao's visit to Kazakhstan, Turkmenistan, and Kyrgyzstan between 1993 and 1995 promised a fresh approach to the region, which was still seen as Russia's backyard. Rao proclaimed that Central Asia for India is an area 'of high priority, where we aim to stay engaged far into the future. We are an independent partner with no selfish motives. We only desire honest and open friendship and to promote stability and cooperation without causing harm to any third country' (cited in Roy 2011, 161). Rao's proclamation was to offer the discursive genesis of the 'Look North' policy, which soon emerged as the narrative framework of India's relations with Central Asia (Kavalski 2010). It identified several key areas of cooperation for forging a new partnership: establishing air connectivity to aid trade, investments, tourism, strategic partnerships in defence and security affairs; promoting ties in spheres of higher education, medicine; and providing developmental assistance (Pradhan 2015).

The 'Look North' Policy emphasized secular values and cultivating mutual interest in combating religious fundamentalism, terrorism, narcotics-funded violence, and crime. It was also a benign representation to the newly emergent Central Asian states of India as a model of secular, multiethnic order and as a normative actor, guided by shared concerns to promote stability and cooperation. Unlike the 'Look East' policy, which successfully reset India's economic and strategic relations with Southeast Asia, the goals set in the 'Look North' were overshadowed by India's complex relationship with China, the lack of a strategic vision and tools for pursuing the goals. 'Look North' Policy denoted an attempt, albeit unsuccessful, to 'break out of the claustrophobic confines of South Asia' (Kavalski 2010, 43).

Atal Bihari Vajpayee was the next prime minister to visit the region in 2002, where he also attended the first Conference on Interaction and Confidence Building Measure in Asia (CICA) in Almaty. CICA was the first major Central Asian regional cooperation structure initiated by Kazakhstan, of which India became a member and has remained its consistent supporter and an active participant. Vajpayee was to underscore the 'new geopolitical reality' in the region following the independence of the Central Asian states, the end of the Cold War, and India's significant role in Afghanistan. He was also the first Indian prime minister to visit Tajikistan in 2003, in an affirmation of Tajikistan's important role in supporting the Northern Alliance and its vital contribution to realizing India's strategic goals in the region.

Notwithstanding the NDA government's emphasis on a closer engagement with the extended neighbourhood as a core element in foreign policy (Scott 2009), Central Asia continued to remain peripheral to all major foreign policy initiatives. Lacking shared borders, transport links, trade, and economic leverage, India had been content to follow a 'do no harm' policy in the Central Asian region. During his visit to Central Asian states in 2003, Minister of External Affairs Yashwant Sinha had averred that 'we are not in Central Asia to replace anyone. We see Central Asia as part of India's extended neighbourhood and our presence there is to promote a mutually inclusive relationship' (Aneja 2003). Such pronouncements reinforced the image of India as a relative bystander in a region that has historically been described as an arena of the 'Great Game' between European powers and again as the site of a 'New Great Game' denoting competition for energy resources and security objectives between the emerging powers. During the 1990s and early 2000s, when numerous Western diplomatic establishments, China, Japan, and Korea began playing close attention to the region, training experts and policymakers to learn languages of Central Asia, India was visibly lagging behind in imparting appropriate Central Asian language training to its diplomatic staff, many of whom appeared self-satisfied in the belief that as Indians they already had the cultural and linguistic affinity to understood the Central Asian societies.[1]

Central Asia is perhaps the only region in India's extended neighbourhood where India's image ranged from being positive to neutral, untainted by perception of dominance, conflict, or political or ideological contestation. The positive image based on 'goodwill without depth' (Dave 2016) in many ways stemmed from the absence of an effective engagement with the region. As Subrato Mitra (2003, 399) notes, Central Asia as a neutral space masked the 'hiatus between India's self-perception as a status quo power and its perceptions by the neighbouring states as a regional bully'. From this standpoint, India's cautious 'do no harm' approach under Look North Policy, combined with a benign presentation of its secular model, sought to build on existing goodwill, without a long- or medium-term strategy (Mehta 2009). It approached Central Asia still as a backyard of Russia, failing to apprehend the profound, though chaotic process of post-Soviet transition and sovereignty consolidation among Central Asian states on the one hand and respond to the rapid expansion of China's economic activities, energy investments in the region on the other. With China asserting its first-mover advantage, India's policy inadvertently had to work on calibrating responses to the actions of China and Sino-Pakistan cooperation in the region.

India-Central Asia Relations under the UPA Rule

The new self-confidence and major power image gained by rapid economic growth gave a boost to India's cultural and economic diplomacy in Central Asia during the first phase of the UPA rule with a series of medium to high-level exchanges facilitating a gradual shift from symbolic utterances of friendship to concrete steps at establishing energy, transport and security partnership.

However, As far as launching a decisive presence in Central Asia was concerned, India was constrained by still a weak economy, lack of connectivity, absence of a meaningful trade and investment, struggling to link its policies in Afghanistan and Central Asia under a single strategy and operating in a context where China had already seized numerous initiatives. Unlike China, India did not yet have the credibility to portray itself as an emerging economic power or as a more 'developed' partner (Sachdeva 2011). India had averaged just under 5% annual growth between 2000 and 2005, which was just over half of China's annual per capita GDP growth exceeding 8%. Though economic growth accelerated further during the second term of UPA, it also fluctuated and still lagged behind that of China's.

During a visit to Uzbekistan in April 2006, Prime Minister Manmohan Singh reiterated the importance of Central Asia in India's extended neighbourhood and pledged 'to build on our traditional ties in providing them with new meaning and substance including in the political, economic, defence, energy, science and technology and cultural fields' (cited in Scott 2009). The pledge to provide new substance to ties broke away from much of the normative baggage of the Look North policy while incorporating its emphasis on establishing close economic and cultural cooperation in subsequent policy iterations. Though it sought to signal India as a 'rising power' parallel to China (Dave 2016, 5), the Look North policy failed to emulate the success that the Look East policy had achieved by establishing closer economic, trade, and cultural linkages with South East Asian countries (Sikri 2009a). While India's aspiration for closer engagement with Central Asia had remained unfulfilled, China had steadfastly established itself as a formidable economic and strategic partner for the region. It was China, and not Central Asia, that India encountered everywhere where it looked North (Kavalski 2010).

As noted earlier, Central Asia was seen as culturally very proximate and at the same time geographically quite distant. India's efforts at forging meaningful economic, political and cultural, people-to-people linkages have been stymied primarily by geographical barriers and lack of connectivity. As the strategist K. Subramanian (2015) said, 'the Central Asian Republics (CARs) posed the most excruciating and complex challenges to Indian diplomacy judged whether by geostrategic compulsions or by India's energy concerns'. The UPA Government sought to overcome this geographical barrier and establish closer connections with the region through the 'Connect Central Asia' policy.

The 'Connect Central Asia' policy, launched in 2012, sought to promote India's new image, define its objectives and priorities in the region and align them with its emerging power status. The Policy was unveiled at the first meeting of India-Central Asia Dialogue in June 2012 in Bishkek, Kyrgyzstan, by India's Minister of State for External Affairs E. Ahamed.[2] Ahamed reiterated the priorities placed on establishing economic and cultural cooperation under the Look North policy pointed to the urgency of formulating a cohesive solution to the unfavourable geography that had plagued transport and trade connectivity. The lack of suitable transport connections and direct flights had deterred potential Indian investors who otherwise may have been willing to brave language and cultural barriers, cumbersome visa procedures, and challenging business climate in the region.

The pronouncements under 'Connect Central Asia' policy emphasized Central Asia's ongoing political and economic integration with the world, highlighted the region's place in India's extended neighbourhood, and called for enhancing strategic and security cooperation, including close consultations on Afghanistan, energy, and other natural resources, as well as connectivity. By establishing a template for finding innovative solutions for overcoming transport and infrastructural connectivity and forming comprehensive partnerships in the development of energy and natural resources, it set many concrete objectives, departing from the ritualistic affirmations of historical ties, amity, and friendship.

During the visit to Tajikistan a month later in July 2012, Minister of External Affairs S. M. Krishna summed up the priorities of the Connect Central Asia Policy as the four C's—'commerce, connectivity, consular and community' (*The Economic Times*, 3 July 2012b). The four C's targeted for expansion of activities included a broad list of goals and targets— establishment of Central Asian University at Bishkek; connecting Central Asia through an E-Network in telemedicine and other critical areas of commercial activities; opening up of hospitals, centres of excellence in IT sector, enhancing defence and strategic partnership through training and joint research between India and the Central Asian Republics, opening of 14 direct flights between India and the 5 Central Asian countries to give a boost to tourism, trade and commerce, cultural contacts, relaxation of visa regimes, and energy cooperation.

As elaborated below, India's approach towards the Central Asian region during the UPA period can be summarized under four rubrics: Forging Connectivity to Central Asia, Quest for Energy, Quest for Strategic Engagement, and Shift to Multilateralism.

Forging Connectivity to Central Asia

Overcoming the Geographical Barrier

The geopolitical and logistical difficulties of obtaining a transit passage to the Central Asian region through Pakistan had confined India into a rigid frame of fractious relations with Pakistan and lingering suspicion of China. India's Central Asia policy, in many ways, had remained trapped in South Asian constraints.

Afghanistan became an area of strategic priority for India after the defeat of the Taliban by U.S.-led forces, in which India and Russia-backed Northern Alliance played a vital role. India offered $2 billion in developmental aid, forging a close partnership with the United States in the rebuilding of Afghanistan. After the United States acquired military bases in Central Asia (K-2 in Uzbekistan, Manas in Kyrgyzstan) for strategic and humanitarian operations to Afghanistan, discussions in the U.S. centred on devising ways of forging a closer connectivity between Afghanistan and Central Asia through cooperation with India as well as Pakistan. The concept of a 'Greater Central Asia' (Starr 2005) had been gaining currency in the U.S. foreign policy-making circles. It envisaged forging a single integrated unit of South and Central Asia through the building of an NSR for forging economic and security relations. It was an attempt to build on the Western-sponsored Northern Distribution Network (NDN) that sought to establish alternative routes to the traditional access to Afghanistan via Pakistan via a system of air, land, and sea supply routes through Central Asia and Caspian to Europe. The key rationale of the NSR was to stabilize the region through transport and trade connectivity, building economic, strategic, and cultural links following the withdrawal of NATO troops from Afghanistan in 2014.

The United States was betting on India's positive image and close historical-cultural ties with the region to bring South and Central Asia together and curtailing China's growing hold over the region. A Bureau of South and Central Asian Affairs was set up in the State Department in 2006. The NSR concept appeared to be an excellent opportunity for India to leverage its position in Afghanistan and the goodwill in Central Asia with the strength of its growing partnership with the United States.

However, the actual establishment of connectivity between South and Central Asia with Afghanistan as the hub was a formidable task given a number of constraints: the complicated India-Pakistan and Pakistan-Afghanistan relations, the continued U.S.-Iran confrontation, lack of trust and cooperation among the various Central Asian states, and absence of meaningful trade between Afghanistan and Central Asia as well as South and Central Asia and the limited potential for enhancing trade.

The strategic role and cultural capital of India were far from sufficient for it to play a pivotal role in forging trade and transport connectivity under the NSR given its negligible economic presence in Central Asia, which counted for about 0.25% of total Indian trade, with India representing only 0.4% of Central Asian trade. Planned energy security initiatives such as that in the form of developing a Central Asia wide power grid (CASA-1000) connecting resource-rich Central Asia to supply energy to Afghanistan, Pakistan, and India were key objectives that had also led the United States to pin hopes on the construction of the Turkmenistan-Afghanistan-Pakistan-India (TAPI) pipeline.

The NSR idea continued to be debated by the Obama administration but without seeking a consistent participation of India. These proposals did not find much resonance in India. First, the United States did not provide a comprehensive aid package or hold discussions on its strategic elements to bring the plan to fruition. Second, the launching of the NSR initiative was contingent on some degree of goodwill and sustained dialogue among Afghanistan, Pakistan, and India, which did not happen. Third, the advantages of this connectivity to the Central Asian states were mixed—while they could enhance options for the export of energy resources, they also came with the fear of spillover of terrorism and illegal drug trade from Afghanistan and Pakistan into Central Asia.

The failure of the NSR project to materialize due to lack of finances and commitments (Kuchins 2013) and the waning of the U.S. commitment to Afghanistan after 2014 weakened the leverage that India could have developed in the Central Asian region via Afghanistan and its close partnership with both the United States and Russia. By this time, China had already launched its own connectivity initiative, inaugurated in September 2013 by Xi Jinping at Nazarbaev University in Astana as the SREB Initiative. SREB incorporated several elements of the NSR concept, albeit it was China and not India, that was spearheading connectivity between Afghanistan, Pakistan, and Central Asia as part of what later came to be known as the Belt and Road Initiative (BRI).

Developing Connectivity via Iran and Afghanistan

With China and Pakistan developing close transport and infrastructural connectivity, India had to engage in out-of-box thinking to pursue innovative solutions that would bypass the conventional constraints. The solution centred on bringing Iran, a crucial supplier of oil and gas, into the regional geopolitical equation for solving the connectivity conundrum. The Chabahar port, with which India had well-established maritime linkages and had harboured a long-term interest in its expansion, was recognized as the new access point through which rail links could be built to Afghanistan and onwards to Central Asia. The UPA government also renewed the pledge to develop the International North South Transport Corridor (INSTC) and to explore alternative routes. In 2000 Russia, India and Iran had reached an agreement in St Petersburg to establish the INSTC, a 7,200-km-long multi-mode network of ship, rail, and road route for moving freight between major cities such as Mumbai, Moscow, Tehran, Baku, Bandar Abbas, Astrakhan, Bandar Anzali, etc.[3] While the INSTC is currently routed via Iran's Bandar Abbas port, India began exploring the options of connecting it with Central Asia via Chabahar port and thereafter overland corridors passing through Afghanistan. INSTC's membership has since expanded to include all Central Asian states which have pledged to support in completing the missing links along the corridor.

Chabahar was estimated to result in a 60% reduction in shipment costs and a 50% reduction in shipment time from India to Central Asia. India, Iran, and Afghanistan had already agreed in 2003 on a joint development of transportation links to Afghanistan. A finalized plan to construct a 900-km railway line to connect Chabahar port to Afghanistan's mineral-rich Hajigak region unveiled in 2011 (*Hindustan Times*, 1 November 2011) also proposed to build a road from the Uzbek city of Termez to Herat in Afghanistan, to be linked by railways to Chabahar. Dry runs of two routes were conducted in 2014, the first was Mumbai to Baku via Bandar Abbas and the second was Mumbai to Astrakhan via Bandar Abbas, Tehran, and Bandar Anzali. India has spent $134 million during 2005–09 to construct a road from Delaram in Afghanistan to Zaranj at the Iran-Afghanistan border and connect Chabahar and Zaranj by rail, as Iran completed 70% of the first phase of the Chabahar project at the cost of $340 million. Further development of the railway links is contingent on Chabahar becoming fully functional.

Chabahar's development has stalled due to numerous complex issues—the differences between India and Iran on construction contracts and financial commitments and the effects of Western sanctions on Iran that complicated India's relations with Iran. The souring of India-Iran relations after India voted twice voted against Iran at International Atomic Energy Agency (IAEA) (*Hindustan Times*, 28 November 2009) slowed the progress on the Chabahar port and the INSTC as well as India's investments in Iran's energy sector.

While India had supported Iran's development of the civilian nuclear programme, its vote against Iran at IAEA also conveyed an attempt to garner the U.S. support to realize its major power status and ambitions in the region. At the same time, India could not afford to alienate Iran, which was an integral component of its Afghanistan strategy as well as the best option for connectivity with Central Asia. Having agreed to reduce its oil imports from Iran in response to the U.S. stance, the UPA government was subsequently able to assert its strategic autonomy from the United States by refusing to support the sanctions on Iran. Given their significant dependence on Iran for oil and transport routes, the position of India and China also converged with both supporting Iran's right to 'peaceful uses of nuclear energy consistent with its international obligations' at the BRICS summit in 2012 (*The Economic Times*, 29 March 2012a). China, in the meanwhile, had already become Iran's largest trading partner and oil importer, also supplying it with technological know-how to develop its energy resources, military facilities, and shield against the effects of international sanctions (Harold and Nader 2012).

India was able to negotiate a waiver from the expansion of the U.S. sanctions by reducing oil imports from Iran. India's decision in 2011 to become an SCO member (*The Hindu* 2011) also factored in the realization that India's interests with Iran could be advanced further within its multilateral framework in which Russia and China were Iran's allies and opposed the U.S. sanctions. Iran has been keen to upgrade its observer status to become a full SCO member.

The Quest for Energy

A Latecomer in Central Asia's Energy Field

India's rapidly rising energy requirements had already turned it into the fifth largest consumer of energy and placed it to be the third largest by 2030 (Madan 2006). In 2006, then Petroleum and Natural Gas Minister, Mani Shankar Aiyar, stated, 'we are fortunate to be placed at the vortex of an extended neighbourhood which has some of the largest gas resources in the world'. He also referred to the need to tap into the energy potential of Uzbekistan, Kazakhstan, Azerbaijan, and the Astrakhan littoral on the Russian shore off the Caspian to justify the proposed North–South energy corridor from the Kazakhstan port of Aktau to the Iranian port of Chabahar on the Arabian Sea 'as another exciting prospect' for India (Aiyar 2006).

Recognizing the urgency for India, already a latecomer, to be seen as a serious player in carving out a presence for itself in the exploration of the Caspian's rich resources, Aiyar actively lobbied for contracts for Indian firms in the region, targeting Russia's Transneft built Bluestream to bring Caspian oil into the Black Sea as well as Kazakhstan-China pipelines bringing oil to China's Xinjiang region.

In 2005, India came very close to securing the take-over of the Canada-based PetroKazakhstan, then Kazakhstan's second-largest foreign producer after Chevron, after ONGC Videsh Ltd (OVL) made a bid for

$3.9 billion against China's National Petroleum Corporation's (CNPC) $3.6 billion. China clinched the deal last minute after offering $4.18 billion in what India saw as an unfair auction in which 'the goal posts were moved midway [through the auction]' (Ramachandran 2008). Moreover, CNPC's bid is already believed to have been approved a few months earlier during the visit of then Chinese President Hu Jintao with Nazarbaev (Petroleum Economist 2005).

OVL was again on the verge of acquiring what could have been its biggest overseas deal of nearly $5 billion following an agreement in November 2012 with the U.S. energy giant ConocoPhillips to buy its 8.4% stake in the Kashagan oilfield. In 2013 Kazakhstan, at the last minute, blocked the deal by exercising its pre-emptive right to first buy ConocoPhillips' stake, only to sell it to CNPC, which secured the deal (*The Financial Times* 2013, Modi 2013).

A year after India's failed bid in the previous year, Kazakhstan in 2014 offered OVL a stake in medium-sized Abai oil block in the Caspian Sea. It was adjacent to the Satpayev exploration block in which OVL and KMG had signed agreements for the exploration of oil and gas in the Satpayev block in the Caspian Sea, with OVL acquiring a 25% share in 2011 following Manmohan Singh's visit to Astana. Plans to drill two exploration wells on Satpayev in 2014 and 2015 were delayed. Eventually, after having spent almost $300 million on the block, OVL decided to exit it in 2018 as it did not find commercially viable oil (*The Economic Times,* 18 September 2018).

Expansion of India-Kazakhstan Energy Cooperation

An impressive achievement of the UPA government was on forging a comprehensive relationship with Kazakhstan, endowed with rich energy and mineral resources. President Nursultan was the first Central Asian leader to visit Delhi as the Chief Guest at the Republic Day celebrations in 2009, a visit that resulted in a joint declaration of Strategic Partnership. Manmohan Singh's official visit to Astana in 2011 sealed agreements on cooperation over legal issues, peaceful use of nuclear energy, cooperation in agriculture, healthcare, and IT. The meeting between visiting Secretary of the Kazakhstan Security Council Marat Tazhin in February with the

National security advisor Shivshankar Menon paved the way for agreements on Kazakhstan supplying over 2,000 tons of uranium by 2014 (*The Economic Times* 2019). Trade volume between India and Kazakhstan has experienced rapid growth, rising from roughly $80 million in 2004 to $253 million in 2009 and $314 million in 2010.

Turkmenistan-Afghanistan-Pakistan-India Pipeline (TAPI) Project

The prospects of Turkmenistan's abundant gas resources reaching the energy-deficient regions of Afghanistan, Pakistan, and India via a new pipeline (TAPI) generated considerable optimism, notwithstanding the recognition of enormous geopolitical, security, and logistical challenges. The TAPI project, together with Central Asia-South Asia Regional Electricity Trade Project (CASA-1000), was actively promoted by the U.S. State Department as integral components of its New Silk Route Strategy, which were also seen as delivering energy security to Afghanistan (Ashraf 2013). The TAPI project was first proposed by the Asian Development Bank (ADB) in the mid-1990s and later incorporated into the U.S. concept of Greater Central Asia for delivering energy security to Afghanistan and Pakistan in particular. CASA-1000 was a $1.16 billion project with funding from the World Bank to allow for the export of surplus hydroelectricity from Kyrgyzstan and Tajikistan to Afghanistan and Pakistan (Kucera 2011).

The United States saw promoting TAPI also as a counterforce to Iranian, Russian, and Chinese influences and as part of its objective of promoting multiple pipelines from the Caspian and Central Asian region to numerous destinations by bypassing Russia. Indeed, in an ideal geopolitical setting of secure borders, close regional cooperation, and determination of all parties to develop the pipeline, TAPI promised to be the perfect solution to the potential of delivering enormous benefits to all.

In May 2006, India officially approved its participation in the $5 billion TAPI gas pipeline project. The death in December 2006 of president Saparmurat Niyazov, who had built a bizarre personality cult, maintained personal control over the country's resources, and shown little interest in foreign investment, kindled hopes of an active commitment on the part of his successor on developing TAPI. Pakistan, Afghanistan, and India signed a framework agreement to buy natural gas from Turkmenistan in April 2008. Following up on this, India and Turkmenistan signed a Memorandum of Understanding during Vice President Mohammad Hamid Ansari's visit to Ashgabat in April 2008 to cooperate on conducting further explorations (*The Economic Times*, 5 April 2008). Keen to tap into Turkmenistan's enormous energy potential, OVL–Mittal joint venture acquired a 30% share in the exploratory Block 11–12 in October 2007 in offshore Turkmenistan, only to surrender it in 2013 after the explorations failed to yield any commercially viable success (*Business Standard*, 20 January 2013).

Difficult relations between Afghanistan and Pakistan, insurgency in the border regions, and continuing tensions between Pakistan and India dimmed the prospects of TAPI's realization. Making the prospects of the project's realization dim further, President Gurbanguly Berdymukhammedov of Turkmenistan displayed little commitment to the project beyond periodic references to it, which seemed to be directed at an international audience (Durdiyeova 2007). The pipeline, as a result, is yet to see the light of the day.

Hydroelectricity

Tajikistan's hydroelectricity potential is estimated to be around 4% of the world's potential. India's efforts to enter its hydroelectricity sector were timid in view of its complex structure of ownership and control and huge infrastructural costs. Though India attained a toehold in developing the Varzob I hydropower station, it has opted to focus on agriculture, tourism, education, research, and skills development to build a bilateral relationship.

The Quest for Strategic Engagement

In articulating India's distinct approach to its neighbours, several foreign policy strategists in India have evoked the framework of concentric circles (raja mandala) from Kautilya's Arthashastra to define India's foreign policy strategy (Menon 2014; Mohan 2005). This logic calls for bolstering India's role in the extended neighbourhood by also utilizing the support of the United States to counteract the influence of China and enhance the leverage against its more prickly immediate neighbours. It identifies plausible scenarios for India, ranging from its role as a stable democratic ally of the United States in the region to a reluctant partner in the Sino-Russian anti-hegemonic coalition (Mohan and Khanna 2006).

India's Ministry of Defence officials reportedly have tended to view India-Central Asia relationship and India's developmental efforts in Afghanistan within the conventional Indo-Pak rivalry framework and look upon Central Asian states as vital in 'building strategic space for India in the region and to encircle Pakistan' (Blank 2004, 8). Some Western scholars have tended to analyse India's growing engagement with the Central Asian states in the post-2001 context as driven primarily by the need to counter Pakistan's role in Central Asia and Afghanistan (Cooley 2012). However, if any plan of 'encircling' Pakistan through forging closer ties with Central Asia did exist, it would still leave India in a catch-22 phase, unable to act effectively due to the clear strategic geopolitical advantage Pakistan has over India in connecting to Central Asia, China as well as Afghanistan. Even if India had this objective, it still lacked the leverage to restrain Pakistan from expanding its interests in Central Asia in light of the expanding role of SCO and the development of CPEC.

India's Ambiguous Security Engagement: The 'Military Base' in Tajikistan

Tajikistan, which also shares a 1,400 km border with Afghanistan through the restive Badakhshan region, was of utmost importance from a strategic and security point of view in aiding India's developmental and peacebuilding efforts in Afghanistan. It is also the closest to New Delhi in terms of geographical distance. India's support to the former Northern Alliance headed by the Afghan Tajik commander Ahmed Shah Masood between 1996 and 2001 had already established close security and strategic cooperation. India was using the Farkhor airbase, about 130 kilometres southeast of Dushanbe, as an extension of the field hospital in the late 1990s to help the Northern Alliance in its fight against the Taliban regime in Afghanistan.

A Defence Agreement in 2002 resulted in India acquiring its first foreign military facility in Tajikistan in 2003 in an airfield at Ayni north of Dushanbe (Central Asia Newswire 2012). India spent $70 million in technical assistance to renovate the Ayni airbase between 2004 and 2010 by extending the runway, building a control tower, and three new hangars. Then Russian Minister of Defence Sergei Ivanov declared in 2005 that Russia was using the Ayni base together with the Tajik and Russian air forces for conducting joint operations. In September 2010, Tajik Ministry of Defence spokesperson confirmed that the Ayni airbase has state-of-the-art navigational and defence technology and a 3200-metre runway—one of the longest in the world—able to accommodate all types of aircraft (RFE/RL, 9 September 2010). Russian sources claimed Russian officials were training Indian air forces at the Ayni airbase in lieu of renovation of the Ayni base (Savenikov 2011).

India had continued to deny the reports that it had a military base in Ayni but did not offer any further clarification on its reported activities.[4] Tajikistan and Russia also remained silent on this issue. During his visit to Tajikistan in October 2011, India's Defence Minister A.K. Antony finally denied reports that India was using Ayni Air Base for military or strategic purposes (Shukla 2011).

The much-talked-about security cooperation between India and Central Asia did not go beyond the pledges to regional security and combating Islam-based insurgency. Indian army conducted some joint training exercises with Central Asian states focusing on counterinsurgency and counter-terrorism. Uzbek special forces have trained at India's prestigious counterinsurgency jungle warfare school in the state of Mizoram (Jha 2011). The participation of Indian armed forces in counter-terrorism military exercises in Tajikistan had been limited in contrast to the joint exercise by the Chinese PLA and the Russian military in June 2012 (Tanchum 2013).

Keen to pursue a close security cooperation with India, President Rahmon visited India six times between 1995 and 2016. His fifth state visit to India in 2012 elevated bilateral relations to a strategic partnership.

Overall, India was unable to garner multilateral support and establish important security cooperation with Tajikistan for its operations in Afghanistan and build on its repeated references to Tajikistan as India's 'gateway to Central Asia' (Mishra 2017) as a narrow strip of territory connects India with Afghanistan and Tajikistan at the Wakhan corridor.

Tajikistan is also one of the biggest beneficiaries of the ITEK programme, with many Tajik officers graduating from Indian military academies.

India's aspirations for permanent membership of the UN Security Council too found sympathetic ears in the region. Kazakhstan has been most active in extending support for India's proposals for reforms of the UN and its bid, together with the G4, for a permanent membership of the UN Security Council. India and Kazakhstan have also actively supported each other's bid for the non-permanent seat of the UN Security Council. Kazakhstan subsequently withdrew from the electoral race in 2006 to ease the path for India (*India Today*, 11 May 2011), with India holding the seat for the seventh time in 2011–12 and Kazakhstan for the first time in 2017–18 (*The Economic Times,* 24 April 2010).

A Shift to Multilateralism

To its credit, the UPA administration sought to disengage India's role and objectives in Central Asia both discursively and in policy terms from the prevalent 'Great Game' rhetoric, including the references to the 'New Great Game' (Swanström 2005) in Eurasia with China as a major actor.

Delivering a speech at the Shanghai Institute of International Studies, the Indian Foreign Secretary Shyam Saran (2011) declared that the theories of 'balance of power' or 'conflict of interest' are 'outdated in today's fast-emerging dynamics of Asia's quest for peace and prosperity and its interconnectedness'. He further asserted that 'India and China, as two continental-sized economies and political entities, are too big to contain each other or be contained by any other country'. The Connect Central Asia Policy reflected this flexible thinking of avoidance of traditional rivalries and shift to multilateralism (Singh 2011).

Seeking Full Membership of SCO

Though India did obtain an observer status in SCO in 2005, the decision at that time lacked a long-term objective and was limited to issues of energy and supporting the measures to combat cross-border Islam-based radical ideology. While all SCO members and observers attending the annual meeting are represented by the heads of the government, India was represented by Murli Deora, Minister of Petroleum and Natural Gas, from 2005 to 2008, denoting that energy cooperation remained India's priority. Manmohan Singh attended the SCO summit for the first time in 2009, held in Yekaterinburg, Russia. Minister of External Affairs S.M. Krishna represented India in 2010 SCO summit in Tashkent and at 2011 SCO summit in Astana.

It was at the Astana summit in 2011 that Krishna conveyed India's desire to join the SCO as a full member 'to add value but also to enhance the stature of the organization' (*The Hindu Business Line*, 15 June 2011). The decision was a belated recognition of the Central Asian region's incorporation into a broader geopolitical space dominated by Russia and China through regional cooperation arrangements and a declining influence of the United States and Western Europe.

India's admission together with Pakistan into the SCO in 2017 had been in the making behind the scene, with Russia brokering a consensus on India joining SCO and negotiating China's objections for India's membership. Though the concept of the Russia-China-India triangle or 'trilateral cooperation' promoted by Russian Prime Minister Yevgeny Primakov failed to gain traction, it offered an initial synergy to the effort to bring India within the SCO (Pant 2006).

India's participation in BRICS, as well as sporadic engagement with the Russia-China-India triangle, enabled it to assert a significant policy autonomy from the United States, whose half-hearted efforts to build an NSR have been criticized for 'geopoliticizing' the establishment of trade and transport network and 'deliberately exclude Russia, Iran, and China' (Peyrouse and Raballand 2015).

The waning of the U.S. role in the region reflected the exhaustion of the potential of the U.S.-India cooperation in Afghanistan and the limits of India's bilateral approach to Central Asia. As China assumed a vital strategic role in Afghanistan, India's position increasingly came to converge with that of Russia and China on key issues in Iran and Afghanistan. It also led to a recognition on the part of UPA foreign policy establishment that membership of multilateral structures that engage other regional stakeholders such as Iran and Afghanistan (both are candidate members of SCO) can boost India's strategy in the Central Asian region.

In August 2013, in what were the first-ever official bilateral talks on the Central Asian region held between the two countries, senior officials from India's Ministry of Foreign Affairs met with their counterparts in Beijing to discuss cooperation and areas of potential complementarity between them with discussions centred on 'regional security and counter-terrorism, SCO, energy security, development partnerships, and people-to-people contacts with the countries of the region' (*The Indian Express*, 18 April 2013). These were followed by a visit by a Chinese delegation to New Delhi to discuss Afghanistan and the consequences of NATO withdrawal in 2014.

The lingering suspicions about China's intents among Indian foreign policy establishment gradually gave way to a more pragmatic thinking as India also began cooperating with China on a number of global issues—environment, climate change, terrorism in various multilateral fora. A consensus was emerging among Indian experts on the region who argued that India could be more effective by cooperating with China and joining the SCO. To quote Rajiv Sikri, India's former Ambassador to Kazakhstan, 'in order to protect and preserve its interests in the region, India has no alternative but to closely consult and cooperate with the other major powers who have an interest and a presence in Central Asia' (Sikri 2009b).

Conclusions

This chapter has argued that the UPA Government, especially through the 'Connect Central Asia' policy adopted in 2012, marked a welcome, though belated, departure from routine affirmations of cultural ties and friendship and projected a transformed image of India as an emerging power, with a thriving economy and advanced capability and innovation in science and technology. The policy identified the strategic directions along which bilateral relationship and multilateral ties were to evolve. A number of incremental changes during the UPA rule enabled India to expand its engagement in the region, especially in the energy sphere. However, India has continued to lag behind other major actors in the region due to being a peripheral actor in terms of geography and a late mover, in contrast to China, Western states, and even Turkey (Wheeler 2013).

After a decade of a close strategic partnership with the United States on Afghanistan and the pursuit of the goal of establishing a 'Greater Central Asia', which also portended to complicate India's relations with allies such as Iran, alienate Russia and enhance suspicion among adversaries that India was acting as a U.S. proxy, the UPA government was able to assert India's autonomy by not endorsing the sanctions on Iran as India's hopes for establishing road and rail connectivity with Central Asia and acquiring a strategic foothold in the region hinged precariously on transport links through Chabahar and cooperation with Iran, which is also critical to its oil imports.

The development of the Chabahar port was still a distant option, though the Manmohan Singh government could draw some comfort in having finally identified the trajectories for connectivity and pledged investments in its development. At the time of writing this chapter in late 2019, Chabahar had not yet become a fully functioning port. Many questions remain about its ability to deliver the promise and also about the railroads connecting it with Central Asia. The Modi government has pledged an investment of $500 million in building the Chabahar port, which is a fraction of what China has invested in building Gwadar and the CPEC.

India's quest for energy resources, especially in Kazakhstan and Turkmenistan, was one of the driving factors behind the salutary shift from platitudinous references to cultural ties to the appreciation of the region's resource potential and negotiations over specific projects. While the UPA government displayed a pro-active approach towards establishing close energy partnerships and looking for investments, as a late actor in devising a strategic plan and objectives in defining its place in the region, it found itself outpaced and outplayed by China in every sphere.

Towards the end of its second term, the UPA policies shifted to the inevitable recognition of the importance of joining multilateral institutions in the region by seeking membership of the SCO and collaborating with China-led regional security and strategic cooperation initiatives.

The eventual admission of India and Pakistan to SCO in 2017, facilitated actively by Russia and aided by Kazakhstan, was also made possible by the growing multilateral cooperation between India and China on a number of global concerns in multilateral organizations. The Connect

Central Asia Policy initiated by the UPA Government also reflected the pragmatic realization that India's policies towards Central Asia as an extended neighbour could not be separated from 'the management of a host of triangular relationships among China-Pakistan-India, China-India-United States, United States-Pakistan-India, Russia-China-India, and India-Russia-United States, not to mention the Iranian factor' (Sahgal and Anand 2010).

Notes

1. Personal observations of the author. As a fluent Russian speaker with proficiency in Kazakh, the author has regularly visited the Central Asian region since 1992 for doctoral research and subsequently for ongoing academic research and interacted with a range of Indian diplomatic officials posted in the region.
2. E. Ahamed, 'Keynote Address by MOS Shri E. Ahamed at First India-Central Asia Dialogue', 12 June 2012. https://www.mea.gov.in/Speeches-Statements.htm?dtl/19791/
3. Intergovernment Agreement on International North-South Transport Corridor, https://instc.org/Include/ReadFile.asp?qsFileName = Agreement.pdf&qsFilePath = Earchiverad742BC.pdf
4. Amar Sinha, then Indian ambassador to Tajikistan, resolutely denied the existence of a base during a conversation with the author in Dushanbe in July 2008.

References

Aiyar, Mani Shankar. 2006. 'What lies beneath: getting to all that oil and gas'. *Indian Express*, 25 February 2006.

Aneja, Atul. 2003. 'Central Asia is our extended neighbourhood, says Sinha'. *The Hindu*, 2 February 2003.

Ashraf, Malik Muhammad. 2013. 'TAPI and CASA-1000', *The Nation*, 23 March 2013. https://nation.com.pk/23-Mar-2013/tapi-and-casa-1000

Blank, Stephen. 2004. 'India's Continuing Drive into Central Asia'. *Central Asia Caucasus Analyst*, 14 January 2004: 8–9.

Business Standard. 2013. 'ONGC-Mittal exit Turkmenistan oil block'. 20 January 2013. https://www.business-standard.com/article/companies/ongc-mittal-exit-turkm enistan-oil-block-110012000159_1.html. Last accessed 3 December 2019.

Central Asia Newswire. 2012. 'Tajiks Likely to Grant Russia Access to Ayni Air Base'. 7 July 2012. https://archive.is/20120707044711/http://centralasianewswire.com/Security/Tajiks-likely-to-grant-Russia-access-to-Ayni-air-base-says-analyst/viewstory.aspx?id=3252#selection-367.8-367.124. Last accessed 5 November 2019.

Cooley, Alexander. 2012. *Great Game: Local Rules*. Oxford: Oxford University Press.

Dave, Bhavna. 2016. 'Resetting India's Engagement in Central Asia: From Symbols to Substance'. *RSIS Policy Report*, January 2016. https://www.rsis.edu.sg/wp-content/uploads/2016/02/PR160202_Resetting-Indias-Engagment.pdf

Durdiyeova, Chemen. 2007. 'Berdimuahammedov Launches Turkmenistan-China Gas Pipeline project'. *Central Asia-Caucasus Analyst*, 20 September 2007. http://www.cacianalyst.org/?q=node/4701. Last accessed 15 November 2019.

Harold, Scott W. and Alireza Nader. 2012. *China and Iran: Economic, Political, and Military Relations*. Santa Monica: RAND Corporation. https://www.rand.org/pubs/occasional_papers/OP351.html

India Today. 2011. 'India to Be Elected as Non-Permanent Member of UNSC'. 11 May 2011. https://www.indiatoday.in/world/story/india-to-be-elected-as-non-perman ent-member-of-unsc-puri-73932-2010-05-11. Last accessed 7 November 2019.

Jha, Saurav. 2011. 'India's Strategic Footprint in Central Asia: Part II'. *World Politics Review*, 14 December 2011. https://www.worldpoliticsreview.com/articles/10933/indias-strategic-footprint-in-central-asia-part-ii

Kavalski, Emilian. 2010. 'An Elephant in a China Shop? India's Look North to Central Asia ... Seeing Only China'. In *China and India in Central Asia*, edited by M. Laruelle, J. F. Huchet, S. Peyrouse and B. Balci, 41–60. The Sciences Po Series in International Relations and Political Economy. New York: Palgrave Macmillan.

Kucera, Joshua. 2011. 'SCO Hopping on New Silk Road?' *Eurasianet*, 9 November 2011. http://www.eurasianet.org/node/64482. Last accessed 1 February 2012.

Kuchins, Andrew C. 2013. 'Why Washington needs to integrate the new silk road with the pivot to Asia'. *Asia Policy* 16 (July):175–8.

Madan, Tanvi. 2006. 'India: A growing appetite for energy'. *The Brookings Foreign Policy Studies* (November 2006). https://www.brookings.edu/wp-content/up loads/2016/06/2006india.pdf

Mehta, Pratap Bhanu. 2009. 'Still Under Nehru's Shadow? The Absence of Foreign Policy Frameworks in India'. *India Review* 8, no. 3: 209–33. DOI: 10.1080/14736480903116750

Menon, Shivshankar. 2014. 'Kautilyan Approach Useful in Multi-Polar World'. *IDSA Press Release*, 9 April 2014. https://idsa.in/pressrelease/KautilyanApproachUsefuli nMultiShivshankarMenon

Mishra, Anish. 2017. 'Tajikistan: Pakistan's Gateway to Central Asia'. *The Diplomat*, 7 August 2017. https://thediplomat.com/2017/08/tajikistan-pakistans-gateway-to-central-asia/

Mitra, Subrata. 2003. 'The Reluctant Hegemon: India's Self-perception and the South Asian Strategic Environment'. *Contemporary South Asia* 12, no. 3: 399–418.

Modi, Ajay. 2013. 'Chinese Firm Foils ONGC Videsh's $5 Billion Kazakh Deal'. *Business Today*, 3 July 2003. https://www.businesstoday.in/sectors/energy/ovl-ongc-kazakh-kashagan/story/196401.html

Mohan, C. Raja. 2005. 'The Return of the Raj'. *The American Interest* 5, no. 5 (1 May 2005). https://www.the-american-interest.com/2010/05/01/the-return-of-the-raj/

Mohan, C. Raja and Parag Khanna. 2006. 'Getting India Right'. *Policy Review*, 1 February 2006. https://www.hoover.org/research/getting-india-right

Pant, Harsh V. 2006. 'Feasibility of the Russia-China-India "Strategic Triangle": Assessment of Theoretical and Empirical Issues'. *International Studies* 42, no. 1: 51–72. https://doi.org/10.1177/002088170504300103

Petroleum Economist. 2005. 'China Beats India to PetroKazakhstan'. 1 October 2005.

Peyrouse, Sebastien and Laruelle, Marlene. 2011. *Mapping Central Asia: Indian Perceptions and Strategies*. London: Routledge.

Peyrouse, Sebastien and Gaël Raballand. 2015. 'Central Asia: The New Silk Road Initiative's Questionable Economic Rationality'. *Eurasian Geography and Economics* 56, no. 4: 405–20.

Pradhan, Ramakrushna. 2015. 'Mapping India's Look North Policy: Why Central Asia Matters'. *IUP Journal of International Relations* 9, no. 4 (October 2015). https://www.questia.com/library/journal/1P3-3906226271/mapping-india-s-look-north-policy-why-central-asia. Last accessed on November 12, 2019.

Ramachandran, Sudha. 2008. 'India Learns Its Oil Lessons'. *Asia Times*, 15 April 2008.   http://www.worldsecuritynetwork.com/India/Ramachandran-Sudha/ India-learns-its-oil-lessons

Raman, B. 2006. 'Shanghai Summit: Indian Misgivings'. 15 June 2006. https://www. c3sindia.org/geopolitics-strategy/shanghai-summit-indian-misgivings/ Last accessed on 1 December 2010.

RFE/RL. 2010. 'Tajik Military Air Base Completed with Indian Help'. 9 September 2010.   https://www.rferl.org/a/Tajik_Military_Air_Base_Completed_With_Indi an_Help/2152731.html. Last accessed on 1 November 2019.

Roy, Meena Singh. 2011. 'India's Policy towards Central Asia: The Pakistan factor'. In *Mapping Central Asia: Indian Perceptions and Strategies*, edited by Marlene Laruelle and Sebastien Peyrouse, 161–79. Berlington, VTL: Ashgate.

Sachdeva, Gulshan. 2011. 'India-Central Asia Economic Relations'. In *Mapping Central Asia. Indian Perceptions and Strategies*, edited by M. Laruelle and S. Peyrouse, 123–41. Farnham: Ashgate.

Sahgal, Arun and Vinod Anand. 2010. 'Strategic Environment in Central Asia and India'. in *Reconnecting India and Central Asia: Emerging Security and Economic Dimensions*, edited by Nirmala Joshi. Central Asia and Caucasus Institute (CACI).   https://www.silkroadstudies.org/resources/pdf/Monographs/1004Joshi-Frontmatter.pdf

Savenikov, Viktor. 2011. 'Aviabaza Ayni: Protiv kogo budut druzhit' russkie, tadzhiki i indiitsy?' *Svobodnaya Pressa*, 22 December 2011. https://svpressa.ru/society/arti cle/51212/. Last accessed on 21 November 2019.

Scott, David. 2009. 'India's "Extended Neighborhood" Concept: Power Projection for a Rising Power'. *India Review* 8, no. 2: 107–43 https://doi.org/10.1080/ 14736480902901038

Shukla, Vinay. 2011. 'Anthony non-committal on Ayni air base in Tajikistan'. *The Outlook*, 5 December 2011. https://www.outlookindia.com/newswire/story/ antony-non-committal-on-ayni-air-base-in-tajikistan/737337\

Sikri, Rajiv. 2009a. 'India's 'Look East' Policy'. *Asia-Pacific Review* 16, no. 1: 131–45. DOI: 10.1080/13439000902957624

Sikri, Rajiv. 2009b. *Challenge and Strategy: Rethinking India's Foreign Policy*. London: Sage Publications.

Singh, Swaran. 2011. 'Paradigm Shift in India-China Relations: From Bilateralism to Multilateralism'. *Journal of International Affairs* 64, no. 2 (Spring/Summer): 155–68. https://www.jstor.org/stable/24385540

Starr, S. Frederick. 2005. 'A Partnership for Central Asia'. *Foreign Affairs* 84, no. 4 (July/August): 164–78.

Subramaniam, K. 2015. 'Caught in the Central Asian Vortex'. *The Hindu*, 17 May 2017. https://www.thehindu.com/books/caught-in-the-central-asian-vortex/article7215033.ece. Last accessed on 15 November 2019.

Swanström, Niklas. 2005. 'China and Central Asia: a new Great Game or traditional vassal relations?'. *Journal of Contemporary China*, 14, no. 45: 569–584.

Tanchum, Micha'el. 2013. 'India's ailing strategic policy in Central Asia'. *East Asia Forum*, 6 September 2013. https://www.eastasiaforum.org/2013/09/06/indias-ailing-strategic-policy-in-central-asia/

The Economic Times. 2008. 'India, Turkmenistan Ink MoU on Cooperation in Oil Sector'. 5 April 2008. //economictimes.indiatimes.com/articleshow/2928106.cms?utm_source=contentofinterest&utm_medium=text&utm_campaign=cppst

The Economic Times. 2010. 'India for Reform in 'Working Methods' of UN Security Council'. 24 April 2010. https://economictimes.indiatimes.com/news/politics-and-nation/india-for-reform-in-working-methods-of-un-security-council/articleshow/5852872.cms. Last accessed on 11 November 2019.

The Economic Times. 2012a. 'BRICS Summit: Solve Iran Nuke Programme Issue through Talks'. 29 March 2012. https://economictimes.indiatimes.com/news/politics-and-nation/brics-summit-solve-iran-nuke-programme-issue-through-talks/articleshow/12457514.cms

The Economic Times. 2012b. 'Eurasia Has Potential to Address India's Energy Needs: S. M. Krishna'. 3 July 2012. https://economictimes.indiatimes.com/news/economy/foreign-trade/eurasia-has-potential-to-address-indias-energy-needs-sm-krishna/articleshow/14637804.cms?from=mdr

The Economic Times. 2018. 'OVL to Exit Kazakhstan's Satpayev Oil Block'. 18 September 2018. //economictimes.indiatimes.com/articleshow/65855647.cms?utm_source=contentofinterest&utm_medium=text&utm_campaign=cppst. Last accessed on 15 November 2019.

The Economic Times. 2019. 'India, Kazakhstan in Talks to Renew Deal with Higher Uranium Imports'. 16 April 2019. https://economictimes.indiatimes.com/news/politics-and-nation/india-kazakhstan-in-talks-to-renew-deal-with-higher-uranium-imports/articleshow/68898103.cms?from=mdr. Last accessed on 15 November 2019.

The Financial Times. 2013. 'CNPC to Take $5bn Stake in Kashagan Oilfield'. 2 July 2013. https://www.ft.com/content/58c1a322-e326-11e2-9bb2-00144feabdc0. Last accessed on 25 November 2019.

The Hindu. 2011. 'India Poised to Join the Shanghai Group'. 15 June 2011. https://www.thehindu.com/news/national/india-poised-to-join-shanghai-grouping/article2107005.ece. Last accessed on 15 November 2019.

The Hindu Business Line. 2011. 'S.M. Krishna to Attend SCO summit in Astana'. 14 June. https://www.thehindubusinessline.com/economy/S.M.-Krishna-to-attend-SCO-summit-in-Astana/article20254938.ece. Last accessed on November 15, 2019.

The Hindustan Times. 2009. 'India Votes against Iran's Nuclear Programme in IAEA'. 28 November 2009. https://www.hindustantimes.com/world/india-votes-against-iran-s-nuclear-programme-in-iaea/story-aoD2CGKgU4mJhtBYxqIMgJ.html

The Hindustan Times. 2011. 'India's Track 3: Afghan-Iran Rail Link'. 1 November 2011. https://www.hindustantimes.com/delhi/india-s-track-3-afghan-iran-rail-link/story-A5GU8YuXxaPJRFjrdvx5dO.html. Last accessed on 15 November 2019.

The Indian Express. 2013. 'No Clash between India, China to up Stakes in Tajikistan, Says Ansari'. 18 April 2013. www.indianexpress.com/news/no-clash-between-india-china-to-up-stakes-in-tajikistan-says-ansari/1104015/

Wheeler, Thomas. 2013. 'Turkey's Role and Interests in Central Asia'. *Saferworld Briefing* (October): 7–8.

PART IV
MAJOR THEMES

This part examines five key thematic issues in India's foreign policy. They are: nuclear diplomacy, diplomacy to secure permanent membership of the UN Security Council, maritime diplomacy, energy diplomacy, and India at the WTO negotiations.

11

Integrating into the Global Nuclear Order as a Responsible Nuclear-Armed State

India's Nuclear Diplomacy, 2004–14

Ramesh Thakur

Introduction

India's nuclear policy can usefully be divided into three timeframes: 1947–68, 1968–98, and 1998–present.[1] From independence until 1968, it was two-track: pursue the development of indigenous capabilities in nuclear power generation in order to master the full nuclear fuel cycle and harness nuclear energy across the entire range of peaceful applications; and, in parallel, promote global nuclear disarmament. During the next thirty years, two more planks were added. The Nuclear Non-Proliferation Treaty (NPT) was signed in 1968, entered into force in 1970, and has been the normative anchor of the global nuclear order ever since.[2] Condemning it for fostering nuclear apartheid by dividing the world into five nuclear-weapon states (NWS) as the nuclear haves and all others as non-NWS have-nots, India refused to sign and became the world's most prominent nuclear dissident, keeping its nuclear option open but not crossing the threshold. The option of the nuclear-weapon acquisition was kept open by developing the requisite expertise, physical infrastructure, and sensitive materials as a threshold nuclear-armed state.[3] The first nuclear test, called a 'peaceful nuclear explosion' (PNE),[4] was carried out in 1974 by the Indira Gandhi Government. The final period dates from May 1998, when India conducted five more nuclear tests and openly proclaimed

Ramesh Thakur, *Integrating into the Global Nuclear Order as a Responsible Nuclear-Armed State* In: *Forging New Partnerships, Breaching New Frontiers*. Edited by: Rejaul Karim Laskar, Oxford University Press. © Oxford University Press 2022. DOI: 10.1093/oso/9780192868060.003.0011 itself a nuclear-weapon possessing state. Since then, India's nuclear diplomacy has focussed on integrating India into the global nuclear order as a non-NPT de facto nuclear-armed state.

This book's timeframe is the 2004–14 decade of UPA rule with Dr Manmohan Singh as prime minister (PM). Nevertheless, a critically important point is worth stating upfront. On nuclear policy, the main storyline shows a fundamental continuity across the Congress, NDA, and UPA governments despite differences in nuances and emphases in the pursuit of essentially the same goals. The chapter begins with a brief background to establish the continuities until 2004, documents in detail the main thrust of the country's nuclear diplomacy during 2004–14 and concludes with a comment on the same thrust being maintained by the Narendra Modi government since 2014. The chapter does not address the merits, wisdom, utility, or dubiousness of the decision to cross the nuclear threshold, as that occurred in 1998,[5] which is outside the timeframe of this book.

Background: 1947–2004

Independent India searched for nuclear self-reliance as a matter of conviction. The Atomic Energy Commission was established in 1948, and eight years later, Canada and the United States agreed to help India build a nuclear research reactor for power generation without requiring independent oversight. India was lobbied hard to sign the NPT being negotiated in 1966–67 but took a militant stance against its discriminatory division of the world into five states with and the rest without nuclear weapons. There was a consensus in the Secretaries' Committee, which examined the draft text in detail, that India should not sign the NPT. Its views were supported by Foreign Minister M.C. Chagla and PM Indira Gandhi and endorsed by the cabinet in May 1967.[6]

The Long Walk to Nuclear Weaponization

Of the nine countries that currently possess nuclear weapons, the public record shows India to have been the most reluctant to walk down that path, with the longest gap between developing the infrastructure and acquiring the technical expertise and sensitive nuclear materials, on the one hand, and getting the bomb, on the other. The subcontinent became a much-touted region for nuclear-weapon proliferation in the 1980s. Both India and Pakistan were assumed to have the nuclear-weapon capacity, but not nuclear-weapon power status.

PM Zulfikar Ali Bhutto had ordered the Pakistani nuclear capability to begin in 1972.[7] The decision flowed from India's role in the secession of East Pakistan in 1971; India's 1974 test merely confirmed Bhutto in the correctness of his decision. In 1983 a U.S. State Department report concluded that 'China has provided assistance to Pakistan's program to develop a nuclear weapons capability'. Pakistan had built 7–12 nuclear warheads 'based on the Chinese design, assisted by Chinese scientists and Chinese technology'.[8] According to the Senate Governmental Affairs subcommittee on international security and proliferation, China sold proliferation-sensitive weapons technology to Iran and Pakistan at least nine times between 1995 and 1997.[9]

India became increasingly exasperated at Washington's inability or unwillingness to address its rapidly worsening geostrategic environment with Chinese nuclear assistance to Pakistan. As the nuclear calculus changed dramatically in the 1990s, New Delhi decided to break out of the dead-end of an unexercised nuclear option. From the perspective of an Indian security planner, the world was firmly in denial mode on two vital questions. Why was China providing such assistance to Pakistan in the 1990s? The most likely answer is that China wished to constrict India to the status of a subcontinental power. What was India to do? India and Pakistan were thus caught in a self-ratcheting nuclear capability spiral which culminated in matching nuclear tests: five by India on 11 and 13 May 1998 and six by Pakistan on 28 and 30 May.

The nuclear option has been a party-political issue in India's elections only sporadically. On 24 September 1989, the manifesto of the Bharatiya Janata Party (BJP) opted for 'optimum defence preparedness, including production of nuclear bombs and delivery systems'.[10] But in general, there has been a remarkable continuity across different governments on the key parameters of India's nuclear policy. The quest for nuclear self-reliance was begun by Jawaharlal Nehru; the nuclear option was kept open by all successive governments; the 1974 test was ordered by Indira

Gandhi; the infrastructure preparations for weaponization were authorized by Rajiv Gandhi in the late 1980s; P.V. Narasimha Rao decided upon a test in December 1995 only to retreat under intense international pressure; the Comprehensive Nuclear Test-Ban Treaty (CTBT) was rejected by I.K. Gujral in 1996; five more tests were conducted by the Atal Bihari Vajpayee Government in 1998, along with the public declaration that India had become a nuclear-weapon possessor state; India's integration into the global nuclear order as a responsible nuclear-armed state was mostly accomplished by the Manmohan Singh UPA Government in the 2004–14 decade; and the process is close to being completed by the Modiled BJP Government.

The policy continuity has been underpinned by a broad national consensus. 'Had the [1998] tests been motivated simply by electoral exigencies, there would have been no need to test the range of technologies and yields demonstrated in May. In the marketplace of Indian public life, a simple low-yield device would have sufficed.'[11] In the immediate aftermath of the tests, the more telling criticism was not that they had been conducted in 1998, but that they had not been conducted in 1995–96 when China and France were doing the same. Criticisms directed at India (and Pakistan) under those circumstances would have been substantially more muted and refracted. In a 2013 public opinion poll, an overwhelming majority of Indians (79%) said nuclear weapons are important for achieving national goals.[12]

India as a Nuclear-Armed State

After the 1998 tests, the most pressing challenge was 'to reconcile India's security imperatives with valid international concerns regarding nuclear weapons.'[13] The sense of initial nuclear drift in India was replaced with a stress on responsibility and restraint. The rudiments of its strategic posture emerged after the shock tests of May: an acknowledgment of the nuclear reality vis-à-vis Pakistan; a 'minimum' deterrent against China; unilateral promises of no use of nuclear weapons against non-nuclear states and no first use against nuclear adversaries; unilateral moratorium on any further testing; a willingness to convert this into a binding obligation under the CTBT in return for a satisfactory outcome of discussions with 'key interlocutors', meaning largely the United States; and a commitment to work towards nuclear disarmament.

India's nuclear arsenal is growing. It is currently estimated to possess some 130–140 warheads for delivery by missiles and aircraft and is working to create survivable nuclear forces based on a mix of different launch platforms. India also continues to develop the naval component of its nuclear triad with the indigenously developed nuclear-powered Arihant class submarine. Aircraft provide the most mature component of India's nuclear strike capabilities. India operates land-based tactical and longer-range nuclear ballistic missiles, with the Agni III nuclear-capable ballistic missile putting Beijing within reach. India has developed road-mobile nuclear-capable ballistic missiles. India is significantly increasing its fissile material production capacities, both highly enriched uranium and weapon-grade plutonium. The growth in India's nuclear arsenal could accelerate with ambitious plans to build additional fast-breeder reactors.

Nuclear Doctrine and Force Posture

India's declared aim is to 'pursue a doctrine of credible minimum nuclear deterrence'. It will not be the first to use nuclear weapons but would 'respond with punitive retaliation should deterrence fail'. India has pledged not to use nuclear weapons against non-aligned non-NWS.[14] It has, however, reserved the right to use nuclear weapons in response to biological or chemical weapons attack.[15] A paper entitled 'Evolution of India's Nuclear Policy', tabled by PM Vajpayee in Parliament shortly after the 1998 tests,[16] was the first comprehensive document on this subject and also contained elements of what would later become the 'nuclear doctrine'. It categorically stated India's stand that 'nuclear weapons were not weapons of war' and 'a nuclear-weapon-free-world would enhance not only India's security but also the security of all nations'. India's nuclear arsenal was for self-defence and 'to ensure that India was not subjected to nuclear threats or coercion'. India declared 'a voluntary moratorium' on further testing and committed to participation in the fissile material cut-off treaty (FMCT) negotiations and the maintenance of 'stringent export controls to ensure that there is no leakage of our indigenously developed know how and technologies'.

India's National Security Advisory Board published its draft report on nuclear doctrine on 17 August 1999. It affirmed that India 'will not resort to the use or threat of use of nuclear weapons against States which do not possess nuclear weapons, or are not aligned with nuclear weapon powers'.[17] The draft doctrine was formally adopted by the Cabinet Committee on Security, chaired by the PM, on 4 January 2003.[18] While 'credibility' is defined by retaliatory capability, command-control-communications survivability, and political will on the part of the national command authority, 'minimum' defines size, cost, posture, doctrine, and use. Linked to the 'right to self defence' under the UN Charter, the doctrine requires survivable and operationally prepared nuclear forces, a robust command-and-control system, effective intelligence and early warning capabilities, the will to employ nuclear weapons, and effective conventional military capabilities.

The 1999 draft provided for 'punitive retaliation with nuclear weapons to inflict damage unacceptable to the aggressor' only in case of a nuclear attack 'on India and its forces'. These elements were modified in the 2003 document—nuclear retaliation would be launched in response to a nuclear attack on 'Indian territory or on Indian forces anywhere'; retaliation would be 'massive and designed to inflict unacceptable damage'; and the trigger for nuclear retaliation was broadened to be able to respond to 'a major attack against India, or Indian forces anywhere, by biological and chemical weapons'.

The defensive role of nuclear weapons and the fact that these are not war fighting weapons, the conviction that a nuclear-weapon-free world is a desirable objective not just in terms of a moral goal but from a national security point of view, and broad-based restraint implied by no-first-use, testing moratorium, engaging in FMCT negotiations and implementing stringent export controls on sensitive technologies are elements which were spelt out in the paper.

The UPA Decade of Consolidating India's Nuclear-Armed Status

India does not provide details of its nuclear arsenal regarding size, composition, and deployment, but much is known based on publicly accessible information.[19] India has decided against a strategy that requires launch-on-warning and has structured its nuclear forces accordingly. Its nuclear arsenal is dispersed in different locations, with warheads separated from delivery systems. Different organizations have custody of weapons and delivery systems in peacetime. At a 2012 conference at the Institute of World Economy and International Relations in Moscow, Russian experts advised India and Pakistan to do more to enhance mutual transparency and set up verification mechanisms to build on confidence-building measures (CBMs) already agreed to, like the commitment not to attack each other's civil nuclear installations. When the Indian participants responded that the Russians needed a reality check because of the prevailing levels of distrust between India and Pakistan, they were reminded that the trust divide was just as stark between Moscow and Washington when they began their nuclear arms talks in the 1970s.[20]

The contours of this policy were established by the NDA Government in the 1998–2004 period and maintained undisturbed by the UPA Government during its decade in power. The arsenal was modestly but steadily increasing each year alongside a growth in the stock of nuclear materials, facilities, and delivery capability. The command-and-control systems were gradually put in place and made more robust. The delivery platforms were progressively expanded across the air, land, and sea-based triad.

Foreign Minister S.M. Krishna described nuclear weapons as integral to India's national security and said that they would 'remain so, pending non-discriminatory and global nuclear disarmament'.[21] National Security Adviser Shivshankar Menon observed that India's possession of nuclear weapons had, 'empirically speaking, deterred others from attempting nuclear coercion or blackmail against India'. India's nuclear weapons are not meant, however, to counter the superior armed strength of others or for use in theatre-level conflict.[22] Its primary objective is to strengthen its strategic deterrent against China. With respect to Pakistan, the Indian establishment continues to believe, as said openly by Defence Minister George Fernandes in 2002, that India can survive a nuclear attack, but Pakistan cannot.[23]

Doctrine

Rakesh Sood, Dr Singh's special envoy on nuclear non-proliferation, notes that India's nuclear doctrine reflects 'the long held conviction that nuclear weapons are political in nature and not weapons of war fighting'. In addition, it seeks 'to explain India's quest for security in a nuclearized environment, the unique restraint and finally its emergence as a reluctant nuclear-armed state'. The doctrine helps 'to establish India's role as a responsible nuclear-armed state that is willing to pursue confidence-building measures (CBMs) and nuclear risk reduction measures in its region, can be a responsible member of multilateral non-proliferation export control regimes, and is prepared to support measures towards a nuclear-weapon-free-world'.[24]

India has not signed the CTBT but has maintained a voluntary moratorium on nuclear test explosions since 1998. In 2005 India committed to continuing its unilateral moratorium on nuclear testing as part of the joint U.S.-India statement establishing the basis for renewed bilateral peaceful nuclear cooperation. It is not known whether India is able to conduct 'subcritical' tests of nuclear material, but it is not generally believed to have such capability. India supported the commencement of FMCT negotiations.

On 2 April 2014, outgoing PM Singh called for the establishment of a global convention on a no-first-use policy for nuclear weapons, based on the argument that if all states recognize that nuclear weapons are for deterrence only, and 'are prepared to declare it', the world 'can quickly move to the establishment of global no-first use norm'.[25]

India was an active and engaged participant in the Nuclear Security Summits (NSS), which were a signature Obama administration initiative, between 2010 and 2016.[26] Of the four, Dr Singh attended the first two in Washington in 2010 and Seoul in 2012. PM Modi attended the final NSS in Chicago in 2016. India joined several other countries in pledging to establish nuclear security centres of excellence, training centres, workshops, and conferences. The approach taken by its Global Centre for Nuclear Energy Partnership recognizes the importance of an integrated approach to security, safety, and safeguards in the design of these 'centres of excellence'.

The release of the 2014 Nuclear Threat Initiative (NTI) Index, which ranked India 23 out of 25 states with weapon-usable nuclear materials (below Pakistan), caused consternation among Indian experts and officials. India's lack of transparency was cited by the NTI Index as one reason why India's score was so low. Indian officials responded that they did not think it was wise to 'put all information about how India guards its nuclear establishments in the public domain' and believed the NTI's quest for inside information on such sensitive issues to be a 'fishing expedition for information'.[27] NTI's response was to highlight the importance of confidence-building through transparency and international peer review.[28] NTI explained that the vast majority of the countries surveyed, including six nuclear-armed states, had participated in some sort of international peer review, but not India, which, with no independent regulatory agency, has 'few "checks and balances"'.

U.S.-India Nuclear Cooperation Deal

In the perspective of history, the signature nuclear legacy of the UPA Government, and Dr Singh personally, is likely to be the bilateral civil nuclear cooperation deal with the United States. This unlocked the global strategic frame in which India had been frozen after the 1998 tests. It permitted the successor Modi Government to pursue similar bilateral deals with other countries and was the curtain raiser to India's de facto acceptance as a responsible nuclear-armed state.

After the 1998 tests, the NDA government had set about trying to ease the resulting concentric circles of diplomatic, economic, and technological sanctions imposed by various countries, angered and shocked at India's nuclear breakout. The ultimate prize was to have India accepted as a nuclear-armed state. The centrepiece of India's campaign was to woo Washington. The BJP government left the task unfinished, but PM Singh picked up the ball and completed the difficult and tortuous journey. In opposition in 2004–14, the BJP thought it was brilliant politics to make Singh's task—to bring to fruition the process initiated by the BJP government in the 1998–2004 years—even harder.

The bilateral joint statement between India and the United States on civilian nuclear cooperation, issued during Dr Singh's visit to Washington on 18 July 2005, was highly contentious in Indian domestic politics as well as in the international disarmament community. Yet it served the strategic goals of both countries while also advancing the global nonproliferation agenda more realistically than any conceivable alternative. To single-issue activists, the agreement was a sell-out that would only make it more difficult to secure NPT compliance from other pro-liferators. For example, India was not required to commit to sign the CTBT nor undertake a moratorium on the production of fissile mater-ials. The agreement imposed no constraint on India's nuclear weapons program: 'this Agreement shall be implemented in a manner so as not to hinder or otherwise interfere with … military nuclear facilities' (para-graph 4); nor on its right to reprocess transferred nuclear material: 'the Parties grant each other consent to reprocess or otherwise alter in form or content nuclear material transferred pursuant to this Agreement' (para-graph 6.iii). The activists lobbied the U.S. Congress to block the deal, or at least to seek much more substantial concessions from India. They noted that Iran was pointing to the sweetheart deal with India as yet another example of double standards whereby Washington discriminates against Muslim countries.

To Indian hawks with a single-minded focus on rapidly expanding and modernizing India's nuclear-weapon capability, the agreement was a sell-out that would significantly constrain India's nuclear options in asymmetric comparison to the freedoms of the five NPT-licit NWS. They tried to embarrass the government into repudiating the deal. India had secured only promises of future assistance subject to all the unpredict-able vagaries of the U.S. Congress. In the meantime, its U.S.-aligned vote on Iran in the International Atomic Energy Agency (IAEA) overturned three long-standing major planks of Indian foreign policy: the NPT is il-legitimate because discriminatory; no country can be bound to obliga-tions arising from international agreements that it has not signed (the IAEA Model Additional Protocol); and the unreformed UN Security Council is itself illegitimate because it is an unreconstructed vestige of 1945. The passion, depth of anger, and strength of opposition to the vote among allies within the ruling coalition government as well as in the op-position parties must have shaken the government.

Washington had three strategic goals riding on the agreement. The first, with a long historical pedigree, was preventing the emergence of China as a regional hegemon. The second was courting India as a popu-lous, democratic, and friendly rising power. The third was drawing India, which is not a party to global nuclear arms control agreements, into the web of non-proliferation obligations through verifiable bilateral com-mitments instead of unilateral policy. According to the U.S. Ambassador to India (2001–03), Robert D. Blackwill, for the Clinton administration, India had been 'a persistent non-proliferation problem that required an American-imposed solution'. By contrast, President George W. Bush and National Security Adviser Condoleezza Rice 'perceived India as a strategic opportunity for the United States and not a constantly irritating recalcitrant'.[29]

The result was that India-U.S. relations became the best ever. India's strategic goals dovetailed with these, including deepening India-U.S. ties without courting client-status dependency. India also has an additional strategic goal to ensure energy security by investing heavily in nuclear power. Sanjaya Baru, the media adviser to PM Singh during the period of negotiations of the India-U.S. civil nuclear deal, has written an authoritative insider account of the process.[30] U.S. motives, based on the recognition of India as a potential major power, were to co-opt New Delhi as a strategic counterweight to China in the Asian regional balance and an equally strategic bulwark against Islamist extremism. India's motives were to break out of the strangulation of its nuclear policy since the 1974 PNE that was tightened after the 1998 tests; and to ensure energy security as a key to economic development.

Both sides used the language of India being 'a responsible nuclear power' to sell the deal to sceptics in Washington. In a formula carefully crafted to avoid challenging the definition of an NWS in the NPT, the joint statement of 18 July 2005 recorded U.S. acknowledgment that 'as a responsible state with advanced nuclear technology ... India should acquire the same benefits and advantages as other such states'.[31] The administration would not merely seek Congressional approval; it would also lobby the Nuclear Suppliers Group (NSG) to exempt India from existing restrictions on nuclear commerce with non-NPT states.

During a visit to India in 2008, then-Senators Joe Biden and John Kerry advised Singh to conclude the deal with the Republican Bush, as a Democratic administration would have more difficulty overcoming entrenched non-proliferation opposition in Washington. As it happens, neither Barack Obama (subsequently elected president for two terms, 2009–16) nor Hillary Clinton (later President Obama's Secretary of State 2009–13) voted in favour of the deal in the Senate. Although several senators did not believe the deal was 'as good as it should have been', Biden explained, their hesitations on substance were 'overcome by their belief in the India–US relationship'.[32]

It is clear that India-U.S. deal would not have been consummated without the personal commitment and directives of President Bush and PM Singh. Bush came to recognize the incongruity of more high-technology commerce with communist China than democratic India and overrode bureaucratic and political resistance in Washington from the habitual 'non-proliferation ayatollahs' and India-baiters. The U.S. Embassy in India, led by Blackwill, had been recommending that the United States 'should set aside its standing nonproliferation policy in regard to India as a means of building the latter's power to balance China'.[33] Singh submitted his resignation to party supremo Sonia Gandhi who rejected it, stared down and outmanoeuvred the communist party allies in the UPA coalition, assuaged Muslim concerns about dealing with the Bush administration, and cajoled and coaxed into acquiescence the instinctive suspicion of the U.S. motives in a bureaucracy deeply burnt by and hostile to Washington because of its long history of technology denial and strategic dependency policies towards India.

Singh stood firm with Washington on some non-negotiable issues (for example, a limit of 14 of India's 22 reactors to be declared as civilian and thus subject to IAEA safeguards, with the two fast-breeder research reactors at Kalpakkam to be kept outside international safeguards, in order to protect strategic autonomy), but conceded ground on other issues, including voting with the Western majority at the IAEA on Iran. At times the negotiations needed the direct intervention of the patient president in Washington. Even so, the vote of confidence in the deal was carried in India's Parliament on 22 July 2008 by the narrow margin of 275-256 (with ten abstentions and absences),[34] and that too only because Singh was prepared to accept defeat in Parliament rather than delay or retreat. In the Congress-led coalition, India's communist parties, which have never hesitated to subordinate India's interests to those of their ideological fellow-travellers in Moscow and Beijing, attacked Singh mercilessly for wanting to sell out to the United States. At one stage, Singh said in frustration but also with grim determination: 'I will not allow these communists to dictate our foreign policy'.[35] Hence Baru's conclusion: 'The assertion of political leadership over bureaucratic and technocratic objections, in both camps, made all the difference'.[36] And his damning judgment that

'While the diplomats had done India proud, negotiating a historic agreement, India's politicians let the country down.'[37]

The bilateral agreement with Washington was India's first tangible integration into the global non-proliferation regime. This was an advance on the existing unsatisfactory status quo, not a setback. The UPA Government signed bilateral deals in quick succession with France (2008), Russia (2008), Namibia (2009), Mongolia (2009), the United Kingdom (2010), Canada (2010), Argentina (2010), Kazakhstan (2011), and South Korea (2011).[38] The Australia-India civil nuclear deal is a perfect example of the interlinkages with other bilateral agreements that followed. John Howard's government (1996–2007) prioritized bilateral relations over multilateralism as the bedrock foreign policy setting and was also influenced by the growing interest in nuclear energy under the pressure of increasing fossil fuel scarcity, rising oil prices, and heightened consciousness of climate change impacts which together were altering Australia's international market opportunities. In 2006–07 Australia announced in-principle willingness to sell uranium to China, Russia, and India. The shifting global energy environment coincided with major readjustments to U.S. policy settings vis-à-vis India which opened opportunities for broadening and deepening Australia's relations with India.

In August 2007, with the India-U.S. deal facing difficulties, Howard endorsed India as being qualified to be a recipient of Australian uranium, thereby buttressing the political position of the supporters of the deal in both India and the United States.[39] After the return of Labor Party Government (2007), negotiations were successfully concluded with China in 2008 and Russia in 2010 as NPT States Parties with safeguards agreements in place to permit international inspections of their civilian (but not military) nuclear facilities. But India was still outside the NPT. Australia joined Washington in the NSG vote on the India-specific waiver to rewrite the rule book for India's benefit, leaving Canberra with an illogical and untenable policy of supporting open access to global nuclear trade for India but not selling Australian uranium to it so as not to breach Labor Party policy. This put Australia at odds with the global backdrop of growing commerce with India by a number of uranium suppliers. As with Washington vis-à-vis the global order, Canberra concluded that the bilateral partnership with India would strengthen the global/Asian economic and security architecture to mutual benefit. PM Julia Gillard's call

for a policy shift in November 2011 was endorsed at the Labor Party national conference on 4 December 2011. Manish Tewari, speaking for the
Congress Party, commented to a senior Australian journalist: 'This may
be the most important single step in the past three decades in furthering
India–Australia relations'.[40]

Export Control Regimes

As part of the effort since 1998 to integrate into the NPT-centric global
nuclear order as a non-NPT nuclear-armed state, in addition to pursuing
bilateral civil nuclear cooperation agreements, India has given parallel priority to membership of four key export control regimes. This, it
was believed, would burnish India's credentials as a responsible nuclear
power from inside the non-proliferation architecture for regulating the
global trade in strategic materials involving weapons of mass destruction.

The NSG, known originally as the 'London Club', was established in
1975 after India's PNE provided evidence of the misuse of nuclear technology transferred for peaceful purposes. It includes the five NPT NWS
and works on a consensus basis. Its guidelines are implemented by
participating governments in accordance with their national laws and li-
censing practices.[41] In September 2008, the NSG controversially decided,
under strong U.S. pressure, to exempt India from the requirement for application of comprehensive safeguards to trigger-list items. This enabled
the Bush administration to sign a bilateral peaceful uses ('123') agreement[42] with India, which exempted India from the undertaking given by
all NPT non-NWS to abandon nuclear-weapon programs as a condition
of access to civil nuclear technologies. The India-U.S. deal removed all
non-proliferation barriers to nuclear trade on the argument that partial
controls—with civilian facilities safeguarded—were better than none.

During a visit to India in November 2010, President Obama declared his support for Indian membership of the NSG and three other
export control regimes—related to missile proliferation (MTCR—
the Missile Technology Control Regime), chemical and biological
weapons (Australia Group), and conventional weapons (Wassenaar
Arrangement). While the NSG is India's priority, it considers itself well-
qualified for membership of all four regimes given its firm commitment

to non-proliferation, effective export controls, and capacity to produce regime-regulated goods and technologies.

The NSG first considered this question at its meeting in Noordwijk, Netherlands, in June 2011. No decision was expected, and none was taken. The United States apparently suggested two possible ways forward for the group: one would be to revise the admission criteria 'in a manner that would accurately describe India's situation'. The other would be to 'recognize' that the 'Factors to be Considered' are not 'mandatory criteria' and a candidate for membership does not necessarily have to meet all of them. A public statement issued at the end of the plenary meeting in Seattle on 21–22 June 2012 said only that the NSG 'continued to consider all aspects of the implementation of the 2008 statement on Civil Nuclear Cooperation with India and discussed the NSG relationship with India'.[43]

The Modi Government: 2014–18

PM Singh's political epitaph on India's nuclear policy in the decade of 2004–14 will read: 'He ... secured for India a new status as a nuclear power'.[44] The UPA Government could not have secured acceptance of India as a nuclear power without the NDA Government having tested in 1998 and invested substantial political capital in convincing Washington to accept India as a responsible nuclear-weapon possessor state. Similarly, the Modi-led BJP Government could not have succeeded in additional bilateral deals without the crucial breakthrough first with the United States achieved by Dr Singh in 2005/2008 and the NSG waiver. The Modi Government has maintained the trajectory of the UPA Government's nuclear policy on all fronts: an annual growth of around 10 in the stock of nuclear weapons based in an expanding stock of weapon-grade nuclear materials, a steady accretion of missiles of growing range and sophistication, continuing efforts to diversify delivery platforms on land, sea, and air, maintenance of the moratorium on testing without signing the CTBT, and strict mechanisms to ensure non-proliferation.

Modi was also able to build on the UPA legacy to conclude negotiations successfully for civil nuclear cooperation deals with other countries like Australia (2014),[45] the United Kingdom (2015), and Japan (2016). Australia's Labor Party changed policy on uranium sales to India in 2011, formal talks began in March 2013, and the draft agreement on civil nuclear cooperation was signed in New Delhi on 5 September 2014 in the presence of PMs Modi and Tony Abbott of the Liberal Party-led Coalition Government. The two directed their bureaucracies to finalize the administrative arrangements expeditiously.[46] And on 25 November 2015, Foreign Minister Julie Bishop announced the finalization of the Australia-India Nuclear Cooperation Agreement that will permit Australian companies to export uranium to India.[47]

The 1999/2003 nuclear doctrine remains in place despite calls for change among some Indian nuclear strategists, who argue that it is not credible because they believe no Indian government would follow through on the threat of massive retaliation in response to a sub-strategic WMD attack.[48] After the 2014 general election and the return of a BJP Government led by PM Modi, some Indian hardliners, driven by the news that Pakistan had developed a short-range nuclear-capable missile Hatf IX (Nasr), called for India to review its no-first-use policy. The party's election manifesto, issued in April, promised to 'study in detail India's nuclear doctrine and revise and update it, to make it relevant to challenges of current times … in tune with changing geostrategic realities'.[49] However, after the election, in August 2014, PM Modi put an end to speculation that his government would amend it when he stated in public that he does not plan to initiate a doctrinal review.[50] Nonetheless, this fails to address the doubts regarding the asymmetrical requirements of 'minimum' vis-à-vis China and Pakistan: 'what is credible toward China will likely not be minimum toward Pakistan; and what is minimum toward Pakistan cannot be credible toward China'.[51]

The continuity from the UPA to the Modi Government can also be seen in the global governance architecture of nuclear security. India is a party to the Convention on the Physical Protection of Nuclear Material (CPPNM) (date of accession 12 March 2002), the 2005 Amendment to the CPPNM (ratification 19 September 2007), and the International Convention for the Suppression of Acts of Nuclear Terrorism (ICSANT) (ratification 1 December 2006). India ratified the Convention on Nuclear Safety on 31 March 2005. India is also on the IAEA Board of Governors for 2018–9.

Similarly with regard to export control regimes. India was admitted to the Australia Group in January 2018, the MTCR in June 2016, and the

Wassenaar Arrangement in December 2017. But its quest for membership of the NSG has so far been frustrated by China's veto despite wide support from the other members.[52] In keeping with the central argument of this chapter, we can expect this ambition to be pursued by the Modi Government during its second term (2019–24).

Notes

1. I would like to record my appreciation to Ambassador (retired) Rakesh Sood, who served as Prime Minister Manmohan Singh's special envoy for nuclear non-proliferation and disarmament, for helpful (and sometimes critical) comments on an earlier draft. The chapter also draws on many private conversations with senior former and current Indian and UN officials that cannot be attributed.
2. See Jane Boulden, Ramesh Thakur and Thomas G. Weiss, eds., *The United Nations and Nuclear Orders* (Tokyo: United Nations University Press, 2009).
3. Only the five NPT nuclear powers (China, France, Russia, UK, and United States) can legally be called NWS. In this chapter, 'nuclear-armed' is used for any country that possesses nuclear weapons, including the five NWS.
4. In describing the test as a PNE, the Government may have been influenced by the language in Article V of the NPT, 'peaceful applications of nuclear explosions'. This was disingenuous, firstly, because the Article V language cannot simply be conflated into a PNE. More importantly, secondly, the test was self-defeating because India duly paid a heavy political and economic price for many years, without in the event gaining any nuclear weapons. In my view, it had tripped over its own cleverness.
5. See Ramesh Thakur, 'The Inconsequential Gains and Lasting Insecurities of India's Nuclear Weaponization', *International Affairs* 90:5 (2014), pp. 1101–24.
6. This paragraph is a distillation of Chapter 17 of C.S. Jha, *From Bandung to Tashkent: Glimpses of India's Foreign Policy* (New Delhi: Sangam Books, 1983). Jha was Foreign Secretary at the time and a member of the Secretaries' Committee.
7. Neil Joeck, 'Pakistani Security and Nuclear Proliferation in South Asia', *Journal of Strategic Studies* 8:4 (1985), pp. 86–87.
8. Tim Weiner, citing US officials and declassified US government documents, in 'U.S. and Chinese aid was essential as Pakistan built bomb', *International Herald Tribune,* 2 June 1998.
9. *Defense News,* 14–20 April 1997, pp. 3, 26.
10. *Statesman Weekly*, 30 September 1989, p. 4.
11. Jaswant Singh, 'Against Nuclear Apartheid', *Foreign Affairs* 77:5 (1998), p. 49.
12. http://www.lowyinstitute.org/publications/india-poll-2013.
13. Singh, 'Against Nuclear Apartheid', p. 52.

14. *Draft Report of the National Security Advisory Board on Indian Nuclear Doctrine*, 17 August 1999; http://www.fas.org/nuke/guide/india/doctrine/990817-indnucld.htm.

15. http://www.armscontrol.org/factsheets/indiaprofile.

16. Atal Bihari Vajpayee, 'Evolution of India's Nuclear Policy', 27 May 1998, http://pib.nic.in/focus/foyr98/fo0598/Foc2705982.html.

17. Ministry of External Affairs, 'Draft Report of National Security Advisory Board on Indian Nuclear Doctrine' (New Delhi: 17 August 1999), paragraph 2.5, http://mea.gov.in/in-focus-article.htm?18916/Draft + Report+of + National+Security + Advisory+Board + on+Indian + Nuclear+Doctrine.

18. Ministry of External Affairs, Press Release, 'The Cabinet Committee on Security Reviews Operationalisation of India's Nuclear Doctrine' (New Delhi: 4 January 2003), https://www.mea.gov.in/press-releases.htm?dtl/20131/The + Cabinet+ Committee + on+Security + Reviews+perationalization + of+Indias + Nuclear+ Doctrine.

19. See, for example, Manpreeth Sethi, *Nuclear Deterrence in Second Tier Nuclear Weapon States: A Case Study of India*, Centre de Science Humaine, CSH Occasional Paper no. 25, December 2009.

20. Vladimir Radyuhin, 'Cold War lessons for India and Pakistan', *The Hindu*, 19 November 2012.

21. 'India Says Nuclear Weapons "Integral" to Security', *Global Security Newswire*, 22 August 2012.

22. 'India Says Nuclear Weapons "Integral" to Security'.

23. Michael Richardson, 'Q&A George Fernandes: India and Pakistan Are Not "Imprudent" on Nuclear Option', *International Herald Tribune*, 3 June 2002.

24. Rakesh Sood, 'Should India Revise Its Nuclear Doctrine?', *APLN/CNND Policy Brief* No. 18 (Canberra: December 2014), http://www.apln.network/briefings/briefings_view/Policy_Brief_18_%E2%80%93_Should_India_Revise_its_Nuclear_Doctrine, paragraph 20.

25. Manmohan Singh, 'A Nuclear Weapon-Free World: From Conception to Reality', Inaugural Address, Institute for Defence Studies and Analyses, New Delhi, 2 April 2014, https://idsa.in/keyspeeches/InauguralAddressShriManmohanSingh.

26. See Rajeswari Pillai Rajagopalan, Rahul Krishna, Kritika Singh and Arka Biswas, *Nuclear Security in India* (New Delhi: Observer Research Foundation, 2016), https://www.researchgate.net/publication/313221201_Nuclear_Security_in_India.

27. Sandeep Dikshit, 'Transparency No Index of Nuclear Security Says India', *The Hindu*, 12 January 2014.

28. NTI, 'Letter to The Hindu', 15 January 2014, http://ntiindex.org/news-items/letter-to-the-hindu/.

29. Robert D. Blackwill, 'The India Imperative', *The National Interest*, 1 June 2005, https://nationalinterest.org/article/the-india-imperative-578.

30. Sanjaya Baru, *The Accidental Prime Minister: The Making and Unmaking of Manmohan Singh* (Gurgaon: Penguin India, 2014), Chapters 11 and 12.

31. Baru, *The Accidental Prime Minister*, p. 208.

32. Baru, *The Accidental Prime Minister*, p. 239.

33. Robert D. Blackwill and Ashley J. Tellis, 'The India Dividend: New Delhi Remains Washington's Best Hope in Asia', *Foreign Affairs* (September/October 2019), https://www.foreignaffairs.com/articles/india/2019-08-12/india-dividend.

34. Baru, *The Accidental Prime Minister*, p. 255.

35. Baru, *The Accidental Prime Minister*, p. 227.

36. Baru, *The Accidental Prime Minister*, p. 207.

37. Baru, *The Accidental Prime Minister*, p. 229.

38. Gareth Evans, Tanya Ogilvie-White and Ramesh Thakur, *Nuclear Weapons: The State of Play 2015* (Canberra: Centre for Nuclear Non-Proliferation and Disarmament, 2015), pp. 115–16.

39. Rory Medcalf, 'Australia's Uranium Puzzle: Why China and Russia but Not India?', *The Fearless Nadia Occasional Papers* (Melbourne: Australia India Institute, November 2011), p. 11.

40. Greg Sheridan, 'India on Highway to Prosperity', *Weekend Australian*, 17–18 December 2011.

41. Nuclear Suppliers Group, http://www.nuclearsuppliersgroup.org/en/.

42. The reference is to agreements pursuant to s.123 of the U.S. Atomic Energy Act that is commonly referred to as '123 agreements'.

43. National Nuclear Security Administration, Nuclear Suppliers group Plenary Meeting Public statement, Seattle, 22 June 2012. http://nnsa.energy.gov/mediar oom/pressreleases/nsgstatement062212.

44. Baru, *The Accidental Prime Minister*, p. 229.

45. See Ramesh Thakur, 'Follow the Yellowcake Road: Balancing Australia's Security, Commercial and Bilateral National Interests against International Anti-Nuclear Interests', *International Affairs* 89:4 (July 2013), pp. 943–61.

46. 'Agreement between the Government of Australia and the Government of India on Cooperation in the Peaceful Uses of Nuclear Energy' (Canberra: Department of Foreign Affairs and Trade), 5 September 2014, http://www.aph.gov.au/Parliam entary_Business/Committees/Joint/Treaties/28_October_2014/Terms_of_Re ference.

47. Julie Bishop, 'Australia-India and Australia-UAE Nuclear Cooperation Agreements'. *Media Release*, 25 November 2015, http://foreignminister.gov.au/releases/Pages/2015/jb_mr_151125a.aspx.

48. Abhijit Iyer-Mitra, 'India's Nuclear Imposture', *The New York Times*, 11 May 2014.

49. Quoted in Sood, 'Should India Revise Its Nuclear Doctrine?' p. 1.

50. 'No Review of Nuclear Doctrine, Says Modi', *The Hindu*, 29 August 2014.

51. Vipin Narang, 'Five Myths about India's Nuclear Posture', *The Washington Quarterly* 36:3 (Summer 2013), p. 144.

52. See Rajeswari Pillai Rajagopalan, 'Can India Make Headway in the Nuclear Suppliers Group in 2018?', *The Diplomat*, 14 June 2018, https://thediplomat.com/2018/06/can-india-make-headway-in-the-nuclear-suppliers-group-in-2018/.

12

India's Quest for Permanent Membership of the UN Security Council, 2004–14

Kate Sullivan de Estrada and Babak Moussavi

Introduction

The United Nations Security Council has been a focus of debate and contestation ever since the Council's size, composition, and prerogatives were debated at the San Francisco Conference in 1945 (Luck 2007, 659–60). After Independence, India's official stance on the existence of the Security Council and the power of the veto of its five permanent members (P5) was that these were necessary to achieve conciliation among the post-WWII great powers and to ensure the survival of the UN as a whole (Indian Council of World Affairs 1957). Throughout the Cold War, India's primary efforts focused on 'empowering the General Assembly and making it a place of meaningful action' (Bhagavan 2015, 599). In parallel, India regularly sought the greater influence and status of non-permanent representation on the Security Council, serving as an elected member of the Council five times during the Cold War and again just as the Cold War ended. India's UN representatives were proactive on the subject of non-permanent Council membership, co-sponsoring a draft resolution in 1979 proposing an increase in non-permanent membership (Fassbender 1998, 222). Initially, the 1979 proposal bore no fruit. However, in the early 1990s, an international political window of opportunity for reform opened up as the post-Cold War Security Council's effectiveness grew. The Council's greater influence also underscored its unrepresentative nature (Fassbender 1998). The majority of UN Member States, including India, became animated by the need for reform of the Security Council. India both sought to drive forward and benefit from

Kate Sullivan de Estrada and Babak Moussavi, *India's Quest for Permanent Membership of the UN Security Council, 2004–14* In: *Forging New Partnerships, Breaching New Frontiers*. Edited by: Rejaul Karim Laskar, Oxford University Press. © Oxford University Press 2022. DOI: 10.1093/oso/9780192868060.003.0012 this momentum. On 3 October 1994, India's then Minister of Commerce and later President, Pranab Mukherjee, delivered a speech before the UN General Assembly in which he officially staked India's claim to a permanent seat on the Council (UNGA 1994, 16).

This article takes as its focus the intense diplomatic efforts that India pursued in seeking a permanent seat on the United Nations Security Council under the two United Progressive Alliance (UPA) governments between 2004 and 2014. This period saw significant activism in India's efforts to achieve reform. These included the development of collective positions such as the Group of Four (G4) from late 2004 and the L69 grouping from 2007, efforts that directly shaped the reform process. The ten-year period saw the cultivation of numerous individual country pledges in support of India's candidature. It also saw India take up a two-year stint as a non-permanent member of the Security Council from 2011 to 2012 in what many saw as a dry run for permanent membership.

India's Development of Collective Positions on Security Council Reform

The UPA I government came to power at a moment when the expansion of the UN Security Council was high on the international political agenda. In 2003, UN Secretary-General Kofi Annan had invited UN Member States to discuss UN reform with renewed urgency. In the aftermath of the 2003 invasion of Iraq, undertaken without a UN Security Council resolution authorizing the use of force, and with the 2005 milestone of the UN's 60th anniversary on the horizon, there was a strong impetus for change. Annan appointed a High-level Panel to consider UN reform, including reform of the Security Council (von Freiesleben 2013). The Panel's 2004 report proposed two models for Security Council enlargement, both of which would increase the existing membership from 15 (5 permanent and 10 two-year non-permanent seats) to 24 members. Model A proposed an expansion via six new permanent seats, but with no veto power, and three new two-year non-permanent seats. Model B proposed a new category of eight seats, renewable every four years, and one new two-year non-permanent seat. Pressure for reform gathered. Prime Minister Manmohan Singh (2005) reported to the Lok Sabha in

May of 2005, 'this is the first time in many years that a certain momentum has been built up for thoroughgoing reform of the United Nations. It is a window of opportunity we must make every effort to take advantage of as developing countries'.

One of the central drivers of momentum towards reform was the diplomatic efforts of India, Germany, Japan, and Brazil. From 2004 onwards, India chose to mobilize for an increase in the number of permanent seats on the Council as part of this 'Group of 4' or G4. The G4 centred its blueprint for reform broadly on Model A, although initially, its members were not supportive of foregoing the veto. India was especially firm on this point and Prime Minister Manmohan Singh declared in parliament that India would not accept a permanent seat without the veto (Nafey 2005, 6–7).

The G4's 2004 founding joint statement signalled their 'will and capacity to take on major responsibilities with regard to the maintenance of international peace and security' and set out the intention to improve the representativeness, legitimacy, and effectiveness of the Council (MEA 2004). They also stressed their mutual support for one another's candidature as permanent members.

In seeking an expansion on the basis of Model A, the G4's expansion plans drew fierce opposition, animating counter reform efforts. A group of states initially known informally as the 'Coffee Club' in the 1990s rallied to restate their original opposition to the notion that adding new permanent members would improve representativeness. The group became known as the Uniting for Consensus (UfC) movement, including prominent members such as Italy, Canada, Mexico, Pakistan, Turkey, and the Republic of Korea (Swart 2013). The UfC grouping advocated expansion on the basis of Model B, aiming solely for a proportionate expansion in the number of non-permanent positions. Their argument against permanency and veto power ran on principle: what mattered was the greater accountability of the Council, not a nominal increase in representativeness through the addition of more permanent members. However, at the same time, the UfC's opposition appeared also to stem from geopolitical interests. The UfC's membership continues to comprise regional rivals to each of the G4 members—for example, just as Pakistan vehemently opposes India's quest for a permanent seat, Mexico and Argentina too have signalled their own opposition to Brazil's bid (Estrada Harris 2015). As one expert on Security Council reform argued, the UfC group has been driven by 'the fear that the delegation of enormous prestige and influence of permanent membership to a single country in their respective regions would lead to the establishment of a regional hegemony of a single country over the entire region' (Bourantonis 2005, 61).

By June 2005, the G4 strategy had run into trouble. China had signalled that it would veto any plan to include Japan as a permanent member, and the United States was pressuring India to 'unbundle' its bid from those of the other G4 members (Nafey 2005, 13). As a means of showing flexibility in the negotiations, the G4 opted to 'dilute their demand for a veto' by suggesting that they join the Security Council initially as permanent members without a veto, but with the decision on granting the veto to be reviewed after 15 years (Nafey 2005, 14).

By the time of the Kofi Annan's ambitious 'World Summit' agenda in September 2005, a vote appeared plausible on the two reform options. At one stage, the G4 believed they could garner 150 votes for their preferred option (Traub 2007, 360). However, the African Union cast doubt on the G4's calculation of votes by declaring its commitment to the 'Ezulwini consensus' that demanded two permanent, veto-wielding seats for African countries (von Freiesleben 2013; Mukherjee and Malone 2013). Meanwhile, the Chinese and the U.S. delegations had met to coordinate their positions, hinting that they would block the G4 proposal (von Freiesleben 2013). Sino-Russian opposition also began to manifest (Nafey 2005, 15–17). According to one biographer, Kofi Annan 'knew very well that everyone is in favour of your plan until it comes to a vote' (Traub 2007, 371). The G4 came to realize this, too and did not seek a vote on their reform proposal.

Against the backdrop of this stalemate on reform, in 2007, India facilitated the formation of the L69 group, a cross-regional bloc of developing countries committed to achieving lasting and comprehensive changes to the UN Security Council. India served as the key sponsor behind the 'L69' draft—also known as the 'India proposal'—authored by 25 countries. The proposal was withdrawn, but it did succeed in prompting the commencement of intergovernmental negotiations on Security Council reform (von Freiesleben 2013). Unlike the G4, the L69 does not argue specifically for its own members to acquire permanent seats. Rather, its broad and flexible membership seeks a reform package 'to better reflect contemporary world realities, and achieve a more accountable, representative, transparent and more importantly a "relevant" Security Council' (Rambally 2015). The group claimed to have been endorsed by 80 Member States by 2012 (Swart 2013).

Progress for the G4 after 2005 was slow, though officially, intergovernmental negotiations were ongoing. In the seventh round of these negotiations, in 2011, the G4 circulated a draft resolution document, with a proposal that 'decides that the reform of the Security Council shall include enlargement in both the permanent and non-permanent categories and improvements on its working methods' (Swart 2013, 37). While intended to hasten the reform discussions, it had the opposite effect of freezing them for nine months, with the G4 and the rival UfC group blaming one another for the stalemate. When negotiations did resume they were more productive, but the G4 initiative did not advance. Over 2012 and 2013, the chair of the negotiations, Afghan Ambassador Zahir Tanin, pushed for the consolidation of the different proposals into a concise, draft working document. The G4 endorsed this idea, as well as a proposal to hold another high-level working group on the topic. But by the time of the ninth round of negotiations, in April 2013, it was clear that there was significant opposition. It took until September 2015 for the General Assembly to agree to a text that would serve as the basis for further debate (UN 2015).

The G4 has remained active since its formation. Its diplomats meet regularly, and the process of intergovernmental negotiations has permitted the G4 to maintain its cohesion. Since the G4 comprises those countries who are generally perceived to have the strongest claim to permanent membership, joining the G4 has cemented India's place in the international imagination as an obvious candidate for a permanent seat (Blum 2005). India's public identification with Japan and Germany, in particular, has been significant. Since the early 1990s, Japan and Germany's justifications for a permanent seat have focused on their financial contributions, while India's and Brazil's early calls for inclusion tended to emphasize how their membership would enhance developing country representation on the Council (Blum 2005; Browne and Blanchfield 2013). In mobilizing with Japan and Germany in particular from 2004, India signalled a materially new dimension to its bid in the form of a willingness to burden share, a commitment that would come under international scrutiny during India's two-year temporary membership of the Security Council from 2011 to 2012.

India continues to align itself with the G4 and the L69 group, whose membership now numbers 42 countries. India's reluctant agreement in 2005 to temporarily forgo the veto as the price for gaining a permanent seat demonstrated flexibility and is a policy that has been continued (Singh and Razdan 2017). By building a common stance with a broad developing country constituency, as well as the most plausible candidates for permanent membership, India has gained powerful allies in its own quest.

The Cultivation of Individual Country Support for India's Candidature

The heated debates that followed UN Secretary-General Kofi Annan's well-intended effort to enlarge the Security Council demonstrated the difficulties in generating widespread consensus on any single model for reform. Consensus is essential because any amendment of Chapter V, which governs the composition and functioning of the Security Council, must first overcome formidable procedural hurdles. Chapter XVIII of the UN Charter sets out the terms of a Charter amendment process. Its Article 108 delineates four necessary steps. First, in order for a vote on Charter amendment to pass, at least two-thirds of the Assembly membership must support the proposal. This requirement was confirmed in 1998 through Resolution A/RES/53/30 (UNGA 1998). Second, after voting on the proposal, a minimum of two-thirds of the Assembly membership must ratify it according to their domestic constitutions. Third, all of the existing five permanent members of the Security Council (the 'P5'), the United States, Russia, China, the United Kingdom, and France, must support the proposal. Finally, each member of the P5 must also ratify it according to their domestic constitutions. Between 2004 and 2014, India made considerable headway on the first step and some headway on the third step (the second and fourth steps are not considered here, as they pertain to domestic decision-making in the respective Member States).

On the first step, by 2014, the United Nations General Assembly (UNGA) had a total membership of 193 Member States. This meant that 129 Member States needed to give their explicit support for any proposal

for an amendment to Chapter V. The UPA I and UPA II governments lobbied hard to seek support from Member States not just for an India-friendly
reform proposal but also for India's individual candidature for permanent
membership.

The precise number of Member States who support India's bid for a
permanent seat on the Security Council has not been clearly advertised
by India's Ministry of External Affairs (MEA). Similarly, questions posed
in parliament and in MEA press briefings tend to be answered only with
vague references to widespread support (MEA 2011, 2016, 2018). Research
conducted by the authors[1] and presented in Figure 12.1 finds, however,
that the two UPA governments' activism in soliciting individual country-
support for India's candidature for permanent membership had steady and
significant results. Between 2004 and 2014, a total of 82 Member States had
expressed support for India's bid. Pledges of support for a reform proposal
may not directly translate into votes, as loyalties and governments can
change over time. But the figure of 82, in so far as it represents reliable supporters, means that by the end of the UPA's second term, India was at least

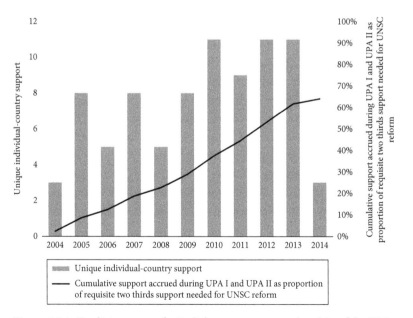

Figure 12.1   Explicit support for India's permanent membership of the UN
Security Council under UPA I and II

64% of the way towards the goal of reaching the requisite support of 128 other UN Member States. Moreover, of the 82 pledges, 66 (80%) came in the form of official MEA statements, either as bilateral statements or media briefings, arguably elevating their credibility.

On the third step, the P5 (China, France, Russia, the United Kingdom, and the United States) have veto power, and the agreement of all five on any reform proposal is essential. No clear consensus among the P5 on the question of Council reform emerged between 2004 and 2014, although it may be argued that the deadlock on reform is precisely in the common interest of all P5 members because it means a continuation of the status quo and thus their privileged position.

The P5 may be ambivalent to reform more generally. But on India's specific claim, between 2004 and 2014, the UPA government secured explicit support from four of them—France (MEA 2013a), the United Kingdom (MEA 2013b), the United States (2013c), and Russia (MEA 2007).

The final P5 member, China, stood as a central and major obstacle to India's bid, however, and it continues to do so today. It is procedurally impossible for India to become a permanent member without explicit support from China. While relations with China were generally positive under the UPA governments, and China expressed support for 'India's aspirations to play an active role in the UN and international affairs' in 2005, this did not translate into Chinese support for India's aspirations to join the Council as a permanent member (MEA 2005). Regardless of whether peace holds between the two countries, the biggest obstacle to Chinese support for India is to be found in Horsburgh's (2015, 48) observation that 'the nature of China's rivalry with India is more related to status concerns ... than actual strategic matters'. Above all, a permanent seat for India stands as a marker of high status and implicit, institutionalized equivalence with China. The status parity that a permanent UNSC seat would grant to India may therefore prove a long-term bar to a Chinese endorsement of India's bid.

India's Tenure as Elected Member on the Security Council, 2011–2

In 2011, India took up a non-permanent seat on the Security Council some two decades after its previous tenure. The election of India for the

2011–2 period was described by one commentator as 'a well deserved acknowledgement of its growing importance in terms of global economic and security governance' (Murthy 2011, 2). Viewed by many as India's dry run for permanent membership, New Delhi set out to pursue a 'strategy of demonstrating responsible diplomacy in the leagues of the great powers while also making the UNSC a more legitimate and representative organisation' (Mukherjee and Malone 2013, 110). For this reason, India adopted a proactive stance within Council activity on counter-terrorism, anti-piracy, and UN peacekeeping in particular, even as the significant international challenges of the political uprisings in Libya and Syria brought dissent and fragmentation to the decision making of the Security Council at that time (Whittington 2014).

In the domain of counter-terrorism, India's then permanent representative to the United Nations, Hardeep Singh Puri, served as Chairman of the Counter-Terror Committee for the duration of India's non-permanent membership on the Security Council. By 2012, India had pledged $2bn in development assistance to Afghanistan, partly to support counter-terrorism in the country, and Puri had also championed a paradigm of 'zero tolerance' in the international community's counter-terrorism agenda. On anti-piracy, India contributed ships to international anti-piracy patrols, co-sponsored UNSC Resolution 1976, the first ever to tackle piracy, and promoted financial and technical capability-building with the Government of Somalia to tackle the social and economic causes of piracy stemming from Somalia. Where UN peacekeeping was concerned, given India's sizeable contribution of troops, Puri stressed the need for a greater representation of troop-contributing nations in decision making related to peacekeeping, especially where the original mandate for a mission might shift in response to changes in the ground situation (Whittington 2014).

At the same time as India played a proactive role in forward movement on these issues of international peace and stability, however, the 'Arab Spring' presented the Security Council with significant challenges on the issue of intervention. The year 2011 saw uprisings in both Libya and Syria that drew international attention for the repressive responses of the Libyan and Syrian leaderships. India voted in favour of UNSC Resolution 1970, which had unanimous support and 'which reminded the Libyan state of its responsibility to protect its population, demanded an end to the violence, referred the situation to the Prosecutor of the International

Criminal Court (ICC), imposed an arms embargo on the country, placed travel bans on leading members of the government and froze regime assets overseas' (Hall 2013, 85). On Resolution 1973, however, which authorized a no-fly zone, India abstained. The Indian position was that the sovereignty, unity, and territorial integrity of Libya must be respected. However, India's failure to endorse the use of force in the Libyan case drew criticism from Western capitals (Mohan 2011).

In the case of Syria, both a 2011 and a 2012 resolution were blocked by China and Russia. India abstained on the first, which 'would have condemned human rights violations in Syria, demanded the cessation of the use of force against civilians by Syrian authorities, and threatened the use of sanctions' (Sullivan de Estrada and Foot 2019, 579). India voted, however, in favour of the second, which supported the Arab League's January 2012 decision to facilitate a Syrian-led political transition, although Puri stressed that the resolution of the crisis should be led by the Syrians themselves and should respect the country's sovereignty, unity and territorial integrity (Sullivan de Estrada and Foot 2019).

In this sense, the Indian tenure on the Security Council from 2011 to 2012 India sent two, at times conflicting, signals. On the one hand, India sought to live up to the G4 pledge of demonstrating the 'will and capacity to take on major responsibilities with regard to the maintenance of international peace and security', for example, by supporting UNSC resolution 1970 on Libya and through a proactive strategy in the domains of counter-terrorism and anti-piracy. On the other hand, India also sought to challenge the interventionist tendencies of the Western members of the Security Council by projecting a commitment against the threat or use of force, supporting non-intervention, seeking greater inputs for troop-contributing nations on UN peacekeeping operations, and advocating negotiated solutions to conflict. This complex picture was emblematic of what Sullivan (2015, 17) has theorized as India's broader rising power strategy, which 'can be understood in terms of two competing, and at times overlapping, rising power practices: compliance with and resistance to the hegemonic norms and institutions of the existing international political and economic order'.

Conclusions

Throughout the decade of UPA I and II leadership, New Delhi often energized the nature and direction of the deliberations over Security Council reform within the United Nations by building solid relationships with the proactive G4 and the broad-based L69 grouping. At the same time, however, this period offered additional confirmation of how difficult it is to achieve an agreed reform outcome. Geopolitical tensions and international status contests precluded straightforward solutions—the adoption of collective positions saw opposition from counter collectives and competing reform formulas. Normatively, the reform process also stalled in the face of questions over the legitimacy of an expanded Council. Against this backdrop, a significant achievement for India was the securing of a number of individual country pledges in support of India's candidature as a permanent member. Explicit individual pledges from 82 UN member states were secured between 2004 and 2014. However, India's period of elected membership on the Council coincided with high-profile and difficult challenges for that international body— the emergence of civil wars in Libya and Syria. Nonetheless, India was proactive on the issues of counter-terrorism, anti-piracy, and UN peacekeeping. All in all, the period of 2004 to 2014 saw India, in the context of UN Security Council reform, cement itself in the international imagination as a clear candidate for any future additional permanent seat, whether as a powerful ally or a powerful force to oppose. The period also provided important cues for the analyst of India's rise to read and understand the tensions that India faces between complying with the expectations of some existing powers within multilateral institutions or forging a path more calibrated to India's own interests and values.

Note

1. This research was primarily conducted using the MEA web archive (https://www.mea.gov.in/index.htm). We searched for documents relating to each UN Member State on the MEA website and manually sorted through for joint statements or media briefings relating to official visits either to or by India. Where a document referred to a UN Member State's support for India's bid, we marked this as

an instance of explicit support. Documents were restricted to the time period of the UPA government. In 16 instances, past research had informed us that certain countries had backed India's bid, but a corresponding document did not appear on the MEA website. In these instances, we gathered the evidence from other sources, including reputable media outlets or the respective country's foreign ministry. We carried out the research in October and November 2018.

References

Bhagavan, Manu (2015): 'India and the United Nations: Or Things Fall Apart', in: David M. Malone, C. Raja Mohan, and Srinath Raghavan (eds.) *The Oxford Handbook of Indian Foreign Policy*, Oxford: Oxford University Press, pp. 596–608.

Blum, Yehuda (2005): 'Proposals for UN Security Council Reform', *The American Journal of International Law*, Vol. 99, No. 3 (July), pp. 632–649.

Bourantonis, Dimitrios (2005): *The History and Politics of UN Security Council Reform*, London: Routledge.

Browne, Marjorie Ann and Luisa Branchfield (2013): 'United Nations Regular Budget Contributions: Members Compared, 1990–2010', Congressional Research Service, 15 January, URL: https://www.fas.org/sgp/crs/row/RL30605.pdf [Last accessed: 27 December 2015].

Estrada Harris, Gilberto (2015): "The Other Pacifist': Mexican Views on India's Quest for Great-Power Status', in: Kate Sullivan (ed.) *Competing Visions of India in World Politics*, London: Palgrave Macmillan, pp. 128–144.

Fassbender, Bardo (1998): *UN Security Council Reform and the Right of Veto: A Constitutional Perspective*, Leiden: Martinus Nijhoff Publishers.

Hall, Ian (2013): 'Tilting at Windmills? The Indian Debate over the Responsibility to Protect after UNSC Resolution 1973', *Global Responsibility to Protect*, Vol. 5, No. 1, pp. 84–108.

Horsburgh, Nicola (2015): 'Chinese Views of a Nuclear India: From the 1974 Peaceful Nuclear Explosion to the Nuclear Suppliers Group Waiver in 2008', in: Kate Sullivan (ed.) *Competing Visions of India in World Politics*, London: Palgrave Macmillan, pp. 34–48.

Indian Council of World Affairs (1957): *India and the United Nations*, New York: Manhattan Pub. Co.

Luck, Edward C. (2007): 'Principal Organs', in: Thomas G. Weiss and Sam Daws (eds.) *The Oxford Handbook on the United Nations*, Oxford: Oxford University Press, pp. 653–74.

MEA (2004): 'Joint Press Statement—India, Brazil, Japan and Germany Meeting on UN Reforms', 21 September, URL: https://www.mea.gov.in/bilateral-docume nts.htm?dtl/7464/Joint+Press+Statement++India+Brazil+Japan+and [Last accessed: 2 November 2018].

MEA (2005): 'Joint Statement of the Republic of India and the People's Republic of China', 11 April, URL: https://www.mea.gov.in/bilateral-documents.htm?dtl/

6577/Joint_Statement_of_the_Republic_of_India_and_the_Peoples_Republic_o f_China [Last accessed: 2 November 2018].

MEA (2007): 'Joint Statement on the Outcome of the Official Visit of H.E. Mr. Vladimir V. Putin, President of the Russian Federation to the Republic of India', 25 January, URL: https://mea.gov.in/bilateral-documents.htm?dtl/5475/joint+ statement+on+the+outcome+of+the+official+visit+of+he+mr+vladimir+v+ putin+president+of+the+russian+federation+to+the+republic+of+india   [Last accessed: 2 November 2018].

MEA (2011): 'Briefing by Secretary (West) on PM's Visit to Ethiopia and Tanzania', 17 May, URL: https://www.mea.gov.in/media-briefings.htm?dtl/3195/briefing+ by+secretary+west+on+pms+visit+to+ethiopia+and+tanzania [Last accessed: 2 November 2018].

MEA (2013a): 'Joint Statement Issued by India and France during the State Visit of President of France to India', 14 February, URL: https://www.mea.gov.in/bilate ral-documents.htm?dtl/21175/joint+statement+issued+by+india+and+france+ during+the+state+visit+of+president+of+france+to+india   [Last   accessed: 2 November 2018].

MEA (2013b): 'Joint Statement on the India-United Kingdom Summit 2013—India and The UK: A Stronger, Wider, Deeper Partnership', 19 February, URL: https:// www.mea.gov.in/bilateral-documents.htm?dtl/21197/joint+statement+on+the+ indiaunited+kingdom+summit+2013++india+and+the+uk+a+stronger+wider+ deeper+partnership [Last accessed: 2 November 2018].

MEA (2013c): 'Joint Statement on Prime Minister's Summit Meeting with President Barack Obama in Washington D.C.', 27 September, URL: https://www.mea.gov.in/ bilateral-documents.htm?dtl/22265/joint+statement+on+prime+ministers+sum mit+meeting+with+president+barack+obama+in+washington+dc+september+ 27+2013 [Last accessed: 2 November 2018].

MEA (2016): 'Question No.1775 India's Permanent Membership Of UNSC', 1 December,   URL: https://www.mea.gov.in/rajya-sabha.htm?dtl/27725/quest ion+no1775+indias+permanent+membership+of+unsc   [Last   accessed: 2 November 2018].

MEA (2018): 'Question No.4299 Permanent Membership Of UNSC', 21 March, URL: https://www.mea.gov.in/lok-sabha.htm?dtl/29686/question+no4299+ permanent+membership+of+unsc [Last accessed: 2 November 2018].

Mohan, C. Raja (2011): 'India, Libya and the Principle of Non-Intervention', *ISAS Insights*, No. 122, 13 April, URL: https://www.files.ethz.ch/isn/128706/ISAS_In sights_122_-_Email_-_India,_Libya_and_the_Princple_of_Non-Intervention_ 19042011144243.pdf [Last accessed: 8 November 2018].

Mukherjee, Rohan and David M. Malone (2013): 'India and the UN Security Council: An Ambiguous Tale', *Economic and Political Weekly*, Vol. 48, No. 29, pp. 110–17.

Murthy, Changavalli Siva Rama (2011): 'India as a Non-permanent Member of the UN Security Council in 2011–12', *Perspective*, May, Berlin: Friedrich-Ebert-Stiftung, URL: https://library.fes.de/pdf-files/iez/08143.pdf [Last accessed: 2 November 2018].

Nafey, Abdul (2005): 'Permanent Membership in the UN Security Council: India's Diplomatic Initiatives and Strategies', *India Quarterly*, Vol. 61, No. 4, pp. 1–38.

Rambally, Menissa (2015): 'Statement on behalf of the L.69 Group', UN document, 30 October, URL: http://papersmart.unmeetings.org/media2/7654976/saint-lucio-on-behalf-of-the-l69-group.pdf [Last accessed: 8 November 2018].

Singh, Manmohan (2005): 'PM's Reply to the LS Debate (rule 193) on Foreign Policy', 12 May, New Delhi, URL: https://archivepmo.nic.in/drmanmohansingh/speech-details.php?nodeid=119 [Last accessed: 5 November 2018].

Singh, Bhairavi and Nidhi Razdan (2017): 'India Ready to Let Go of Veto Initially for UN Security Council Seat', NDTV, 9 March, URL: https://www.ndtv.com/india-news/india-offers-to-give-up-veto-power-temporarily-at-un-security-council-1667565 [Last accessed: 5 November 2018].

Sullivan, Kate (2015): 'India's Ambivalent Projection of Self as a Global Power: Between Compliance and Resistance', in: Kate Sullivan (ed.) *Competing Visions of India in World Politics: India's Rise Beyond the West* (Basingstoke: Palgrave Macmillan, 2015), pp. 15–33.

Sullivan de Estrada, Kate and Rosemary Foot (2019): 'China's and India's Search for International Status through the UN System: Competition and Complementarity', *Contemporary Politics*, Vol. 25, No. 5, pp. 567–585.

Swart, Lydia (2013): 'Reform of the Security Council: 2007–2013', in: *Governing and Managing Change at the United Nations*, Vol 1, September 2013, New York: Center for UN Reform Education, pp. 23–60.

Traub, James (2007): *The Best Intentions: Kofi Annan and the UN in the Era of American Power*, Paperback edition, London: Bloomsbury.

UN (2015): 'General Assembly Adopts, without Vote, 'Landmark' Decision on Advancing Efforts to Reform, Increase Membership of Security Council', 14 September, URL: http://www.un.org/press/en/2015/ga11679.doc.htm [Last accessed: 8 November 2018].

UNGA (1994): 'Forty-Ninth Session, 14th Meeting' [A/49/PV.14], 3 October, URL: http://undocs.org/A/49/PV.14 [Last accessed: 8 November 2018].

UNGA (1998): '53/30. Question of Equitable Representation on and Increase in the Membership of the Security Council and Related Matters', 1 December, URL: https://undocs.org/A/RES/53/30 [Last accessed: 4 November 2018].

von Freiesleben, Jonas (2013) 'Reform of the Security Council: 1945-2008', in: *Governing and Managing Change at the United Nations*, Vol. 1, September 2013, New York: Center for UN Reform Education, pp. 1–22.

Whittington, William (2014) 'The Elephant in the Room: India's Pursuit of 'Great Power' Status at the UNSC 2011–12', *MSc dissertation*, University of Oxford. URL: https://www.southasia.ox.ac.uk/south-asian-research-publications#collaps e616836 [Last accessed: 4 November 2018].

13

India's Maritime Diplomacy, 2004–14

Rahul Roy-Chaudhury

When I published my second book on the Indian navy in the year 2000, titled 'India's Maritime Security', I strongly lamented the 'abysmal neglect of maritime affairs by successive governments and pessimism over the importance it has been accorded in future security policy considerations'.[1] My subsequent stint in the National Security Council Secretariat (NSCS) during the first Bharatiya Janata Party (BJP)-led government of Prime Minister Atal Bihari Vajpayee made me all too aware of the inherent difficulties in the formulation of an official maritime security policy for the country, largely owing to strong bureaucratic turf battles.

Yet, during the decade of the Congress-led United Progressive Alliance (UPA) government in 2004–14 tentative steps in this direction were made, with a greater focus on India's maritime affairs, including maritime diplomacy and the intrinsically linked issue of maritime security. The reasons for this were threefold:

First, greater realization of the impact of the import of energy resources across the seas in terms of both fuelling high economic growth for prosperity as well as the consequences of its disruption leading to domestic economic and political instability. Over 90% of India's foreign trade in volume and 77% in value was seaborne, accounting for over 40% of the country's total GDP. India had also increased its oil imports from about 40% of demand in 1990 to more than 70% by 2011.

Second, growing concern over China's assertive policy towards India. This was seen through tensions on the Line of Actual Control (LAC) as well as the expansion of China's naval influence in the Indian Ocean. In terms of the former, Prime Minister Dr Manmohan Singh's uncharacteristic public remarks on a 'certain amount of assertiveness' by China in late 2009 were significant.[2] In terms of the latter, the UPA government

Rahul Roy-Chaudhury, *India's Maritime Diplomacy, 2004–14* In: *Forging New Partnerships, Breaching New Frontiers*. Edited by: Rejaul Karim Laskar, Oxford University Press. © Oxford University Press 2022.
DOI: 10.1093/oso/9780192868060.003.0013

assessed that China was, for the first time, seeking to establish a permanent naval presence in the Indian Ocean as an attempt to 'encircle' India strategically.

Third, the arrival by sea of the perpetrators of the November 2008 Mumbai terror attacks focused attention on the vulnerabilities of India's coastal security. As a result, the UPA government undertook a major overhaul of India's coastal and maritime security. Notably, in February 2009, it formally gave the navy an expanded responsibility for the overall maritime security of the country, including coastal and offshore security; this was the first time any of the armed services had formally been given such overall responsibility (being limited in the past to assistance to civilian authority).

As a result, the UPA government began to develop a robust posture towards maritime diplomacy and security. This was primarily seen in terms of India's rising naval profile and diplomacy, alongside an expansion of influence in the Indian Ocean. The most notable of these included taking on greater roles and responsibilities in the maritime domain and the announcement of India's role as a 'net security provider' in the Indian Ocean.

Alongside, India began anti-piracy patrols off the coast of Somalia; published the navy's official maritime doctrine and strategy (the latter for the first time); deepened joint naval cooperation and exercises with friendly navies (including the first quadrilateral naval exercise); and acquired technologically capable naval arms from the United States as part of its naval expansion and modernization programme (including the Indian navy becoming the first international customer of the P-8 maritime surveillance aircraft, with the signing of the $2.1 billion agreement in January 2009, for eight aircraft). The burgeoning security relationship with Japan, especially on maritime security affairs, was also begun by the UPA government.

Notably, all these developments and actions were publicly welcomed and encouraged by the major powers, including the United States, Japan, and Australia. This was in marked contrast to the late 1980s when India's naval expansion was viewed with suspicion by some of the same major powers as well as a few of the Indian Ocean littoral countries.

Publication of India's Maritime Doctrine/
Maritime Military Strategy

In a welcome development, the Indian navy published its Maritime Doctrine for the first time in April 2004, just before the swearing-in of the first UPA government. This confidently stated that 'the Indian maritime vision for the first quarter of the 21st century must look at the arc from the Persian Gulf to the Straits of Malacca as a legitimate area of interest'.[3]

Clearly, the Indian navy's primary area of influence and operations was the Indian Ocean. Traditionally, this has included India's maritime zones including the Exclusive Economic Zone (EEZ), the Arabian Sea, and the Bay of Bengal. But, the navy's rising profile, India's 'look east' policy, and the expansion of the Chinese navy's presence and influence in the Indian Ocean began shifting the Indian navy's focus beyond the Bay of Bengal and the eastern Indian Ocean to areas east of the Straits of Malacca-Singapore, including the South China Sea. Not surprisingly, the navy's 2009 updated doctrine categorized for the first time India's 'secondary areas' of maritime interest as including the 'South China Sea, other areas of West Pacific Ocean and friendly littoral countries located herein', along with 'other areas of national interest based on considerations of diaspora and overseas investments',[4] although none of this was elaborated upon. Indeed, the navy's 2007 military strategy specifically noted the importance of 'establishing and retaining influence over the maritime neighbourhood'.[5] Both the navy's 2007 military strategy and the 2009 updated doctrine were published during the UPA government.

In effect, the UPA government's strategic objective for the navy appeared to be to seek 'cooperative engagement' amidst a dynamic and rapidly transforming regional security landscape. This was important as trade and energy flows of the Indian Ocean are primarily extra-regional, accounting for 80% of total trade, alongside global concerns of energy security. Most major international shipping lanes in the Indian Ocean are located close to India's island territories. Some 66% of the world's maritime oil trade, 50% of the global container traffic and 33% of global cargo trade flow through the Indian Ocean. In June 2012, Admiral Nirmal Verma, Chief of Naval Staff, stated at the International Institute for Strategic Studies (IISS) in London that with any adverse development in the region affecting the global economy 'this translates into an appreciation of the need for cooperative engagement … Indian policy is that transnational peace and security must be regarded as global public goods which no state can assure by its efforts alone'.[6]

In terms of the eastern part of the Indian Ocean, more than half of India's trade passed through the waters of the Straits of Malacca; and in terms of commercial interests, Indian oil firm ONGC Videsh was involved since 2006 in Vietnam in the conduct of oil and gas exploration and exploitation activities on land and on its continental shelf and EEZ. More importantly, arguably, the western Indian Ocean and Arabian Gulf region hosted over 6 million expatriate Indians; was the source of over half of India's oil imports; and increasingly was becoming a key source of investments and defence and security cooperation.

India as a 'Net Security Provider'

India's interest in becoming a 'net security provider' in the Indian Ocean is related to the U.S. interest in the Indian navy playing a larger role in the region. U.S. Defence Secretary Robert Gates first used this term at the IISS' Ministerial-level Asian Security Summit, the Shangri-La Dialogue, in Singapore, in May 2009, when he stated the United States looked to India 'to be a partner and net provider of security in the Indian Ocean and beyond'.[7] A senior Indian delegate at this Security Summit, Manish Tewari, Member of Parliament and National Spokesperson of the Indian National Congress, asked Gates to elaborate on this remark. Gates cited the example of India's participation in counter-piracy operations in the waters around Somalia and stated 'what we see in India is a great power that has tremendous potential to be a major player in bringing international security and stability in a lot of places, as a part of the international community'.[8]

Towards the end of 2011, India's Defence Minister A.K. Antony, addressing the naval commanders conference for the first time, reportedly said the navy had been mandated to be a 'net security provider' to island states in the Indian Ocean region. He added that since most of the major international shipping lanes were located along India's island territories, India had the ability to be a potent and stabilizing force in the region.[9] Prime Minister Dr Manmohan Singh used this term for the first time at the foundation-laying ceremony of the Indian National Defence University, when he said that India had also sought to assume its 'responsibility for stability in the Indian Ocean Region. We are well positioned, therefore, to become a net provider of security in our immediate region and beyond', he added.[10]

In this regard, India began to bolster its defence and naval links with littoral and island states of the Indian Ocean. This included coordinated anti-piracy and air surveillance patrols off the Seychelles coast; EEZ surveillance and anti-piracy patrols with Mauritius, alongside enhancing its coastal security; and the provision of patrol boats and aircraft to island states, along with training.

Anti-Piracy Patrols

India played an active role in enhancing the stability and security of the Arabian Gulf's sea lanes through its participation in anti-piracy patrols off the coast of Somalia. As Minister of External Affairs Salman Khurshid told the 2013 IISS Manama Dialogue in Bahrain since October 2008, the Indian navy had continuously deployed one ship in the Gulf of Aden for anti-piracy duties, with operational turnarounds at Salalah, Oman. Indian navy vessels had escorted 1,104 ships (139 Indian- and 965 foreign-flagged, from 50 countries) through the Internationally Recommended Transit Corridor. In the first five years of this activity, the Indian navy reportedly captured 100 pirates and foiled over 40 piracy attempts.[11]

Although India was not engaged in Combined Task Force 151 on counter-piracy efforts in the Gulf of Aden, it began coordinating patrols with China, Japan, and South Korea. It also interacted with other naval representatives involved in anti-piracy through the Bahrain-based Shared Awareness and De-confliction mechanism, formed in December 2008 for sharing 'best practices'. India's participation in these anti-piracy patrols came despite some initial reluctance on the part of the civilian leadership, though not the navy. The UPA government procrastinated for over a year until finally it was moved to action by Somali pirates' hijacking of the Japanese-owned but largely Indian-crewed chemical tanker MT *Stolt Valor* in the Gulf of Aden in September 2008.[12]

Trilateral Maritime Security Cooperation

Significantly, in July 2013, a trilateral agreement on maritime security co-operation was signed by India, Sri Lanka, and the Maldives (although it was earlier launched in 2011). This reflected a consensus on key issues of maritime security among three countries who shared a common maritime boundary in the Arabian Sea. This focused on counter-terrorism, anti-piracy and operational coordination. It essentially enhanced co-operation in Maritime Domain Awareness (MDA), strengthened mechanisms for EEZ surveillance, expanded bilateral exercises, coordinated maritime Search and Rescue (SAR) operations, and enhanced the sharing of intelligence on illegal maritime activities. On 6 March 2014, National Security Advisor (NSA)-level officials of the three countries agreed to boost cooperation on hydrography and training in search and seizure operations at sea. They also agreed to strengthen the biennial trilateral naval and coast guard exercise *Dosti* (friendship).

Indian Ocean Naval Symposium

In another significant development, the Indian navy chief Admiral Sureesh Mehta piloted and led the formation of the Indian Ocean Naval Symposium (IONS) in February 2008. It was a 'voluntary' initiative that sought to bring together navies and navy chiefs to increase maritime co-operation in the Indian Ocean. This focused on a Leadership meeting of navy chiefs and warships hosted by different countries every two years. At its inauguration, it had 35 Members.

Relief Operations

The Indian navy's operational footprint in terms of disaster and emergency relief also increased. This included non-combatant Evacuation operations in Libya in 2011 and Lebanon in 2006, as well as Humanitarian Assistance and Disaster Relief operations such as the Tsunami relief in December 2004 and cyclone relief (in 2007, 2008, and2013). With the disappearance of Malaysian Airlines flight MH370 in March 2014, Indian navy warships and long-range patrol aircraft were involved in the search in the Bay of Bengal, the Andaman Sea, and west of the Andaman Islands.

Defence and Naval Cooperation

In the Gulf region, for example, in November 2008, India, for the first time, signed a maritime-focused defence cooperation agreement with Qatar. A defence cooperation agreement involving greater information exchange and training was signed with Saudi Arabia in February 2014. Regular Indian naval ship deployments take place in this region. India's most notable (but equally low-key) defence cooperation has been with Oman. An MoU on defence cooperation was signed in December 2005; visits to Oman by Indian navy ships have since increased, and Royal Navy of Oman sailors have travelled to India for training in hydrography, diving, and dockyard management. Defence Minister A.K. Antony travelled to Oman in May 2010, a rare overseas visit. India's state-owned Goa Shipyard delivered three 12-tonne tugboats to Oman in 2010 amid global competition. The bilateral defence relationship was extended for another five years when Omani defence minister Sayyid Badr bin Saud bin Harib al-Busaidi visited India in December 2011.[13]

Joint Naval Exercises

An increase in Chinese naval activities in the Indian Ocean was countered by India stepping up naval interactions and engagements with the United States, Japan, and Australia, as well as with Southeast Asian states in the Indian Ocean and the South China Sea. India also sought to further build strategic relations with Singapore and Vietnam. In May 2013, the first visit of an Indian Defence Minister to Australia took place.

The first trilateral joint naval exercise with the United States and Japan took place in 2009 as part of the annual *Malabar* series of exercises with

334 FORGING NEW PARTNERSHIPS, BREACHING NEW FRONTIERS

the U.S. Navy. In the aftermath of the devastating Indian Ocean tsunami of December 2004 and the subsequent successful naval and air coordination for humanitarian and disaster relief among India, the United States, Australia, and Japan, the first quadrilateral naval exercise among these countries took place in September 2007 in the Bay of Bengal, along with Singapore. This large naval exercise involved three aircraft carriers (two of which were nuclear-powered), a nuclear submarine, several frigates and destroyers, and over three dozen fighter aircraft. But, following a 'demarche' by China, this was shelved.

A key security partnership that emerged during the UPA government was with Japan. This included a December 2009 action plan to advance security cooperation between the two countries, based on their joint declaration of October 2008; the operationalization of a Senior Officials 2 + 2 dialogue; a maritime affairs dialogue; a foreign ministerial level bilateral strategic dialogue; a comprehensive security dialogue at Director General/Joint Secretary level; a Vice Minister/Defence Secretary level regular Defence Policy Dialogue; and bilateral military, naval and coast guard exercises and ship visits (including the participation of the Japanese Maritime Self Defence Force in the multilateral maritime exercise *Malabar*; and cooperation in anti-piracy operations).

In the Gulf region, the first bilateral naval exercise with the Royal Navy of Oman was carried out in 1993. Since then, a series of biennial naval exercises named *Naseem Al Bahr* has been developed, held in the waters off Mumbai, on India's west coast, and in the Gulf of Oman. The ninth *Naseem Al Bahr* took place in September 2013; four Indian naval ships, including the destroyer *Mysore* and the replenishment and repair ship *Aditya*, exercised alongside Omani naval vessels and air-force combat aircraft, focusing on surface warfare, search and seizure, anti-air warfare, air operation, advanced helicopter operations, and maritime-interdiction operations. The Omani government also provides critical support to Indian Navy ships at Salalah to sustain their deployment for anti-piracy patrols in the Gulf of Aden. In October 2009, India and Oman also conducted their first joint air exercises, *Eastern Bridge*, at the Omani air-force base at Thumrait. The second in this series was held in Jamnagar in October 2011, and the third in October 2013 at Masirah Island, Oman. The first India-UAE joint air force exercise took place in September 2008.

Conclusion

In terms of maritime diplomacy and the critically related issue of maritime security, the UPA government, between 2004 and 2014, began to lay the framework for India's rising naval profile and maritime diplomacy, alongside an expansion of influence in the Indian Ocean. Most notably, this included taking on greater roles and responsibilities in the maritime domain and the announcement of India's role as a 'net security provider' in the Indian Ocean. Alongside, India began anti-piracy patrols off the coast of Somalia; continuously updated the navy's official maritime doctrines and strategy; deepened joint naval cooperation and exercises with friendly navies (including the first quadrilateral naval exercise); and acquired technologically capable naval arms from the United States as part of its naval expansion and modernization programme. The burgeoning security relationship with Japan, especially on maritime security affairs, was also begun by the UPA government.

Yet, the UPA government remained cautious of signing formal defence and logistics agreements or beginning a maritime security dialogue with the United States in view of its concern over China's reaction and implementation of its own hedging strategy between the United States and China. It was not a surprise, therefore, that when U.S. Defence Secretary Leon Panetta described India as a 'lynchpin' to its new Asia-Pacific 'pivot' in mid-2012, there was alarm in some quarters of South Block, on the basis that this would appear as if India was preparing to counter China with U.S. support. The UPA government also refrained from articulating a vision for the Indian Ocean and was reluctant to endorse the concept of the Indo-Pacific or revive the 'quad' grouping.

Notes

1. Rahul Roy-Chaudhury, *India's Maritime Security* (2000), p. xviii.
2. Outlook, 'India has taken note of Assertiveness by China: PM', 24 November 2009, https://www.outlookindia.com/newswire/amp/india-has-taken-note-of-assertiveness-by-China-pm/669976.
3. Integrated Headquarters, Ministry of Defence (Navy), *Indian Maritime Doctrine* (INBR 8) (2004), p. 56.

4. Integrated Headquarters, Ministry of Defence (Navy), *Indian Maritime Doctrine* (INBR8) (2009), p. 68.

5. Integrated Headquarters, Ministry of Defence (Navy), *Freedom to Use the Seas: India's Maritime Military Strategy* (2007), p. 87.

6. Admiral Nirmal Kumar Verma speaking at the International Institute for Strategic Studies, 'Metamorphosis of Matters Maritime: An Indian Perspective', 25 June 2012, https://www.youtube.com/watch?v = 7PvjyryY1AM.

7. Dr Robert Gates, 'America's Security Role in the Asia–Pacific', The IISS Shangri-La Dialogue: 14th Asia Security Summit, 30 May 2009.

8. Ibid.

9. Press Information Bureau, India, 'Indian Navy-Net Security Provider to Island Nations in IOR: Antony', 12 October 2011, http://pib.nic.in/newsite/PrintRelease.aspx?relid = 76590.

10. Press Information Bureau, India, 'PM's Speech at the Foundation Stone Laying Ceremony for the Indian National Defence University at Gurgaon', 23 May 2013, http://pib.nic.in/newsite/mbErel.aspx?relid = 96146.

11. Rahul Roy-Chaudhury, 'India: Gulf Security Partner in Waiting?' in Toby Dodge and Emile Hokayem (eds.), *Middle Eastern Security, the US Pivot and the Rise of ISIS* (Adelphi Book 447–448. London, UK: Routledge, 2014), p. 235.

12. Ibid, p. 236.

13. Rahul Roy-Chaudhury, 'India: Gulf Security Partner in Waiting?', op.cit. p. 236.

14

India's Energy Diplomacy during the UPA Rule, 2004–14

Carolyn Kissane

Introduction

Securing energy resources for a population of over one billion and a growing economy presents myriad challenges. Along with the challenges, there are also opportunities to forge closer ties and new relationships with countries positioned to meet demand. Governments in India, United Progressive Alliance (UPA), as well as those before the UPA, recognized the emerging risks associated with India's rapidly changing energy profile. A country with historically some of the lowest energy demand per capita was quickly becoming a large energy importer for oil, gas, and coal. Domestic production could not meet India's shifting demands. As the country grew economically, with many analysts seeing India's rise as the next China, energy diplomacy, amidst the global competition to secure adequate resources, became an important, even critical, part of India's diplomacy.

According to the International Energy Agency (IEA), energy security is defined as 'the uninterrupted availability of energy sources at an affordable price' (IEA 2019). India, during the UPA period, confronted the challenges of meeting both long-term and short-term energy security. Both required strategic investments and resource diplomacy. India is considered resource insecure because it depends on imported oil, gas, and even coal to meet its energy security demands. The decade of UPA rule proved to be an especially challenging period for energy diplomacy due to the country's development imperative and commitment to reducing

Carolyn Kissane, *India's Energy Diplomacy during the UPA Rule, 2004–14* In: *Forging New Partnerships, Breaching New Frontiers.* Edited by: Rejaul Karim Laskar, Oxford University Press. © Oxford University Press 2022.
DOI: 10.1093/oso/9780192868060.003.0014

energy poverty, which during the period of UPA rule was the highest of any other country in the world.

Over the past 20 years, India harnessed inexpensive coal to fuel its economic expansion. The country's aim to lift hundreds of millions of people out of energy poverty requires more energy. India has the dual challenge of increased hydrocarbon demand and the global push to diversify beyond fossil fuels, especially coal. To confront these challenges in India, while at the same time facilitating continued economic growth and alleviating energy poverty, requires a deeper focus on efficiency, cost-effectiveness, and a more targeted commitment to deploying renewable energy, especially wind and solar since costs have dramatically come down for both sources of energy. The country needs to ensure access to inexpensive and reliable energy while at the same time meeting India's goals to reduce pollution and confront climate change without compromising economic growth.

This chapter studies India's energy diplomacy during the decade of the Congress party-led UPA rule, i.e., the period 2004 to 2014. It specifically examines the strategies adopted by the UPA Government to secure oil, gas and coal, nuclear fuel, and technologies from foreign countries to meet the burgeoning energy needs of India's rapidly growing economy.

The chapter starts by examining India's burgeoning Energy Needs amidst rising global prices during the period of the UPA rule in India. Then it provides an in-depth look at the diplomatic strategies for securing energy resources and technologies employed by India during the same period. The chapter concludes by summarizing its findings.

India's Burgeoning Energy Needs Amidst Rising Global Prices

In the early 1990s, India, under the government of P.V. Narasimha Rao (1991–96), began to shift its Cold War-era policies away from economic protectionism towards a more open economy in order to spur economic growth. As a result, the Indian economy entered a higher growth trajectory than earlier. This process continued till the inauguration of the UPA Government in 2004. As a result, during this time period, India witnessed growth in per capita demand of energy driving a large increase in gross energy demand. By the time the UPA came to power, India's energy demand was not only high but also increasing rapidly.

The period of UPA rule from 2004 to 2014 in India was characterized by rapid economic growth, averaging over 6% per year concurrently, leading to higher energy demand and consumption. At the beginning of 2004, India was the world's fifth-largest consumer of energy; in the decade to follow, the country became the second-largest consumer of energy, with Indian oil demand emerging as a macroeconomic indicator of global financial health. Historically, oil and coal have been India's primary energy sources. Starting in 2004, India's demand for oil increased at an average rate of 2.9% annually over the decade, panning out the UPA rule; translating to an increase of 0.15 mb/d annually. However, India has only 0.41% of the world's proven oil reserves and domestic production flat-lined over the last two decades.

As a result, India, during the UPA period, confronted the challenges of meeting both long-term and short-term energy security. Both required strategic investments and resource diplomacy. India is considered resource insecure since it depends on imported oil, gas, and even coal to meet its energy security demands.

The decade of UPA rule proved to be an especially challenging period for India's energy diplomacy due to the country's development imperative and commitment to reducing energy poverty, which during the period of UPA rule was the highest of any other country in the world.

The UPA Government, between 2004 and 2014, experienced unique energy market challenges. Oil and gas prices hit record levels during this period. By the summer of 2008, Brent crude was trading at $147 a barrel, and natural gas in Asia was in the high teens. India's increasing demand for fossil fuels coincided with the market perception that global oil supply was limited and hitting a supply peak, referred to as peak oil. This perception of supply scarcity contributed to the price going from the high teens in 2000 to over a hundred dollars a barrel between 2007 and 2008, before a rapid price decline due to the global recession. Global gas prices also hit new highs during this period, and Asia paid the highest prices due to the regional price model for gas, where Asia paid the highest premium. This environment of the scarcity of supply is important to consider when examining India's energy diplomacy during the period of UPA rule. It created record high prices for oil and gas, and for import dependent countries such as India, the cost to ensure energy security was high and created political vulnerabilities for the ruling party.

Under the UPA, India added on average, more than 12 GW power generation capacity per year from 2005 to 2014 (Indian National Congress 2014). During that same period, the government instituted massive fuel subsidies, 15 rupees per litre of gasoline and 25 rupees per litre for diesel (Moily 2018). The UPA was intent on increasing urban electricity access rates to 100% and improving access for rural communities. The increased domestic energy demand helped guide foreign policy by sparking interest in foreign energy assets. The Indian state invested in a diverse range of what it saw as sure bets for the future, some of which did not pan out, including gas fields in Mozambique and oil assets in Iran. In 2004, India expected to meet 75% of its energy demand by 2020 with imported oil and gas (Munee et al. 2004). The government did intend to rely completely on domestic petroleum production by 2030 (Veerappa, 2018). Almost a decade later, the Singh Government implemented policies to double its renewable energy capacity to 55 GW, within four years (2017) (Economic Times 2013).

Energy Diplomacy of UPA Government

Securing sufficient energy supplies for a rapidly growing economy became a critical part of India's diplomacy during the UPA's rule. Though India did not have comparable diplomatic tools as China to use, such as big national banks and an open wallet, and clear government mandates to 'go out' and exploit energy resources to meet energy demand, it did try and use diplomatic means to achieve some level of energy security, which, albeit, often fell short given internal economic and political constraints.

Understanding India's energy diplomacy during the 10-year period between 2004 and 2014 starts with an examination of the 2006 Planning Commission's 'Integrated Energy Policy Report of the Expert Committee'. This ambitious report, dedicated to energy security, access, and availability, affordability, and pricing, efficiency, and environment, followed President Abdul Kalam's 2005 Independence Day speech calling for 'energy independence'.

Among numerous policy recommendations of the report, using diplomacy as a tool to ensure energy security was explicitly mentioned five times. The report says,

> 'We are energy secure when we can supply lifeline energy to all our citizens irrespective of their ability to pay for it as well as meet their effective demand for safe and convenient energy to satisfy their various needs at competitive prices, at all times and with a prescribed confidence level considering shocks and disruptions that can be reasonably expected'. (Integrated Energy Policy Commission 2006, 2)

During the period of UPA rule, an increasing deployment of diplomatic and economic tools was used in an effort to gain an advantage in the global oil market. A former Indian diplomat described successful energy diplomacy as 'getting in first with exploration contracts, negotiating bilateral, trilateral and multilateral agreements, and ensuring that our future energy security is safeguarded through all this' (Madan 2006, 47). Diplomatic efforts included but were not limited to bilateral visits, conferences, trade agreements, and offers of various kinds of aid.

Indeed, at the heart of the UPA Government's diplomacy was economics. Indian foreign policy from 2004 to 2014 was driven by its developmental priorities. The government was keenly aware of the critical importance of energy security in sustaining high economic growth. The UPA Government made use of a number of instruments in its energy diplomacy to secure India's energy security. Some of these are examined below.

Visits to and from Oil Rich Countries

The decade of UPA rule saw a dramatic increase in visits to oil rich countries by Indian officials. Similarly, there was a striking increase in the number of invitations issued to leaders and officials from oil producing nations to visit New Delhi. India, as an import dependent country for oil and gas, looked at the Middle East as part of its grand strategy around energy security. India welcomed the Saudi Minister of Petroleum and Mineral resources in January 2005, and a year later, it welcomed the Saudi

King Abdullah. The king was invited as the guest of honour for India's Republic Day celebrations. It was the first visit by a Saudi monarch to the country in 51 years.

Additionally, there was an emphasis on improving ties with Central Asian nations, especially Uzbekistan and Kazakhstan. Prime Minister Singh hosted the Uzbek president twice during his term and founded the Indo-Uzbek Intergovernmental Commission on Trade, Economic, Scientific, Technical and Cultural Cooperation. In an effort to bolster relations with Kazakhstan, President Nursultan Nazarbayev was the Chief Guest at the Republic Day parade in New Delhi on 26 January 2009.

Over the course of 10 years, India's Ministry of External Affairs and Ministry of Petroleum hosted over 50 energy conferences in the capital with the intention of attracting OPEC members. The UPA government also established the SAARC Gas Buyers Summit in an effort to increase cooperation in the region.

Acquiring Oil and Gas Assets Overseas

As part of India's quest for security of hydrocarbons supply; policymakers implemented various strategies to attract investment in the domestic oil infrastructure as well as acquiring assets overseas. The state-owned oil and gas company acquired oil assets in places like Sudan, Syria, Iran, and Myanmar putting it in direct conflict with its relatively new ally, the United States (Economic Times 2012). When trying to acquire overseas assets, India emulated China in offering resources beyond the actual bid as a means of winning the equity asset. For instance, the Indian government encouraged private sector entities to invest in Uzbekistan, particularly in the information technology sector.

India's state owned ONGC's overseas arm called ONGC Videsh Limited (OVL), concentrated efforts on acquiring upstream assets for enhanced energy security. Between 2004 and 2014, OVL invested $4.5bn in exploration projects in Brazil, Vietnam, and Egypt. In addition, OVL acquired a 20% stake in Russia's Sakhalin–1 and invested $1.77bn in the offshore field—the single largest foreign investment by India in any overseas venture (Tanvi 2006, 34).

Apart from oil, India, during the period, also sought to acquire natural gas assets. Indeed, during this period, there was a growing consensus among Indian policymakers regarding the critical need for diversification of the country's energy mix. Policymakers involved in India's energy diplomacy emphasized the role of natural gas as a solution to India's over-dependence on oil increasingly endorsed it as a preferred source of energy. The fact that the same period saw an increase in global gas production further buttressed this argument. Gas was considered preferable to oil for a number of reasons: oil prices are more volatile and unpredictable; gas is seen as having more development potential, while oil production is expected to peak; although gas still has to be imported, it is closer in terms of sources of supply; and gas is cleaner than oil and coal (Tanvi 2006, 32).

Efforts around Gas Diplomacy Coincided with Oil Diplomacy

India signed a deal with Iran for the supply of 7.5 million tonnes of LNG between 2005 and 2015. There was great interest from the UPA government in building pipelines in order to ensure the security of the natural gas supply. During this period, there was an ongoing dialogue about building three pipelines: Iran-Pakistan-India pipeline, Turkmenistan-Afghanistan-Pakistan-India pipeline, and Myanmar-Bangladesh-India pipeline. Regrettably, none of them materialized for various political, economic, and security reasons.

In addition, there was growing interest in constructing gas-fired power plants in the exporting countries, with power to be transmitted over high-voltage direct current lines. Advocates suggested that a comparative analysis determined this as the most economical option. However, this alternative didn't get much traction (Mahajan 2007, 122).

The Coal Question

Nothing better demonstrates the scale, intensity, and challenges of India's energy sector than coal. Despite having the fifth largest deposits in the world, extractable coal reserves were estimated to run out in 45 years, per a consistent 5% production growth rate.

Despite the importance placed on 'energy independence' in the 2006 report of the Planning Commission, India's total coal imports have increased tenfold between 2004 and 2015 under the UPA government (Cornot-Gandolphe 2016). Coal consumption far-outpaced coal production in the UPA era (9.4% annual growth rate v/s 4.7% annual growth rate) (IEA, 2018). To understand why India's biggest energy sector was set on this path, it is important to understand existing issues within the coal sector in India. Another strategy adopted by the UPA Government to ensure India's energy security was investing in power plants in energy resource rich countries with a view to import electric power directly through power transmission cables.

Coal India Limited (CIL) is the largest domestic producer and the world's largest coal company. Centralized in 1973 until 2015, it was 90% government-owned (Economic Times of India 2015), hence subject to vast subsidies from the central government. (It paid Rs 38,150 crore in dividends to the central treasury between 2008 and 2014.) As a result, CIL has almost exclusive control over India's mines. There were also several significant shortcomings, as per a Brookings Institute report in 2006:

'The company is considered inefficient (production costs are estimated at 50 percent higher than in leading countries), with too many employees (it is the second-largest employer in the world), strong unionization, too few funds, and low productivity. The company lacks the technical (and sometimes financial) capacity to mine efficiently and access coal in deeper areas' (Madan 2006)

CIL also lacked the capacity to mine deeper and more efficiently, with its output/employee/year ratio being 1,200 tonnes, compared to Australia's 10,000 tonnes (Clemente 2014). There is also the issue of geography: coal-abundant states are clustered in the east. Transportation, coordination, and land regulation issues are compounded by local insurgent movements and corrupt non-state actors. Even the Planning Commission understood that importing coal for the west and southern coastal areas is more cost-effective (Integrated Energy Policy 2006). As a result, transmission capabilities did not meet generation capacities and load requirements (Mukherjee and Biswas 2015). The Electricity Act of 2003 de-licensed power generation, easing restrictions to set up power plants. As a result, 'coal-based power capacity went up from 84 GW in March 2010 to 165 GW in March 2015, a 95 percent increase, while production increased by only 15 percent during the same period' (Inamdar 2013). This further compounded the need for steam coal imports, which saw an increase from 25 metric tonnes (MT) in 2010 to 91 MT in 2015.

The UPA coalition delivered an average of 8.1% GDP growth, largely aided by the availability of coal powering steel factories, general industrialization, and electrification. At the same time, they oversaw a shift in India's largest energy sector to become reliant on imports, susceptible to international trade and volatility. The varying ratios of private and public sector involvement in India's coal trade make it difficult to assess the true impact of the UPA government in 'coal diplomacy'.

It is ironic, therefore, that the UPA is unlikely to be remembered as heralding India into an era of major coal expansion and industrialization, but rather, for allegations of misappropriating funds and deals related to the coal industry. Top UPA officials were accused of involvement in the 'Coalgate' scandal. Between 2004 and 2009, the government allegedly allocated coal blocks to private and public entities in a non-transparent manner. As a result of this ad-hoc allocation, competitive bids were not encouraged, and the exchequer allegedly faced an estimated loss of Rs. 1.86 lakh crore (Cornot-Gandolfe 2016). Although the ultimate verdict by a Standing Committee found unlawful allocation going back to 1993, the UPA government bore the political weight of the scandal.

One significant international investment in a coal power plant made under the UPA government was in Bangladesh. The National Thermal Power Corporation pledged $1.5bn to build a 1,320 MW power plant in Rampal, Khulna Division (Sengupta 2016). Expected to supply 10% of the country's electricity, the project has been criticized by UNESCO, Greenpeace, and elicited local protests over the expected environmental impact on the neighbouring Sundarbans (Mathiesen 2016). Despite continued bilateral support, progress remains slow, with the first dispatches sent to Bangladesh only in 2018.

India's per capita income for 2013 was estimated at about US$1,499, while that of China for the same year was US$6,807. India's per capita carbon emission from 2010 to 2013 was estimated at about 1.7 metric tonnes, compared to China's 6.2 metric tonnes for the same period. India's carbon intensity, counted in kg per kg of oil equivalent energy use, for 2010–3, was calculated at 2.8, in comparison to 3.3 kg for China and 2.5 kg for the United States (Jones and Saran 2015).

Additionally, the National Thermal Power Corporation Limited (NTPC) and India's private sector energy giant *Reliance Energy* developed joint power projects in Saudi Arabia and in the United Arab Emirates (Tanvi 2006, 48).

Securing Technology and Fuel for Nuclear Energy

A watershed moment for the UPA government's energy diplomacy was the conclusion of the Indo-U.S. Nuclear Deal. Concluded in 2006 and signed by the U.S. House of Representatives in 2008, this landmark civil nuclear agreement aimed for the United States to have 'full civil nuclear energy cooperation and trade with India' (Ministry of External Affairs, 2007), essentially ending the country's 30+ years of nuclear isolation. As a non-signatory to the Non-Proliferation Treaty (NPT), India was excluded from the Nuclear Suppliers Group (NSG) and thus denied access to information, technology, and trade, as well as intermittently subjected to sanctions for nuclear testing. Although former PM Singh touted the signing of the agreement as his 'best moment' (NDTV.com 2014) in office, navigating this deal did not prove to be an easy task, and a fruitful implementation arguably evades the UPA as well as the current NDA government.

For India, this agreement initially promised multiple successes. India would maintain control of its nuclear arsenal while simultaneously benefiting from international civilian cooperation and remaining a non-signatory of the NPT. In terms of significant concessions, India allowed for IAEA independent inspections on 14 of 22 plants while reserving the right to build future plants and independently determine them to be civilian or military (CFR 2019).

This path was essential to realizing India's nuclear energy generation ambitions, and ultimately, its energy security goals. The Singh administration aimed for nuclear energy to provide 25% of India's electricity needs by 2050, a significant leap as compared to the approximate 2–4% it provided at the time. This was especially important to meet the anticipated domestic demand of 1084 GWe base-load capacity in conjunction with a growing population (World Nuclear Association 2019), as well as international environmental commitments for curbing carbon emissions such as the Kyoto Protocol. In addition to not having access to knowledge from Nuclear Suppliers Group (NSG) signatories, India was also historically under-resourced in nuclear fuels such as uranium. Access to nuclear-related imports, technology, and trade were primary considerations guiding the UPA's actions, combined with broader strategic ambitions of cementing its role as a global power.

Perhaps the most significant outcome of the deal was the NSG's 'unique waiver' for India allowing access to uranium, which will enable India to meet its nuclear electricity generation capability goal of 60,000 MW by 2030 (Kumar and Kumar 2010). The first deal signed under this new era of 'uranium diplomacy' was with French energy firm Areva for 300 tons of uranium annually. France will also set up six atomic power reactors, each with a capacity of 1,650 MW, while the United States signed up to build 12 nuclear reactors. The Press Trust of India confirmed that uranium import deals were also signed with Kazakhstan, Australia, Canada, and Russia, which has, in turn, strengthened existing bilateral relationships and will enable 80% efficiency of existing plants (Press Trust of India 2018).

Energy Diplomacy Post-UPA Rule: 2014 and Beyond

Post-UPA India remains energy hungry, with demand for all sources of energy on the rise. Over the last decade, energy consumption has grown over 60% to 1269 TWh in 2017, from 793 TWh in 2010. The population during that same period grew by almost 10%. Today, India's energy demand is met by coal, hydro, and natural gas, and oil demand is forecast to put it in line with China's oil demand trajectory. India is the world's third largest producer of electricity but is plagued by frequent outages. The government somewhat controversially contends that 90% of India is now electrified.

Since taking office in early 2014, Indian Prime Minister Narendra Modi has made energy policy a driver of his domestic and foreign policy.

Having campaigned on an 'energy revolution', Modi began his term publicly pushing for renewables. In the first years of his term, SoftBank formed a JV with local conglomerate Bharti Enterprises to form a solar company. As a part of that JV, the following year, SoftBank pledged to invest $20bn in 20 GW of Indian solar projects. Last year, Softbank's Vision Fund announced a $60bn–$100bn in Indian solar projects. India currently has a 100 GW by 2022 target. The current deployment is roughly 20 GW. Modi unveiled a large renewable target of 175 GW by 2022, which includes: 100 GW solar, 60 GW wind, 10 GW biomass, and 5 GW of small hydro.

Since 2014, India has opened 52 coal mines. Since 2014, foreign energy investments in India grew by over 12%, the highest growth of energy investment anywhere in the world during that same period. Modi has further opened India up to outside investment while expanding Indian energy investments abroad. This policy has not been limited to traditional allies or groups but includes countries like Russia, the United States, Vietnam, China, Iran, and Saudi Arabia. Modi's goal seems to be to hedge energy risk in an attempt to secure economic inputs for the coming decade. Called 'strategic autonomy', the philosophy espoused by Modi pushes the unconstrained pursuit of relationships with various powers in an effort to diversify imports and maximize the benefit to India. This policy includes defense and energy agreements with both the United States and Russia and energy relations with Saudi Arabia while maintaining friendly, diplomatic ties with Tehran.

Imports have in recent years provided 80% of India's oil demand. Historically Iran was a major supplier of crude oil to India. The Indian–Iranian relationship has been tested by the Trump Administration's maximum pressure campaign. Initially, granted sanction waivers, India continued to import crude from Iran, reaching a historical peak in mid-2018 but rapidly weaned itself off of Iranian imports by August 2019, when the Administration announced that it would not renew sanction waivers. Unrest in the middle east and unknowns regarding American foreign policy have forced Modi to diversify his country's energy ties. From Russian natural gas to American shale oil, gas exchanges with Myanmar to energy trade agreements with Saudi Arabia, India has worked to walk a fine line somewhat reminiscent of the non-aligned philosophy of the 20th century.

Modi's aggressive energy goals depend primarily on foreign investment, which has led his government to pursue wide-ranging and sometimes incompatible foreign relations. In 2016, Russia and India agreed to a large energy and defense package. Russian companies had already been developing nuclear reactors in India and now agreed to the largest foreign takeover in Indian history and Russia's largest outbound deal. Rosneft will acquire 98% of Essar Oil and a 400k bpd refinery and port for $12.9bn. The deal followed a string of upstream investments in Russia by Indian companies worth $5.5bn. Indian firms, meanwhile, are investing $4bn in the United States shale assets, and though until recently, Indian–American ties were considered strong, the trade tensions between Trump's and Modi's administrations do not reflect the continued expansion of American solar companies in India.

At the same time, energy resource, finance, and expertise exports have increased significantly. Regionally, Modi has worked to deepen India's relationships as China continues to flex its muscle. As part of a defense cooperation agreement, Vietnam and India agreed to joint oil exploration and development along Vietnam's territorial waters and exclusive economic zone. India, meanwhile, has also started exporting refined petroleum to Myanmar, which received its first shipment of Indian-refined diesel in September 2017. India has pushed development in the Pacific, launching solar development partnerships in Fiji and other Pacific Island Countries, starting in November 2014. China soon followed in an attempt to build similar ties. India apparently also led the development of the regional cooperation agreement on electricity trade during the 2015 SAARC summit at Kathmandu. Under this agreement, Pakistan, India, Sri Lanka, and Bangladesh would be able to import electricity from hydropower-rich Nepal and Bhutan. While India has been asserting its role in the region, vis-à-vis China, that has not stopped the two from engaging in energy trade. In 2016, India helped launch talks for a natural gas swap in which Russia would sell gas to China, which would then deliver a portion of that gas to Myanmar and then to India.

Conclusion

As Prime Minister Singh, an economist, oversaw a period of wide-ranging economic liberalization, Indian foreign policy from 2004 to 2014 was driven by its own development principles. India was keenly aware of its own energy insecurity and also laid the groundwork for expansive renewables deployment. Like, its predecessor government, the Singh government pursued a sort-of realpolitik, ideologically free energy, and foreign policy. Under UPA rule, India signed numerous energy cooperation agreements, establishing secured channels of knowledge and civil-society exchange. Of particular importance was the India–United States Civil Nuclear Agreement, signed in 2005, under which India agreed to implement IAEA safeguards and grant full access to its civilian nuclear facilities in exchange for U.S. civil engagement in developing India's nuclear power industry. Singh managed to push the agreement forward despite significant domestic opposition, recognizing the dire need for expanded electricity capacity. One year later, India signed a nuclear and defense cooperation agreement with Moscow (Khan 2006). In 2007, Japan and India signed a joint cooperation agreement in recognition of the need for enhanced energy security. At the same time, in pursuit of its new energy goals, freed from ideological constraints, the state-owned oil and gas company acquired oil assets in places like Sudan, Syria, Iran, and Myanmar putting it in direct conflict with its relatively new ally, the United States (Economic Times 2012).

Under the UPA, India added, on average, more than 12 GW per year from 2005 to 2014 (Indian National Congress 2014). During that same period, the government instituted massive fuel subsidies, 15 rupees per litre of gasoline and 25 rupees per litre for diesel (Veereppa 2014). The UPA was intent on increasing urban electricity access rates to 100% and improving access for rural communities. The increased domestic energy demand helped guide foreign policy by sparking interest in foreign petroleum assets. The Indian state invested in a diverse range of what it saw as sure bets for the future, some of which did not pan out, including gas fields in Mozambique and oil assets in Iran. In 2004, India expected to meet 75% of its energy demand by 2020 with imported oil and gas (Munee et al. 2004). The government did intend to rely completely on domestic petroleum production by 2030 (Veerappa 2018). Almost a decade later, the Singh Government implemented policies to double its renewable energy capacity to 55 GW within four years (2017) (Singh 2013).

The overall legacy of the numerous joint energy cooperation agreements, however, is mixed. By the time Primer Minister Singh left office, India remained highly dependent on imported energy resources, and while foreign developers had helped expand India's electricity capacity, overall electrification remained a major obstacle to economic growth. Despite technical improvements, electrification growth remained sluggish and was marked by regular outages and production shortages. The accomplishments of the Singh government have been marred by charges of corruption, including in the process of coal-block allocation (Padmanabhan 2004). It is believed by critics that the alleged widespread corruption within both UPA-led governments substantially hindered growth and development.

During the period of UPA rule, India's energy diplomacy focused on purchasing oil, gas, and coal assets overseas. This increased thirst for energy resources happened at the same period when China was voraciously buying up equity stakes in oil and gas as part of China's internationalization strategy. While China had the economic resources to buy its energy security, India relied on diplomatic strategies to secure energy resources focusing on higher reliability and access. A foreign policy accomplishment during the first Manmohan Singh government was to persuade the United States to lift international sanctions against India's nuclear power sector, a process that began in 2005 and was completed in 2008. An energy security challenge to which India was exposed during the period of UPA rule was the risk associated with providing energy requirements of a rapidly growing economy amidst lack of sufficient domestically available resources combined with the price and supply volatility of an international market already tilted by other big buyers like China.

The UPA Government's energy diplomacy sought to ensure India's energy security in such a complex and difficult scenario through a number of strategies, notable among them may be summed up as: strengthening relations with oil and gas resource rich countries such as Saudi Arabia and other oil and gas rich countries of West Asia and Central Asia through exchange of bilateral visits; hosting of energy conferences and summits including the SAARC Gas Buyers Summit; acquiring oversees oil and gas assets in countries like Russia, Brazil, Vietnam, Egypt,

Sudan, Syria, Iran, and Myanmar through India's state owned company ONGC Videsh Limited (OVL); signing of agreements for the supply of natural gas from countries like Iran; investing in power generation projects in coal resource rich countries such as Bangladesh through India's state owned company NTPC; and concluding agreements with nations having advanced nuclear technology such as the United States, France, and Russia as well as those having large deposits of nuclear fuels such as Kazakhstan, Australia, and Canada for securing advanced technology and nuclear fuel for India's nuclear power program.

The UPA Government also showed interest in the construction of international gas pipelines such as the proposed Iran-Pakistan-India pipeline, Turkmenistan-Afghanistan-Pakistan-India (TAPI) pipeline, and Myanmar-Bangladesh-India pipeline. Unfortunately, none of them materialized due to various political, economic, and security reasons.

The energy mix under the UPA rule was dominated by fossil fuels. The next leaders of India must achieve deeper and more expansive energy diplomacy to account for a required rise in renewable energy while at the same time securing oil and gas to support growth and India's economy (Griffiths 2019). India needs to better prepare and reform its approach to energy policy as it moves through the energy transition. The global shift from reliance almost entirely on fossil to a much greater reliance on renewable energy demands more innovative policies and practices, and it's up to the government and India's growing private sector to cooperate and collaborate on making sure India's energy system moves the country forward as a rapidly emerging global leader. The decisions India makes with regards its energy mix matters, not just for the region but for the global energy outlook. India is the next China, but it can take a different path that is less fossil fuel dependent, especially around coal. As Griffith's (2019) study of the energy transition highlights, 'the rise of renewable energy will be accompanied by increased electrification and digitalization across all energy sectors as well as decentralization of energy supply', and the world will be watching how India responds.

The UPA navigated a challenging time for energy diplomacy, with 2004–14 being one of the most volatile in decades. India's current leadership must find ways to chart a comprehensive pathway forward and do so through bilateral partnerships, regional cooperation, and astute planning at both the state and more federal levels.

References

Clemente, Jude. *India Will Be Using and Importing More Coal* Forbes Magazine, 10 November 2014.

Cornot-Gandolphe, Sylvie. *Indian Steam Coal Imports: The Great Equation.* Oxford Institute for Energy Studies, 2016.

Economic Times. *India to Double Renewable Energy Capacity by 2017: Manmohan Singh* 18 April 2013: https://economictimes.indiatimes.com/industry/energy/power/india-to-double-renewable-energy-capacity-by-2017-manmohan-singh/articleshow/19595092.cms?from=mdr

Economic Times, *ONGC Videsh in Talks to Buy Shale Gas Assets in US, Canada* 29 August 2012: https://economictimes.indiatimes.com/industry/energy/oil-gas/ongc-videsh-in-talks-to-buy-shale-gas-assets-in-us-canada/articleshow/15946571.cms?from=mdr

Griffith, Steven. Energy Diplomacy in a Time of Energy Transition Energy Strategy Reviews, 26, 2019, November 2019, 1–10.

IEA, *Coal 2018*, Paris: International Energy Agency, 2018. https://www.iea.org/reports/coal-2018

Inamdar, Nikhil. *7 Things You Wanted to Know about 'Coalgate'* Business Standard 15 October 2013: https://www.business-standard.com/article/companies/7-things-you-wanted-to-know-about-coalgate-113101500366_1.html

Indian National Congress. *Power Generation Has Doubled under UPA*, 3 April 2014: https://www.inc.in/en/in-focus/power-generation-has-doubled-under-upa

World Nuclear Association. *Nuclear Power in India* 2019: https://www.world-nuclear.org/information-library/country-profiles/countries-g-n/india.aspx

Integrated Energy Policy, Indian Planning Commission. 2006: http://planningcommission.nic.in/

Jones, Bruce and Samir Saran. *An India Exception and India–U.S. Partnership on Climate Change* The Brookings Institution, 2015: www.Brookings.edu: http://www.brookings.edu/blogs/ planetpolicy/posts/2015/01/12-india-us-partnership-on-climate-change-jones-saran

Khan, Anwar Ahmad *India, Russia Sign Agreements to Further Strengthen Ties* outlookindia.com, December 2006: https://web.archive.org/web/20090411192950/http://www.outlookindia.com/pti_news.asp?id=339943

Mahajan. Accessing Neighbourhood Energy. in Khosla (ed.) Energy and Diplomacy, 2005. New Delhi: Konark Publishers.

Mathiesen, Karl. *U.N. Tells Bangladesh to Halt Mangrove-Threatening Coal Plant* The Guardian, 19 October 2016: https://www.theguardian.com/environment/2016/oct/19/un-tells-bangladesh-to-halt-mangrove-threatening-coal-plant

Ministry of External Affairs. 2007. Annual Report 2006-2007. New Delhi: Ministry of External Affairs, Government of India.

Moily, Veerappa. *NDA's Costly Fuel Policy: In Contrast to UPA's Pro-People Record, NDA Is Driving India to Energy Poverty* Times of India, 7 June 2018: https://timesofindia.indiatimes.com/blogs/toi-edit-page/ndas-costly-fuel-policy-in-contrast-to-upas-pro-people-record-nda-is-driving-india-to-energy-poverty/

Mukherjee, Maitreyee and Asit Biswas. *India's New Stand on Energy* The Diplomat, 19 May 2015: https://thediplomat.com/2015/05/indias-new-stand-on-energy/

Muneer, Tariq, Muhammad Asif, and Saima Munawwar. *Sustainable Production of Solar Electricity with Particular Reference to the Indian Economy* Renewable and Sustainable Energy Reviews. Pergamon, 6 July 2004: https://www.sciencedirect.com/science/article/abs/pii/S1364032104000693?via=ihub

NDTV Elections. *Q&A with Prime Minister Manmohan Singh: Highlights* 3 January 2014: www.ndtv.com/elections-news/q-a-with-prime-minister-manmohan-singh-highlights-546631

Padmanabhan, Anil. *2004 to 2014-India's Lost Decade* Livemint, 9 January 2014: https://www.livemint.com/Opinion/pJn6VtNuSyLCIkQFwx5OqN/2004-to-2014Indias-lost-decade.html

Press Trust of India. *10 Years of Indo-US Nuclear Deal: What India Gained from the Historic Pact* Business-Standard, 10 October 2018: https://www.business-standard.com/article/current-affairs/10-years-of-indo-us-nuclear-deal-what-india-gained-from-the-historic-pact-118101001045_1.html

Rajiv, Kumar and Kumar Santosh. *In the National Interest a Strategic Foreign Policy for India*. New Delhi: B.S. Books, 2010.

Sengupta, Debjoy. *Bhel Bags NTPC's Bangladesh Project* The Economic Times, 14 July 2016: https://economictimes.indiatimes.com/industry/energy/power/bhel-bags-ntpcs-bangladesh-project/articleshow/53210731.cms

Madan, Tanvi. *The Brookings Energy Series: India*. The Brookings Institute, 2006.

The Economic Times. *CIL Mega Share Sale Sails through; Government to Get Rs 22,600 Crore* 30 January 2015: https://economictimes.indiatimes.com/markets/stocks/news/cil-mega-share-sale-sails-through-government-to-get-rs-22600-crore/articleshow/46066139.cms

15

India at the WTO Negotiations, 2004–14

Vinícius Rodrigues Vieira

Introduction

Being a member of the multilateral trading system since 1948, India, however, significantly changed its views and approaches to prospective liberalization at the global level after the formation of the World Trade Organization (WTO). Indian negotiators began to go beyond traditional defensive approaches and learnt how to play with the rules of international trade to advance Indian interests. The Congress-led United Progressive Alliance (UPA) contributed to this new approach by balancing defensive demands from agriculture and small-scale industries, on the one hand, and offensive positions in services, on the other, in the negotiations of the Doha Development Agenda (DDA), launched in 2001. Yet, as the prospective international crisis finally arrived in 2008, the UPA government had no choice but to defend that 'no deal is better than a bad deal'. Consequently, India was again regarded in the West as a protectionist emerging power despite remaining committed with economic liberalization.

This chapter explores the domestic and international constraints that led India under the UPA government to find a middle ground between liberalizing interests and defensive demands as the DDA negotiations advanced amid growing fears of economic turmoil. While at the domestic level, stakeholders became more active, then complicating bureaucrats' and elected officials' task of defining the national interest in trade, the international scenario gave further leverage to India to adopt stronger stances vis-à-vis developed world's hypocrisy in demanding liberalization from the Global South without conceding on points that would yield development opportunities de facto. Moreover, the country's rising

Vinícius Rodrigues Vieira, *India at the WTO Negotiations, 2004–14* In: *Forging New Partnerships, Breaching New Frontiers.* Edited by: Rejaul Karim Laskar, Oxford University Press. © Oxford University Press 2022.
DOI: 10.1093/oso/9780192868060.003.0015

profile as an emerging power facilitated establishing alliances with developing nations outside the WTO, then allowing Indian policymakers to stick with a balanced view in trade without becoming at odds with traditional partners such as Brazil, whose negotiators pursued more market openness than Delhi.

The chapter begins by contrasting National Democratic Alliance (NDA)'s and UPA's views upon the DDA, then explains how domestic stakeholders in three major sectors—agriculture, industry, and services—organized themselves to influence the government to incorporate their interests into the national interest. The following section adds more complexity to the analysis by unfolding the impact of international factors over such a process, which in turn lays the ground for a debate on the effects of the expansion of preferential trade agreements (PTAs) upon Indian policymakers. The conclusion recasts the main arguments and discusses whether any other governing coalition but the UPA would have adopted similar positions and strategies within the same context.

Balancing Offensive and Defensive Interests

Conventional wisdom claims that there is a consensus in Indian politics that agriculture cannot be liberalized. Yet, a brief comparison between government positions under the NDA and the UPA suggests a more complex reality. The 2002 Indian Trade Policy Review (TPR) submitted to the WTO explicitly mentioned that the DDA would be an opportunity for 'maximising export opportunities for Indian agricultural products' (WTO 2002, 16). Five years later, in the TPR submitted by the middle of UPA's first term in power, there was no reference to opening agricultural markets, then portrayed as a 'vulnerable sector of the economy' that required 'special care and protection' (WTO 2007, 13).

In fact, preliminary evidence indicates the need to consider seriously that UPA's victory in the 2004 elections was in part a response from peasants to NDA's dubious plans for Indian agriculture in a globalized world. In its manifesto for the 2004 bid for re-election, the NDA had expressed the desire to expand opportunities for food exporting rather than just keeping the sector focused on the domestic market. The manifesto stated the goal of making India an economic superpower through a seven-pronged strategy which listed as its first goal making the country the 'the food factory of the world' (NDA 2004).

NDA aligned India with Brazil in the Cancun Ministerial, in September 2003, to counter the developed world's agenda that circumvented liberalization *de facto* in agriculture, which implies phasing out subsidies to farmers in the Global North. The Agricultural G-20, a coalition composed of developing countries, predominantly with offensive interests in agriculture, lost importance for India's diplomacy under the UPA administration. Instead, the UPA emphasized membership in the G-33, which advocated special treatment in agriculture for developing countries. The prominence of defensive over offensive positions is evident in the emphasis the UPA government gave to the G-33 right after coming into power, in May 2004. Even though India belonged to the G-33 since its foundation in September 2003 (when the G-20 also started its activities), the newsletter 'India & the WTO' (the official publication of the Indian mission in Geneva to report the state of affairs in the negotiations) had never mentioned that the country was a member of the group before the UPA came to power.

It is worth noting that the Agricultural G-20's demands were not at odds with the defence of small peasants. The coalition simply claimed for the fulfilment of the DDA that had been launched in 2001, which had determined the discussion of market access, domestic support, and export subsidies in agriculture. The group also encompassed the defence of special and differential treatment (SDT) to developing countries, which still had large shares of people dependent upon agriculture. G-20 even adhered to the defence of special safeguard measures (SSM) and the exclusion of special products (SP) from potential liberalization. Yet, those commitments seemed not to suffice to meet the defensive interests that the UPA Government came to represent. In fact, India's emphasis on the G-33 only grew with the lack of progress in the negotiations after the Hong Kong Ministerial in December 2005. Until then, there were still hopes for significant gains in services, the sector that concentrated most of India's liberalizing interests, particularly for information and communication technology (ICT) entrepreneurs and workers who would benefit from mode 4 liberalization—that is, the exemption of visa for temporary service providers from abroad.

From 2005 to the major deadlock the DDA talks faced in 2008, India's position under the UPA government only became more balanced—not to say cautious—regarding the main effects of liberalization. That is, rather than being circumstantial, Indian opposition to finishing the negotiations in 2008 derives from a long duration process. Certainly, in 22 July 2008, during the Geneva meeting after which the DDA negotiations went into a deadlock, the UPA faced a vote of no confidence, then reducing the chances that the round would be ever finished. This happened because the Left Front, formed by communist and other leftist parties of India, withdrew support to the government as it opposed the conditions of the Indo-U.S. Nuclear Deal. Commerce Minister Kamal Nath (often regarded as the main factor for explaining UPA's supposed turn towards protectionism) himself had to go to Delhi and returned only on 23 July to Geneva, when the mini-ministerial was on its third day (South Centre 2008, 5). Two days later, the negotiations started to break apart and on 29 July, the meeting came to an end (Ibid.). Part of the deadlock was attributed to the constraints India's negotiators faced because of the parliamentary election of April 2009 (Wolfe 2009, 27), when the UPA successfully secured a second consecutive term.

Playing with Domestic Stakeholders

UPA's move towards a more cautious approach in multilateral liberalization had led to relevant changes in the state-society relationships in trade policymaking in India. Until 2004, there was an Advisory Committee on International Trade with stakeholders and state actors.[1] In the committee, industrial associations were more represented than civil society organizations in general,[2] thus signalling a preference of the government for liberalizing opinions. UPA's minister Nath limited the role of this committee (Sharma 2007, 24). Evidence from interviews in general suggests that it was extinguished in practice after 2004. Nevertheless, interactions between private stakeholders and the Government of India remained strong but happened through other channels.

Indian agriculture was far from having a single, coherent organization of its interests even when there was a convergence of interests among some of its players, as it is the case with the defensive small farmers.

They were constantly mobilized, yet did not prevail until after May 2004, when the UPA came into power with a more balanced agenda between the need to reform Indian agriculture in the long term while retaining people's livelihood goals in the short term. The farmers' concerns were not unheard of by the Government of India. The specific organizations that offered inputs, however, are hardly identifiable given that there is a plethora of them in the country. In 2001, prior to the launch of the DDA, the NDA government consulted farmers' organizations about their preferences regarding agriculture (Lok Sabha 2001). Consultations continued as the DDA negotiations evolved and were maintained under the UPA government (Rajya Sabha 2004). Farmers' awareness about the DDA was further enhanced after the implementation of the project Strategies and Preparedness for Trade and Globalisation in India, an initiative of the United Nations Conference on Trade and Development (UNCTAD). The initiative (henceforth the UNCTAD-India project) aimed to improve Indian societal actors' ability to participate in international trade negotiations, including the DDA talks. With the financial support of the Department for International Development of the United Kingdom (DFID), the project was launched in 2003, when NDA was still in power (UNCTAD-India 2010, 1). It focused not only on players within agriculture but also within marine goods, small and medium enterprises, and textiles and clothing (Ibid.).

Grassroots organizations then had opportunities to engage in direct lobbying with bureaucrats rather than just relying on *ad hoc* mass mobilization as it seemed to be common before 2004. The UNCTAD-India project organized a meeting between farmers' organizations and government officials between 19 and 20 July 2005 simply to discuss India's strategy in agriculture for the Hong Kong Ministerial in December of that year. Another meeting between 28 and 29 November, which also included NAMA topics, involved peasant associations too (Ibid., 16). The archives list 19 different farmers' associations attending at least one of the meetings. The participants include members of the five organizations that claim to have a national scope (AIKS, AIAWU, BKS, BKU/ICCFM, and the Farmers' Forum) (Rajya Sabha 2005).[3] The other 14 associations represent agricultural labourers and small farmers from only seven out of 35 states or territories that composed the Union at that time. The southern Indian states of Andhra Pradesh, Karnataka, Kerala, and Tamil

Nadu—which tended to side with UPA members—are the basis for nine of these regional associations (Ibid.).

The organization of defensive interests in manufacturing also contributed to UPA's adoption of a balanced approach between liberalizing and protectionist demands from domestic stakeholders. Lobbying outside federations like the Confederation of Indian Industries (CII) and the Federation of the Indian Chambers of Commerce and Industry (FICCI) happened through regional and/or sub-sectoral business associations or quasi-statist organizations, such as area-specific export councils (Lok Sabha 2003). The textile industry, especially apparel, is such a case.[4] It feared foreign competition and loss of markets abroad, particularly after 2005, when the quotas provided by the Agreement on Textiles and Clothing (ATC) were phased out. Players within the chemical and pharmaceutical sub-sectors had similar concerns.[5] Automobile industries (including manufacturers of car components) also opposed a Non-Agricultural Market Access (NAMA) agreement unless it provided enough exceptions for their products to be protected from foreign competition.[6] Out of all these defensive sectors, only the automobile complex does not have many medium or small firms. Hence its lobby was organized at the national level and was more evident than other manufacturing sub-sectors.[7] It is conducted by the Society of Indian Automobile Manufacturers and, to a smaller extent, the Automotive Component Manufacturers' Association of India. As for chemicals, pharmaceuticals, and textiles producers, representation of interests outside the federations happened mainly via state-based industrial associations.[8]

In opposition to the conventional wisdom that attributes to India superpowers in services, we clarify that not all sub-sectors within that economic segment involve activities that would have been directly impacted by any agreement in the DDA context. Besides the well-known organization in ICTs through the National Association of Software and Services Companies (NASSCOM), the medical and law sub-sectors were also following the developments of the round through their respective class associations.[9] Players in education, which had initially been listed amongst the activities with potential for liberalization, also expressed their defensive interests, although they were later in 'limbo'.[10] There were also concerns with finance (a heavily regulated activity in the country) and retail[11] (the opening of which has been suspended since 2011 in spite of parliament's consent of the sector's liberalization).

NASSCOM reports to be disappointed with the deadlocks in the DDA negotiations.[12] This is understandable considering that the organization is engaged in trying to expand liberalization in ICTs through trade agreements.[13] It participated actively in the process of forming India's positions for the negotiations.[14] Apart from NASSCOM's lobby, the ICT sub-sector relied on direct connections between firms and the field of the state.[15] The support for a liberalizing deal, in particular in mode 4, was consensual among players within the sector. State actors also embraced such a position insofar as ICTs correspond to about a third of its exports of goods and services together. Also, as a senior bureaucrat argues, ICTs reached a level of internationalization that makes it impossible for anyone to oppose further liberalization in the sub-sector.[16]

A Changing International Environment

India's participation in the DDA talks under the UPA government should, however, be understood not only in the light of the constraints domestic stakeholders impose upon any administration. The UPA also had to cope with a changing international environment where India itself consolidated its status as an emerging power after concluding the shift of its international strategy from 'nonalignment to multialignment' (Jaffrelot and Sidhu 2013, 319). As Narlikar (2006, 59) argues, a rising India developed greater engagement with economic partners while de-emphasizing Third World rhetoric. Notwithstanding these shifts, India did not have to leave aside its Global South allies to improve relations with the systemic core—that is, the West (Ibid., 74)—and to gain international power (Narlikar 2007, 984). Given the increasing costs of only ever saying no in international fora, policymakers dealt with regimes to satisfy domestic interests in parallel with the enhancement of national power abroad. UPA's approach to the DDA exemplifies such a trend, notwithstanding the absence of a grand strategy in India's foreign policy at that time (Mehta 2009, 210).

Multialignment was a means of sustaining economic growth and empowering the nation abroad (Jaffrelot and Sidhu 2013, 319). This had been crucial since the aftermath of the 1991 crisis but gained more relevance in the 2000s as rising India portrayed itself as a responsible stakeholder that, for instance, would no longer obstruct multilateral talks such as the DDA. In such a context, further integration into the world economy became possible insofar as a sense of national sovereignty over the domestic market could be maintained (Norbu 1998, 303) and economic development be addressed (Ibid., 313). Those trends only became more prominent while the UPA held power. In the 21st century, as Mohan argues, India moved from a defensive to a responsible multilateralism, using international regimes to demonstrate a willingness to cooperate within a globalized order, while enhancing its power.

In fact, at the transition from the NDA to the UPA government, the Government of India expressed the view that foreign policy should be conceived as being part of a larger effort to enhance economic development and national security (MEA 2004, 1; MEA 2005, 1). Nevertheless, insofar as the UPA had significant support within rural areas in South India, the understanding of the limits for development through the government changed after 2004. Moreover, the rise in international food prices in 2007 and 2008 contributed to reducing the scope for concessions in agriculture (Malone 2011, 262). The perspective of international crisis also generated uncertainty about whether the country could still gain from multilateral liberalization. Embarking on the race for PTAs looked like a more worthwhile strategy to advance national interests without exposing much protectionist interests, particularly in agriculture. However, prior to the launch of the DDA, India had already been engaged in the advancement of economic integration at the regional level, within the context of the 'Look East' strategy (Jain 2011, 217), launched in the 1990s and which gained further relevance with the rise of China and its consequent growing influence in East and South-East Asia. Therefore, while the pursuit of PTAs did not stem only from gloomy perspectives for the DDA negotiations, lack of progress at the multilateral level stimulated first policymakers and thereafter stakeholders to look for bilateral alternatives in economic liberalization.

India was in the process of negotiating framework agreements with the goal of signing PTAs with five economic blocs at the beginning of 2005 (that was before the DDA took its final route towards deadlock in the aftermath of the Hong Kong Ministerial in December of the same year): the Association of South East Asian Nations (ASEAN, composed of Brunei Darussalam, Cambodia, Indonesia, Lao PDR, Malaysia, Myanmar, Philippines, Singapore, Thailand, and Vietnam), the Bay of Bengal Initiative for Multi-Sectoral Technical and Economic Cooperation (formed by Bangladesh, Myanmar, India, Sri Lanka, and Thailand), the Gulf Cooperation Council (composed of Bahrain, Kuwait, Oman, Qatar, Saudi Arabia, and the United Arab Emirates), the South African Customs Union (SACU, made up by Botswana, Lesotho, Namibia, South Africa, and Swaziland). Also, the country conducted bilateral talks with Afghanistan, Chile, Korea, Singapore, and Mauritius to form separate agreements with each of them.[17]

In 2007, India initiated conversations to form an overreaching PTA with the EU that would exclude substantial reform in the agricultural sector given the sensitivities of both parties in the area (European Commission 2014). After the DDA deadlock of July 2008, the UPA government engaged the country in other initiatives that may result in at least in comprehensive economic cooperation agreements (CECAs) with the European Free Trade Association (which comprises Switzerland, Iceland, Norway, and Liechtenstein, in December 2008), Canada, Israel, New Zealand (2010), Australia, and Indonesia (2011). The Asia-Pacific Trade Agreement, with five members (Bangladesh, China, India, Korea, Lao PDR, and Sri Lanka), it has been planning since 2009 to expand its system of preference. Moreover, China demonstrated interest in establishing a bilateral economic agreement with India.

Preliminary evidence suggests that the PTAs have limited effects, insofar as they are restricted to markets with limited importance for the country (Nataraj 2007, 14). Nonetheless, their negotiation is evidence that the UPA has not placed India on an old-fashioned protectionist track: instead, the government had just downplayed the multilateral negotiations as the DDA stalled and domestic demands could no longer be satisfied at the WTO level. In 2014, by the end of the UPA rule, only four bilateral negotiations that were still under negotiation nine years before resulted in some trade liberalization. Economic cooperation with Afghanistan and Singapore started in 2005, whereas the PTA with Chile has been in place since 2007. In 2010, a comprehensive economic partnership agreement with Korea came into effect, and, a year later, a similar pact was celebrated with Japan. The agreement with the Brazilian-led Common Market of the

South (MERCOSUR) came into effect in 2009, as well as the PTA with ASEAN, whose services part was approved by India in 2013. Negotiations with the EU—whose conclusion would meet particularly the interests of ICT services[18]—were advanced yet suspended at the end of 2013 due to the 2014 general elections in India. Moreover, PTAs with partners in Asia have more political clout than economic objectives (Sally 2011, 9), but had the potential in the medium and long term to create trade rather than just diverting it. The great recession of 2008, however, placed more caution over liberalization in the whole world, not just in India.

Conclusion

The participation of India in WTO negotiations under the UPA government should therefore be understood less in terms of partisan preferences rather than because of transformation in both international and domestic environments during the period 2004–14. Certainly, both the Agricultural G-20 and the G-33 expressed not only economic interests but also the opportunity to revive the partnership with Brazil during the GATT era and the solidarity ties forged with the old Third World in the Non-Aligned Movement during the Cold War (Rodrigues Vieira 2015). With the rise of the BRICS and of the India-Brazil-South Africa (IBSA) group throughout the 2000s, the political costs of leaving aside the Agricultural G-20 in favour of the G-33 diminished, thus opening further space for pursuing the interests of small-scale producers. Other spaces to coordinate shared political interests with emerging powers like Brazil emerged. UPA remained faithful to that logic even in the later attempts to revive the DDA negotiations, like in the Bali Ministerial Meeting of December 2013, when India was at the forefront of the negotiations by defending SDT to agriculture (Rodrigues Vieira 2016).

Politics is the art of the possible, realists say. Being the consequence of both international and domestic politics rather than of the economic dynamic, trade negotiations reflect a complex game of power in which partisan preferences (if existent) are just a small piece of a large puzzle. The UPA probably did as any other government would have done in the same context: it played at the best of its ability with both internal and foreign constraints. 'No WTO deal better than a bad deal', minister Nath said in

2006 in reference to the lack of advancement in the DDA talks. The following years proved that, in fact, liberalization without considering development needs is anything but a false promise that brings instability that no superficial prosperity can afford.

Notes

1. Interview with Bipul Chatterjee, CUTS officer, Delhi, 6 Sep 2011.
2. Interview with senior bureaucrat, Delhi, 15 Sep 2011.
3. The All India Kisan Sabha (AIKS) is associated with the Communist Party of India (CPI), whereas the All India Agricultural Workers Union (AIAWU) has links to the Communist Party of India-Marxist (CPI[M]) (Rajya Sabha 2005). In turn, the Bharatiya Kisan Sangh (BKS) integrates the Sangh Parivar, the group organizations that form the Hindu nationalist movement (Jaffrelot 2002). The Bharat Krishak Samaj (Farmers' Forum) and the Bharatiya Kisan Union (BKU) have no partisan affiliation. The latter has strong connections with the Via Campesina, a global social movement composed by peasants' and small farmers' associations from all over the world (Lindberg 1995, 115).
4. Interview with Rahan S. Ratna, MoC senior bureaucrat (2001–08), Delhi, 14 Sep 2011.
5. Interview with Bipul Chatterjee, CUTS officer, Delhi, 6 Sep 2011; interview with former senior bureaucrat, 26 Sep 2011; interview with senior bureaucrat, 21 Mar 2012.
6. Interview with T. S. Vishwanath, CII representative in Geneva (2003–05) and consultant, Delhi, 21 Sep 2011.
7. Interview with Dr Biswajit Dhar, RIS director and former negotiator, Delhi, 12 Sep 2011.
8. Interview with former senior bureaucrat, 26 Sep 2011; interview with senior bureaucrat, 21 Mar 2012.
9. Interview with MoC senior bureaucrat, Delhi, 7 Sep 2011.
10. Interview with Dr Biswajit Dhar, RIS director and former negotiator, Delhi, 12 Sep 2011.
11. Interview with MoC senior bureaucrat, Delhi, 7 Sep 2011.
12. Interview with Gagan Sabharwal, NASSCOM officer, Delhi, 29 Sep 2011.
13. Interview with consultant, Delhi, 12 Sep 2011.
14. Interview with Dr. Abhijit Das, MoC senior bureaucrat (2000–05) and member of UNCTAD-India Project (2005–10), Delhi, 12 Sep. 2011.
15. Interview with Rahan S. Ratna, MoC senior bureaucrat (2001–08), Delhi, 14 Sep 2011.
16. Interview with MoC senior bureaucrat, Delhi, 7 Sep 2011.

17. India & the WTO, Mar–Apr 2005, 26.
18. Interview with Gagan Sabharwal, NASSCOM officer, Delhi, 29 Sep 2011.

References

European Commission. 2014. Countries and Regions: India. Available from http://ec.europa.eu/trade/policy/countries-and-regions/countries/india. Accessed 13 February 2014.

Jaffrelot, Christophe. 2002. Hindu Nationalism and Democracy. In Transforming India: Social and Political Dynamics of Democracy, edited by Francine R. Frankel et al, 353–78. Oxford: Oxford University Press.

Jaffrelot, Christophe, and Waheguru Pal Singh Sidhu. 2013. From Plurilateralism to Multilateralism? G-20, IBSA, BRICS, and BASIC. In Shaping the Emerging World: India and the Multilateral Order, edited by Waheguru Pal Singh Sidhu, Pratap Bhanu Mehta, and Bruce Jones, 319–40. Washington, DC: Brookings Institution.

Jain, Rajendra K. 2011. From Idealism to Pragmatism: India and Asian Regional Integration. Japanese Journal of Political Science 12 (2):213–31.

Lindberg, Staffan. 1995. New Farmers' Movements in India as Structural Response and Collective Identity Formation: The Cases of the Shetkari Sanghatana and the BKU. In New Farmers' Movements in India, edited by Tom Brass, 95–125. Ilford: Frank Cass.

Lok Sabha. 2001. Unstarred Question No 3104: Consultation with Farmers before Signing WTO Agreement. Available from <http://164.100.47.132/LssNew/psearch/QuestionArchive.aspx>. Accessed 14 November 2012.

Malone, David. 2011. Does the Elephant Dance? Contemporary Indian Foreign Policy. Oxford: Oxford University Press.

MEA. 2004. Annual Report 2003–2004. Available from <http://www.mea.gov.in/Uploads/PublicationDocs/165_Annual-Report-2003-2004.pdf >. Accessed 5 May 2014.

MEA. 2005. Annual Report 2004–2005. Available from <http://www.mea.gov.in/Uploads/PublicationDocs/166_Annual-Report-2004-2005.pdf >. Accessed 5 May 2014.

Mehta, Pratap Bhanu. 2009. Still under Nehru's Shadow? The Absence of Foreign Policy Frameworks in India. India Review 8 (3):209–33.

Narlikar, Amrita. 2006. Peculiar Chauvinism or Strategic Calculation? Explaining the Negotiating Strategy of a Rising India. International Affairs 82 (1):59–76.

Narlikar, Amrita. 2007. All That Glitters Is Not Gold: India's Rise to Power. Third World Quarterly 28 (5):983–996.

Nataraj, Geethanjali. 2007. Regional Trade Agreements in the Doha Round: Good for India? ADB Institute Discussion Paper No. 67. Tokyo: Asian Development Bank Institute.

NDA. 2004. National Democratic Alliance: An Agenda for Development, Good Governance, Peace, and Harmony—Elections to the 14th Lok Sabha, April–May

2004. Available from <http://www.indian-elections.com/partymanifestoes/party-manifestoes04/nda.html>. Accessed 1 October 2011.

Norbu, Dawa. 1998. After Nationalism? Elite Beliefs, State Interests, and International Politics. International Studies 35 (3):295–315.

Rajya Sabha. 2004. Unstarred Question No. 613: Strategy at WTO. Available from <http://164.100.47.5/qsearch/qsearch.aspx>. Accessed 1 October 2011.

Rajya Sabha. 2005. List of Farmers' Organizations which Participated in the 'Pre-Hong Kong Ministerial Meeting—Consultation Workshop'. Organized Jointly by Government with the United Nations Conference on Trade and Development (UNCTAD), 19 and 20 July 2005. Available from <http://164.100.47.5/qsearch/qsearch.aspx>. Accessed 1 October 2011.

Rodrigues Vieira, Vinícius. 2015. 'The 'Eastern Brother': Brazil's View of India as a Diplomatic Partner in World Trade'. In Competing Visions of India in World Politics India's Rise beyond the West, edited by Kate Sullivan. Basingstoke: Palgrave, pp. 111–127.

Rodrigues Vieira, Vinícius. 2016. Beyond the Market: The Global South and the WTO's Normative Dimension. International Negotiation 21(2): 267–94.

Sally, Razeen. 2011. Indian Trade Policy after the Crisis. ECIPE Occasional Paper No. 4. Brussels: European Centre for International Political Economy.

Sharma, Shefali. 2007. India and the Agreement on Agriculture: Civil Society and Citizens' Engagement. Working Paper 278. Brighton: Institute of Development Studies.

South Centre. 2008. The WTO's July 2008 Mini-Ministerial: Agriculture, NAMA, Process Issues and the Road Ahead. Available from <http://www.southcentre.int/wp-content/uploads/2013/08/AN_MA_AG_The-WTO-July-2008-Mini-Ministe rial_EN.pdf>. Accessed 22 July 2014.

UNCTAD-India. 2010. Strategies and Preparedness for Trade and Globalization in India: Key Outcomes of the Project. Delhi: UNCTAD, MoC, and DFID.

Wolfe, Robert. 2009. Sprinting during a Marathon: Why the WTO Ministerial Failed in July 2008. Group d'ÉconomieMondiale, Science-Po Working Paper. April.

WTO. 2002. Trade Policy Review: Report by the Government—India (WT/TPR/G/100). Available from <https://docs.wto.org/dol2fe/Pages/FE_Search/FE_S_S006. aspx?Query=((%20@Title=%20india)%20or%20(@CountryConcerned=%20in dia))%20and%20(%20(%20@Symbol=%20wt/tpr/g/*%20))&Language=ENGL ISH&Context=FomerScriptedSearch&languageUIChanged=true#>. Accessed 15 June 2014.

WTO. 2007. Trade Policy Review: Report by the Secretariat—India (WT/TPR/S/182). Available from <https://docs.wto.org/dol2fe/Pages/FE_Search/FE_S_S006. aspx?Query=((%20@Title=%20india)%20or%20(@CountryConcerned=%20in dia))%20and%20(%20(%20@Symbol=%20wt/tpr/s/*%20))&Language=ENGL ISH&Context=FomerScriptedSearch&languageUIChanged=true#>. Accessed 30 April 2014.

PART V
CONCLUSION

This concluding part summarizes the findings of this book to reach a number of important conclusions about the foreign policy of India during the UPA period.

16

Decade of Transformations

India's Foreign Policy under the United Progressive Alliance, 2004–14

Rejaul Karim Laskar

Introduction

The contributors to this volume belong to a diverse set of geographical, national, and institutional backgrounds. Most of them are distinguished academics belonging to some of the leading universities or think tanks around the world. Some of them have held in the past senior positions in the Government of India or in the United Nations. What is common to all of them is that they are among the leading experts in the areas with which their respective chapters deal. We wanted a rich and kaleidoscopic perspective on the various aspects of India's foreign policy as they evolved through the period of the United Progressive Alliance (UPA) rule in India (2004–14). The editor, therefore, resisted the temptation to straightjacket the contributors with any rigid theoretical or methodological framework. Rather, it was left to the discretion of the individual contributors to choose the theoretical and methodological approach they find most suitable for their respective chapters based on the theme of the chapter as well as on the expertise and experience of the contributor.

The result is that we have a collection of chapters that are rich in their analyses and diverse in their perspectives. However—sheathed in this diversity of perspectives, methodologies, and theoretical and analytical frameworks—certain core strands of findings are discernible in these chapters, summarizing which we can reach several important conclusions about India's foreign policy during the UPA rule, especially in terms of the objectives sought, the instruments used, the principles adhered to,

Rejaul Karim Laskar, *Decade of Transformations* In: *Forging New Partnerships, Breaching New Frontiers*. Edited by: Rejaul Karim Laskar, Oxford University Press. © Oxford University Press 2022.
DOI: 10.1093/oso/9780192868060.003.0016

the role of ideology and leadership, the problems of implementation, and finally the continuities and changes with the previous NDA Government.

Economy First

Scholars of India's foreign policy are more or less unanimous that India's economic development was the core goal of the foreign policy of the two UPA governments (Panda 2013, 2014; Scott 2013, 351). In other words, securing access to foreign resources, technologies, and markets—through trade, investment, and technology transfer agreements—to fuel India's rapid economic growth has been the highest priority objective of the foreign policy of the two UPA governments.

The findings of this volume largely support this view. Several of the chapters of the present volume find that enhanced trade was the key priority in India's approach to several of its bilateral partners. Isabelle Saint-Mézard, for example, in her chapter finds that the UPA governments viewed India-Pakistan relations through 'neoliberal prism', which is based on the belief that increased economic interdependence and prospects of mutual economic gains can transform their conflictual relations. Moreover, India's less overbearing approach towards its South Asian neighbours—during this period—too was underlaid by the belief that a peaceful and friendly neighbourhood was a sine qua non for India's rapid and unobstructed economic growth. Similarly, Mervin Bain and Shutaro Sano, in their respective chapters, find that economic cooperation was a key area in India's relations with Russia and Japan. Several other contributors find similar emphasis on economic cooperation in India's approach to key geographical regions of importance. In the case of India's relations with ASEAN—as John D. Ciorciari finds in his chapter—even while UPA brought strategic content in the relations, emphasis on the objective of economic development of North East India through increased trade and connectivity with ASEAN members was noticeable.

Securing access to foreign natural resources was critical to sustaining the rapid economic growth that India saw during the UPA period. Naturally, ensuring secured supply of natural resources was an important objective of UPA's foreign policy. Findings of several chapters of this volume support this argument. Barnaby Dye and Ricardo Soares de Oliveira, for example, in their chapter, find that one of the 'drivers for India's interest in the continent' was the 'desire to secure natural resources'.

Perhaps the most important instrument used by the UPA governments to give a boost to India's trade was trade agreements. Major trade agreements signed by India during the UPA period include, Japan-India Comprehensive Economic Partnership Agreement (CEPA) signed in 2011; ASEAN-India free trade agreement (FTA) signed in 2009; and the partial-scope trade agreement with the MERCOSUR (Southern Common Market countries, namely, Argentina, Brazil, Paraguay, Uruguay) signed in 2009. Other notable bilateral trade agreements signed during the period were with Singapore, Thailand, Malaysia, and Chile. Similarly, the UPA government signed a number of investment treaties, notable among these are those with China, Bangladesh, Myanmar, and Brunei.

Proof of the pudding is in the eating! The touchstone to evaluate the economic thrust in any foreign policy must be the spurt seen in trade and investment. In this regard, the findings of the chapters of this volume give thumbs-up to the two UPA administrations. John D. Ciorciari, for example, finds in his chapter that the economic thrust of the 'Look East' policy during the period 'yielded clear benefits in investment and trade'. To bolster his argument, Ciorciari cites FDI figures to show that by 2014, India became the second largest destination of FDI among developing countries (the first being China). He also finds that a 'sizable share of that investment came from Asian partners including Japan, China, South Korea, and Singapore'. He also finds that the trade between India and ASEAN members saw a manifold increase from U.S.$17 billion in 2004—the year the UPA administration was inaugurated—to U.S.$81 in 2014—the year the UPA left office—around a five-fold increase in just ten years! Similar findings are reached by Barnaby Dye and Ricardo Soares de Oliveira in their chapter on India-Africa relations. They find that India-Africa trade figures which stood at a meagre U.S.$7.2 billion at the turn of the century, grew to U.S.$78 billion by the end of the UPA period—again a whopping ten-fold increase!

However, the economic thrust of UPA's foreign policy does not mean a single-minded focus on free trade without concern for weaker sectors in the Indian Economy, which are not well prepared to face international competition. Indeed, as Vinícius Rodrigues Vieira in his chapter shows, the UPA was unyielding in its determination to protect the 'vulnerable sector of the economy'—namely the agricultural sector. Indeed, Rodrigues Vieira finds that the protectionism shown by the UPA vis-à-vis the agricultural sector contrasts strongly with the approach of the previous NDA administration.

Energy

In ensuring rapid and sustained economic growth, the role of unhindered and secured access to energy resources at affordable prices can hardly be overemphasized. UPA's focus on using its foreign policy to propel and sustain high-speed growth of India's economy, therefore, naturally translated to the use of diplomacy by it to ensure India's access to reliable and affordable energy resources from foreign countries. Several contributors to this volume have found this emphasis on securing resources and technologies related to energy in UPA's diplomacy.

Carolyn Kissane, for example, in her chapter, while pointing out that during the ten-year period of UPA rule India became the second largest consumer of energy from fifth largest, argued that the UPA government was 'keenly aware of critical importance of energy security' in sustaining India's high economic growth. She finds that energy diplomacy was an 'important even critical' part of UPA governments' diplomacy.

The findings of several other contributors to this volume uphold her assertion. Barnaby Dye and Ricardo Soares de Oliveira, for example, find that India's quest for energy resources was one of the most important drivers of India's relations with Africa during the period. Similarly, Bhavna Dave, in her chapter, finds that the most important driver of India's increased focus on Central Asia was 'India's growing energy needs'. Dave points out the emphasis that the 'Connect Central Asia' policy initiated by the UPA-II government gave to energy resources available in the region. She also mentions UPA minister Mani Shankar Aiyar actively lobbying on behalf of Indian firms for exploration rights of energy resources in the region.

Kissane, in her chapter, finds a number of instruments that UPA used in its drive to secure foreign energy resources and technologies. These are: strengthening relations with oil and gas resource–rich countries through exchange of bilateral visits; hosting of energy conferences and

summits such as SAARC Gas Buyers Summit; offers of various kinds
of aid to energy resource–rich developing countries; acquiring overseas oil and gas assets in countries like Russia, Brazil, Vietnam, Egypt,
Sudan, Syria, Iran, and Myanmar through India's state-owned company
ONGC Videsh Limited (OVL); signing of agreements for the supply of
natural gas from countries like Iran; investing in power generation projects in coal resource–rich countries such as Bangladesh through India's
state-owned company National Thermal Power Corporation Limited
(NTPC); and concluding agreements with nations having advanced nuclear technology such as the United States, France and Russia, as well as
those having large deposits of nuclear fuels such as Kazakhstan, Australia
and Canada for securing advanced nuclear technology and nuclear fuel
for India's nuclear power generation projects. Kissane also mentions the
interest shown by the UPA government in proposed pipeline projects
such as the Iran-Pakistan-India pipeline, Turkmenistan-Afghanistan-
Pakistan-India (TAPI) pipeline, and Myanmar-Bangladesh-India pipeline, none of which were ultimately materialized due to 'various political,
economic, and security reasons'. Barnaby Dye and Ricardo Soares de
Oliveira, in their chapter, give example of another instrument of India's
energy diplomacy, namely Buying shares of foreign oil companies. They
give some examples of the use of this instrument by India during the
UPA period, such as the ONGC Videsh Limited buying 25% share in the
Greater Nile Petroleum Operating Company.

A discussion of India's energy diplomacy will be incomplete without a
mention of the India-US nuclear agreement signed during the UPA period. Ramesh Thakur, in his chapter, points out that ensuring energy security was an important 'strategic goal' of the agreement.

One of the most interesting developments in India's energy diplomacy in recent times, perhaps, is the development of cooperation between India and China as the two largest international buyers of energy
resources. Although India and China are rivals on several issues, the
leadership of the two countries apparently have realized their convergent
interests in cooperating as buyers. The foundation for such cooperation
was laid during the UPA period. Srikanth Kondapalli, in his chapter, details the institutionalization of a framework for such cooperation during
the UPA period such as the signing of the January 2006 agreement on energy cooperation between India and China.

Emphasis on Negotiations

Scholars of India's foreign policy such as Kanti Bajpai (2012, 107–10) have observed that reliance on negotiations rather than coercion or force has been a hallmark of UPA's foreign policy, especially that towards Pakistan and China.

The findings of the present volume agree with this observation. Isabelle Saint-Mézard, for example, in her chapter finds that the first UPA government's approach towards Pakistan (especially before the Mumbai terror attack of 26 November 2008), 'mostly focused on negotiations'. Saint-Mézard finds that the UPA government sought to manage the relations with Pakistan through 'three channels' of negotiations, namely, the composite dialogue, secret backchannel talks and, high-level political engagement. The UPA preferred quiet diplomacy involving a low-key style of negotiations. She proffers three reasons behind UPA's preference of diplomacy over coercion or force in its dealings with Pakistan. *First*, the lesson learned from the 2002 military standoff with Pakistan, which cost India about U.S.$2 billion giving India 'limited strategic gains' in return. *Second*, the presence of nuclear arsenals of the two countries, which entails high risk of a military confrontation eventually escalating beyond nuclear threshold. *Third*, intense pressure from the international community, especially the United States and the United Kingdom, to avoid military confrontation with Pakistan. Saint-Mézard finds that though the UPA avoided direct military confrontation with Pakistan, it nevertheless sought to build up pressure on Pakistan through a 'relentless diplomatic and media campaign'.

With China, too, the UPA governments preferred an approach that prioritized negotiations and communication. Srikanth Kondapalli, for example, in his chapter, finds that the main feature of India's approach towards China during the UPA rule was 'institutionalization of process of communication at almost all levels'. As detailed by Kondapalli, these institutions of communications are strategic dialogues, *Special Representative* meetings, financial dialogues, strategic and economic dialogues, annual defence dialogues, and maritime dialogue.

Forging Strategic Partnerships

The signing of *strategic partnerships* has been a hallmark of India's diplomacy during the UPA rule. While the previous NDA government led by Atal Bihari Vajpayee signed six strategic partnerships, the UPA governments signed as many as fifteen (Hall 2016, 277). These *strategic partnerships* give India access to markets, finance, technology, arms, and intelligence (Hall 2016, 282).

Several contributors to the present volume, too, find special emphasis by the UPA governments to forge strategic partnerships with a range of nations. Timothy J. Lynch finds that India, during the period, was busy with 'forging of treaties across a range of issues, not least defence'. Mervin Bain, in his chapter, gives the example of the *joint declaration* of 2007 between India and Russia, which upgrades their relationship to *strategic partnership*. Similarly, as Shutaro Sano points out in his chapter, it was during the UPA rule that India-Japan relations developed into a *strategic partnership*. The 'Eight-fold Initiative for Strengthening Japan-India Global Partnership' signed by India and Japan in 2005 paved the way for enhanced security dialogue and cooperation, especially on issues such as counter-terrorism, non-proliferation, energy, and environment. Subsequently, in 2006, the two nations elevated their relationship into 'Global and Strategic Partnership'. Another notable strategic partnership, initiated during the previous NDA government but developed during the UPA period was that with the Central Asian nation Tajikistan. As Bhavna Dave points out in her chapter, between 2004 and 2010 India spent $70 million in technical assistance to renovate the Ayni airbase in Tajikistan.

Breaking Free of the South Asian Box: Reaching out to the Extended Neighbourhood

One notable feature of the two UPA governments' foreign policy was to take India out of the *South Asian box* and reach out to the larger extended neighbourhood. Three factors help explain this approach. *First*, with

the emergence of India as a rapidly growing major economy, its immediate neighbourhood, that is, South Asia, became 'too small an economic
space for India' (Scott 2013, 351). *Second*, as our contributor Thomas
P. Cavanna points out in his chapter, '(m)ajor obstacles' such as historical divisions in the region, the limitations of India's power to influence
the developments in the region, and Pakistan's unhelpful policies were
preventing the region from achieving its full potential of economic cooperation with the result that by the time the UPA left office, the South
Asian region accounted for a meagre 5.6% of India's exports and an even
meagrer 0.5% of its imports. This lack of scope of economic cooperation
with immediate neighbourhood forced India to look elsewhere for markets and resources to fuel India's economic growth. Extended neighbourhood came as a natural choice. *Third*, as Bhavna Dave argues in her
chapter, the 'raja mandala' theory of 'concentric circles' of ancient Indian
strategic thinker Kautilya—who has a profound influence on the Indian
strategic community—also had an influence on India's new policy of
reaching out to the extended neighbourhood. Simply put, Kautilya's 'raja
mandala' theory of 'concentric circles' implies competitive relations with
the immediate neighbourhood and cooperative relations with the extended neighbourhood. The logic of the Kautilya's 'raja mandala' theory,
in Dave's words, 'calls for bolstering India's role in the extended neighbourhood … to counteract the influence of China and enhance the leverage against its more prickly immediate neighbours'. The then foreign
minister in the UPA Government, Pranab Mukherjee, hinted at the influence of the 'concentric circles' theory on the government's outreach to
the extended neighbourhood with the following words, 'India's foreign
policy today looks at India's environment in expanding circles … starting
with the immediate neighbourhood … moving on to … the extended
neighbourhood' (quoted in Scott 2013, 350).

The regions of the extended neighbourhood that received maximum
attention in the two UPA Governments' foreign policy were *South East
Asia* and *Central Asia*. As John D. Ciorciari, finds in his chapter, India's
relations with *South East Asia* were upgraded substantially during the
UPA period as the 'Look East' policy took a 'strategic form' and India
made 'deeper investment in regional markets and diplomatic institutions'.
Similarly, Bhavna Dave finds in her chapter that while India was 'practically invisible as a strategic or diplomatic actor' till the middle of the first

decade of the twenty-first century, during the UPA rule, especially during its second term, a 'gradual shift' became discernible in India's policy towards Central Asian region, when the government of India began looking towards the region as an energy resources–rich region having the potential to help India meet its growing energy needs. Moreover, to overcome the geographical barrier—that hitherto prevented India from establishing closer relations with the region—the second UPA government initiated the 'Connect Central Asia' policy.

Breaching Geographical Barriers through Connectivity Infrastructure

One major instrument that the UPA Government used to build closer relations with the extended neighbourhood was breaching the geographical barriers to cooperation by building physical infrastructure for connectivity. John D. Ciorciari, in his chapter, finds that one of the main thrust areas of India's relationship with ASEAN during the UPA period was infrastructure connectivity. According to Ciorciari, this thrust for connectivity was motivated by two concerns: *first*, the desire to address the chronic underdevelopment faced by India's North East region; and *second*, the rise of China—to balance which forging closer cooperation with the South East Asian region was deemed necessary. Similarly, as Bhavna Dave points out in her chapter, breaching the geographical barrier in India's relations with Central Asia through building infrastructure for connectivity was the central thrust area of the UPA governments' approach towards the region.

Competition-Cooperation Mix in Relations with China

Managing relations with China is perhaps the most difficult task any government in India has to face. On the one hand, the two countries are rivals and competitors in a number of issues including the long and disputed boundary they share. On the other hand, as emerging economies, their interests converge on a number of international issues. Little wonder, scholars of India's foreign policy such as Ankit Panda (2014) consider how a government in India manages relations with its northern neighbour as a major touchstone to evaluate the foreign policy of that government.

This volume finds that the UPA managed to devise a delicate mix of Competition and Cooperation in India's relations with China. The UPA policy towards China, on the one hand, made a range of diplomatic moves including partnerships with other nations—who are worried about a rising China—to check the latter's assertiveness and competed with the latter for resources, markets, and influences in different regions. On the other hand, it sought to collaborate with China on a number of issues where the two countries' interests converge. As Srikanth Kondapalli puts it in his chapter, the two UPA governments established a 'cooperative and competitive cycle' in India's relations with China. This competition-cooperation mix was most visible in UPA governments' handling of the boundary question. On the one hand, the two UPA governments sought to enhance India's defence capabilities vis-a-vis China, esp. the defence capabilities in India-China border by, among others, strengthening the China-centric mountain division and creating a new 'Strike Corps' to be stationed in that border. On the other hand, it worked with the latter to institutionalize communication between the forces of the two sides and confidence-building measures in a bid to minimize chances of escalation in the border. At the same time, the UPA continued with the *Joint Working Group* meetings and *Special Representative* meetings to find out a lasting solution to the boundary dispute. The signing of the 'Political Parameters and Guiding Principles for the settlement of the India-China Boundary Question' was an important milestone in this regard and will indeed be remembered as UPA's legacy in the two countries' quest to find a lasting solution to the boundary dispute.

As emerging maritime powers facing two adjacent oceans, one notable area of competition between India and China is maritime competition. Srikanth Kondapalli, in his chapter, finds that the UPA period was marked by increased maritime competition between India and China in the Indian Ocean as well as in the South China Sea. The UPA government resisted Chinese pressure on India to reduce the latter's presence in the South China Sea. As pointed out by Kondapalli, nearly half of India's global trade goes through the South China Sea, and consequently, freedom of navigation in South China Sea is of paramount importance to India. India, under the UPA, adopted a two-pronged approach to rebuff Chinese pressure to reduce India's presence in this important maritime space. *First*, in its interactions with its Chinese interlocutors, India maintained that its presence in the region is 'commercial in nature'. *Second*, India bluntly and publicly asserted that the South China Sea is 'not China's sea' and repeatedly called on all concerned to respect *freedom of navigation* in this important transit point of international trade.

Another major irritant in India-China relations during the UPA period was the mounting imbalance in the bilateral trade in China's favour. As Kondapalli points out, the UPA governments sought to address this problem by trying to persuade China to help India overcome this imbalance through a range of measures, such as investing in the manufacturing sector in India, increasing purchase of value-added goods from India, and removing non-tariff barriers on Indian products' entry into China. However, this approach failed to get the desired results, as is clear from the fact that the trade imbalance, instead of getting reduced, actually worsened throughout the UPA period.

In a bid to balance an emerging and assertive China, India—during the UPA period—sought to forge and strengthen strategic partnerships with a number of other powers who were worried about China's rise and assertiveness. As Shutaro Sano finds in his chapter, 'increasing assertiveness of China's maritime activities' was an area of emphasis in India-Japan security cooperation as developed during the period. Similarly, John D. Ciorciari finds in his chapter that addressing 'mounting strategic concerns about China' was one of the major objectives in India's engagement with ASEAN during the period. Barnaby Dye and Ricardo Soares de Oliveira, in their chapter, find that 'concerns about China's dramatic push in diplomatic, economic and development-cooperation activity' in Africa was one of the two key drivers of India's enhanced ties with the countries of that continent.

Along with these competitive and balancing behaviour, the period also saw evolving cooperation between the two Asian giants on a number of international issues ranging from global economic governance and multi-lateral trade regime to climate change. As Srikanth Kondapalli points out in his chapter, the UPA decade saw coordination and cooperation between India and China in international economic forums such as G-20 and BRICS to promote common economic interests. Kondapalli finds that cooperation between the two countries has been significant during the period, especially in the context of BRICS. As he points out, in BRICS, the two nations have coordinated their positions on a range of issues including the proposal on the creation of the New Development Bank to finance infrastructure projects in BRICS member countries. On the issue of *climate change* the two countries coordinated their international positions as a part of the BASIC (Brazil, South Africa, India, and China) grouping to fend off international pressure on the emerging economies to take on greater emission reduction responsibilities. Kondapalli also finds significant cooperation between India and China on regional security issues including Afghanistan, Iraq, North Korea, and Syria during the period. Even a maritime dialogue process was initiated to coordinate position on maritime issues. In this competition-cooperation matrix, the most positive aspect of the bilateral relations was the growing economic relations. As pointed out by Kondapalli, India-China bilateral trade saw major growth during the UPA rule. This growth in economic relations and consequent economic interdependence, argues Kondapalli, greatly reduced the possibility of the competitions and disputes in other areas escalating into conflict. A major development towards institutionalization of cooperation was the signing of the 'Strategic and Cooperative Partnership' in 2005. As pointed out by Kondapalli, the agreement paved the way for the institutionalization of cooperation at multiple levels including *strategic dialogues* between the foreign ministries of the two countries and the *annual defence dialogue* between the two defence ministries.

Integrating India into the Asian Security Architecture

The UPA period saw India becoming an important part of an evolving Asian security order. Although a favourable international situation helped this development, the two UPA governments' conscious efforts in this regard cannot be overlooked.

John D. Ciorciari, in his chapter, finds that the two UPA governments capitalized on India's rising capabilities, as well as uncertainty surrounding China's rise and waning U.S. primacy, to secure a pivotal position for India in the emerging security order in Asia. Ciorciari also finds that the two UPA governments used India's close relations with the United States, Japan, and ASEAN countries to secure for India this pivotal position. One important indicator of India's rising profile in the security order of Asia during the period was India's increased presence in the disputed waters of the South China Sea. To increase India's influence in these disputed waters, the UPA adopted a two-pronged approach. *First*, it enhanced security cooperation with the littoral states of that sea such as Vietnam, Singapore, and the Philippines. For example, the SIMBEX exercises between India and Singapore that began in 2005 gave a significant boost to India's presence in these disputed but extremely important waters. *Second*, UPA leaders issued public statements and declarations calling for freedom of navigation in this sea. One tentative but promising initiative in the direction of an emerging security order in Asia was the 'Quadrilateral Security Dialogue' (QUAD) between the United States, Japan, India, and Australia. The first meeting of this QUAD took place in 2007. However, facing strong backlash from China, this initiative had to be shelved the very next year and remained dormant until its revival a decade later.

One major success in India's efforts to integrate itself into the emerging Asian security order was getting membership in the *East Asia Summit* in 2005. John D. Ciorciari argues, in his chapter, that India's inclusion in the *East Asia Summit* was a watershed in the former's relationship with the evolving institutional architecture in the region and was a 'clear indication' of increasing recognition among the stakeholders of its important role in the evolving power balance in the region. As Ciorciari points out, before the UPA period, India remained an external power vis-a-vis the Asia-Pacific regional order. He credits the UPA for changing that. Ciorciari details, in his chapter, how the UPA government positioned India to be a key player in the evolving Indo-Pacific order by 'securing a more prominent place within Asia's multilateral institutional framework', thus redefining India's role in the regional security order. He argues that the UPA was successful in moving India from being a 'peripheral actor' in the Asia-Pacific region to being a 'major node' in the evolving security order in that region. While acknowledging that the term 'Indo-Pacific' came to be widely used in regional security discourse only in 2016—two years after the UPA left office, Ciorciari argues that the foundation for this geopolitical conception was laid during the UPA period by India's securing of a major role in the security order of the region.

Building up India as a Major Maritime Power

One of the discernible developments during the UPA period was India's emergence as a Maritime Power. Rahul Roy-Chaudhury, in his chapter, finds that three factors motivated the UPA in building up India as a maritime power. *First*, the realization of the importance of security of the transport—through sea route—of energy resources and other imports and exports for ensuring the sustainability of India's high-speed economic growth. As he points out, over 90% of India's foreign trade in volume and 77% in value was seaborne during the UPA period, which accounted for over 40% of the country's total GDP. *Second*, China's rising maritime profile, not only in the Pacific but also in the Indian Ocean—which the UPA viewed as an attempt to encircle India—convinced the UPA governments to make countermoves in the form of raising India's maritime profile not only in the Indian Ocean but also in China's backyard—the South China Sea. *Third*, the 2008 terror attack in Mumbai—the perpetrators of which entered India through sea route—made the UPA government strengthen India's naval capabilities, among others, to enhance the coastal security of India. Indeed, as Roy-Chaudhury points out, after this terror attack, the UPA government formally transferred the responsibility for the coastal security of the country from the Coast Guard to the Indian Navy.

The two UPA governments took a number of initiatives towards building India into a major maritime power. The most notable among them are: modernizing Indian Navy; declaring India as a 'net security provider' in the Indian Ocean; expanding India's maritime 'area of interest' to include the South China Sea and other areas of West Pacific Ocean; shifting eastward a significant portion of India's naval capabilities; participating in maritime activities such as anti-piracy patrols and disaster response operations; and forging naval partnerships with important littoral countries of the Indian Ocean and the Pacific Ocean.

Of course, the most basic effort towards building India as a maritime power is naval modernization. As detailed by Roy-Chaudhury in his chapter, the two UPA governments took a number of initiatives for India's naval modernization such as the acquiring of the P-8 maritime surveillance aircraft.

While naval modernizations can be considered as 'hardware upgradation' for building India as a maritime power, doctrinal evolution such as declaring India as a 'net security provider' in the Indian Ocean and expanding India's maritime 'area of interest' can be considered as 'software upgradation' for the same. The term 'net security provider' in the context of the Indian Navy's role in the Indian Ocean was first used by the then Defence Minister in the UPA government A. K. Antony in 2011 while addressing a conference of India's naval commanders. This policy got the stamp of approval from the highest level of the UPA government in 2013, when Prime Minister Dr. Manmohan Singh in his speech at the Indian National Defence University, as quoted by Rahul Roy-Chaudhury in his chapter, declared that India is 'well positioned … to become a net provider of security in our immediate region and beyond'. As regards expanding India's maritime 'area of interest', as pointed out by Roy-Chaudhury, while the maritime doctrine—issued just before the inauguration of the UPA government—declares India's maritime area of interest to be 'the arc from the Persian Gulf to the Straits of Malacca', the UPA government expanded this 'area of interest' to include 'South China Sea, and other areas of West Pacific Ocean' through the upgraded maritime doctrine issued in 2009. One natural corollary of including the South China Sea and other areas of the West Pacific Ocean in India's maritime 'areas of interest' was the shifting of a significant amount of naval capabilities eastward. As described by John D. Ciorciari in his chapter, this included shifting a significant amount of naval capabilities from the Western Command based in Mumbai to the Eastern Command headquartered at Visakhapatnam and facing the Bay of Bengal and the relocation of annual Indo-U.S. Malabar joint naval exercises from the Arabian Sea to the Pacific Ocean.

What can be considered as both an indicator and facilitator of India's growing maritime profile during the UPA period were the Indian Navy's involvement in activities such as disaster response efforts and anti-piracy patrols in far-flung areas of the Indian Ocean and the Pacific Ocean. Indian Navy's disaster response activities such as the relief and reconstruction efforts in the Maldives, Sri Lanka, and Indonesia in the wake of the December 2004 Indian Ocean Tsunami made a significant contribution to increasing India's maritime profile. Similarly, anti-piracy patrols that Rahul Roy-Chaudhury details in his chapter, such as those in areas like off the coast of Somalia and the Seychelles coast in which the Indian Navy took part, must be credited to have contributed significantly in increasing India's maritime profile in the Indian Ocean.

Forging Naval Partnerships

The role of India's naval partnerships with important littorals of the Indian Ocean and the Pacific Ocean—that were initiated or intensified during the UPA period—in facilitating India's emergence as a major maritime power in the Indo-Pacific region can hardly be overemphasized. The importance placed by the UPA on developing such partnerships can be gauged from the creation of the Directorate of Foreign Cooperation in the Indian Navy in 2006. Indeed, as pointed out by Rahul Roy-Chaudhury in his chapter, India during the UPA period stepped up naval engagements with important naval powers such as the United States, Japan, and Australia, as well as with several Southeast Asian states. Shutaro Sano, too, in his chapter, finds that India and Japan—during the UPA period—developed closer cooperation in the field of maritime security. One important specific aspect of enhanced maritime security cooperation between India and Japan, as described by Sano, is the strengthening of information sharing between their respective navies, including the beginning of exchange of their respective schedules of escort operations in the Gulf of Aden. John D. Ciorciari, too, finds in his chapter, significant increase in naval cooperation with the ASEAN member countries. Naval agreements with ASEAN member states such as the 2006 agreement to combat piracy contributed to building the framework for closer cooperation with ASEAN nations in the field of maritime security. The immediate neighbourhood, too, were part of the two UPA governments' spree of forging maritime partnerships. As pointed out by Thomas P. Cavanna in his chapter, the agreements on Maritime Security Cooperation Framework for counter-terrorism and anti-piracy, as well as intelligence sharing on illegal maritime activities agreed with the Maldives, the Seychelles, Sri Lanka, and Mauritius, contributed substantially to increase India's maritime profile in the region.

As detailed by Rahul Roy-Chaudhury, in his chapter, the two UPA governments between 2004–14, through a number of initiatives, laid the framework for India's rising maritime profile. However, in spite of such efforts to enhance India's maritime profile, there were certain hesitations visible in UPA's approach. These hesitations were mostly motivated by a reluctance to provoke China by overplaying the anti-China maritime alliance card. Such hesitations were visible in, as mentioned by Roy-Chaudhury, UPA's reluctance to initiate a formal naval defence agreement or even a maritime security dialogue with the United States, as well as in its reluctance to formally endorse the concept of the Indo-Pacific.

Transformations in Relations with the United States and Japan

The UPA period saw a transformation in India's relations with major powers, especially the United States and Japan. These transformations were the results of both the increasing realization by these major powers of India's importance as a pillar of the liberal international order and the conscious efforts by the two UPA governments towards achieving these transformations. Indeed, scholars of India's foreign policy are more or less unanimous that the Indo-U.S. relations was not only the core thrust area of the foreign policy of the two UPA governments (Bajpai 2012, 104) but also reached what Ian Hall terms as their 'highest point' during the UPA period (Hall 2016). Scholars like Sylvia Mishra (2017), too, agree that the UPA period saw a decisive shift in India's relations with the United States.

Arguably, it was the previous NDA government led by A. B. Vajpayee which made the initial moves towards this transformation by signing the *Next Steps in Strategic Partnership* (NSSP) at the fag-end of its term. However, as Kanti Bajpai (2012, 102) points out, it was the UPA who 'quickly build on the NSSP' to bring about a transformation in the relationship.

Contributors to the present volume, too, share this assessment. In an indication of the realization by the UPA of the importance of India-U.S. relations, John D. Ciorciari finds in his chapter that the UPA governments viewed the U.S. as 'the principal gatekeeper' which can facilitate an enhanced role for India in the East and Southeast Asian region.

It will not be an exaggeration to say that the pivot of the transformation of the Indo-U.S. relations in recent times has been the nuclear cooperation agreement signed in 2008. Indeed, there is a near unanimity among the scholars of India's foreign policy that the signing of the nuclear cooperation agreement transformed the Indo-U.S. relations (Bajpai and Pant 2013, 16; Tremblay and Kapur 2017, 6).

Contributors to the present volume, too, agree with this assessment. Ramesh Thakur, for example, argues that the result of the signing of the nuclear agreement was that 'India–US relations became the best ever'. This is so because, Thakur argues, as a result of this agreement, the respective strategic goals of India and the United States 'dovetailed' with each other. Indeed, Thakur asserts that '(i)n the perspective of history, the signature nuclear legacy of the UPA Government … is likely to be the bilateral civil nuclear cooperation deal with the US', which according to him 'unlocked the global strategic frame in which India had been frozen after the 1998 tests'.

The Indo-U.S. relations entered a qualitatively upgraded track of cooperation during the UPA period in a number of other areas, too, most notably in defence cooperation and trade relations. The *Framework Agreement on Defence Cooperation*, signed in 2005, can be considered as the lynchpin of the transformation in defence cooperation between the two countries. As pointed out by Timothy J. Lynch in his chapter, this *framework agreement* helped make the United States the third largest arms supplier to India. Lynch bolsters his conclusion that military cooperation with the United States was 'transformed during the UPA years' with relevant statistics—by pointing out that while between 1999 and 2003, the United States supplied only 0.2% of India's imported arms; by 2013, it was supplying 7.4%. The trade relations too were not outside this transformation. As pointed out by Lynch, the bilateral trade between the two countries increased five-fold during the period 2004–14. In the light of these developments, one cannot but agree with the conclusion reached by Lynch in his chapter that the relations between India and the United States were 'stronger at every level of analysis in 2014 than they were in 2004'.

Similarly, the transformation of India's relations with Japan during the UPA period was too discernible to miss. As Shutaro Sano finds in his chapter, '(t)he foundation for a strong multifunctional strategic partnership' between these two major Asian nations was developed 'during the ten years of the UPA rule'.

Projecting India as an emerging Global Power

Scholars like Kanti Bajpai (2012, 102) have noted the UPA's efforts to project for India the image of a global player. Others like Malone, Raja Mohan, and Raghavan (2015, 16) have observed India's 'enhanced international profile' as one of the achievements of the two UPA governments' foreign policy.

The findings of several chapters of the present volume agree with these observations. One of the contributors to this volume, Bhavna Dave, for example, finds that one of the major objectives in India's approach towards the Central Asia region during the UPA period was to project the image of India as an 'emerging power'. Another contributor Srikanth Kondapalli finds in his chapter that it was during the UPA period when China and India for the first-time included cooperation 'at global levels' in the agenda of cooperation between them. This, as Kondapalli points out, was a departure from the earlier Chinese policy that attempted to deny India a larger global role with the intent to confine the latter to the South Asian region.

Lobbying for Permanent Membership of the UNSC

The most important endeavour of the two UPA governments to build India as a global power was the efforts to secure for India a permanent membership of the United Nations Security Council (UNSC). As detailed by Kate Sullivan de Estrada and Babak Moussavi in their chapter, the two UPA governments mobilized, from 2004 onwards, international support for an increase in the number of permanent members of the UNSC as part of 'Group of Four' (G4). What is more important, the two UPA governments not only lobbied for increasing the number of permanent members but also for the specific goal of India's permanent membership in a reformed UNSC. Research conducted by Sullivan de Estrada and Moussavi reveals that lobbying by the two UPA governments resulted in

India getting significant support from the international community for its bid for UNSC permanent membership. They find that between 2004 and 2014, a total of 82 Member States of the United Nations had declared their support for India's candidature for permanent membership of the UNSC.

In the meanwhile, India's image as an emerging global power got a boost with India's election as a non-permanent member of the UNSC for a two-year period beginning in 2011. This was the first time in nearly two decades that India was elected as a non-permanent member of the UNSC. Sullivan de Estrada and Moussavi quote a commentator viewing this election as 'a well-deserved acknowledgement of (India's) growing importance in terms of global economic and security governance'. Indeed, this election, according to them, was viewed by many as India's 'dry run' for the permanent membership of the UNSC.

Ambivalent Power

However, Sullivan de Estrada and Moussavi find that India, as a non-permanent member of the UNSC from 2011 to 2012, sent 'conflicting signals'. As they point out, India sought to demonstrate the 'will and capacity to take on major responsibilities with regard to the maintenance of international peace and security' through measures like supporting UNSC resolution 1970 on Libya and also through a proactive role in the UNSC on counter-terrorism and anti-piracy actions. However, they find India at times challenging the 'interventionist tendencies of the Western states' in the UNSC. This they observe as India's 'broader rising power strategy' which they put as 'compliance with and resistance to the hegemonic norms and institutions of the existing international political and economic order'.

Non-alignment

Non-alignment was enshrined as a foundational principle of India's foreign policy by the first Prime Minister Jawaharlal Nehru at the dawn of independence. Since then, the principle has remained a sheet anchor of

India's foreign policy, albeit with major adjustments from time to time in response to changing international as well as domestic situations. These adjustments have, sometimes, been so radical as to make some observers of India's foreign policy assert, at frequent intervals, that the principle has been done away with. However, the core of the principle survived even though under different names such 'strategic autonomy', 'nonalignment 2.0' (Khilnani et al. 2012), and 'multi-alignment' (Hall 2016). Put simply, the core principle of non-alignment—which is keeping India's option open and not keeping all eggs in one basket—has survived the many radical reorientations that India's foreign policy saw from time to time in the seven decades since independence.

The UPA government made major adjustments in India's non-alignment principle without abandoning the core of that principle, namely, 'strategic autonomy'. These adjustments were so profound that scholars such as Ian Hall (2016, 275) argue that the UPA governments have shifted India from non-alignment towards 'multialignment'. Hall lists three aspects of this new principle of 'multialignment', as developed by the UPA government: *first*, 'accelerated push for membership of-and great engagement in-emerging global and regional multi- and mini-lateral institutions and forums'; *second*, 'forging a series of "strategic partnerships" and deepening some existing partnerships'; and *third*, 'normative hedging'. While these three strands were indeed visible in the UPA government's foreign policy and giving them the moniker of 'multialignment' makes sense, what is problematic is the haste to write the epitaph of non-alignment. Indeed, critics have written the epitaph of non-alignment several times in the past—most notably when Indira Gandhi drew India closer to the Soviet Union and later when the Government of P. V. Narasimha Rao made radical reorientation in India's foreign policy in response to the end of the Cold War—only to find its uncanny ability to survive by adapting to changing situations. What I would like to argue in response to the 'multialignment' theory of Hall is that non-alignment as a principle of India's foreign policy—as developed in practice through the last seven decades—is broad enough to accommodate 'multialignment' within itself.

Several of the contributors to the present volume have found the two UPA governments to jealously guard India's *strategic autonomy* and even restore it in areas where it was perceived as compromised by the previous

NDA dispensation. John D. Ciorciari, for example, in his chapter on India's 'Look East' policy during the UPA rule, finds that India during the period 'preserved a strong degree of diplomatic autonomy' which helped it to act as a 'swing state' and significantly influence outcomes on certain divisive issues. Another contributor, Bhavna Dave, finds in her chapter on India's relations with Central Asia during the UPA rule, that 'After a decade of close strategic partnership with the US on Afghanistan' which had a negative effect on India's traditionally good relations with Iran and Russia, the UPA was finally able to restore India's strategic autonomy in its approach towards the region. Even on such initiatives as the India-U.S. nuclear agreement, which were dubbed by critics as compromising India's strategic autonomy, the findings of this volume go contrary to the assessment of these critics. Indeed, Ramesh Thakur, in his chapter on India's nuclear diplomacy during the UPA rule, finds that while this agreement deepens India-U.S. relations, it does not by any means usher in a 'client-status dependency' for India.

Role of Ideology and Leadership

A pertinent question regarding the two UPA governments' foreign policy is, what has been the role of ideology and leadership in shaping it? Any serious student of India's foreign policy will be aware of the fact that role of ideology and leadership is a blind spot in the literature on India's foreign policy. With a few notable exceptions, some of whom were mentioned in the introductory chapter of this volume, existing literature on India's foreign policy largely follow the neorealist tradition, which tends to believe that the foreign policy of a country is exclusively shaped by systemic forces and the ideology and leadership of the ruling dispensation does not play any role, at least not significant enough a role to merit detailed scholarly examinations.

Ideology

The neglect of the role of ideology in shaping India's foreign policy in the existing literature is the reason scholars like Kanti Bajpai feel that future research in the field of India's foreign policy should 'pay much greater attention to ideology—its influence but also its limits' (Bajpai 2012, 111). Bajpai suggests that the differences in the foreign policies of the NDA Government led by Atal Bihari Vajpayee and the UPA Government led by Manmohan Singh can be explained by the differences in 'political worldviews' of the two leading parties of the NDA and the UPA, namely the BJP and the Congress (Bajpai 2012, 111). To quote Bajpai, 'The BJP is a conservative party in its ideological leanings, and the role of force and violence in its understanding of politics is that these are more or less inescapable ... The Congress remains a "left liberal" party ideologically, and the role of force and violence in politics is one that it finds repugnant' (Bajpai 2012, 111).

Tremblay and Kapur (2017, 3) delineate three ideological strands co-existing in Indian foreign policy: Nehruvian (which emphasizes diplomacy and soft power); neoliberal (which prioritizes economic objectives and instruments); and hyper-realism (which relies on use and threat of use of force and seeks to pursue balance of power). Going by this taxonomy, the two UPA governments' foreign policy—as per the findings of this volume—can be considered as largely a blend of the first two strands, with the second strand, that is neoliberalism, having a more pronounced presence than the first strand that is Nehruvianism. This, However, does not mean the third strand was completely absent as any foreign policy in operation—as opposed to mere academic conceptualization of it—cannot completely do away with realist elements.

Isabelle Saint-Mézard, in her chapter, finds that the UPA governments viewed Indo-Pak relations through 'neoliberal prism'. Saint-Mézard's analysis of India-Pakistan relations explains UPA's approach towards Pakistan by three neoliberal beliefs that, she finds, motivated the UPA leaders: *first*, peaceful neighbourhood is an essential condition for sustaining India's rapid economic growth; *second*, economic interdependence can make India and Pakistan transform the relations between them by making them more accommodative to each other's interests and concerns; and *third*, peace with Pakistan will bring great economic dividends to India by lessening the huge cost of protecting the border and by reopening India's trade and commerce with Central Asia and Eurasia through Pakistan.

Leadership

Several of the contributors of this volume have found the leadership of Prime Minister Manmohan Singh to have a significant impact on the evolution of India's foreign relations during the UPA decade. Timothy J. Lynch, for example, maintains that the transformation in the relations between India and the United States that has been observed during the UPA period owes to '(Manmohan) Singh-inspired resolve'. Lynch also argues that the rapport between prime minister Singh and U.S. President George W. Bush played a significant role in this transformation. In Lynch's words, 'Bush and Singh … shared enough of a worldview to make their diplomacy work'. Another contributor, Ramesh Thakur, shares this assessment. Thakur maintains that the nuclear agreement between India and the United States would not have been possible were it not for the 'personal commitment and directives of President Bush and PM Singh'.

Similarly, another contributor Isabelle Saint-Mézard finds leadership style of prime minister Singh—his preference for low-key style and quiet diplomacy-had an impact on India's approach towards Pakistan. Saint-Mézard contrasts Singh's quiet diplomacy with Pakistan, mostly on the side-lines of multi-lateral meetings, with the spectacular diplomacy of his predecessor Vajpayee such as the latter's bus sojourn to Lahore. She argues that such quiet diplomacy on the side-lines of multi-lateral meetings offered India two advantages. It helped maintain the channel of communications open at the highest level. At the same time, it limited the 'media frenzy' and high expectations in both the countries that inevitably accompany spectacular diplomacy and thus make it difficult for the negotiators to arrive at a mutually acceptable solution.

Hiccups in Implementation

The gap between announcement and implementation is a perennial problem of public policy in India (Singh 2017, xxiv). UPA governments' foreign policy was no exception to this endemic issue besetting public policy in India. Indeed, several contributors to this volume have found such lacunae in the implementation of the UPA government's foreign policy in their respective chapters.

Timothy J. Lynch, in his chapter on India-U.S. relations, details the 'bureaucratic inertia' that hamstrung the prime minister from driving policy. Lynch gives the example of the nuclear agreement, which transformed the bilateral relations, and yet became a victim of 'procedural obtuseness within Indian political and legal circles'. Indeed, based on what he terms as 'disconnection between promise and delivery' in the context of the nuclear agreement, Lynch comes to somewhat harsh judgement that the UPA government 'often lacked the ability to walk the procedural path'.

Another contributor John D. Ciorciari, too, finds in his chapter on India's 'Look East' policy during the UPA rule that trade and investment relations with the East and Southeast Asian nations could not reach their full potential as the technocrats in major Indian institutions responsible for formulation and implementation of economic policy such as the Commerce Ministry, Ministry of Finance, and Reserve Bank of India as well as the 'broader domestic political environment' were found to be unhelpful in bringing about the necessary economic policy measures to realize these potentials.

Barnaby Dye and Ricardo Soares de Oliveira, in their chapter, similarly find a discernible gap between 'rhetoric and reality' in India's approach towards Africa during the period. In particular, Dye and Soares de Oliveira give examples of how the lack of proper coordination between different departments and agencies of the government of India prevented the energy cooperation between India and African states from realizing their full potential. They also point out the 'lack of integration' between the different ministries in India, due to which different parts of India's civil service remain 'isolated from one another'. One interesting example of such lack of proper coordination relates to two programmes: subsidized ExIm credit and the ITEC development cooperation. As Dye and Soares de Oliveira find in their chapter, these two related programs remain disconnected in effect even though the Ministry of External Affairs oversees both the programmes.

Continuities and Changes

Some of the scholars of India's foreign policy, notably Harsh V. Pant (2008), Shivshankar Menon (2016), and Tremblay and Kapur (2017), hold that the UPA's foreign policy maintained a remarkable continuity with that of its predecessors. Others, such as Kanti Bajpai (2012), Ian Hall (2016, 275), and Ankit Panda (2013), maintain that the UPA have indeed brought significant changes in India's foreign policy.

The findings of this volume are mixed in this regard. The contributors to this volume have found strands of continuity in some areas coexisting with significant changes in others. However, the scale has been found to be titling towards the side of change.

Continuity

One notable area of continuity, as found in this volume, is India's nuclear diplomacy. Despite significant progress made by the two UPA governments in this direction including nuclear agreement with the United States and subsequent relaxation by the Nuclear Suppliers Group of its rules in favour of India, the basic direction of the policy has been found to remain unchanged from UPA's predecessor Vajpayee government. As Ramesh Thakur points out in his chapter, the contours of India's nuclear policy as set up by the Vajpayee government were 'maintained undisturbed' by the UPA throughout the decade it was in power. The core of that policy being, in the words of Thakur, 'integrating India into the global nuclear order as a non-NPT de facto nuclear-armed state'.

Changes

Several other contributors, however, find discernible changes, either in content or in style, brought by the UPA government in the area they examined. Timothy J. Lynch, for example, finds in his chapter on India-U.S. relations that the UPA governments showed an 'openness' in dealing with the United States that 'stood in contrast to' the predecessor Vajpayee government. Isabelle Saint-Mézard, in her chapter on India-Pakistan relations, find that there were changes in both content and style. For example, unlike its predecessor, the UPA preferred a 'low-key style' and 'quiet diplomacy' on the 'sidelines of multilateral meetings'. Saint-Mézard notes the reluctance of the UPA governments to hold stand-alone summits with Pakistan, which she contrasts with Vajpayee's Lahore visit. Another change she found is the reluctance of the UPA to resort to the threat of force—and initiate an intense diplomatic and media campaign against Pakistan instead—in the face of the Mumbai terror attack by Pakistan based elements, which, again, Saint-Mézard contrasts with the military mobilization that the Vajpayee government ordered in a similar situation. Bhavna Dave, too, in her chapter, finds that India's Central Asia policy during the UPA period was 'a departure from the complacency, lethargy and lofty iterations of cultural ties' that hitherto marked the policy. It, rather, sought to make a practical move in building the foundation of a closer relations by investing in connectivity infrastructure through the 'Connect Central Asia' policy. Another notable change observed by Dave is the change of earlier focus on bilateral ties and opening up for engagement with multi-lateral groupings such as the *Shanghai Cooperation Organization*, in which India got observer status in 2011. Vinícius Rodrigues Vieira, in his chapter, finds that the UPA government brought about a fundamental change in India's position regarding the multi-lateral trade negotiations at the WTO. As Rodrigues Vieira points out, while the earlier Vajpayee government sought to maximize export opportunities for Indian agricultural products, the UPA government rather opted for more protectionist policy in this regard considering the sector as a 'vulnerable sector of the economy' needing 'special care and protection'.

Conclusion

Jacob and Layton (2009) use three pertinent questions as a conceptual framework to assess the UPA Government's foreign policy: *first*, whether the UPA foreign policy was 'status quoist, tactical or strategic?'; *second*, did India during the UPA period 'behave as a rising international power?'; and *third*, has India, during the period, 'asserted a positive influence over developments in its neighbourhood?'. The answers they find lead them to conclude that the foreign policy of the UPA government failed to live up to the criteria set up by these three questions. To be specific, they assessed that UPA's foreign policy was 'status quoist'; India under the UPA did not behave as a rising power; and India was unable to assert 'positive influence' over the developments in the immediate neighbourhood. The findings of this volume contradict the first two of these assessments, though they, more or less, corroborate the third.

As elaborated in the previous sections of this conclusive chapter, the findings of this volume suggest that the foreign policy of India during the UPA rule was driven by a number of medium- and long-term objectives. To recapitulate briefly the most notable among them:

1. Securing and increasing access to foreign resources including energy resources, technologies, and markets to fuel India's rapid economic growth. At the same time, working towards achieving technological, logistical, institutional, legal, and ideational capabilities to secure the maritime routes in the Indian Ocean and the Pacific Ocean through which foreign natural resources including energy resources reach India and India's exports reach foreign markets.
2. Seeking to manage and transform the historically troubled relations with neighbouring states such as China and Pakistan through quiet diplomacy and institutionalization of communication as well as through deepening of economic interdependence and cooperating on select areas where interests converge even while competing on areas where the interests diverge.
3. Breaking free of the 'South Asian box' and forging closer trade, investment, and security relations with the extended neighbourhood, especially Southeast Asia and Central Asia.
4. Integrating India into the evolving security architecture in the Asia-Pacific as one of the lynchpins of that architecture.
5. Building up India as a major maritime power.
6. Projecting India as an emerging global power, especially by making intense diplomatic efforts to secure for India permanent membership of the UN Security Council.

In light of these findings, it can plausibly be argued that India's foreign policy during the UPA rule was indeed strategic.

As regards the second question—i.e., did India during the UPA period behave as a rising international power?—the findings of the present volume suggest that it did. We can draw this conclusion on the basis of the following findings of this volume:

1. India's area of interest and influence saw significant extension both in the land and maritime domain. In land, as explained earlier in this chapter, the period saw India finally overcoming the traditional image of a South Asian power by making serious inroads into the extended neighbourhood especially, South East Asia and Central Asia through a number of trade, investment, and strategic partnership agreements as well as though initiatives to breach geographic barriers—which hitherto frustrated India's attempts to forge closer relations with these regions—by investing in physical connectivity infrastructure.

2. India's largely successful efforts, during the UPA period, to secure a prominent maritime profile in the Indian Ocean and the Pacific Ocean as exemplified by the development of closer naval cooperation with the United States, Japan, and other important naval powers; expansion of India's maritime areas of interest by adding the South China Sea, and other areas of West Pacific Ocean to the earlier NDA government's comparatively modest definition of maritime areas of interest, namely 'from the Persian Gulf to the Straits of Malacca'; declaration of India as a 'net security provider' in the Indian Ocean; and significantly increased activities of the Indian Navy in maritime patrolling and anti-piracy operations in far-flung areas such as off the coasts of Somalia and Seychelles as well as in disaster relief operations such as that undertaken in places like Indonesia in the wake of the December 2004 Indian Ocean Tsunami.

3. The intense diplomatic moves to secure, for India, permanent membership of the UN Security Council—not only the collective diplomatic endeavour to secure wide support for reform of the council through the 'Group of Four' (G4) but also securing pledges for support to India's individual candidature from as many as 82 member states of the United Nations. India's election to the UNSC for a two years period beginning in 2011, for the first time in nearly two decades, was another indicator of India's successful projection of itself as a rising international power.

4. China's acceptance to work with India on important issues 'at global levels', which was an interesting contrast to China's earlier policy of seeking to confine India to the *South Asian box*.

As regards the third question, however, the findings of the present volume largely agree with the assessment of Jacob and Layton. Our findings confirm that India's efforts to positively influence the developments in the immediate neighbourhood did not achieve significant success, especially with respect to Pakistan, India's largest and most difficult neighbour in South Asia. Although, the UPA government did make some novel policy shifts including greater reliance on quiet diplomacy and institutionalized negotiations in place of earlier reliance on spectacular diplomacy punctuated by military mobilization. The results achieved by the two contrasting approaches of NDA and UPA were, puzzlingly enough, not much different. The neoliberal approach of the UPA of seeking transformation of the troubled relations with Pakistan by deepening economic interdependence failed to take off. However, as Isabelle Saint-Mézard explains in her chapter, this failure had more to do with the domestic politics of Pakistan than with India. As she points out, the relations indeed improved while Musharraf was in power—peace prevailed on the Line of Control, terrorist attacks in India reduced significantly, and both the nations even came closer to finding a lasting and mutually acceptable solution to the Kashmir issue that troubled relations for decades. However, Musharraf's exit in mid-2008 finally unravelled all the gains made till then and the relations were back to square one. However, as Saint-Mézard argues, a portion of the blame must be shared by what she terms 'over-cautious' approach of the UPA government and failure 'to take advantage of the unique historical opportunity that Musharraf's unorthodox approach offered for the resolution of Kashmir'. However, as she herself clarifies, it is easy to make this judgement of UPA as 'over-cautious' with the benefit of hindsight than appreciating the political difficulties and risks that the UPA might have perceived during its time in office in trusting Musharraf given his reputation as the architect of the Kargil misadventure. As regards other South Asian neighbours, as Thomas Cavanna points out in his chapter, the UPA government 'made the most of limited resources and adverse circumstances'. However, given the existing and entrenched mistrust among the smaller neighbours as well as domestic 'political and bureaucratic constrains' that limits India's ability to offer out of the box solutions to intractable problems besetting its relations with its smaller South Asian neighbours, '(u)ltimately, promises did not fully materialize'.

The UPA used a range of instruments to secure its foreign policy objectives. For securing the objective of giving boost to economic growth, it signed a series of trade and investment agreements including agreements that provide India access to foreign energy resources. For enhancing India's strategic profile, it signed strategic partnership agreements with a number of important nations; modernized the Indian Navy and at the same time took some bold policy decisions such as declaring India as a 'net security provider' in the Indian Ocean and expanding India's maritime 'area of interest' to include the South China Sea, and other areas of West Pacific Ocean; increased the number and geographical reach of naval exercises with friendly navies; took part in anti-piracy patrols in far-flung areas of the Indian Ocean; and, undertook disaster response operations in the wake of the Indian Ocean Tsunami of December 2004 in places such as Indonesia. For projecting India as an emerging global power, it did intense lobbying—both individually and as a member of the 'Group of Four'—for securing permanent membership of the UN Security Council; and successfully contested the election for non-permanent membership of the UNCS for a two-year term beginning 2011. For managing the troubled relationship with Pakistan, the instruments preferred by the UPA government was quiet diplomacy and low-key negotiations, including backchannel negotiations, before the terror attack on Mumbai, and diplomatic and media campaign against Pakistan after the attack to create international pressure on the latter to change its hostile policy towards India. For managing another difficult neighbour, namely China, the UPA devised a delicate mix of instruments of competition and cooperation. On the one hand, it strengthened the defence capabilities on the India-China border; deepened defence relations with the United States, Japan, and ASEAN countries; and increased presence in the South China Sea. On the other hand, it sought to increase cooperation with China on areas of convergent interests such as global economic governance, multi-lateral trade regime, and climate change. Another notable instrument, which received priority from the UPA government, was building physical infrastructure for connectivity to enable enhanced trade, investment, and energy cooperation with extended neighbourhood such as South East Asia and Central Asia.

As regards ideology, going by the findings of this volume, neoliberalism had the strongest influence on the UPA government's foreign policy. This is evident in the emphasis on economic objectives as well the belief in the potential of increasing economic interdependence to transform troubled relations with neighbouring countries like China and Pakistan. However, the influence of neorealism cannot be dismissed either, going by the proclivity to increase naval capabilities and profile as well as the signing of defence cooperation agreements with nations such as the United States and Japan. The influence of Nehruvianism—in particular, emphasis on diplomacy and negotiations as instrument, strategic autonomy as principle, and a global leadership role as objective—too has been discernible, as evident by a number of findings discussed earlier in this chapter. The findings of the volume also confirm the influence of the leadership style of Prime Minister Manmohan Singh on India's external relations, especially on important bilateral relations such as those with the United States and Pakistan.

Several chapters of this volume also find that the alacrity in reaching international agreements did not automatically translate into similar alacrity for their implementation on the ground. This, several of the contributors find, was a lacuna in UPA Government's foreign policy. Indeed, this problem is not limited to UPA's foreign policy. This problem has been seen to persist regardless of the political complexion of the administration in New Delhi. In fact, such problems of implementation have been found in almost every sphere of public policy in India. To say this is not to dismiss the gravity of the problem or to belittle these concerns. Rather, this is a serious issue and needs a thorough study to trace the complex interplay of diverse domestic factors—political, bureaucratic, and cultural—that contribute to this lethargy in the implementation of public policy in India in order to help find a permanent solution to this vexing problem. Ad-hoc solutions such as finding the lacunae in the implementation of one particular policy initiative may be a stop-gap arrangement but cannot offer a long-term solution to this perennial problem of policy implementation in India.

The findings of this volume point to some interesting continuities as well as changes in the foreign policy of the two UPA governments vis-à-vis that of the previous NDA government led by A. B. Vajpayee. While in areas like nuclear policy and relations with the United States, the UPA seemed to maintain continuity in the essential direction of the policy, although the latter brought to fruition the objectives set by its predecessor and achieved the transformations that its predecessor aspired for. In other areas like policies regarding China, Pakistan, extended neighbourhood, and WTO negotiations, the contributors find that the UPA government made notable policy innovations and made significant changes in objectives as well as instruments.

The chapters of the present volume made detailed examinations of various important aspects of India's foreign policy as they evolved through the decade of the UPA rule in India. Their findings helped make, in this conclusive chapter, a number of conclusions about the objectives and instruments of the foreign policy of the two UPA governments. Significant changes in policy were found in some areas, as well as marked continuities in some other areas. The volume fills a glaring gap in the existing literature on India's foreign policy—which is the absence of a detailed and comprehensive scholarly examination of India's foreign policy during the ten-year period of the UPA rule. As mentioned in the introductory chapter of this volume, in contrast to the absence of a detailed examination of India's foreign policy during the UPA period, there are several volumes that examine the foreign policy of its predecessor Vajpayee government and perhaps an even larger number of volumes that examine the foreign policy of the successor Modi government. By filling this gap, our volume will not only complement these other volumes but will also help future researchers examine the commonalities and differences in the foreign policy approaches of India's two leading coalitions, namely the centre-right NDA and the Centre-left UPA.

Finally, I would like to conclude by offering three suggestions for future researchers in the field of India's foreign policy. *First*, there are a number of volumes that examine the foreign policy of the NDA governments led by Vajpayee and that led by Modi and the present volume complements these volumes by offering a detailed examination of the foreign policy of the UPA government led by Manmohan Singh. Future researchers are now well positioned to undertake the task of making a comparative study of NDA and UPA's foreign policy. Such research will not only enrich the otherwise monotonous literature on India's foreign policy—dominated largely, as it is, by one single theoretical strand, namely neorealism and concomitant 'black-boxing', i.e., neglecting domestic politics as a determinant of India's foreign policy—but will also have substantial policy relevance as it can reasonably be expected that over the foreseeable future the government of India will alternate between NDA and UPA. *Second*, as mentioned earlier in this chapter, the role of ideology is the most neglected aspect of the existing literature on India's foreign policy. Examining how the ideology of the ruling coalition influences, or does not influence, foreign policy of India has the potential to greatly contribute to theory development in International Relations, particularly in Foreign Policy Analysis. This is a promising and fascinating area waiting to be discovered by the researchers on India's foreign policy. *Finally*, future researchers can also attempt to find linkage, if any, between the electoral support bases of India's two leading coalitions and the foreign policies they pursue when in power. This, if undertaken properly with appropriate methodological rigour, has the potential to contribute immensely to the development of not only foreign policy analysis but also of the liberal theory of International Relations.

References

Bajpai, Kanti. 2012. 'The UPA's Foreign Policy, 2004–9' in Lawrence Sáez and Gurharpal Singh (eds.) *New Dimensions of Politics in India: The United Progressive Alliance in Power*. New York: Routledge.

Bajpai, Kanti P. and Harsh V. Pant. 2013. 'Introduction' in Kanti P. Bajpai and Harsh V. Pant. (eds.) *India's Foreign Policy—A Reader*. New Delhi: Oxford University Press.

Hall, Ian. 2016. 'Multialignment and Indian Foreign Policy under Narendra Modi'. *The Round Table*. Vol. 105, No. 3: 271–286.

Jacob, Happymon and Kimberley Layton. 2009. 'UPA's Foreign Policy: A Critique'. *Economic and Political Weekly*. Vol. 44, No. 25, Jun. 20–26, 2009: 13–5.

Khilnani, Sunil et al. 2012. *Nonalignment 2.0: A Foreign and Strategic Policy for India in the Twenty First Century*. New Delhi: Centre for Policy Research.

Malone, David M., C. Raja Mohan, and Srinath Raghavan. 2015. 'India and the World' in David M. Malone, C. Raja Mohan, and Srinath Raghavan (eds.) *The Oxford Handbook of Indian Foreign Policy*. New York: Oxford University Press.

Menon, Shivshankar. 2016. *Choices: Inside the Making of India's Foreign Policy*. Washington, DC: Brookings Institution Press.

Mishra, Sylvia. 2017. 'Modi and America: Great Expectation and Enduring Constrains' in Sinderpal Singh (ed.) *Modi and the World: (Re)Constructing Indian Foreign Policy*. Singapore: World Scientific.

Panda, Ankit. 2013. 'Did India's "Manmohan Doctrine" succeed?: What were the greatest foreign policy successes and failures of Manmohan Singh's tenure?'. *The Diplomat*. November 06, 2013. https://thediplomat.com/2013/11/did-indias-manmohan-doctrine-succeed/ (accessed January 22, 2020).

Panda, Ankit. 2014. 'India's UPA government and foreign policy: How did India's UPA government perform in terms of foreign policy during its 10 years in power?'. *The Diplomat*. January 18, 2014. https://thediplomat.com/2014/01/indias-upa-gov ernment-and-foreign-policy/ (accessed January 23, 2020).

Pant, Harsh V. 2008. *Contemporary Debates in Indian Foreign and Security Policy: India Negotiates Its Rise in the International System*. New York: Palgrave Macmillan.

Scott, David. 2013. 'India's "Extended Neighbourhood" Concept: Power Projection for a Rising Power' in Kanti P. Bajpai and Harsh V. Pant (eds.) *India's Foreign Policy—A Reader*. New Delhi: Oxford University Press.

Singh, Sinderpal. 2017. 'Introduction' in Sinderpal Singh (ed.) *Modi and the World: (Re)Constructing Indian Foreign Policy*. Singapore: World Scientific.

Tremblay, Reeta Chowdhari and Ashok Kapur. 2017. *Modi's Foreign Policy*. New Delhi: SAGE.

Index

For the benefit of digital users, indexed terms that span two pages (e.g., 52–53) may, on occasion, appear on only one of those pages.

Tables and figures are indicated by *t* and *f* following the page number